BIOFUTURE
Confronting the Genetic Era

BIOFUTURE
Confronting the Genetic Era

Burke K. Zimmerman

Plenum Press • New York and London

Library of Congress Cataloging in Publication Data

Zimmerman, Burke K.
  Biofuture, confronting the genetic era.

  Includes bibliographical references and index.
  1. Genetic engineering—Social aspects. 2. Genetic engineering—Moral and ethical
aspects. 3. Genetics—Social aspects. 4. Genetics—Moral and ethical aspects. I. Title.
QH442.Z56 1984   575.1   83-26932
ISBN 0-306-41315-9

© 1984 Burke K. Zimmerman
Plenum Press is a Division of
Plenum Publishing Corporation
233 Spring Street, New York, N.Y. 10013

Printed in the United States of America

Foreword

Anyone writing on scientific matters for the lay public must try to avoid a number of hazards. He must not use excessive technical jargon or dwell too much on the many important scientific details, or his readers will desert him. Equally he must avoid oversimplification, or the science will become vacuous. In addition he must not try to side-step difficult political, religious, and ethical problems, otherwise his writing will smack too much of the ivory tower. And yet he will do no one a service, if, in an attempt to grab readers, he sensationalizes the issues involved.

It seems to me that Dr. Burke Zimmerman has very successfully circumvented these many dangers. His book is readable, but informed. He deals with many aspects of his topic, yet in a balanced manner. Common sense keeps breaking through, so much so that his pages can be read with profit not only by the layman but also by the professional.

And what a marvelous topic it is! Starting from academic knowledge, acquired because of the thirst to unravel the most intimate secrets of biology, so that we may better understand this remarkable universe in which we find ourselves, the work on DNA, RNA, and protein synthesis—in a word, gene structure, gene replication, and gene action—has developed a whole new world of biotechnology, which not only promises to produce considerable medical benefits, but industrial and agricultural ones as well. Not surprisingly, this new knowledge, and the power it brings with it, is likely to have profound effects on our civilization, not merely in the distant future but within the life-time of most of the readers of this book. An educated citizen will ignore these remarkable developments at his cost. In Dr. Zimmerman he will find a knowledgeable and companionable guide to introduce him to this exciting new world.

FRANCIS CRICK

Preface

As a small boy, I was hooked on several radio serials. For an hour or so before supper, I would sit glued to the speaker, sharing the most amazing adventures with Tom Mix, Superman, Dick Tracy, Jack Armstrong (the All-American Boy), and more. For 15 minutes (actually, it was more like 11, after you subtract the time spent urging our plastic minds to send in a quarter and a boxtop from Kellogg's Pep—or was it Shredded Ralston—to receive, if we were lucky, a genuine whistling sheriff's badge, or whatever), I would be swept into the latest episode to the brink of—"Tune in tomorrow to find out . . ." And, faithfully, I tuned in again tomorrow.

Much like yesterday's radio serials, every day the new biology brings new thrills and raises new questions. And when we tune in tomorrow to find the answers, we get, into the bargain, 10 more questions for each one that is answered. This book is an attempt to allow the general reader to tune in on today's exciting adventures in molecular and cell biology. If that description sounds a bit dull, then genetic engineering and cloning and test-tube babies—the vernacular of the popular press—may be a better one. These terms are misleading, as you will see after venturing inside the next few pages. But when you begin to appreciate what is really behind the hype in the newspapers, it is far more interesting than some overblown science-fiction scenario.

This book deals with the knowledge of life, which we have been accumulating at an extraordinary rate in recent years. With that knowledge comes the responsibility to use it wisely. Much of this volume is devoted to the power that this knowledge is putting into the hands of man,[1] and the ethical dilemmas with which it challenges us. How much can we ever know about ourselves? How much of our future is already set for us? Can and will the human race be transformed into something a bit different, now that we have the power to direct our own evolution? These are some of the questions I worry over in these pages.

It is difficult to start in the middle of any adventure story, so I have recapitulated the previous episodes, briefly, within the limits allowed by the publishing process. And since there are many more segments of the this thrilling series that lie ahead, and as most of us just can't wait to see what happens, I give you my own perceptions of where we may be going from here, but they are only my own educated guesses. To find out what *really* is going on, you must tune in again tomorrow.

Burke Zimmerman

Oakland, California

Contents

Introduction

Have you noticed that nowadays it seems to be necessary for any book worth the paper its printed on to begin with an appropriate quotation? Indeed, often every chapter begins with a profound line or paragraph that is intended to summarize the essence of what is to follow. To me, however, this practice has now become so tiresome that I would rather try my luck at being original.

Still, the reader who has made it this far may feel a gnawing uneasiness because there has been no nice quotation to serve as a summary for the book. Thus, so that such people will not feel deprived, I am including *two* selected quotations here in the beginning, which do not summarize the book at all but capture succinctly certain widespread public views of science and the revolution in genetics.

The first was uncovered during the exercise of my weekly obsession with the *New York Times Magazine* puzzle page. Lo and behold, the solution to the double-crostic puzzle in the February 1, 1981, issue turned out to be a quotation from Art Buchwald:

> Professor Heinrich Applebaum chortled, ''You know the gene I was splicing? Well, I think we can sell it to the Telephone Company people to put in their Princess phones so they can reproduce any color they want without painting them.''

Although I have long enjoyed Buchwald's art for both its humor and its satirical value, this brief commentary contains something more. Encompassed in the above quotation is a very clear statement of the popular conception of what science is all about. In the first place, science exists only to provide new ideas and technologies to be exploited. No distinction is made, of course, between science, the quest for knowledge, and engineering or technology— the application of knowledge. Second, it shows how the practitioners of science are perceived. In one sense, they are screwballs, but at the same time, they are the revered gods who are providing all of the discoveries that will keep our society undergoing a rapid rate of ''progress.''

At least, everyone knows that Buchwald was joking. But the public understanding of science is not helped in the least by the fact that a large fraction of the population acquires its sole knowledge of science and all its attendant wonders as processed by Hollywood and delivered through the entertainment media: television and movies. Thus, my second quotation is provided by the 1978 remake of the *Invasion of the Body Snatchers,* in which the following line is gasped desperately into Donald Sutherland's anxious ear:

> "These things could get into our systems and start screwing us up like DNA— recombining us!"

Thus, one Hollywood writer who, like most of us, had heard the catch-word of the late 1970s, *recombinant DNA,* and knew that it had something to do with altering life and that a lot of people were scared of it, did his part to help educate the moviegoing public, believing, perhaps, that he understood correctly that recombinant DNA was this nasty stuff that had been discovered by these weird scientists and that could wreak disaster. Indeed, the cartoons spawned by the recombinant DNA controversy, and, in fact, much of the controversy itself, were inspired far more by the mythology that surrounded the spectacular achievements in molecular biology than by the reality of these advances. The exploitation of the sensational, the lurid, and the ominous has always been more successful in arousing the public than an accurate presentation of facts or events. Thus, even the existence of some excellent science journalism and public-television science programs can do little to dispel the public impressions that can be created by a single popular movie or even a clever editorial cartoon. The message is simpler and easier to understand; it appeals to basic human drives and emotions and reaches far more people.

If one looks at the history of the last 50 years, at least, there has usually been at least one scientific miracle in vogue at any given time. Although such miracles may in reality be changing our society in profound ways, a popular mythology surrounds them too, projecting the mysterious powers of the new phenomenon into the future, both in ways that are scientifically plausible and in those that are pure fantasy. The boundary between the plausible and the preposterous is usually rather blurred.

The cult surrounding radiation began decades ago. Even the prewar Superman's astounding powers were in some way linked to radiation from a mysterious element called kryptonite. Yet, exposure to the rays from kryptonite, which was found only on Superman's original planet, was the only thing in the universe that could do Superman in. When the realities of nuclear fission were finally grasped by the people of the world, the reaction was a mixture of expectations of wondrous things in the future with a dread and a fear of the awesome power of The Bomb. This manifestation of what was, in fact, very exciting basic research in physics was viewed as some great new powerful force embodying both good and evil. Not long after World War II, the scenarios of the future—that is, the 1950s or perhaps the far distant 1960s—would have everything running on nuclear power, which would propel not only all of our earthbound vehicles but space ships as well. Ionizing radiation would cure everything from acne to cancer, preserve our fruits and vegetables, and do all sorts of miraculous, wonderful, undreamed-of things.

The cloud of unrestrained hopes—and apprehensions—about radiation and nuclear power, of course, was and still is far more interesting than the reality. Two decades of monster movies sprung from the notion that some intense source of radiation buried deep in the ocean—perhaps as a result of nuclear tests in the Pacific—somehow caused wild mutations[1] in the surrounding life, creating the Creature from the Black Lagoon, Godzilla, and God knows what else. Poor Dr. David Banner, as most young kids know nowadays, owes his Incredible Hulk-ishness to an overexposure to gamma rays. And where would Spiderman be if it weren't for his close encounter with ionizing radiation?

Looking back on the radiation/nuclear-energy mystique, we see that most of the expectations people held for radiation and nuclear fission in the 1940s and 1950s never came to pass, at least not to the degree projected. Many were tried but abandoned, for many different reasons. It is true that we have been able to use nuclear power as a source of the generation of electricity, one that is quickly becoming the most expensive and impractical way to generate power. Concern about the biological effects of ionizing radiation is far greater than it was two decades ago, as evidence accumulates that cancer and perhaps other debilitating effects are directly traceable to radiation exposure. It was given up long ago as an acne treatment for this reason. It is also true that we have made more and more terrible weapons, which, fortunately, have not been used deliberately for military purposes since the first human experiments at Hiroshima and Nagasaki. The legacy of tens of thousands of nuclear weapons is by far the most important consequence of the development of nuclear technology, presenting the political institutions of the world with their greatest challenge in history: How can the destruction of the "civilized" world be prevented?

This was not exactly the forecast 35 years ago. What was promised as a miracle, made possible by some fundamental discoveries by Albert Einstein, Enrico Fermi, and others concerning the nature of matter and the universe, turned out to be a technology of much more mundane dimensions than was once predicted. Its initial applications for destructive purposes, the Atomic Energy Act of 1947[2] notwithstanding, have predominated from the beginning. It is not surprising that the mystique of radiation and nuclear energy has faded considerably. But, of course, science was to provide the public with yet another miracle.

The current major miracle—there are many minor miracles—has come about gradually through a series of discoveries which have elucidated the basic nature of the structure of the genetic material—deoxyribonucleic acid, or DNA—and how it stores information and can duplicate itself. In recent years, we have also learned a great deal about how DNA is organized into genes, the functional units of heredity which determine the form and the function of all living things, and about how their expression is controlled in living cells. To be sure, much more is yet to be discovered. Nevertheless, these advances have greatly increased man's ability to manipulate the biological environment. As we understand more and more about cells and their subcellular structures and how they reproduce and how they are put together chemically, we are gaining the capacity to alter life in its most fundamental aspects.

A dramatic event, like the dropping of an atomic bomb, or at least something unique or startling that takes the public by surprise, is usually required for a scientific discovery to capture the public's attention. In the case of genetic manipulation, it was first reported to the public as a profound scientific advancement that was potentially hazardous—possibly even extremely dangerous. Some genuine scientific concerns had led a group of scientists to call attention to the unknown consequences of putting genes normally found in one organism into a completely unrelated organism, and to recommend that research proceed with caution until the risks, if any, could be assessed. Most scientists, however—even those asking for cautious restraint for certain experiments saw the extraordinary potential of using "recombinant DNA" to elucidate and understand the most fundamental of biological mechanisms. The possibility of inadvertent hazards called for prudence, as do many types of scientific research, not hysteria. Other scientists jumped immediately to the relevance of science to the real world, to its exploitation and its practical applications, including both its beneficial uses and its misuses. These musings made much better press copy than the science itself.

Thus, the public was informed simultaneously of the profound potential of genetic manipulation as well as the possible dangers inherent in altering the most basic components of living systems. A few individuals—some with impeccable scientific credentials—and the public statements and magazine articles which reflected their views could genuinely be described as "fearmongering." Horror scenarios were described in which, simply accidentally, in the course of conducting a benign experiment, a molecular biologist might render cancer an infectious disease or might completely disturb the ecology of the planet or turn harmless intestinal bacteria into raging pathogens. The nature of the public reaction to these announcements and the contentious years of the debate over safety policies for research involving recombinant DNA are the subjects of Chapter 3 of this book.

At the same time, the techniques were extolled as providing miraculous new ways of providing rare biologicals and drugs for the sick, a safe and inexpensive way to make antigens for vaccines, and a way for doing genetic surgery on individuals with hereditary diseases. Of course, the speculations did not stop there. The promises of many public benefits were countered with the prediction that evil dictators might manufacture armies of identical super-soldiers—strong, obedient and heartless. The possibility was raised that one might someday be able to order the genetically controlled traits of one's children: intelligence, strength, beauty, and other qualities that a parent might value. Might this list not also include being well behaved and amenability to early toilet training? And what of biological warfare? This question was asked early in the debate over recombinant DNA. Would genetic manipulation methods allow us to create new virulent pathogenic organisms or novel biological toxins? It has even been suggested that these could be made so selective that they would infect or attack only black people or only those with blue eyes, or that they could be linked to some other appropriate combination of population traits, so as to wipe out the enemy, however he were to be defined, provided that there was a genetic basis for distinguishing your enemy from your ally. How much of all this speculation is mythology of the type that surrounded radiation in the 1940s and the 1950s? How much is probable? And how much is reality already?

Although an accurate parallel exists between much of the public perception of the wonders/dangers of radiation and the wonders/dangers of the new biology, there is an important difference between the two phenomena. On its most fundamental level, ionizing radiation is essentially destructive. It breaks chemical bonds and, thus, damages molecules. There are instances in which this property of radiation is useful, as in cancer therapy, but I would guess that after more than 40 years of technological development in radiation and nuclear fission, we have found most of the applications that might be useful to contemporary society. On the other hand, the manipulations now possible with genes and cells are essentially constructive. These techniques enable scientists to take apart genes and cells and put them back together in novel ways, and perhaps even to design and build genes with new functions. It would seem, therefore, that the possibilities would be infinite. Thus, many of the original speculations about the new biology, unlike those about radiation, not only have come to pass in a mere decade, but have been greatly surpassed by more recent developments that were not even imagined in the early 1970s. Although there are, to be sure, some inherent limitations in all of the applications of modern genetics and cell biology, there appear to be relatively few. Many of the things which we would like to do in the 1980s but cannot are very likely to be realities by the 1990s.

Perhaps it would be enough if this knowledge were used only for the cultural enrichment that comes from understanding the mysteries of life. To me, that in itself is ample justification for doing research, and for the governmental support of research, just as it is a justification for the sponsorship of creative activities in the arts and the humanities. However, society and its political and economic institutions have a tradition of building ''progress''— and, in fact, economic growth—on the discoveries of science, as they are applied through the various branches of engineering and technology. It is therefore not surprising that what was considered a probable area of commercial exploitation a few years ago has seen a boom of speculation among venture capitalists and the creation of countless ''biotechnology'' companies, small and large, gambling on what the future may bring.

These developments present society with a responsibility to deal with the increasing power of knowledge in a just, equitable, and ethical manner. Many of the ethical questions have never been raised before in a serious way because they concerned phenomena which were not believed to be possible. Yet, implicit in the subjects discussed in this book are questions fundamental to the integrity of our society and to our very existence. As long as man's power is insufficient to disturb his universe[3] in any but very small ways, then it is not quite so urgent to anticipate the future. But it does not require complex analytical methods to see that man continues to deviate further and further from any semblance of a steady-state equilibrium with his environment. The rate at which we are perturbing the ecology exceeds the rate at which it is able to reach a new equilibrium. The rampant exploitation of resources, industrial development, energy production, manufacturing, and so on, have been very costly in terms of values that many of us hold very dear. Society as a whole—and by this I mean the totality of worldwide human culture—blunders ahead to gratify its immediate needs, oblivious of the earth's delicate ecological balance which requires active human participation.[4]

The rate of technological advancement is far faster than our political, social, and economic institutions can adjust to in such a rapidly changing world. Human beings evolved in a much different environment; our survival instincts are thus often inappropriate to the world into which we were born.

Alvin Toffler discussed the inability of society to keep up with itself more than a decade ago.[5] In fact, the nuclear arms race, the rapid loss of the variety of plant and animal species,[6] and our increasing encroachment on and disruption of natural ecological systems as our human numbers increase have many people forecasting doom of one sort or another before another century passes. But, as if this weren't enough, there is now a new dimension. Our ever-increasing knowledge of life gives us unprecedented power to control our biological destiny. We have, of course, already intervened in the course of human evolution, if only indirectly. Soon, we shall be able to do so directly and by precise design if we so choose. This knowledge bestows on the human race both an ever-increasing power over its future and a responsibility that is growing proportionately. For it amplifies enormously the consequences of a miscalculation of an error of judgment or the failure to anticipate and assess the effects of the tangible applications of this knowledge.

We can choose to give no heed to our future and simply to continue unconstrained, enjoying each short-term gratification that every new technology provides for us, and ignoring each potentially harmful application that posturing and competing national governments may elect to implement. Or we can attempt to control the course that our planet shall take. Before we can do that, however, it is imperative that we define a technology ethic. Until now, the governing principle, if it is indeed a principle at all, has been to do whatever can be done. But as the power of technology increases to the point where its exercise touches all lives in significant ways, the invalidity of this principle becomes obvious.

War has always been the ultimate expression of technology, pushed to the limit of the knowledge available. But even the terrible destruction of World War II was not so great that a relatively rapid recovery was not possible. Even in view of the terror of the use of two atomic bombs, the war did not contaminate the land with stable poisons, nor inflict irreversible genetic damage on the population, nor destroy the capacity of societies and cultures to regenerate themselves. In some ways, the much "smaller" war in Vietnam has left scars that have been much slower in healing than those of World War II. The sophistication of technology is now such that it takes little reflection to be convinced of the utter irreversibility of any new global armed conflict.

Although war may be the extreme expression of technological capability, there are other expressions that, although not as dramatic, may still have consequences which are equally devastating. It is for this reason that it is more important than ever to define a workable ethic for technology. To do this in any social context would mean agreement on a set of values that we would wish to live by. Our children—or at least our grandchildren—have scarcely any say in the matter. It is up to us. We can no longer trust the outcome to chance or to the forces that have governed the exploitation of knowledge in the past. For the present, and certainly in the future, one mistake may be enough. We probably won't get a second chance.

How, then, can we begin to define the ethics of knowledge? And how is it possible to translate them into a realistic technological policy? We are all continually governed by one or another set of values, whether we are consciously aware of it or not. The time has come when we must attempt to bring them out and address them, define them, and be comfortable with what they really are. Implied are the basic questions of morality—good and evil. One can either argue for an absolute morality—and to do so I know of no other way than to invoke religion—or argue for a relative, and ultimately pragmatic, morality. But here it becomes somewhat more difficult, for a relative morality is not derivable from a set of absolute principles.

If our survival—and, indeed, a purely constructive survival—is to determine our societal ethic, we must reject the arrogance of many human cultures and religions that view man as somehow apart from and superior to the rest of his environment. An inseparable element in man's blueprint for survival, if he is to prove himself a competent architect, must be respect, not contempt, for the remainder of the animals and plants and the inanimate environment, as well as the recognition that we must live in harmony with them. A second principle which must ultimately be included in any workable strategy for the future is that any process used to determine an ethic of technology must include the entire globe. Such a strategy is not up to the United States or the Soviet Union or coalitions of smaller nations competing for power in the continuing drama of world politics. It has to be a truly international effort. Anything short of this will surely fail.

Now, it may be that human beings can never agree on a set of values, particularly ones compatible with modern survival. It may be found, ultimately, that those values which have predominated in society are really a reflection of fundamental animal survival instincts our genetic makeup has carried with us since we evolved from the slime. This possibility brings up another question: Now that we have the power to manipulate genes, do we not then also have, ultimately, the power to manipulate human psychology and the nature of human behavior? Few would argue with the notion that it is fundamental human psychology which is ultimately reflected in the behavior of national governments. Aggression and cruelty are intrinsic elements in human behavior, whether we like it or not. In comparison with all the species that have evolved, man's capacity for cruelty to his own species would seem to be unprecedented. We have a continuum of examples, and no culture is exempt from the most heinous acts possible. The Crusaders murdered and raped in the name of Christ; the Nazis to purify the race. In modern times, we have Vietnam, Cambodia, Guatemala, El Salvador, Lebanon, India—we are constantly reminded of the worst that humans can perpetrate. But these uniquely human characteristics are not manifested only in the atrocities of armed conflicts. In early 1983, an unsuspecting woman entered a bar in Connecticut to get some change. She was held down and raped by four men, while the other clientele—men and women alike—cheered her attackers on. The bartender watched. No one helped, no one called the police. Sadly, this was not an isolated incident.

Are personality and behavior purely cultural phenomena, or do their roots, as the mounting evidence suggests, lie in our genes?[7] If so, then the matter of human values becomes far more complex than if we were to assume that we humans are a constant factor in the equation, or that our behavior, either individual or cultural, is simply a product of our environment. If the application of our knowledge includes the possibility of transforming 1984 human beings into something different, which then may be capable of defining an entirely new set of values, perhaps ones less destructive to survival, how should we then proceed? Obviously, we must assume nothing to be impossible. We must also recognize, therefore, that whatever process we develop and whatever solution we reach in the present age must have built into it a means of change, a means of adaptation, a means to adjust to the future.

The record of current society—*current* here meaning the society of the last 200 years—in dealing with change, even of the type that has been forced upon it, is not comforting. Humans, and the cultures they create, tend to resist change of any type, even when it can be shown conclusively that change is consistent with the values held by most individuals and is in the best interests of the vast majority.

We have many modern examples, such as the failure of the American auto industry to give the consumers what they wanted and needed in an era of increasingly expensive fuel and high-quality foreign imports. We have seen our political systems—certainly both major American political parties—cling to a nineteenth-century Keynesian economic model that fails to take into account the constraints on population and resources operating at the end of the twentieth century. Sacred principles are preached as though they were valid for all time. That is, the current economic system taken as a given in the United States *requires* us to have yearly economic growth. We subscribe to a system that depends on such growth for its survival. But if one looks deeper into the models on which these "principles" are based, one sees that there are certain requirements that cannot be met in the real, contemporary world. Perhaps this shortsightedness, which continues to get us into trouble, is an intrinsic human quality that can be modified through an application of the new biology.

One thing is certain: Regardless of the structure of our political and economic models, or the details of our society, knowledge will continue to increase at a staggering rate. The consequences of its application are therefore potentially far greater than ever before in history. As J. Brownowski put it,

> Knowledge is not a loose-leaf notebook of facts. Above all, it is a responsibility for the integrity of what we are, primarily of what we are as ethical creatures. You cannot possibly maintain that informed integrity if you let other people run the world for you while you yourself continue to live out of a ragbag of morals that come from past beliefs. That is really crucial today.[8]

This book is concerned with the knowledge of life and how it is to be used. Now is the time for society to prepare to deal with it. How it does so will determine our future—our biofuture.

CHAPTER 1

Life: Knowledge and the Loss of Innocence

Life

What is life? What is that magic quality of being alive? We have always been surrounded by it and have taken it for granted. But the beginning and the end of human life—birth and death—have forced mankind and its predecessors to contemplate the nature of life itself[1] and its frailty. Yet it is in many ways a concept which continues to mystify us. The record of human culture is filled with perceptions of life and its significance. Human life is in most cultures described as something special, singled out by the gods for preferred treatment, both good and bad. Perhaps the explanation of life could be argued to be the paramount problem in both religion and science.

Our advances in scientific research—not only in biology *per se,* but in physics and chemistry and in all the ways these disciplines have merged into one continuum of knowledge—have brought us to a remarkable point in history. It is the transition between seeing life as a mystical phenomenon beyond the grasp of human comprehension and being able to understand it in its most elementary form. It is a curious period, in which much of the darkness and dogma of past millennia still linger, while, at the same time, we look ahead to the certainty of understanding life to the point of being able to structure it in every detail. It is a transition that has come about rather quickly, perhaps too rapidly for society to adjust to a perception that is at odds with traditional views. The battle continues to rage between the creationists and the evolutionists. The U.S. Senate has attempted to define the point at which human life begins. But then, adjustment to a new level of understanding has never been easy for any culture.

This time, it is a little different. For this transition from the mystical to the concrete concerns the understanding of our very being, the nature of human existence in its most fundamental form. Thus, each new discovery only heightens the intensity of our fascination with ourselves as living beings. Those who choose to contemplate the nature of life and of man and his place in the world *must* accommodate the knowledge of the molecular basis of man's existence in their world views and must acknowledge the importance of the gene. Perhaps this is carrying "know thyself" far beyond what Socrates had in mind. In a way, knowing ourselves to this degree represents a loss of innocence from which there can be no return.

There is no question that this level of knowledge has made many uneasy. Most people would probably prefer the comfort of taking life for granted, simply having it go on, not being concerned with the details of what it is or how it is, and, particularly, being thankful that it has been beyond our power ever to change it. Therefore, even idle talk about altering the genetic makeup of human beings is unsettling. It is not surprising that many view this new future with both awe and trepidation.

People, like the societies they form, innately resist change. Any change, whether it be for better or for worse, is always responded to with discomfort. It is always difficult to change one's habits or one's world view, particularly if one is forced by circumstances to do so. The individual who suddenly loses his money and goes from rich to poor might be expected to feel a great deal of discomfort. However, I would contend that the poor man who suddenly receives a windfall and thus becomes rich experiences just as much anxiety. It has been comforting to view life over the past centuries as a constant, lying safely within the realm of religion. Any responsibility for the nature of human life, however grim, could be attributed to God. But we cannot do that any more. Now we are beginning to understand the marvel of a complex set of self-sustaining chemical reactions that continues and propagates itself in the most unbelievably clever ways, following a set of natural laws rather than the willful edicts of a supreme intelligence.

There are many ways in which one might choose to describe life. A completely general description, however, must include the following elements: (1) specific structure or form; (2) controlled chemistry; and (3) reproducibility. In this discussion, it is meaningless to quibble over whether or not a virus is living or nonliving. A virus clearly satisfies the above requirements. It is part of the totality of the phenomenon which we call life. One should perhaps include a fourth criterion that acknowledges that the specific structure, controlled chemistry, and reproducibility characteristic of any living thing is more than a reflection of the simple chemical properties of atoms. There must also be a *selection* of specific characteristics to enable a particular entity to exhibit the three conditions in a particular environment. I am not concerned here with a legally valid definition of life that might contain certain arbitrary choices of words and is free of loopholes but, rather, with the nature of the phenomenon itself. Life itself. By some stretching of the imagination, the growth of a crystal of salt might be considered to exhibit a specific structure, controlled chemistry, and reproducibility; that is, all crystals of salt have a certain fundamental similarity. But a crystal of salt is clearly not living. It does not reproduce itself in precise ways, in the manner that even the simplest of viruses or subcellular components do.

Life is at the same time both extraordinarily complex and profoundly simple. Its form and movement are exquisitely aesthetic; its solutions to the problems of adapting to and surviving in the natural environment are ingenious. We are usually so wrapped up in being part of the phenomenon of life and all of its daily machinations that we do not stop to reflect on what we take for granted, and so, perhaps, we lose respect for something which lies far beyond the creative powers of the most brilliant human intellects. Who could have invented a bird, let alone one that could fly with ease, or a fish or a colony of bees or DNA? But as we slowly penetrate each layer of obscurity in which living phenomena have been hidden, to begin at last to understand the nature of the molecular control that ensures that each generation of an organism will look, behave, and function in the same way (almost) as did its ancestors, our respect for the deliberate wisdom of the evolutionary process can only deepen.

What we are currently undergoing in biological research has been described by many as a revolution. The biological revolution. Yet it must be kept in mind that centuries and decades of research have built on the existing body of knowledge to bring us to where we are today. It is a continuous and, by some reckonings, slow process, rather than one of sharp discontinuities or jumps in our understanding. Thomas Kuhn[2] speaks of "paradigm shifts" in describing revolutions in science. But the invention of such jargon does not clarify the overall nature of the creative process in science, nor should it be assumed that the evolution of conceptual understanding is marked by abrupt transitions. Rarely is that the case.

However, sometimes discoveries or inventions, in which a long-outstanding problem is finally solved, give the appearance that advances in science are made in leaps. But "breakthroughs," as they are called in the popular vernacular, always follow an accumulation of knowledge and a long series of small increments in the understanding of the problem. The final tying together of the data and the resolution of the competing hypotheses is, to be sure, a satisfying event for a scientist, and the kind of achievement that bestows fame and perhaps a law named for its discoverer. But I would contend that the rate of acquisition of knowledge and understanding is still, in spite of its deceptive appearance, more-or-less continuous.

However smooth or rough the road to enlightenment may be, it is a fact that many of the phenomena concerning the nature of life which have been uncovered recently were not even imagined as little as five years ago. I am not the first to observe that perhaps our science-fiction writers have predicted more of what is to come than have scientists. True, science-fiction writers' predictions are also accompanied by a great deal of "noise" predictions, which, if not blatant nonsense, have not, at least to date, been borne out. But the caution of scientists in suggesting explanations that they cannot absolutely justify perhaps inhibits the creative process in some ways. We should, of course, presume that scientists' imaginations can soar as freely as those of our science-fiction writers. Playing the hunch is an undeniably important part of scientific discovery. Most scientists, however, would be risking their reputations if they did their creative thinking in public. At least, in the twentieth century this is no longer done as it once was.

The scientific literature of the 300 years preceding 1900 includes some fascinating reading[3]; the style of writing was generally much less confined than that now demanded by scientific journals. The accounts of scientists were most commonly personal accounts of discovery, as one might narrate an adventure tale. Many were also full of speculation and imagination. There was no unwritten proscription of the use of the first-person singular, as there is today. It was much easier to get a flavor of the way in which people thought and the way in which discoveries are really made. Now, however, the publication of the results of a successful line of investigation, complete with the rigorous proof of the hypothesis stated in the first lines, rarely reveals to the reader the actual creative thought process by which the scientist was really driven, or the blind alleys that he may have followed before he succeeded in solving the problem. And if the scientist does not succeed in solving the problem, his hunches and false leads are more often kept to himself. Scientists fear being wrong; negative results and incorrect hypotheses do not win tenure or research grants. Because it is an essential part of the scientific process that all contentions be carefully scrutinized for their logical soundness and be confirmed by observation, scientists, at least in legitimate professional publications and forums, generally avoid too much speculation.

But the science-fiction writer is not so bound. He can say anything he wants to, in the name of entertainment, and no one will hold him accountable for his ravings. There would seem to be a dilemma here for which no immediate resolution is obvious. The cautious professional scientist is apt to have a higher rate of success than the writer about the future, but he takes far fewer chances. The writer, on the other hand, although likely to be wrong a good deal of the time, makes far more unconstrained attempts. So, in fact, he may actually predict a greater number of the things to come than the scientist.

I am attempting here to bring the reader up to date in the domain of the world of molecules known as *genetics* and *cell biology*, current to the date of publication. However, because much of this book is concerned with the future, I have allowed myself additional license to make some educated predictions of what the status of our knowledge is likely to be in five years, a decade, and beyond. In doing so, I am being somewhat less cautious than rigorous science would demand. However, such musings are a useful exercise in an age where the power of knowledge is becoming so great—particularly in the life sciences—that our future depends upon being able to use this knowledge with wisdom.

The Cell Universe

We are living objects, of the order of 1–2 meters in length and 50–100 kilograms in mass. As such, we tend to judge other living objects according to our own dimensions. That is, a redwood is very big, and a whale or an elephant is big, but a cat is small. A mouse is very small, and an ant is tiny. But the resolving power of our eyes can't go much beyond a very small insect, say one tenth the size of a small ant. So anything smaller is called *microscopic*, for in order to see anything of a millimeter or less in length *well*, we need some help, and that help is usually in the form of a microscope.

That remarkable invention, dating back 400 years, provided a window to a new universe and revealed much about the nature of life that had previously escaped man's scrutiny. The remarkable accounts of Antony van Leeuwenhoek (1632–1723)[4] describe all sorts of minute creatures (''animalicules'') everywhere, coming in all sorts of bizarre and weird shapes, with many peculiar habits that were unknown in the living things that we could see with our unaided eyes.

But the discovery that changed the way in which natural philosophers thought about life was that all organisms above a certain size seemed to be composed of smaller units, which we call *cells*. Whether plant or animal, nearly all tissues which could be examined appeared to consist of these small compartments. Of course, the first microscopes, consisting of a small bead of glass, were simply high-power magnifying glasses and couldn't distinguish the individual cells of all tissues. But as the technology improved, the long-hidden world of the minute gradually became revealed.

The history of biology over the past 300 years is really the story of being able to ''see'' the shape of living things and to study the way in which their parts function to smaller and smaller dimensions. First, there were the cells, which comprise all organisms. The simplest forms of life were seen to consist of only a single, specialized cell, whereas the more complex organisms appeared to contain perhaps billions of component cells. Generally, the "higher" or more advanced on the evolutionary scale an organism is, the more *types* of specialized cells it is likely to have, although that measure alone is not a sufficient index of an organism's complexity.

Most of the cells to be found in the tissues and organs of all living things, like van Leeuwenhoek's one-celled animalicules, exhibit the remarkable property of division, by which they increase in number. It was noted that after a cell increased in size past a certain point, it seemed to pinch off in the middle and become two nearly identical cells. This process accounted, at least in part, for how plants and animals grew. The growth of an organism, overall, is usually accompained by an increase in the *numbers* of cells, rather than by an increase in size of individual cells, at least in the animal kingdom. I say "usually" because that is the general rule for a growing organ or tissue. There are, of course, many exceptions to that rule, particularly for certain specialized cells. The number of cells in the human brain, for example, is highest shortly before birth and decreases throughout a person's lifetime, even though the brain obviously increases in size and weight. In green plants, cell division takes place only at the tips of the new shoots, stems, and roots. The elongation of a stem reflects the increase in length of individual cells to many times their original length, with no further cell division taking place once the cells have acquired the specialized characteristics appropriate for a plant stem, root, or leaf.

As microscopes were improved, smaller bodies within cells were seen and studied, particularly after the development of methods of staining biological material, greatly improving the contrast among the cell's component parts. Most cells were seen to contain a nucleus, and the nucleus sometimes appeared to have a mottled appearance or to contain little dark bits. But shortly before a cell split in two, its nuclues would disappear, and the dark bits would become much more distinct, looking like crudely drawn versions of the letters X, V, and Y. These were the chromosomes, which are visible only around the time of cell division. They seemed to line up on the plane along which the cell would fission, with half going to each of the two daughter cells. In his elegant cytological studies of the dividing cells of a developing salamander, published in 1879,[5] Walther Flemming described the longitudinal splitting of individual chromosomes into equivalent, perhaps identical, halves. However, it took more than 20 years to reconcile these observations with Mendel's studies of the inheritance of independent traits and to establish that it was these chromosomes which were themselves the units of heredity.[6]

The limit of resolution of the light microscope was finally reached. As the quality of the optical elements improved, the size of the smallest object that could be discerned was now dependent only on the wavelength of visible light. At the dimensions in question—about 2000 angstrom units (Å),* or two ten thousandths of a millimeter—the diffraction of light begins to destroy the quality of the image. At smaller dimensions, diffraction effects obliterate the coherence of the image so much that it is useless to go to higher magnification, even though that is a relatively simple optical problem.

So, in order to investigate living things at still smaller dimensions, other means had to be developed.[7] Light of shorter wavelengths—ultraviolet and x-radiation—can, in principle, be used by a microscope to take advantage of the higher resolving power of shorter wavelengths. But the human eye is sensitive only to light between 4000 Å (violet) and 7000 Å (red). Ultraviolet light is, therefore, invisible, necessitating some other sort of suitable detector, such as photographic film or, more recently, a television camera, which is not subject to the limitations of the human retina. But even the best quartz glass will not transmit ultraviolet light below about 1800 Å. In this region, it is preferable to utilize reflecting optics—precision curved mirrors—instead of glass. It turned out, however, that most biological tissue is opaque to short ultraviolet light, a consequence of the light's absorption by proteins and nucleic acids. Although this property has sometimes been useful in locating the DNA within a cell, the technology begins to get rather complex at these wavelengths. Thus, such instruments have not been very useful even though there is a small improvement in theoretical resolving power.

In spite of these limitations, light microscopy has remained as the single most powerful tool in understanding the general organization and behavior of cells and tissues. The technology has seen improvements, such as phase contrast and interference microscopy, which have made possible the study of living and unstained preparations at high magnification. However, the real advance in allowing us to peer into the details of cells came with the electron microscope,[8] developed in the late 1930s and improved steadily well into the 1970s until it could resolve even the most minute discrete subcellular structures and even large molecules, the best instruments resolving dimensions of only 2Å. But the electron microscope requires that a specimen not only be dead and cut into very thin sections but have the water removed as well. This procedure, of course, can greatly alter the nature of biological material. Moreover, in order to obtain enough contrast of organic structures, various staining and shadowing methods using heavy metals are employed. There

*1 Å (Ångstrom unit) = 10^{-8}cm.

have been attempts to get around the requirements of desiccating samples and even to observe life in a dynamic state, rather than in a fixed specimen, frozen in time. These efforts have not succeeded particularly well.

Nevertheless, a tremendous amount of knowledge of the cell and its structures has been obtained with the electron microscope. It has been particularly useful in helping us to understand the structure and organization of deoxyribonucleic acid (DNA)—the genetic material—and the way in which it replicates itself and the way it is organized within the cell. The electron microscope has also been of great value in elucidating the way in which more than a meter of human DNA double helix can be folded into those tiny but intricately structured chromosomes of micrometer dimensions.

The first microscopes immediately began to give clues to the nature of the beginning of life. The development of eggs—not necessarily those of the common chicken, although these were among the first studied—provided a fascinating object of study. It was here that the cell theory really began to take form. A frog egg looked like a single sphere. As it developed, it first divided in half, then in quarters, eighths, and so on, until there were countless tiny cells. But the total volume of these new cells was about the same as that of the original egg. Eventually, as development proceeded for a few days, the ball of cells began to acquire distinguishable features, which, in time, became specific parts of the animal. Imagine the excitement that the first observer of the process of development must have experienced!

The development of an animal from a single, nondescript spherical cell has been one of the most baffling mysteries of biology. The size of the original egg cell varies considerably, depending on the species, generally being the smallest in mammals. The human egg, for example, is only 0.14 millimeters in diameter, and it remains about this size for the first week after fertilization before it begins to grow rapidly. But what is remarkable is the fact that every kind of animal—be it fish or frog, pig or penguin, horse or human—looks approximately the same during the early stages of development, or embryogenesis. This observation was heartening to the Darwinians, who subscribed to the thesis that man had evolved, through gradual change and selective adaptation, from the most primitive forms of life. The catchy phrase "ontogeny recapitulates phylogeny" emerged; it simply means that during the course of development of the human embryo, features of the more primitive forms of life from which we have evolved are indeed expressed at various stages. At three weeks' gestation, the human embryo exhibits gill-like structures; at two months, it certainly has a tail. But such catch phrases cannot be taken too seriously. It would be quite impossible to trace the ancestry of the human species by careful observations of the development of the human embryo.

What is revealing, however, is that there *is* so much similarity among species. That we have a great deal more in common with at least a good part of the animal kingdom, especially the vertebrates, than many wished to admit was an inescapable conclusion of the direct observations of development. Viewing only photographs of embryos, where the dimensions are not known, experts have a difficult time telling the species of mammal even at a stage where eyes and distinct limbs have formed. But that this relationship is far more intimate than even morphogenesis would indicate was revealed when we acquired the tools to look in detail into the structure of the molecules that comprise our being, and ultimately those that direct our heredity. There are very few functional differences in the cells and the biochemistry of humans and other mammals. Corresponding enzymes and hormones may differ in only 1 or a few of the amino acids; human DNA overall shows over 90% homology with the DNA of a mouse.[9]

However, before venturing off into the world of molecules and the ways we have discovered to "see" into how certain of these can function in concert to constitute the essence of life, let us linger a bit longer in the domain of cells. DNA isn't everything. It is the cells which constitute the working units of life—and the ways in which they interact—that determine the nature of the organism and the kind of life it will lead. That is, there is a great deal of molecular similarity in all cells. The fundamental molecular chemistry of all cells is, more or less, the same. But cells are vastly different, even those in a single organism which all arose from a single cell and that all contain identical DNA.

But how did they get to be so different, if they all came from a single cell? If the genetic messages contained in the DNA don't change, then what does? Much of that process is still a mystery, but we are slowly beginning to find the clues. Part of the answer, of course, lies in how the information in the DNA is read into reality, and which parts of it are read at a given time in a given place. That is, we know that every cell contains the totality of information necessary to determine every feature of the organism and the manner in which it develops. But we know that, at any given time, most of these directions are simply kept stored and filed away; only a small fraction are being used at any given time to direct the operation and the fate of any given cell.

But after the first few rounds of cell division following fertilization, what determines which parts of the blob of cells present will become the head, or the tail, or the eyes, or the brain, or the toes? Is the egg itself assymetrical, having an intrinsic polarity? Classical embryologists identified the so-called animal and vegetal poles of the egg, which would become the embryo and the nourishing yolk respectively. Does the point of entry of the sperm make a difference? Does gravity have an influence? Chance? Now that we are asking that all the old questions be answered again in molecular terms, these are among the important ones in biology still to be answered.

A typical animal cell is depicted in Figure 1. Most embryonic cells, or those undifferentiated cells that ultimately change with each division to form the specialized cells that comprise tissues and organs, resemble, more or less, this prototype cell. Plant cells are shown in Figure 2. Although each one of these small cellular units contains in its genetic material all of the information necessary to determine its own unique destiny, it also contains the information necessary to specify every other part and feature of the organism—not only its morphology but its chemistry, its functions, its life span, its reproductive

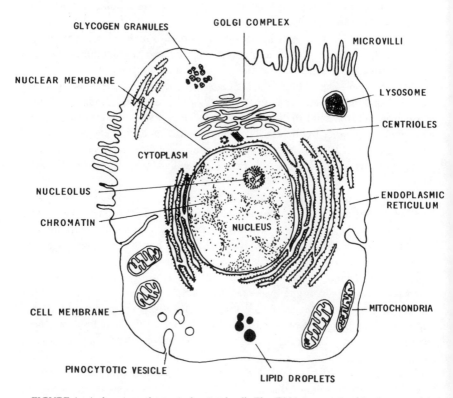

FIGURE 1. A drawing of a typical animal cell. The DNA is contained in the material labeled *chromatin*, which appears even under the electron microscope as a darker, slightly granular material in the nucleus. Only immediately before and after cell division is the chromatin condensed into visible chromosomes.

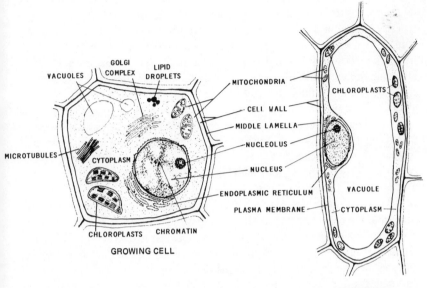

FIGURE 2. Drawings of typical plant cells. A growing, dividing cell, found typically in the growing tips of shoots and roots, is shown on the left. A mature cell, represented schematically on the right, is typical of the elongated cells of the stems of higher plants. It is much larger than its dividing precursor (the drawings are not in relative scale) and is characterized by a large central vacuole. The principal ways in which plant cells differ from animal cells include a rigid cell wall, which gives the plant its structure; chloroplasts, in which photosynthesis takes place; and large vacuoles in the cytoplasms of most mature, differentiated cells, often comprising the bulk of the intracellular volume.

cycle, and, as many now contend, its social behavior.[10] That is, the genetic information contained in each cell, coded in the remarkable molecular structure of DNA, is identical to that in every other cell in that organism (except for the reproductive cells, or gametes, which have only half the usual number of chromosomes).

The intricate programming in the DNA of the cell, regulated to some degree by the precise surroundings of each cell, dictates how, with each cell division, the daughter cells become more and more unlike each other, taking on specific new functions and forming specialized structures (differentiation). The goal of this process is the formation of tissues and organs, which perform separate essential functions in harmony with those carried out by all of the other tissues and organs. The result is a free living organism, capable of fending for itself. In a fully differentiated tissue, there are perhaps several types of cells, but there are millions that are functionally identical. Thus, the damage or loss of a few cells can occur without serious harm to the organ.

When viewed from an evolutionary point of view, it seems obvious that all living things would be composed of cells, a feature that imparts a significant tolerance for injury from the environment. At one level, then, although all cells are important to the function of the organ or the tissue, they function somewhat independently of one another, much as ants or bees do in a colony of millions. Indeed, some of the cell types in an adult human being, such as lymphocytes and phagocytes, behave much as do the independent, single-celled amoebas, carrying out their specialized functions with the predetermination built into their genes.

The cell, thus, has two essential properties. First, it reproduces itself, providing the basis for embryonic development, the formation of new tissues and organs, growth, and the healing of wounds. Second, each provides, in a relatively small space, the complete chemical and structural apparatus for carrying out some necessary functions of the organism. The contained compartment that is the cell allows for a controlled internal environment in which this chemistry can function in an optimal way. The cell must perform all the steps required to convert food or light energy from the outside into energy useful to the organism, and it must be able to generate the substances necessary for growth. In that sense, each cell may be considered a miniature factory, highly organized to process thousands of different chemical substances in precisely specified ways. But as this factory is constructed on the scale of molecules, it is no wonder that under the light microscope, the internal workings of that mysterious, jellylike material called *cytoplasm,* with its smaller nucleus, remained a mystery until indirect methods allowed us to ''see'' the molecular details of the cell in operation. Each of the ''organelles'' distinguished by the cytologists in the early twentieth century contains perhaps thousands of different components in a very specific microstructure which enables it to carry out its functions effectively. By comparison, the most advanced integrated circuits and solid-state electronic components are giant simpletons next to even the most primitive living cell.

Most of the activities directed by the cell are carried out within the cell itself. But, of course, both plants and animals are characterized by extracellular structures and tissues. The circulating blood of an animal is, in a sense, a tissue. It contains living cells, but it also contains many chemical components in suspension and solution. Scales, hair, and fingernails are examples of extracellular structures, and even teeth and, to some extent, bones lose their cellular characteristics. Plants lay down a matrix of polysaccharides (sugar molecules bound together chemically in long chains) that forms the cell walls and gives plants their fibrous nature and wood its unique properties long after the tree itself is no longer alive.

It is true that in highly differentiated structures the characteristics of our prototype cell are not always present as shown in Figure 3. Red blood cells, for example, lose their nucleus, cease cell division, and have, on the average, a life span of only 120 days. Therefore, their supply must be constantly replenished from the undifferentiated cells in the bone marrow where they

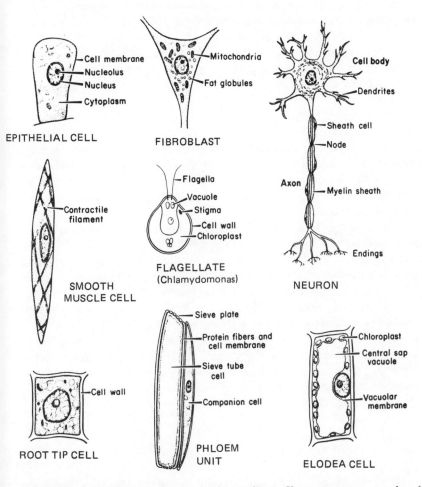

FIGURE 3. Cells differentiate into many diverse forms. Shown are some examples of animal and plant cells. (From A. C. Giese, *Cell Physiology*, 5th ed. © 1979 by Saunders College Publishing/Holt, Rinehart & Winston. Reprinted by permission of Holt, Rinehart & Winston, CBS Publishing.)

develop. Muscle cells, on the other hand, may have many nuclei and are characterized by the fibrous contractile proteins that give muscle tissue the capacity to convert stored metabolic energy into work. Only a small part of nerve cells may be devoted to the nucleus, the bulk of the cell consisting of an axon, or nerve, which can be several meters in length in large animals.

The well-orchestrated harmony that exists among the many different cell types, tissues, or organs of a complex organism perhaps represents the level of life with which we are more familiar, rather than the cellular, subcellular, or molecular levels. But this remarkably coordinated mechanism, including the communication that takes place between the different cells and the organs of the body through the nervous and endocrine systems is all ultimately dependent upon the proper functioning of individual cells. The nature of this coordination is the subject of physiology; the correction of malfunctions in these systems or the ways in which they work together is the object of medicine.

Here, we are concerned not with medicine and physiology, but with the fact that both the whole and all of its parts are directed by an intricate molecular mechanism that must function at a high level of precision in order for the life that springs from this mechanism to function properly. So now we are to probe the cell nucleus and see just what this DNA is all about. It is this remarkable molecular substance in which all of the specifications for all of life on earth are encoded.

Most of the DNA of a cell resides in the nucleus, although in higher plants and animals there are small bits of DNA present in both chloroplasts (the specialized structures that carry out photosynthesis), and mitochondria (tiny cytoplasmic structures that produce the bulk of the metabolic energy which virtually every life-related process requires). Depending upon the species of organism under consideration, there may be from one to several complete copies of the organism's genetic material in a single cell nucleus. It is the understanding of how DNA functions and how the expression of the information contained in its long strands is controlled that is the subject of modern genetics. Genetic engineering, then, is the deliberate manipulation or alteration of the genetic material of the cell, in order to directly produce a change in some feature of the organism.

Genes and Their Function

The concept of the inheritance of traits by children from their parents has been a given principle in human cultures throughout recorded history. Even if nothing was understood about the mechanisms or even the statistical nature of genetics, it was common knowledge that a strong bull or a good milk-producing cow was more likely to yield a calf with similar characteristics than one not so endowed. Children were observed to resemble their parents. Only the direct heirs to royalty were assumed to partake of their superior powers, often imputed to be divine in origin. And proper "breeding" has certainly been an important part of class-conscious Western civilization. The barriers between castes in India were assumed to be genetic; you had to be born into your niche in life. Although all of the mythology surrounding the historical concepts of inheritance is certainly not based in scientific fact, it probably contains many more sound elements than many modern social egalitarians would be willing to accept. In one sense, we may be what we eat, but we are inexorably bound and limited by what our genes specify that we are to be.

The monk Gregor Mendel[11] demonstrated in the mid-1800s that easily defined morphological traits of peas, when bred in controlled crosses, appeared in subsequent generations in the ratio of small whole numbers. Moreover, these traits seemed to be independent of one another. From his remarkable data (some have suggested that he fudged it a bit to fit his model or at least reported only his best experiments), he fashioned the hypothesis that predicts accurately how many hereditary traits are transmitted to offspring. His model included the concept of dominance and of segregation and independent assortment of genetic determinants. He, of course, had no notion of the concept of chromosomes or DNA or the nature of the details of cell division, let alone the development of the reproductive cells (ova, pollen, and sperm).

Around the turn of the century, it was determined that the actual units of inheritance in plants and animals were the several chromosomes,[6] each species having a characteristic number. Perhaps, it was thought, these were the units that carried the traits that Mendel had observed segregated independently. One of the simplest organisms in which chromosomes are observed is yeast, which has four chromosomes or two pairs. The fruit fly, long the favorite object of study of the geneticist because of its short generation time and oversized salavary gland chromosomes, has 8 chromosomes, or 4 pairs; the frog has 26, or 13 pairs; the mouse 40, or 20 pairs; and the human 46 chromosomes, or 23 pairs. The members of each pair begin as those contributed by each parent. That is, each sex cell of a man or a woman, whether ovum or sperm, contains only 23 unpaired chromosomes. During fertilization, the corresponding members find each other and form pairs, each presumably containing the DNA coding for the same traits.

Throughout most of the cell division cycle, the chromosomal DNA is completely dispersed within the cell nuclei. It is during these periods that the replication of the DNA takes place, along with its other functions of specifying and controlling all of the other biochemical and physiological properties of the cell. It is also at this time that "crossing over" can occur. That is, pieces of the maternal and paternal chromosomes actually exchange with one another, and they do so quite readily. Crossing over, or the recombination of genetic material is of no particular importance for most cellular functions (with a few exceptions) except during the process of meiosis, or the formation of gametes: the sperm and the ova. Because of this exchange, each chromosome in each gamete is likely to contain segments of DNA contributed by both parents. Thus, Mendelian segregation, it turns out, occurs even if the genes for the trait in question are on the same chromosome. Only when they are very close together on the same chromosome is what is called *genetic linkage* apparent. The closer two genes are together physically, the less likely they are to cross over, or to experience recombination with a sister chromosome, and the more likely it is that they will be inherited together.

As cell division approaches, the long strands of DNA in each chromosome, now having replicated, must undergo an intricate folding, which is not only necessary for condensing the DNA into discrete chromosomes but essential for the process by which the duplicated chromosomes divide equally between the two daughter cells. The cell division process in animal cells is shown schematically in Figure 4. In bacteria, nuclei are not always visible, and discrete chromosomes cannot be seen. Nevertheless, even in such simple

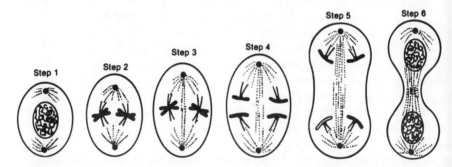

FIGURE 4. A schematic representation of the condensation and separation of the duplicated chromosomes during cell division. During most of the division cycle, the chromatin, a complex structure containing the cellular DNA and proteins important to its packaging in the cell, appears to be dispersed throughout the cell nucleus and cannot be seen with the light microscope. Shortly before division and after DNA replication, the chromatin begins to condense, eventually forming the discrete chromosomes as the nuclear membrane disappears. Each of the doubled chromosomes divides along with the cell itself. As soon as the chromosomes are separated, a nuclear membrane forms around each set to form the nuclei of the two daughter cells, even before the cells have separated completely. (From Congress of the United States, Office of Technology Assessment, *Impacts of Applied Genetics*, 1981.)

organisms, the DNA appears to be organized in space in a way that we now view as moderately complex.

Regardless of the type of molecular organization needed to pack DNA into its tiny cellular compartments, nearly all DNA consists of a unique intertwined double-stranded structure. First elucidated by the pioneering work of Francis Crick and James Watson and published in 1953,[12] the description of the "double helix" represented the culmination of efforts by a number of scientists toying with alternative models of a molecule which could somehow replicate itself faithfully and then split so that each of two daughter cells had a complete and identical copy. There are four distinct types of subunits in a strand of DNA, called bases[13] (A = adenosine, T = thymine, C= cytosine, G = guanine). Although a strand of DNA may contain thousands of each of these bases, it is the sequence of these four substances that encodes the information contained in DNA. In the double-stranded structure of DNA, two of the bases are complementary to the other two (shown in detail in Figure 7), so that they form unique hydrogen-bonded pairs (A:T, C:G), providing the perfect solution for the faithful propagation of the species. That is, one strand is an exact template for the other. Because it is these specific base pair bonds that determine how the DNA chains are assembled during synthesis, each strand directs the synthesis of its complement, with the effect of exactly duplicating the entire structure.

The form in which the information in DNA is coded was a major challenge to molecular biologists 20 years ago. Because there are only four different types of subunits, one may imagine that a strand of DNA is much like a very, very long necklace, containing beads of four different colors. It was postulated that all of the information in DNA is coded in the precise sequence of those colored beads, or bases. How indeed could a substance like DNA, containing only four different unique chemical subunits, possibly code for the intricacy of information necessary to specify every aspect of a human being? That is, the chemical structure of each protein synthesized by the cell, the function of each enzyme, the morphology, the appearance, and every aspect of the organism's life must ultimately be coded in this sequence. Well, computers do it with only 1's and 0's. The text of this book was encoded in such a binary form on just a few magnetic computer discs. DNA, then, is only slightly more complicated than a computer's information storage system in that it uses a quaternary code instead of a binary one. The information it must store is, in a way, somewhat more complex than that stored in the most sophisticated computers. In principle, however, all of the information stored in the DNA of a human being could also be stored in binary form on computer storage discs. But that is a great deal of information. Fortunately, DNA is

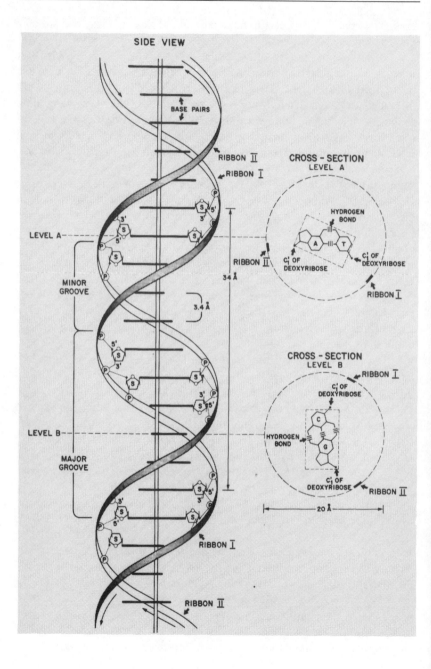

very small. The smallest viruses contain about 3,000 base pairs' worth of information. The single circular piece of DNA in a bacterial cell contains about 4.5 million base pairs. The DNA complement of a single human cell is capable of storing about 1,000 times as much DNA as a bacterium, or a unique sequence of 4.5 billion base pairs, enough to contain the entire plans for a person, including the way he develops, functions, learns, looks, behaves, lives, and dies.

It was once believed by many that all DNA sequences coded for the synthesis of proteins, and that all other properties of a living organism, derived from the sequence of amino acids in the various proteins. Thus, in order to specify the information for 20 different amino acids, each code "word" would have to contain at least three bases. That is, the maximum number of possible unique combinations of two bases is $4 \times 4 = 16$, whereas three bases would make possible $4 \times 4 \times 4 = 64$ different combinations. That would easily allow for 20 amino acids plus a bit of redundancy.

It was never universally accepted that DNA coded *only* for amino acid sequences. There would have to be ways to code for the beginnings and ends of protein chains as well as many other control functions. But these, too, could be easily accommodated by 64 combinations. Nature being true to its predicated efficiency, the "triplet" code was cracked in the early 1960s, principally by the work of Marshall Nirenberg of the National Institutes of Health.[14] The genetic code words for each amino acid and the "start" and the "stop" signals for protein synthesis are given in Table 1.

A gene is a region of DNA which codes for a specific functional or structural unit. That entity might be the sequence of amino acids in a particular protein, or in a larger sense, it may refer to several protein enzymes required for a particular biochemical pathway, where the regions of DNA coding for those proteins are adjacent. There are also control genes that govern the activity of adjacent DNA but which do not themselves code for proteins. As the details of the process of the control of genetic function are revealed, the extraordinary ingenuity with which nature has solved the design problems of living processes becomes apparent.

←───

FIGURE 5. The double helical structure of deoxyribonucleic acid (DNA). The left-hand figure illustrates the spatial orientation of the two strands, which run in chemically opposite directions. The right-hand drawing shows more accurately the actual structural properties of DNA. The open pentagons are the deoxyribose rings; the lines connecting them are the hydrogen bonded bases which are perpendicular to the axis of the DNA. (From R. A. Kellin and J. R. Gear, "A Diagrammatic Illustration of the Structure of Duplex DNA," *Bioscience*, **30**, 110–111, 1980, modified from W. Etkin, *Bioscience*, **23**, 652–653, 1973. © 1980 by the American Institute of Biological Sciences.)

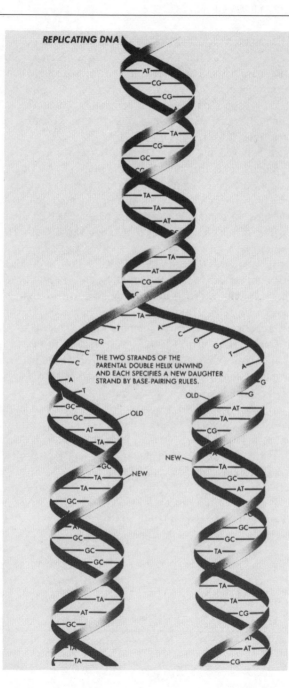

REPLICATING DNA

THE TWO STRANDS OF THE PARENTAL DOUBLE HELIX UNWIND AND EACH SPECIFIES A NEW DAUGHTER STRAND BY BASE-PAIRING RULES.

OLD

NEW

OLD

NEW

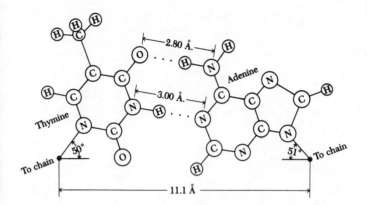

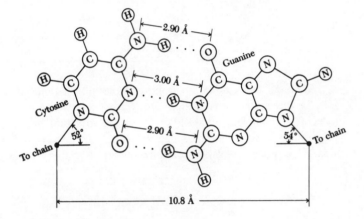

FIGURE 7. The pairing of complementary bases by hydrogen bonding gives DNA its physical stability, as well conferring on it a property essential to its unique mechanism of replicating itself and transmitting its information to RNA and protein structure. The base adenine pairs specifically with thymine (or uracil, its RNA counterpart), and guanine pairs uniquely with cytosine. (From C. Anfinsen, *The Molecular Basis of Evolution*. New York: John Wiley and Sons, Inc., 1959.)

←

FIGURE 6. Schematic representation of the replication of DNA, showing the unwinding of the parent DNA double helix, with each new strand containing a base sequence complementary to that of the strand of parental DNA serving as a template for its synthesis. (From James D. Watson and John Tooze, *The DNA Story.* © 1981 by W. H. Freeman and Co., all rights reserved.)

TABLE I. The Genetic Code

1st ↓ 2nd →	U	C	A	G	↓ 3rd
	Phe	Ser	Tyr	Cys	U
U	Phe	Ser	Tyr	Cys	C
	Leu	Ser	Terminate	Terminate	A
	Leu	Ser	Terminate	Trp	G
	Leu	Pro	His	Arg	U
C	Leu	Pro	His	Arg	C
	Leu	Pro	Gln	Arg	A
	Leu	Pro	Gln	Arg	G
	Ile	Thr	Asn	Ser	U
A	Ile	Thr	Asn	Ser	C
	Ile	Thr	Lys	Arg	A
	Met	Thr	Lys	Arg	G
	Val	Ala	Asp	Gly	U
G	Val	Ala	Asp	Gly	C
	Val	Ala	Glu	Gly	A
	Val	Ala	Glu	Gly	G

Although DNA is the controlling stable informational molecule of the cell, the directions stored therein are ''read'' and stored in another similar molecule, ribonucleic acid (RNA). When a ''structural'' gene is turned on, many copies of so-called messenger RNA (mRNA) are synthesized from that gene. This process is called *transcription* and is entirely analagous to tran-

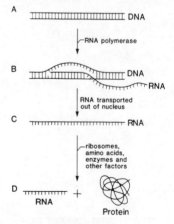

FIGURE 8. A schematic representation of the transcription of information encoded in a gene in DNA into messenger RNA (mRNA), which is then translated into a specific polymer of amino acids (protein).

scribing multiple copies of a single song onto magnetic recording tape from a master tape containing hundreds of selections. The mRNA molecules, in turn, direct the synthesis of proteins, after which they are degraded and the components are used over again to make new mRNA. The conversion of the information coded in messenger RNA to protein is a rather complex process called *translation*. The sequence of events by which information in DNA is transferred to the synthesis of a protein molecule is shown in Figure 8. The study of the mechanisms of DNA replication, transcription, translation, and related processes comprise the heart of what is referred to as *molecular biology*. There are some excellent general references that should be consulted by those who wish to explore these topics more thoroughly.[15]

Enzymes

The working molecules of the cell and of physiological systems in multicellular organisms are, for the most part, proteins. Although some proteins provide structural form for the cell and others perform a regulatory function, most of the hundreds of different types of proteins in a cell are enzymes. An

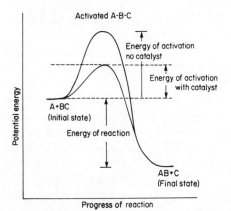

FIGURE 9. An illustration of the energetics of catalysis. The catalyst lowers the energy of activation needed to be overcome by the reactants in order to undergo a chemical transformation. An enzyme specifically lowers the activation energy for only one of the many possible products that may be formed from a particular starting compound(s), thus determining the direction of a biochemical pathway. (From A. C. Giese, *Cell Physiology*, 5th ed. © 1979 by Saunders College Publishing/Holt, Rinehart & Winston. Reprinted by permission of Holt, Rinehart & Winston, CBS College Publishing.)

emzyme is a biochemical catalyst. A catalyst enables a chemical reaction to take place readily. If the reacting chemicals were simply left to their own devices, the desired reaction would occur only very slowly or not at all. Furthermore, a mixture of complex molecules can generally react in more than one way. The reason that not every set of chemicals reacts easily with any other set is not because it can't, but because there exists a certain "activation energy," or an energy barrier which must be overcome before a reaction can take place. Thus, of all of the possible chemical reactions, particularly those involving "organic" molecules (those based on carbon and hydrogen), very few occur spontaneously in nature. In order to direct the very specific chemical pathways that must take place in a living system, some means must be available to determine that the reactions will proceed in one particular direction rather than in the often-numerous other possible directions. Enzymes, which are generally highly specific, provide the necessary directed catalysis.

Energy

We know that carbohydrates, or sugars, which provide much of the energy for life, are broken down in most organisms into carbon dioxide and perhaps other carbon compounds, such as ethanol (yeast), lactic acid (yogurt bacteria), or acetic acid (vinegar bacteria). The energy stored in the chemical bonds of a sugar molecule is transferred to special energy storage compounds, particularly those containing phosphate groups, in which form it is saved until needed. Clearly, there are many possible ways in which sugars could be broken down to provide energy. Yet, when we look at the particular pathways chosen to extract energy from glucose, a basic form of sugar found in most living things at least as an energy intermediate, we see that they are few in number. Moreover, the higher the evolutionary form, the better the efficiency of the system. In primitive organisms, the most universal pathway for the breakdown of glucose is called *glycolysis*, which does not require oxygen and also produces far less usable energy from each molecule of glucose. That is, less than 10% of the energy in a molecule of glucose is released when a yeast converts it to a molecule of ethanol and a molecule of carbon dioxide. Of this energy, only about one fourth can be stored and utilized by the organism. Higher plants and animals have an additional pathway, called the *tricarboxylic acid cycle,* which is closely coupled to a family of iron-containing proteins especially adapted to convert more than half of the usable energy in compounds derived from glucose into high-energy phosphate bonds. This mechanism requires oxygen and is called *oxidative phosphorylation,* or, simply, respiration.

Of course, many kinds of chemical compounds can be utilized as energy sources by most living things. In our diet-conscious modern life, we all know about fats, carbohydrates, and proteins. But there are organisms, most of them microorganisms, that can utilize virtually any kind of stored chemical energy (except for some of the esoteric man-made substances previously unknown in nature). And plants use the abundant energy in sunlight directly. However, at the level of energy storage and utilization within the organisms themselves, there is a great deal of common biochemistry. Glycolysis and oxidative phosphorylation, described above, are the most general. Regardless of the initial source of energy, common intermediates are formed that enter these pathways at key points.

Different systems for producing energy operate, depending on the demands of the organism. The sprinting runner, for example, cannot supply the muscles with enough oxygen fast enough to enable oxidative phosphorylation and to provide the rapidly exercising body with enough of the energy it needs. Thus, glucose is converted to energy through the less efficient glycolysis pathway. The muscle fatigue encountered after the race is due, in part, to the lactic acid, the end product of glycolysis, that builds up in the muscles. The marathon runner, converting energy stores at a somewhat slower pace, is able to avoid significant glycolysis, at least until the final sprint of the race.

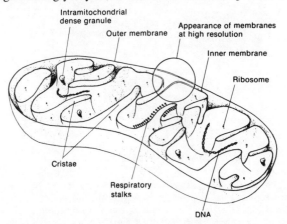

FIGURE 10. A representation of an idealized mitochondrion cut in half, showing the complex structure of the cellular organelle. The physical proximities of the enzymes to each other enhance the reaction rates, and the large surface area is ideally suited to the efficient exchange of CO_2 and O_2. (From B. Tandler and C. L. Hoppel, *Mitochondria.* New York: Academic Press, 1972.)

Through the use of such biochemical catalysts, organisms perform *all* of the necessary chemistry that enables them to survive and flourish. However, the cell contains other substructures that make this process even more efficient. Rather than to rely on the random kinetics of chemicals in solution, nature has devised very specialized structures which greatly increase the probability that the correct substances will react with each other. Mitochondria are small factories in which oxidative phosphorylation takes place. These are generally much smaller than a nucleus and are found in the cytoplasm in most higher organisms. Mitochondria consist of very intricate membranous

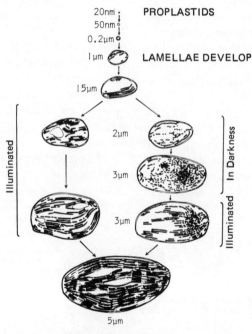

FIGURE 11. The development of chloroplasts, showing the highly complex internal membrane structure that has evolved for the highly efficient energy-conversion process of photosynthesis, by which energy absorbed from light by chlorophyll and accessory pigments is converted into chemical energy in the form of glucose. The overall reaction is similar to the reverse of the breakdown of sugar into carbon dioxide. There is some structural similarity between mitochondria and chloroplasts. Some believe that they may have had a common ancestor. (From K. M. Ühlethaler and A. Frey-Wyssling, "Entwicklung und Struktur der Proplastiden." *J. Biophys. Biochem. Cytol.,* **6,** 507–517, 1959.)

structures, with the enzymes involved in a particular biochemical pathway all in close proximity to each other, so that the products of one reaction will not have far to go before they may enter into a new reaction. The internal structure of a mitochondrion is shown in Figure 10. These may be highly concentrated in the cells needed to convert sugar to energy at a high rate. The honeybee must produce an enormous amount of energy in proportion to its weight in order to fly. Its highly efficient flight muscles are packed full of mitochondria, which allow it to produce energy in the most efficient metabolic way possible. A flying insect simply cannot afford the inefficiency of glycolysis.

Choloroplasts, the site of photosynthesis in higher plants, are subcellular organelles resembling mitochondria in several ways. They contain remarkably efficient structures that extract energy from absorbed light, making it available for storage in chemical bonds, functioning somewhat like a biological solid-state electronic device. Using this energy, glucose is synthesized from water and carbon dioxide from the atmosphere. Both chloroplasts and mitochondria contain DNA and, inside cells, have been seen to divide like miniature cells and increase their number. One theory suggests that they derive from a primordial intracellular parasite, which, at some very early period in the evolution of living organisms, invaded a primitive cell and, fortuitously, imparted a symbiotic advantage to both.

*Revising the Genetic Blueprint**

The amount of knowledge we are still capable of obtaining is still dependent upon the continuous development of more and more clever ways to see into living cells and to study the precise ways in which the components of life—the proteins, the nucleic acids, and the thousands of other molecules—are put together and how they function together and interact with one another to produce that exquisitely well-orchestrated phenomenon we know as life. Our techniques for "seeing" into the nature of molecules have involved methods for determining the sequence of the building blocks of proteins and nucleic acids, and for manipulating and isolating them. With these new tools, we have at last been able to peer into the nature of life at its most intimate and fundamental level. What they are continuing to teach us about ourselves is forcing us to put old dogma aside and to view the phenomenon of life in terms somewhat different from those we have been used to historically.

---

*A considerably expanded discussion of the material presented in this section, with references from the literature, may be found in the Appendix.

Perhaps the most important technique to be developed within the past 10 or 12 years is gene splicing—the isolation of a piece of DNA, including one or more intact genes, from one type of organism and inserting it in a functional way into the cells of perhaps a completely unrelated species. This is "recombinant DNA," often singled out as an entity unto itself, or a specific branch of investigation in science. Yet it is merely a technique (actually, several techniques), a method whose primary value has been to explore the function of genes.

The sensational way in which the subject of genetic manipulation was introduced to the public created a genuine fear in those whose overall perception of scientists was perhaps most inspired by the brilliant but emotionally disturbed antiheroes of science fiction and horror movies. These widely held views allowed a legitimate discussion of safety and prudence within the scientific community to get out of control rather quickly, spreading like a California brushfire and fanned by the winds of ignorance. We shall examine the nature of the controversy and its underlying causes in due course. First, however, it is important to understand the simple reality of what the recombinant DNA technique is, what it can do, and why it has been so important to the advancement of the life sciences.

The problem confronting the molecular geneticist in 1970 was that many of the most interesting phenomena in the structure of genes and in the control of how the information therein was expressed were simply inaccessible. That is, a great deal had been learned about the organization and expression of genetic information in bacterial viruses and in bacteria, but it was clear that much of the picture that had emerged could not be extrapolated to multicelled animals and plants or even to the more complex single-celled organisms (yeast, fungi) that have a nucleus and discrete chromosomes. For example, it was discovered by Donald Brown of the Carnegie Institution of Washington's Department of Embryology in Baltimore than the genes that code for ribosomal RNA in the African clawed frog (a favorite subject of study for embryologists) exist in many identical copies strung together in tandem.[16] But what was more surprising was,that between these multiple genes are stretches of "spacer" DNA—DNA for which no obvious function seemed to exist.

The genetics of even the simplest of these organisms is much more complex than that of bacteria and their viruses, and there is considerably more DNA to contend with. What made it much more difficult was the fact that one could not easily carry out mating and genetic mapping experiments. The more complex the organism, the longer the generation time and the more difficult it is to conduct a controlled genetic experiment.

Animal and plant genetics are, in some ways, highly developed sciences, resulting primarily from attempts to improve agriculturally important species. Human genetics has been understood in terms of the inheritance patterns of obvious physical traits and clinically observable disorders. The enzymatic or structural defect has been identified in some cases. But, until recently, little has been understood about basic genetic mechanisms in higher organisms.

Mammalian genetics are especially difficult to study. Even the smallest, fastest breeding mammal, the mouse, takes at least two months for a generation. Moreover, one could not, even after years of selected inbreeding, produce a "clone" of thousands of genetically identical animals, as it was possible to do in a few hours with bacteria or any other organism not subject to the constraints of sexual reproduction. Moreover, specific pieces of genetically distinct DNA could not be isolated readily from animal or plant cells. Even if it had been possible to do so, there was no way to characterize the miniscule amounts obtained. There had been efforts to separate chromosomes, by electrophoresis, centrifugation, and so on, in order to isolate and study individual genetic regions. But these attempts had been largely unsuccessful. What was clearly needed was a means to study animal DNA, or specific segments thereof, in an experimental context that allowed the ease of handling and the short generation times characteristic of bacteria.

But that was not all that was needed. In 1970, the mechanics of how DNA codes structural information and how this information is translated into specific proteins was fairly well understood. The DNA code words for "start" and "stop" were known, at least in bacterial viruses and bacteria themselves. It was clear, however, that the control of genetic expression was not a simple matter, even in these simple organisms, and that there was more than one way to do it. Protein "repressors" had been isolated. A chemical to be used by a bacterium could, in some cases, stimulate the organism to make the enzymes needed to utilize it. There were thus a great many reasons why scientists needed to be able to determine the base sequence of at least certain regions of the DNA. More interesting than the actual coding sequences for proteins were the stretches of DNA that came before, after, and, as it turned out, interspersed in the middle of these regions, for it was this non-coding DNA which was likely to be very important in the control of gene expression.

The development of techniques for studying isolated segments of DNA from any source transplanted into a simple organism where it did not normally occur gave molecular biologists the means they had been seeking. But it is often not appreciated that one of the main discoveries that made it all possible came from completely unrelated research—research designed to explain why certain bacterial viruses infected certain hosts but not others. This was the discovery of so-called restriction enzymes. These enzymes usually recognize a specific sequence of six bases, a sequence that is complementary to itself. Some of these enzymes make a break in each strand of DNA within this region, so that a small, self-complementary piece of DNA is left at the end of each DNA fragment. When mixed under the proper conditions, these loose ends can find each other and recombine, but at random, because they are all identical. This property allows DNA from two different sources to be treated with the same enzyme and then to be recombined, with some of the resulting fragments containing DNA from both sources. Hence the term *recombinant DNA.* This story is a beautiful demonstration of serendipity in science, which should serve as a lesson to federal funding agencies and corporations that continue to assume that the most productive research is that directed toward a particular goal.

At about the same time that restriction enzymes were first used to reconnect DNA fragments (1972), another method was developed independently for recombining DNA segments without the use of restriction enzymes. Although more tedious, this technique allowed for a more specific recombination of DNA than the restriction enzyme methods. Now, it is common to use both methods, particularly for the construction of so-called expression vectors, which enable *any* DNA fragment to be expressed in a particular host organism.

There were obvious means at hand in 1972 for getting foreign DNA to be incorporated into bacterial cells. The gene of interest could be spliced into the DNA of a bacterial virus, which also possessed the mechanism for getting the DNA inside a cell, where the DNA insert would be expressed along with the viral DNA. Or it could be inserted into a small piece of circular DNA called a *plasmid,* a naturally occurring extrachromosomal piece of DNA that readily

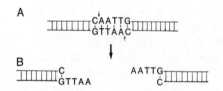

FIGURE 12. A representation of the cleavage of DNA by a restriction enzyme (*Eco*R1 from *Escherichia coli*), showing the pallindromic nature of the recognition sequence. The sequence of the six-nucleotide site recognized by the enzyme not only is identical in both strands of DNA (the two strands of the DNA double helix run in chemically opposite directions), it is self-complementary. This is the unique property that enabled restriction enzymes to constitute the heart of a quick method for the construction of recombinant DNA molecules.

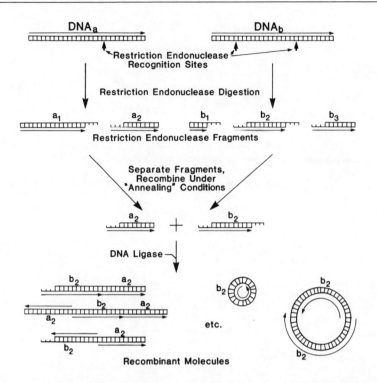

FIGURE 13. The recombination of DNA using restriction enzymes. The self-complementary ends which are left after restriction enzyme digestion are identical, not only at each end of the same fragment of DNA, but for all fragments. Thus, under the proper conditions, these ends become "sticky" and will recombine at random. The remaining breaks in the DNA backbone can be sealed with the enzyme DNA ligase to form stable DNA molecules. Those recombinants of interest must be separated from all other, unwanted combinations.

transfers genetic information between strains of bacteria. Most of the studies that people wished to do involved making large quantities of specific genes or gene products, and bacteria were the ideal vehicles. But there were soon many reasons to wish to insert "new" DNA into the cells of higher plants and animals.

It has now been more than a decade since the first successful demonstrations of gene splicing. Since that time, a variety of means have been developed for inserting genes into the cells of every kind of organism. Methods of animal and plant cell culture have allowed the addition of genes to the cells of

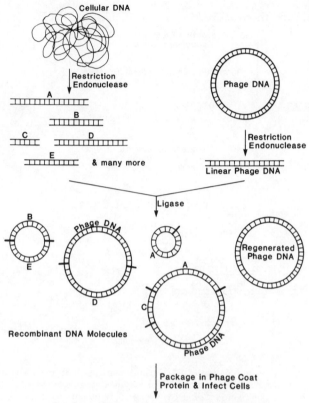

FIGURE 14. A typical recombinant DNA "shotgun" experiment in which the total cellular DNA is cut into fragments with a particular restriction enzyme and is spliced at random into the DNA of a bacterial virus (phage). The DNA recombinants are then repackaged in phage coat protein. Those containing the original phage DNA infect bacteria and multiply. Out of the thousands of different recombinants, the gene of interest must then be selected by some other type of selective assay.

higher organisms with nearly the ease with which they can be added to bacteria. The cells of many species of plants can be isolated and grown in the laboratory. Following the modification of the DNA, they can be induced to differentiate and to develop into intact, normal plants, each cell of which contains the added genes. Similarly, some types of animal cells can be genetically modified and then combined with the cells of an early embryo to produce genetic mosaic animals. Some of these will have sex cells derived from the genetically modified cells and can thus pass the new genes on to their offspring. Perhaps the most successful means of introducing new genes into animal cells has been direct injection into fertilized eggs prior to the first cell division. Although it is not yet possible to control precisely the site at which the added DNA will be integrated into the chromosomes, gene expression has been achieved in a surprisingly high percentage of animals given a properly constructed DNA insert. A number of oversized mice were created in this way by injecting fertilized mouse eggs with DNA containing the gene for rat growth hormone.

The simple insertion and expression of DNA from one organism into another *per se* doesn't really teach us very much. But the experiments that this technique enabled scientists to do revealed a great deal about the structure, organization, and function of genetic material. The first thing that the simple splicing of a foreign piece of DNA into a bacterial host permitted was the production of a large quantity of a specific small segment of DNA from a source where gene isolation had been impossible. That is, a single animal—or human—gene could be cloned. *Clone* simply means a set of identical copies of anything that may be grown. Thus, *DNA cloning,* a much misunderstood expression, refers to the production of millions of identical copies of a specific gene or other fragment of DNA.

By recombining restriction enzyme digestion fragments of the total DNA of an animal with the appropriate plasmid cloning vectors, relatively small regions of DNA could be isolated and grown in any quantity desired. But how does one select for a specific gene to study? There are several methods that allow one to "fish" out the segments of interest from the sea of total DNA. If one knows the protein sequence, it is possible to synthesize DNA probes based on the genetic code and to use them as bait. Or, if the messenger RNA for a certain protein is available, it can be used to make complementary DNA probes, which can then be used to find the DNA one wants. The probes don't have to be nearly as long as the entire gene. They need to have only enough sequence homology to permit a specific recognition of the gene in question.

Simultaneously with the developments in the isolation of single genes, methods to determine the base sequence of DNA were also found. These procedures, along with the techniques of gene splicing, provided the tools needed to permit the detailed analysis of any genetic region. To date, of course, only a small fraction of the many thousands of human genes have been subjected to such thorough scrutiny. But these have yielded some most interesting and unexpected results.

The genes of most animals, it turns out, are not continuous. That is, the coding regions are interspersed with much longer stretches of DNA, which, so far, have not been shown to have a specific function. Messenger RNA is made that is a faithful copy of the entire genetic region, but it is soon edited by a specific cutting and splicing mechanism to give precisely the mRNA needed for the synthesis of a particular protein. Why are these "nonsense" regions there at all? Do they possibly have some control or regulatory function? Are they an evolutionary vestige? Or perhaps an intermediate state in evolution? Do they have some important role in the folding or physical conformation of the DNA in the chromosome structure? The answers to all of these questions could be yes, but we really don't know. We have come to think of nature as being efficient. But in order for an organism to have the capacity for evolution, it needs something to work with. It is possible that this extra DNA baggage is nature's safety margin for survival.

Another revelation made possible by the new gene-splicing techniques came from attempts to isolate the gene coding for a particular protein using the messenger RNA to make a complementary DNA probe. Instead of finding only one region of DNA that binds to the probe, it is not uncommon to find as many as five or even more regions of DNA having considerable sequence homology with the original mRNA. Such genes are usually found physically adjacent to one another and are believed to have resulted from a replication error in which the original gene was duplicated in tandem, creating two copies where only one was needed. Such a situation then confers, on at least one of the genes, a tolerance for mutation. It sometimes turns out that a family of related proteins are made from some of the members of such a gene family. Such an example is found in the human globin genes, which form different types of hemoglobin. All have structural similarities. In some cases, there will be a region of DNA that is very similar to a gene for an important protein but which is itself not expressed at all. Because these DNA regions have no obvious function, they are called *pseudogenes*.

Again, we may be observing here another reason why evolution works. If every bit of DNA coded for an essential function, then nearly all mutations would be lethal. If, on the other hand, there are tandem genes, similar in structure, some of which are expressed and some of which are not, there is ample room for mutations that can be passed on from generation to generation. Eventually, at some very low probability, one of these unneeded regions may express a protein or a function conferring a survival advantage on its host. In time, the presence of the advantageous gene will increase in the gene pool for that particular species until all will have it, and the species will then be slightly different. In this way, it is possible to understand how completely new proteins or other substances could arise in the course of evolution, not from a single mutational event, but from a long, accumulated series of them.

There is no question, then, of the extraordinary value that gene-splicing methods have been and will be in the quest for knowledge about the underlying principles of the phenomenon of life. However, when most people think of gene splicing, it is not about the tremendous boon to the acquisition of new knowledge that these methods are making possible. Rather, it is of the practical use to which genetic manipulation can be put. The manufacture of useful products for the pharmaceutical, food, and chemical industries in these modified bacterial factories was immediately envisioned as soon as the first examples of genetic manipulation were demonstrated. And the ability to alter the genetic makeup of plants and animals immediately suggested dramatic improvements in agriculturally important species. However, the most ominous application of all to excite the imagination was the possibility of the direct intervention into human genetic makeup. The correction of and prevention of hereditary diseases are hard to argue against. But such a capability also suggests that other "normal" traits could be modified as well, giving man control over the genetic destiny of the human species. Indeed, this will soon be technically possible. The way in which we deal with the power of such knowledge and the technology that it can create is a principal subject of this book.

Gene Splicing Is Not Enough

For scientists in biological research, the past decade has brought a deluge of new knowledge. However, the reports finding their way into newspapers and the popular media have been only a trickle. Most of that trickle has concentrated on the truly remarkable achievements in the introduction of specific, functioning genes into virtually any type of living cell.

The gene mystique and perhaps the slightly ominous associations people make with genetic manipulation have nearly overshadowed the equally remarkable advances that have taken place in another important area of biological research, generally referred to as *cell biology*. It is true that some events have been newsworthy, such as the birth of a baby in England who began life in a petri dish (the historic "test-tube" baby). Even the first American success of *in vitro* fertilization managed to make the evening news on television.[17] Still, most of these advances are unknown to the public.

But however quietly these achievements have taken place, the promise they hold for the enhancement of knowledge about the remarkable process of development, from fertilized egg to embryo to adult, is extraordinary. The once-baffling intricacies of the immune system are now understood in remarkable detail. And with the amalgamation and convergence of genetics and cell biology, the possibilities for man's ultimate control over his biological destiny are already being anticipated.

As has happened in all areas of science when the level of knowledge outgrows the artificial boundaries that were once drawn around individual disciplines, it makes increasingly less sense to distinguish "genetics" from "molecular biology" from "biochemistry" from "cell biology." Of course, these terms do have different meanings, but their practitioners are all using the same growing body of knowledge, integrating and correlating the findings of the past decade so as to understand life at a level of detail that was totally unanticipated only a few years ago.

When this fact is fully appreciated, the catchphrases *recombinant DNA* and *genetic engineering* ring hollow and meaningless when used to characterize recent advances in biological science. Equally misleading are the terms *clone* and *test-tube baby*. It seems that the popular concepts of science must either have a wowie-zowie-gee-whiz type of excitement attached to them or conjure up a creepy foreboding of doom. But when what is *really* happening is understood, either concept, each of them the product of cheap, journalistic hype, becomes irrelevant.

Bozo the Clone[18]

Cell biology made the public scene in a big way late in 1977 with the announcement of the publication of what was claimed to be a privileged personal account of the first successful "cloning" of a human being.[19] *Cloning* here refers to the creation of a genetically identical copy of a living organism, in this case a human being. A clone of anything simply means a collection of identical copies derived from a single entity. Thus, a bacterium growing on a petri plate, reproducing by simple cell division, produces a clone of perhaps millions of identical bacteria. Each of several different mutant forms of a single-celled organism growing on the same petri dish will give rise to a separate clone, each organism comprising it containing the original mutation. Similarly, we have referred to techniques for "cloning" genes in bacteria or other types of host cells. Thus, the millions of identical copies of a chemically synthesized piece of DNA comprise a clone of the original piece.

But *clone* has, unfortunately, come to mean something more ominous in the eyes of much of the public. In the 1978 movie *The Boys from Brazil,* three dozen genetically identical copies of Adolph Hitler were turned loose upon the world. With that film, on top of Rorvik's book, not to mention a couple of dismal made-for-television movies, not only did *clone* come to mean a population of identical *people,* but any individual member of that group was called "*a* clone." Erica Jong even published a poem about a clone.[20]

When Rorvik's book came out in early 1978, the chairman of the Subcommittee on Health and the Environment in the House of Representatives was Paul Rogers from Florida, also known as "Mr. Health" for his leadership in the passage of much of the key health and environmental legislation during the early and middle 1970s. Mr. Rogers was, among other things, a shrewd politician, with a keen sense of timing about when Congress, and especially his subcommittee, should bring an issue before the public. Thus, when the hype about cloning humans hit the media, he ordered his staff to put together a hearing on the subject, in which Rorvik would be brought in to defend the allegations in his book, and the leading scientists in the field would inform the Congress about what was *really* possible.

Even though Lippincott published a lukewarm disclaimer at the beginning of the book, the dust jacket of *In His Image: The Cloning of a Man* was full of unrestrained puffery. It seems that there was this wealthy old man who had never had a child but deemed his genes worthy of propagation—all of them—so much so that he was willing to go to extreme heroic measures to have his intact genotype rise again in a new human being. Thus, he set about hiring, at astronomical expense, a world-class scientist, an obstetrician, and all the attendant technical staff, plus a surrogate mother—all of this on a remote South Sea island. The nuclei from some of his own body cells were transplanted into the eggs obtained from suitable donors, which then began to develop just as a normally fertilized human embryo would. When implanted into a suitably receptive human uterus, voila! Soon to appear would be the first cloned human being. Rorvik claimed that this incredible tale was all true.

The subject covered a wide variety of scientific and medical areas in the course of relating the tale. The scientists who bothered to read the book were astounded by the unusually large number of errors committed by the author. He was presumably an experienced science writer and should have done his homework better. Of course, one should have an open mind in evaluating what one claims to be a "breakthrough." But when the background data cited in support of such a wondrous achievement are so seriously misunderstood, it is difficult to take the rest seriously.

Rogers's advisers (I was one) believed that a congressional hearing on the subject would give too much public attention to something that should be relegated to oblivion as quickly as possible. It would cheapen the stature of the U.S. Congress even to admit that there was a question of the book's validity. But the chairman disagreed. He believed that there was already too much public attention focused on the subject and that it was up to Congress and his subcommittee to set the record straight.

Rorvik, fortunately, seemed to be a bit scared of the whole thing and managed to make himself very inaccessible. It was thus possible to avoid a circus, complete with network TV coverage, and to have instead, a high-class scientific review of "advances in cell biology," which was ultimately how the hearing was billed. The hearing would then be less of a personal indictment and public trial of one man, and more of a chance to bring before the Congress and the public the remarkable progress that was being made in our understanding of how animal cells function, particularly during embryonic development, and where we could expect such research to take us in the future.

Meanwhile, a piece appeared in the *Washington Post* [21] by the late Dr. André Hellegers, then director of the Kennedy Institute of Ethics at Georgetown University. The article, generously seasoned with Hellegers's sparkling wit, was a brilliant rebuttal of the assertions in Rorvik's book, which, when critically examined from the viewpoint of an obstetrician, were reduced to absurdity. As it would be impossible to avoid the subject of human cloning and *In His Image* at the hearing, Hellegers seemed—and proved to be—the ideal witness.

Of Frogs, Mice, and Men

The foremost scientists investigating the control of embryonic development came to Washington to educate the Congress—and, indirectly, the public—in the fine points of cell biology, and just what it was that research in this area was trying to accomplish and why. Beatrice Mintz discussed how she had got the cultured cells from a certain type of embryonic cancer to become incorporated into early mouse embryos, where they behaved just like normal embryo cells. The resulting mouse was a genetic mosaic, with two genetically different populations of cells. She explained how this model system had enabled her to alter the genes of the cultured cancer cells to create animal models of human genetic diseases.

Robert Briggs and Thomas King, whose work in the 1950s at Indiana University had shown that it was possible to clone amphibians,[22] and Robert

McKinnel, who had just published a book on animal cloning,[23] came to discuss why people wished to obtain genetically identical animals, and just how feasible it was in 1978. They had found that if a nucleus from certain embryonic frog cells was transplanted into a fertilized frog egg in which the normal nucleus had been destroyed, a normal animal developed. The procedure used to produce genetic clones of amphibians is shown in Figure 15. After a certain stage of development, this procedure no longer worked. They were asking if the nucleus of a cell lost its totipotency (the ability to direct the entire development and cellular differentiation of an animal) after the cells had begun to differentiate. Their cloning studies then were designed to teach us something about the mechanism of the control of genetic expression in the nuclei of a developing animal.

Clement Markert of Yale discussed his studies on embryonic mice and how he was approaching the problem of cloning in mammals.[24] At the time (June 1978), the hearing—and the published record[25]—provided a unique and excellent review of at least one area of cell biology, in terms that the layman could understand.

One question which arose repeatedly during the hearing was whether it was *possible* to clone an animal. The scientists present agreed that, at the present time, it was *not* possible to clone humans, at least not in the way it was done in amphibians or as portrayed by Rorvik. And even if it were, they asked, who would want to do it anyway? Unless someone has a pathological ego problem, like the aging protagonist in Rorvik's book, conventional methods of human reproduction are not only much more reliable and less costly, they are a great deal more fun.

There are good reasons, however, to wish to create a population of genetically identical animals. In many laboratory experiments, the use of such populations would greatly reduce the variability that one observes between individuals, even in strains of highly inbred mice, thus increasing the reliability of experimental results. And if one is able to select, or create by genetic manipulation, a single individual possessing certain highly desirable features, such as a cow capable of producing twice the quantity of milk as an ordinary cow, then cloning might represent a sure way to perpetuate those traits in the progeny, as opposed to conventional mating. If, of course, you find yourself with a steer which is an exceptional choice for beef production, then there is obviously no choice. The cloned offspring of such a steer would be able to reproduce and thus be a prospective prize bull. Or, if a large supply could be created, one could go on cloning the clones, just as seedless oranges or other horticultural varieties are propagated. But aside from any practical benefits that may ensue from the ability to produce clones of animals, research in this

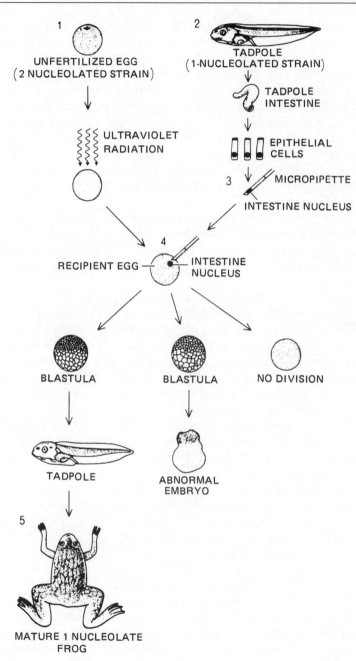

1
UNFERTILIZED EGG
(2 NUCLEOLATED STRAIN)

2
TADPOLE
(1-NUCLEOLATED STRAIN)

TADPOLE
INTESTINE

EPITHELIAL
CELLS

ULTRAVIOLET
RADIATION

3   MICROPIPETTE

INTESTINE NUCLEUS

4

RECIPIENT EGG   INTESTINE
                       NUCLEUS

BLASTULA   BLASTULA   NO DIVISION

TADPOLE

ABNORMAL
EMBRYO

5

MATURE 1 NUCLEOLATE
FROG

area has taught us a great deal about how an intact cell functions, and about the expression of the genetic material contained within it at different stages in the life cycle.

It should not be forgotten that multiple human births, particularly of the "indentical twin" type, result from the separation of zygote cells early in development. This is a rare but "natural" event. In this way, sets of five and six genetically identical humans (quintuplets and sextuplets) have been born, each constituting a small but genuine human clone.

It should be noted here that the techniques of fertilization outside the animal (*in vitro* fertilization) and subsequent transplantation into the uterus of another mouse had been in common use for more than a decade in laboratory studies and were used extensively in the mouse-cloning experiments cited above. It became news, however, when these techniques, which were common to animal research and are now used extensively in animal husbandry, were applied to humans. Louise Brown made history as the first "test-tube" baby" in 1978. In order to allow a couple to bear their natural children, in a case where the mother had blocked fallopian tubes, ova were obtained surgically from the prospective mother and fertilized in the laboratory with her husband's sperm. The fertilized egg was allowed to undergo two or three "cleavages" (cell division cycles) before transplantation into the mother's uterus.

This is a procedure for which enough animal data were at hand to make the chances of success in a human extremely good. For obvious ethical reasons, greater care must be taken in obtaining the ova and in the uterine transplantation procedure than with animals. Neither, however, puts the mother at very great risk. There are now a number of private clinics around the world that routinely perform this procedure, for a substantial fee. The first in the United States, started by Drs. Howard and Georgeanne Jones, is located in Norfolk, Virginia. The first successful fruit of their labor (or perhaps I should say Mrs. Carr's labor) was born in December 1981. The ethical issues concerning the clinical use of these procedures are discussed in Chapter 4.

Exploring the Immune System

Nearly two centuries ago, Edward Jenner discovered that pus from a cowpox lesion was capable of conferring immunity to smallpox.[26] This was

←

FIGURE 15. The procedure by which nuclei can be transplanted into frog eggs in which the nucleus has been destroyed to create clones of genetically identical adult frogs. (From John B. Gurdon, "Transplanted Nuclei and Cell Differentiation," *Scientific American*, **219**, 24–35, 1968.)

the beginning of the science of immunology—or perhaps *art* would be a better term—which has had a profound effect on medicine and society. In the Victorian era, and before, infectious diseases were a major cause of death. Now, very few people, at least in the modern developed nations, die from infections of any sort. Now and then, there is a new disease, or a new version of an old one, that arises unexpectedly and kills people, like Legionnaire's disease or the Asian flu. But yesterday's big killers—such as smallpox, diphtheria, polio, cholera, and yellow fever—are, happily, scarcely more than memories. There are many physicians in practice in the United States today who have never seen a single case of any of these diseases.

At first, immunity and the phenomenon of vaccination were only empirical facts. The hunches and intuition that often guide scientists, even when the true nature of things is not understood, led a number of medical pioneers in the nineteenth and early twentieth centuries to make a great deal of progress in the diagnosis and control of several of the scourges of the day.

During the past 15 years or so, the intricate cellular system that controls the immune response has been elucidated. It is beyond the scope of this book to go into detail describing the human immune system and the nature of the immune response. The interested reader should consult one of the general references given.[27] However, a brief description here is in order.

An antigen is a chemical substance which is recognized by certain cells of the immune system and against which antibodies are produced. An antigen may be a protein or a portion of a protein molecule, a polysaccharide, or other large molecule, or it may be a small molecule attached to a large molecule. Free small molecules, and a few large molecules, are poor antigens. An antibody is a protein molecule that combines selectively with a particular antigen to neutralize it, or otherwise to render it biologically harmless. Antibodies to an infectious bacterium, while not necessarily killing it outright, bind to antigens on its surface so as to prevent it from attaching to and colonizing on cellular or tissue surfaces and causing infection. An antibody molecule is shown schematically in Figure 16.

The system is exceptionally sensitive, as anyone with an allergy can tell you, outdoing some of our best instruments for measuring low levels of chemical substances. Although the immune system evolved to protect animals against invading organisms, it can sometimes work against one. Allergy, which can, of course, produce serious illness or even death in a small number of individuals, is a minor problem in comparison to the autoimmune diseases. These include juvenile-onset diabetes, multiple sclerosis, some types of kidney failure, rheumatoid arthritis, and possibly some psychiatric disorders, in all of which an individual makes antibodies against his own cells and

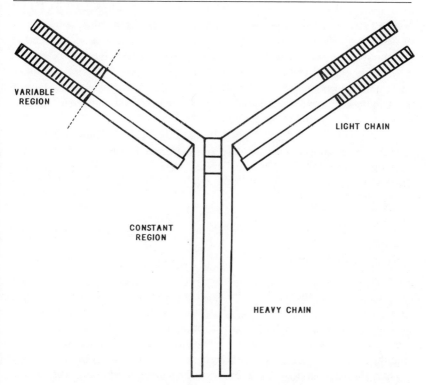

FIGURE 16. A schematic illustration of an antibody molecule. The specificity of the antibody is determined by the variable region, which is synthesized following a complex rearrangement of genetic subunits determined by a specific antigen. A monoclonal antibody is an antibody derived from a single clone of B cells. Such antibodies all have identical variable regions.

tissues. Reactions to antibiotics or other drugs, as well as the host rejection of transplanted tissues, are also undesirable consequences of the immune response. But the system is indispensable. We literally couldn't live without it.

One of the most significant advances in immunology during the past decade was a method that enabled one to produce a large quantity of a single, homogeneous antibody molecule in the laboratory. The cells that produce antibodies can produce only one type of antibody per cell. The reason is that the DNA on three different chromosomes, coding for various parts of antibodies, must rearrange itself in a specific way so that it codes for only a single type of antibody to be made in response to the presence of a specific antigen.

These antibody-producing cells can be isolated and cultured, but these cells usually don't do very well in the laboratory. The trick that revolutionized immunology, however, was the fusion of a type of cancer cell with these "B" cells. This method created an immortal cell line, allowing the production of large quantities of cells that make only one type of antibody.[28] Because each of these antibodies is produced by a single clone of these immortalized B cells, the resulting identical antibodies are referred to as *monoclonal*.

Such purified, homogeneous antibodies are clearly highly useful in research for detecting minuscule quantities of certain substances, and in medicine for both diagnosis and therapy. It is needless to point out that the production of these monoclonal antibodies has become an important element in today's biotechnology business.

Another important property of the immune system is currently under intense investigation. The model of immune surveillance states that there is a scavenger system, perhaps involving several subclasses of T cells, which recognize and destroy potentially harmful substances that don't belong where they are found. These might include virus particles, infectious microorganisms, and even cancer cells. Of particular interest are the so-called killer T cells, and of these, a class called *natural killer* (NK) *cells*. This system appears to be controlled and mediated by a large class of proteins generally referred to as *immunomodulators*. The way in which this system is regulated, and the function of the many specific regulatory proteins, is a mystery slowly yielding to investigation. It is known that the general level of immune competence depends on stress and an individual's ability to handle it. It has been shown, for example, that the hard-driving workaholic business executive has a lower probability of getting cancer than the submissive person who lets pressure get him down. It is also known that many individuals can do quite nicely under protracted periods of extreme stress and pressure. But when the pressure lets up and they look forward to relaxing, they get sick. These observations could reflect the state of immune surveillance in different types of people and under different circumstances.

The immunomodulators generally include the interferons, which are triggered in many cells by a viral infection and subsequently prevent simultaneous infection by a second type of virus. That is why one will probably never get the flu and the measles at the same time. Also included are the thymic hormones and the lymphokines, which individually seem to be able to either stimulate or to suppress the growth of specific cell types.

It was suggested in the late 1970s that interferon was the magic bullet for cancer, although that hypothesis has not been borne out by clinical trials on cancer patients. Of perhaps greater promise are certain of the lymphokines, such as interleukein-2 and tumor necrosis factor, which under certain conditions have been shown to stimulate the proliferation of natural killer cells, which can selectively destroy tumor cells. There is some evidence that the occurrence of abnormal, cancerous cells may be a rather common event, but that these killer cells, when functioning properly, destroy the cancer cells and quell metastases before they have a chance to get started.

The Search for the Fountain of Youth

For thousands of years, man has dreamed of immortality. But, aging and death have been accepted, sometimes reluctantly, as inevitable facts of life—accepted by most, that is, because there is no other choice. The advances in all areas of modern biology have, however, given new hope to those who would prefer not to accept that four score and ten years is forever to be the measure of a man's days on earth.

I would contend that the principal driving force for most scientists is simple curiosity: the thirst to understand the nature of the world in which they live. But research on such a fundamental element of our own existence as aging *cannot* be carried out with the same detached objectivity as virtually any other branch of investigation.

When I worked for Congress, with the subcommittee that had jurisdiction over all National Institutes of Health (NIH) programs, I had occasion to meet several individuals who carried their case directly to the Congress of the United States for greatly expanded research programs specifically directed toward extending the human life span. These men had not been able to convince the NIH grant review process that their ideas merited support by the federal government. So they came to Congress in hopes that they would be able to sway the minds and hearts of the lawmakers, many of whom were getting on in years. After listening to their intensely emotional pleas and reading their proposals, one thing was very clear: These men, all late in life, simply did not want to die.

I wonder, if we all had the chance to make a Faustian bargain with the Devil himself, in return for youth or an extension thereof, how many of us would do it. Isn't it really more important than most of us are willing to admit? Of course, our society spends billions of dollars on all manner of concoctions and treatments that are supposed to make us *look* younger. Some are alleged to make us *feel* younger. What should happen if someone would offer us the chance to actually *be* younger? And what price would we be willing to pay for it?

Even the remote possibility of the extension of youth holds a fascination for most. It would not surprise me if people scanning the table of contents of this book notice the title of this section and start reading here first. But these pages will not reveal the answer.

Some suggestive results have been obtained by cell biologists. In the 1960s, Leonard Hayflick,[29] studied cells in culture from many sources and concluded that normal cells, when grown outside the body (a so-called primary cell culture) could divide only a limited number of times. Cells from a human embryo were capable of perhaps 50 divisions before the culture died. Cells from a newborn would be capable of possibly 30 divisions, and adult cells of only 20. There was a general decline in the number of divisions related to the age of the donor. To demonstrate whether this number could be altered in some way by the presence of younger cells, or by the cells' environment, half of a cell culture was frozen and stored, while the other half was allowed to continue to grow. After perhaps 20 divisions, the frozen cells were thawed and mixed with their cultured counterparts. But their presence did not return youth to the culture. The "older" cells continued to "age," and their preserved siblings outlasted them by the predicted number of cell divisions. This experiment showed that there was no substance released from the newer cells which controlled the rate of aging of the culture.

Cancer cells, on the other hand, or certain cells transformed by a virus, seem to be immortal. That is, they continue to divide indefinitely. Sometimes, a single cell in a culture of primary cells undergoes a change to enable it to grow and divide with the vigor of a cancer cell. These classes of cells comprise the cell "lines" used in research.

Some of Hayflick's conclusions have been challenged. Others, adjusting the substances in the culture medium, have found that the properties of cells in culture can be altered greatly depending upon their environment. But the basic conclusion seems to have held up. Cultures of essentially normal human cells cannot live forever.

Just as frog-cell and mouse-cell nuclei seem to lose their totipotency (their ability to generate any type of differentiated cell) with age and cannot serve as nuclei in a successful cloning experiment, mammalian-cells in culture seem to lose something, too. Are the mechanisms the same? And what are they? Are there irreversible changes in the control of transcription? Are there changes in the DNA itself? One theory of aging[30] postulates that an aging organism accumulates more and more mutations in its total DNA until it simply runs down and one of its vital systems fails.

It is known that there are specific changes in a person's biochemistry with age. Collagen, a simple protein with repeating amino acid sequences that is the principal substance in connective tissue, bones, and cartilage, becomes cross-linked with age and loses its elasticity. This is why the joints stiffen, wrinkles appear, the skin sags, and the bones become brittle in the aging. It is also why the lens of the eye loses its ability to focus closely and, thus, why some of you need reading glasses or bifocals in order to read the print in this book. Why this happens to collagen is not known.

Fat is another substance that shows changes with age. The oxidation of fat that occurs actually turns it rancid in a true chemical sense. In some elderly individuals, these oxidized fats can produce a peculiar or unpleasant smell. Antioxidants, such as vitamin C and vitamin E, have been shown to prevent or reduce the oxidation of fats in animal tests.

Similar phenomena of aging are observed in other physiological systems. No one has yet established that the deterioration of the body is a reflection of alterations in the DNA. And no one has yet been able to reverse any of the changes that take place with age. The failure to do so does not prove that they cannot be reversed. Our present state of knowledge simply does not allow us to conclude whether or not the changes that occur in animal cells during development and during aging can ever be reversed. If they cannot, then two of mankind's hopes, or fears, are impossible.

First, it should not be possible to take a cell from an adult or even from a newborn infant, and cause it to revert to the totipotency of an early embryonic cell. Nor should it be possible to remove a nucleus from such a cell and restore totipotency by transplanting it into an ovum from which the nucleus has been removed. Thus, human cloning, in the manner described in Rorvik's imaginary account, should not be possible.

The second impossibility is that aging cannot be reversed or arrested. The fountain of youth must therefore remain an elusive dream—if, that is, the cellular changes that one observes in either aging cells or aging animals are irreversible. If so, of course, the ethical questions of the future will be much simpler. But are these changes *really* irreversible? One could argue that in the course of the evolution of development, it was desirable for the control of gene expression to become fixed. But is there *any* evidence whatsoever that this apparently fixed position could be unlocked by appropriate manipulation of the control mechanisms? And wouldn't there be an occasional individual with an abnormality of such a kind that this control is disrupted?

One would expect that to be the case. In fact, cancer may be the expression of what happens when a differentiated cell loses the fixed nature of its specialized state. Cancer cells lose the specific characteristics of the tissues in which they arose and divide much more rapidly, resembling embryonic cells. There is no evidence, however, that any human cancer cells are truly totipotent in the sense that those in an early zygote are, nor that they can, in the proper environment, be made to undergo controlled differentiation. But Beatrice Mintz's findings concerning mouse teratocarcinoma cells are highly provocative.[31] When she mixed these cancer cells from a laboratory culture with those from an early zygote, the teratocarcinoma cells became incorporated into the developing mouse and differentiated normally, producing an animal that was a genetic mosaic but otherwise normal in every way.

Could a cancer-cell nucleus, transplanted into an enucleated egg, direct normal development? The answer to this question is not known. Most cancer experts, however, regard cancer as a highly abnormal state, and believe that whatever changes take place—for example, in removing the normal inhibition of cell division in adult cells—are not a precise reversion to a juvenile state. In some types of human bladder cancer, it has been shown that a single base alteration, leading to the change of one amino acid in the protein product of the "oncogene," is sufficient to transform cells in culture to a cancerous state. In another type of cancer, Burkitt's lymphoma, the culprit seems to be a piece of a chromosome that is mistakenly rearranged along with the DNA coding for antibodies. But these studies are not complete explanations of the cause of human cancer. It should be evident to the reader by now that we have barely begun to understand the nature of the control of gene expression in mammalian cells. On the other hand, we must not be so smug as to state that scientists cannot intervene in cellular regulation in any desired way, once the regulatory mechanisms are fully understood. In another decade, our ability to manipulate cells will certainly be far greater than it is today.

But what about aging? If there is accumulated damage in the DNA, which gradually contributes to the eventual demise of the organism, then it would seem to be beyond our control. But the life spans of organisms differ enormously. It is thus difficult to attribute these differences to damage from external sources, such as radiation in the environment. Most organisms seem to have efficient error-correction mechanisms, which correct mistakes made during DNA replication or resulting from radiation or chemical damage. Could the difference in life spans reflect differences in repair efficiency? Perhaps, but probably not. Suppose that each round of DNA replication and cell division introduces a certain number of errors in the DNA. Then, one would expect the life span of a cell, or of an organism, to depend upon how rapidly the cells were dividing.

In general, small animals of short life span have a higher metabolic rate and more rapid cell division than larger, longer-lived animals. Humans seem to do everything slowly. We take longer to grow and mature than most animals, but we also live longer. Thus, what we see is consistent, overall, with a theory of accumulated errors. But there are a few observations that don't really fit this simplistic model (and surely, even if it is on the right track, it can't possibly be this naively simple). Some types of cells are produced in fresh supply during one's lifetime—white blood cells, red blood cells, and spleen cells, for example. Although these arise from specialized precursor cells, there are clearly great differences in the number of cell divisions experienced by the cells of different tissues. Most cells normally divide very slowly, if at all. A wound or an injury, however, stimulates healing and cell division. But there is no evidence that the cells around wounds age any faster than other cells. And is it really impossible to culture certain human cells *in vitro* as immortal cell lines? Just because no one has demonstrated conclusively that "primary" cultures can survive indefinitely does not prove that it cannot be done. Current research seems to be improving methods for *in vitro* cell culture. However, even if it is possible to extend considerably the number of cell divisions exhibited by primary cultures, what does this mean in terms of human aging and its control?

There is some research activity in the United States directed toward the understanding of the fundamental mechanisms of aging, especially through the National Institute on Aging at the National Institutes of Health. The elucidation of the aging process, like most of the other specific problems in the biology of development, will, no doubt, depend upon the gradual unraveling of the complex threads of mystery which still enshroud the mechanisms of gene regulation. Scientists continue to make use of every suitable object of study, however. For example, there is a hereditary disorder, named *progeria,* in which the afflicted individuals age at a greatly accelerated rate and usually die of old age before they reach the age of 20. Laboratory cultures of the cells from these patients are far less hardy than those from normal subjects; they die after half the number of cell divisions usually expected. The study of gene regulation in these cells may yield a clue to the mechanism of cellular aging. It is unlikely, however, that the phenomenon of aging will be understood through directed research designed specifically to find out why people get old, just as the "War on Cancer" of the early 1970s failed to find a cure for cancer.

Genetics and Behavior

There is a field of scientific endeavor which, in comparison with the advances made in the study of gene isolation and characterization, is still in its infancy, but that is, nevertheless, one of the most exciting frontiers in science.

That is the study of the brain and the nervous system. How can they possibly perform the exquisite functions that they can, so quickly and in so little space? Perhaps this comparison is a result of our conditioning by the latest human attempts to invent machines that exhibit a modicum of intelligent behavior. Although there is indeed a technological revolution in the design and function of computers, the term is still an apt one. That is, what they do best is "compute." Even the most sophisticated devices—and mankind's best attempts to program them to think, or to create, or to recognize and analyze spacial patterns—are, at best, pedestrian in comparison with the human mind.

Here, nature is quite far ahead of our best efforts. The painstaking construction and analysis of the brain's circuit diagram has thus far yielded a level of complexity that we have not begun to understand. Studies of the visual cortex (the portion of the brain which processes visual signals) and the nerve connections in the retina suggest that, at the very least, there is a high degree of simultaneous processing and comparing of the signals from all parts of the retina.

The field of neuropharmacology has yielded considerable information in recent years concerning the chemistry of the brain and how it is regulated. The number of compounds which could be classified as neurotransmitters (substances that mediate or modulate the signals between nerve endings) is now believed to be in the hundreds or thousands, instead of being less than 10 as it was thought to be only a few years ago.[32] Some of these substances are found only in the brain; others occur throughout the body. Some seem to be produced by nerve cells and detected by other nerve cells. Others are classified as hormones, being produced far from the brain, but participating in the regulation of brain (and other) functions. Adrenalin (the fright–flight substance) and naturally produced opiates are examples of this type of substance.

It now appears possible that the way these substances are regulated with respect to each other has a great deal to do with a person's state of mind. An imbalance can produce—or is at least correlated with—a variety of abnormal conditions, ranging from inappropriate emotions (common, for example, during pregnancy or menopause) all the way to psychosis. A psychotic state, indistinguishable from that exhibited by mental patients, can be produced temporarily in normal volunteers to whom chemicals resembling certain neurotransmitters are administered.[33] There is growing evidence that the production and the regulation of neurotropic substances is under tight genetic control. It is only logical that it should be, of course, but certain dogma has prevailed in Western society that emotional status, behavior, and psychological parameters could not possibly vary with genetics in the same way that hair, eye, and skin color obviously do.

Approaching the question of genetics and behavior from a completely different direction, the sociobiologists have offered a coherent theory and some evidence that individual behavior (including that between the sexes) has a strong genetic component, as do the cultural differences among the world's societies.[34] In the era of social equality and civil rights, it is understandable that this thesis has been rather unpopular in many quarters. It has also served to rekindle the entire matter of nature versus nurture, and whether or not intelligence and all of its component parts are determined by one's genes or by the environment. Arthur Jensen and others[35] who chose to investigate human intelligence and its determinants ran into trouble when they began to apply to humans principles taken for granted by animal breeders for many years. That is, not only were there ample data to support the hypothesis that the individual variation one observes in intellectual and behavioral traits is primarily genetic in origin, but that the differences among the average values of these parameters measured in racial, ethnic, and geographical population groups are a reflection of the relative differences in the distribution of genes among various human gene pools.

Of course, controlled studies and measurements of features as complex as human behavior and that collection of a large number of traits lumped together under the name "intelligence" are enormously difficult. It is unfortunate that it is so difficult to separate the objective investigation of a very interesting problem in human population genetics from the feeling, emotional human animal living in a society of contemporary, sometimes conflicting, values. It is important that both scientists and the critics of science keep very separate in their minds the free inquiry into the nature of a phenomenon in quest of the Truth, and the possible use and misuse of the knowledge that will ensue. To inject into scholarship and research the bogeymen of ideology and the notion of preferred results is only destructive. This subject is discussed in much more detail in Chapter 4.

But what of the science? Can we now decide the extent to which our behavior, intelligence, and other talents originate in our genes? Published studies continue to indicate differences—significant differences—in such traits among individuals and populations.[36] The clear interpretation of these data is not always easy, but continuing to explain away the data in terms of cultural and environmental differences or biased tests is becoming more and more difficult.

It is my personal opinion, although I cannot support these views with hard scientific evidence, that the winner in the nature/nurture controversy will be nature, hands down. That is not to say that one's environment and experience are not critically important to the development of one's total being.

Rather, the manner in which an individual responds to one's surroundings and his capacity for being influenced by them, in both positive and negative ways, is most probably the reflection of genetic factors. The more we learn about genetics and genetic control, and about neurobiology, the more we must accept the logic that every part of our entire being is genetically determined. So why not our brains, our minds, and our behavior? People have been breeding animals for behavioral traits for centuries. Why should humans be exempt from what otherwise seems to be a universally accepted rule? Closer to my own direct experience, I have been impressed by the fact that the personality and the behavioral characteristics of my children has not changed significantly from the time each was a small baby, although their personalities are very different from each other. The argument that their personalities were somehow drawn on the blank pages of their young minds during the first three months of life is, to me, an untenable hypothesis.

So, the mysteries of the brain, and how it thinks and remembers and feels, are beginning to yield to the scientific sleuths. The phenomenon of consciousness may be a difficult one for us to grasp conceptually. As we get closer to understanding the most basic parts of our existence, can we extricate ourselves enough from our own humanness to retain our objectivity? This may be the most difficult task of all.

Genes and Human Disease

Medical research has, in addition to the objective of expanding our knowledge of how the human animal functions, the following goals: to understand the process of disease, to find out how to prevent its occurrence, and to find a cure for it. In the remainder of this chapter, I shall discuss some of the new insights that the new biology has given us into the causes of disorder in the human system.

Before it may be understood how the body's functions are impaired by disease or malfunction, it is first necessary to understand how they operate normally. Obviously, then, much of medicine must now deal with disorders for which the underlying causes are not understood, although they present clinically observable symptoms to the physician, and usually to the patient, too. Although the clinical basis of most major infectious diseases is now understood in terms of our ever-increasing knowledge of microbial physiology and genetics, there are many classes of diseases, such as cancer, diabetes, arthritis, multiple sclerosis, and numerous genetic diseases, for which our level of knowledge permits neither the prevention nor the cure.

With advances in our methods for studying human genes, we are now beginning to understand, in rather precise molecular terms, the underlying basis for a number of human genetic disorders. The isolation and the characterization of the human beta globin gene family have revealed the source of difficulty in sickle-cell anemia and the beta-thalassemias, both of which lead to abnormal red blood cells of highly impaired function. The detailed knowledge that we now have of these genes may soon permit successful gene therapy in these patients, as well as in their children and subsequent descendants.

In many hereditary diseases, the defective gene product is known. In most cases, it is an enzyme. In the disorder known as Lesch-Nyhan disease, which is linked to the female (X) chromosome and therefore affects only boys, the afflicted are mentally retarded and spastic, mutilate themselves, and usually die before reaching adulthood. The disorder is due to the lack of an enzyme (hypoxanthine phosphoribosyltransferase, or HPRT) involved in nucleic acid metabolism. Beatrice Mintz created teratocarcinoma cells with this defect in the laboratory in order to study the disease in her model system using allophenic mice. This work is discussed in the Appendix.

There are, however, several genetic diseases for which even the specific biochemical, structural, or developmental defect is not known, or at least not well understood. These include Huntington's disease (which killed Woody Guthrie), amyotrophic lateral sclerosis (the disease that killed Lou Gehrig, a New York Yankees star of the 1920s), muscular distrophy, and cystic fibrosis.

It is important here to distinguish these true genetic diseases from another class of congenital disorders that reflect errors in the way the chromosomes are distributed in the parents' gametes. The most well known of these is Down's syndrome, or mongolism, which results from an extra chromosome, Number 21, contributed by the mother, with the incidence rising dramatically in births to women over age 35. There are many other disorders resulting from extra sex chromosomes, most of which include mental retardation and usually other characteristics. (The sex chromosomes, named for their appearance in the condensed form, are denoted X and Y; a female normally has two X chromosomes, and a male one X and one Y chromosome.) Examples include Kleinfelter's syndrome, in which males have two or more X chromosomes in addition to the one Y chromosome, and the disorder receiving recent legal attention, in which it was suggested that males with two Y chromosomes might exhibit excessive aggression and violent criminal tendencies.

There are a number of other serious disorders that may have a genetic basis (such as Alzheimer's disease, alcoholism, atherosclerosis, diabetes, multiple sclerosis, and schizophrenia), but rather of the sort that determines susceptibility, rather than causing the disease directly. It is also well known that a familial history of heart disease (atherosclerosis) is a good predictor of the same affliction in males. Even the occurrence of some types of cancer seems to have a hereditary bias.

In recent years, a line of research into the genetic determinants of a class of human proteins known as human leukocyte antigens (HLA) has suggested a possible cause of at least some of these diseases. Each individual has a characteristic set of HLA proteins, as unique as one's fingerprints. These antigens, originally found on the surface of white blood cells, appear to occur in many other cell types as well. At present, their function is unclear. However, by extensive screening, involving testing human blood samples with antisera for more than 100 different HLA proteins, it has been shown that genetic "linkage" occurs between certain HLA proteins and perhaps 30 human diseases. These include juvenile-onset diabetes, multiple sclerosis, and possibly even human depression.[37]

The term *linkage* means that when the genetic material of a germ cell is divided into two gametes (the ova and the sperm), each of which has only half the number of chromosomes as a normal somatic cell, the two linked genes always, or usually, go to the same cell and thus occur together in the same offspring. Genetically, this means that the two genes must be located close to each other—not only on the same chromosome, but, because the DNA *within* chromosomes also exchanged, rather close to one another on the same chromosome. It is, of course, possible that there is some very direct causal relationship between a particular HLA protein and the disease, in which case the linkage is not by chance but is determined directly by the HLA gene. The HLA genes are located on chromosomes Number 6 and Number 17. These DNA regions have been "fished" out and are being studied extensively.

Thus far, a definitive cause involving HLA proteins for any of these diseases has not been unequivocally demonstrated. However, there is much support for the theory that certain of the HLA proteins resemble, fortuitously, the coat proteins of certain viruses, or possibly bacterial antigens. Thus, if a person is infected by one or more of these diseases (and these might in themselves be very innocuous diseases and ignored as just another cold), antibodies will be induced against these invaders. But, the theory goes, these antibodies might then *also* react with the surface antigens, particularly in certain tissues or organs where they are likely to occur. A possible result might be the destruction of the cells of these tissues.

Further studies of the HLA proteins could provide us with important clues to the so-called autoimmune diseases, which include rheumatic fever and kidney (Bright's) disease among many others. In the case of juvenile-onset diabetes, antibodies appear to be made that destroy certain cells in the pancreatic structures called the *islets of Langerhans,* where insulin is manufactured, but only in individuals possessing one of three specific HLA proteins. If this turns out to be a general mechanism for a large class of diseases, then the new biological techniques offer much promise for both the diagnosis of susceptible individuals and the prevention of the diseases.

The report that human depressive disorder appears to be linked genetically to certain of the HLA proteins on Chromosome 6 is a provocative finding. The correlation is still being questioned by some, and it is not known whether the determinant in the disease is one of the HLA proteins itself or simply another gene that happens to be located in the same region. Nevertheless, if depression turns out to be correlated directly with a specific cell surface protein, it will be the first case in which autoimmunity is implicated as the possible cause of a psychiatric disorder. If antibodies are produced by an infection and then cross-react with antigens on nerve cells, it follows that there should be a disturbance in function. Other psychiatric illnesses that appear to have a strong hereditary component include schizophrenia and alcoholism. Thus, one might expect many experiments to be carried out to determine the extent to which these syndromes follow the model of juvenile diabetes.

Cancer

The causes of cancer, at least at the level of the control of gene expression, still remain a mystery. And so this remains one of the paramount problems in medical research. There appear to be a multiplicity of agents that will induce cancer. In fact, there are probably several steps in carcinogenesis. As a rough approximation, there are two classes of agents involved in the conversion of a normal cell into a cancerous one. The first, called an *initiator,* triggers an event apparently involving DNA, probably a mutational event. Most mutagens are also cancer initiators. The second is called a *promoter,* which, while not actually producing cancer itself, greatly enhances the effect of an initiator. Possibly, the action of both is necessary. For example, the natural chemical aflatoxin, produced by a mold that infects improperly stored grains, nuts and peanuts, is both a potent animal carcinogen and a mutagen. (Aflatoxin is present to varying degrees in about 15% of the peanut butter samples sold in the United States, although, it is claimed, not at dangerous levels). On the other hand, saccharin, which has caused a colossal flap concerning its potential as a carcinogen, appears to be a promoter rather than an initiator. Animal studies[38] have shown that while saccharin is at best a rather weak carcinogen by itself, animals to which it was fed and which were exposed to a single weak dose of an initiator, developed cancer readily. No cancer was observed in those animals exposed only to the initiator, with no subsequent saccharin in their diets. In another type of cancer, human cervical cancer, the causal agent is the herpes Type II virus, which is spread by sexual contact.

Recently, strong evidence has been found to implicate certain specific genes in cancer.[39] These genes, dubbed *oncogenes,* are normally harmless. In human bladder cancer, however, it has been shown that a change in a single base pair leading to one altered amino acid in the protein product, is sufficient to cause the transformation from normal to cancer cells. This finding suggests that the initiation event in cancer may indeed be a simple mutation. It does not, however, account for the phenomenon of promotion, which may well be operating at the level of the control of proliferation of cells in the organism. The breakdown of immune surveillance, which may normally be scavenging and eliminating transformed cells, is possibly one way in which the promoting event may occur. That is, if some external agent suppressed the natural-killer T cells in some way, this action might then allow transformed cells to proliferate and seed metastases.

In Burkitt's lymphoma, another putative oncogene mistakenly gets onto the wrong chromosome during the normal genetic rearrangement that accompanies the immune response to an antigen and the synthesis of specific antibodies.

Although there are now several different examples of oncogenes being implicated in certain types of cancer, the precise mechanism of how these changes cause a differentiated cell to lose control over itself and to begin to grow and divide at a greatly accelerated rate is still not understood.[40] Nor is it known whether oncogenes are causally linked to *all* cancer. It is possible that there are other ways in which control is disrupted and cellular transformation occurs, thus initiating cancer.

Now that sophisticated techniques are available for the detailed characterization of human genes and gene function, it should be only a matter of time before the enigmatic puzzle of cancer is solved. However, as we learn more and more about this cantankerous collection of diseases, the possibility of a magic bullet cure for cancer seems more remote than ever. If one is found, it will be at least partially by chance rather than design. Until that unlikely occurrence, effective cancer therapies that are able to avoid the destructive effects of radiation and present-day chemotherapeutics are likely to be individually tailored to the patient, as well as being of heroic and very expensive proportions. According to Robert Weinberg, one of the leading scientists in today's quest to solve the cancer puzzle, the only effective means to reduce the number of cancer deaths during the next decade, and probably beyond, will be prevention, not a miraculous new cure.[41] If people could be made to stop smoking, the reduction in death and disability from cancer, especially lung cancer, and other diseases as well, would be dramatic. And if Americans could change their eating habits, particularly by reducing the amount of dietary fat, a substantial decline in cancers at many other sites (colon, breast) might be expected. But the difficulty in changing the living habits of people, and in thwarting the powerful commercial interests that promote and profit from their self-destructive habits, may pose the greatest obstacle of all.

CHAPTER 2

Life: The Technology

Science and Technology

In the preceding pages, I have tried to lead the reader, carefully if quickly, through the past 20 years or so of discovery. It has been an exciting period of bringing into focus the conceptual basis of life. Where there was once largely a blur of seemingly unrelated observations, some coherent images are slowly emerging, and the single, integrated picture is beginning to make sense. Although we can still only barely discern some of its features, it is clear that this picture, encompassing the wisdom of the ages, will reduce to irrelevance any questions about why science should be pursued. Continuing to bring this image to crystal clarity is reason enough for scientific endeavor. Just as art justifies itself, so does science.

I hope that by now, my readers share this perception. But this most precious view of the world is rarely seen by those whose concepts of science come from the newspapers and television. Science instead means useful *things,* or inventions, or the perturbing of the natural order by mankind. In the media world, science is equated with technology. And genetics means genetic engineering. There is, however, a fundamental difference between science—the search for knowledge, and technology—its application.

In the course of the scientific exploration of any set of natural phenomena, there comes a time when the body of accumulated knowledge contains enough elements to permit their application to what is "useful," or at least to what human beings desire at a particular point in history. If there is insufficient knowledge, then the technology will never get off the ground, or it will remain surrounded by a mythology or quasi-religious belief system that must be subscribed to by its adherents.

Thus, for centuries, the alchemists, using a very limited body of knowledge of basic chemistry, tried, by means of various hypotheses based more on desire than on fact, to create gold from lead (they were both metals, heavy and relatively soft—therefore, there must be a fundamental similarity). But the contributions that made chemistry a coherent science and which ultimately made a revolutionary industry possible stemmed not from the work of alchemists, but from the discovery of certain fundamental relationships between the components of matter and eventually the atomic theory and the periodic table of elements.

Similarly, in medicine, the attribution of disease to evil humors, demons, bad blood, or a variety of other creations of the imagination (which had to be consistent with the contemporary culture and the religious framework within which societies existed) was ultimately overturned not by the advances made by healers and witch doctors, but by the discovery of microbes. Even though contagion and the transmissibility of disease were well known in the Middle Ages, the development of the microscope was required before the world of microbes could be discovered. Even then, a connection was slow in coming. The work of Edward Jenner, Robert Koch, and Louis Pasteur did much to establish the basis of infectious disease and the beginnings of an understanding of the immune system.

At the beginning of the twentieth century, the concept of electronics and the wireless transmission of voices and pictures was unimagined. The theoretical basis for the transmission of electromagnetic energy through space had been set down elegantly years earlier by James Clerk Maxwell.[1] Only slowly did the experimenters begin to use and appreciate the knowledge that was at hand.

Now we may look back on the development of one of the world's major industries and most useful (as well as desired) technologies stemming from advances in physics. The telegraph depended on electromagnetism. Marconi's transmission of electrical pulses over great distances[2] depended on an appreciation of the fact that electromagnetic waves could be propagated over great distances.

The vacuum tube, now nearly obsolete, once revolutionized electronics. But its development depended on an elucidation of the properties of the electron and the generation of electron beams in a vacuum between oppositely charged plates. With Lee De Forest's invention of the grid,[3] again utilizing the fact that electrons are charged electrical particles which obey the laws of physics, the amplification of electrical signals became possible, and the electronics industry was on its way.

The invention of solid-state devices[4]—the transistor and integrated circuits—did not add any fundamental principles to electronic circuits, but it made possible many things that vacuum tubes could not do, simply because of the great reduction in size and energy requirements, the simplicity of manufacturing methods, and far lower costs. The reduction in size alone enables the computers of today to operate in the nanosecond range. Again, however, basic studies in the structure of matter and the properties of electrical conductance of certain crystalline substances had to be appreciated before today's commonplace applications could be imagined.

Although some technologies far exceed their initial promise, some never make it in quite the way that their proponents thought they would, however correct the exploitation of certain branches of knowledge once appeared. It can scarcely go unnoticed that the hydrogen bombs that now worry increasingly larger portions of the population were a direct corollary of the discovery of fundamental relationships between matter and energy and between the smallest known components of matter itself. Of course, the circumstances of World War II provided the impetus for physicists to devote their energy with great enthusiasm to the construction of a fission bomb. The history of the Manhattan Project is a fascinating study in human motives and the exercise of the creative process.[5]

The result of this technology, however desirable it may have seemed to many at the time, has been a monster that has the globe poised in a metastable state over the abyss of irreversible and total self-destruction. The nuclear power industry, which was an indirect result of fission research, became embroiled in politics very early, with the result that there has been virtually no innovation in reactor technology in two decades, and an intrinsically safe reactor was scrapped in favor of the type that requires a multitude of gadgets, all functioning perfectly, in order to operate safely. Thus, this particular industry, once the darling of the atomic age, has become mired in inefficiency, astronomic costs, radioactive waste which nobody wants, regulation, litigation, and a great deal of bad public will. It is possible—even likely—that the developing solar photovoltaic industry will displace the nuclear industry as a source of electric power generation long before the nuclear industry can solve its problems.

Thus, not all technologies that spring from the well of scientific discovery turn out to be desirable in the long run. But that, too, is a principle of history. There are always intermediate stages to everything. One only hopes that certain of these technologies (e.g., nuclear weapons) will not render meaningless discussions of the next stage.

Repeatedly, then, there is a logical and inevitable progression from science to technology. Both require material support, but for technology to become really useful to society, a substantial financial investment is needed. Just where this comes from is a matter of national economic systems and political values. In most of the world, however, this progression is accomplished by the investment of private capital and the dreams of the true entrepreneurial spirit. In almost every case, the initiative was taken by scientists who were inspired to take the step *after* discovery—that of bringing the practical benefits of science to the people. Of course there is the profit motive. But there is much more.

What Good Is It Anyway?

So here—for those who may have asked after reading this far, "Well, what good is it anyway?"—is a discussion of the practical corollaries of scientific endeavor. Invention, in order to make life easier and more pleasurable, has long been a proclivity of the human race. Thus, the intense proliferation of practical ingenuity that is now characteristic of what has been dubbed *biotechnology* is no different from any other period of technical innovation. It is only that we now have a rapidly growing body of basic biological knowledge on which to build. This increase in knowledge has, in fact, been so rapid, that science and technology are often inseparable in practice, although the two terms remain fundamentally distinct in concept.

Good is a term everyone must define for himself. *Good* and *progress* are often equated with new inventions, particularly material ones. In recent years, however, the view has often been expressed that technology has gone too far, and most of its current contributions to the gross national product are viewed as "bad." New and fiendishly original weapons systems are certainly considered "good" by generals, that is, unless it is the other side that has them. To others, any contribution to the arms race is definitely "bad."

I would argue that knowledge itself is value-free. That is, simply to understand some aspect of nature, in whatever detail, can be neither good nor bad, except possibly in the sense that certain knowledge may be psychologically harmful or beneficial to the one who has it. But here, it is not the knowledge itself that contains moral value, but the effect of that knowledge on the individual's particular psyche and how he relates it to the rest of his experiences, values, and beliefs. Thus, so that I will not be taken to task for making sweeping statements that do not stand up to scholarly scrutiny, I clearly recognize that innocence (or ignorance, if you prefer) might at times be desirable (good) or undesirable (bad) under certain circumstances. If an otherwise responsible and caring mother were also a thief and a prostitute, it might well be bad for her nine-year-old daughter to know the full extent of her mother's activities. Similarly, it is good for children to know that walking in front of a speeding bus could be fatal. In these cases, we are dealing with the practical corollaries of knowledge and its value to the well-being of the knower. Of course, knowledge can have either positive or negative value to the knower.

This section, then, is concerned with the practical corollaries of knowledge, not simply the way in which it affects the behavior or the emotional state of the knower, but the way in which it can and will be used by the knowers and the societies that the knowers comprise. I repeat: Knowledge *per se* is value-free. But its use never can be. I do not wish to split philosophical hairs or belabor what is both a trivial point and a subject about which learned scholars have written volumes. The distinction to be made is between the human, psychological act of knowing, which cannot be separated from the rest of one's humanness, and the information itself. Put another way, a book on how to split the atom is value-free. It is only information. Reading that book might affect the reader's emotional state, but the knowledge would remain free of moral content unless that knowledge were to lead to a particular *action*. Action resulting from knowledge, particularly that which might affect more than the knower, is then subject to evaluation for goodness or badness by a society, or by one or more individuals. If the reader makes an atomic bomb, then that is an act subject to such evaluation and one which would probably be judged by most modern societies to be a bad application of knowledge.

Or someone might read that the sun will someday explode into a supernova, incinerating the earth. This knowledge might make that person so depressed that he commits suicide. It is possible that such an action would affect no one else. But it is also possible that he would leave behind a grieving wife and children. Knowledge, then, has led to an action that has had consequences which might be viewed as undesirable or "bad." It was not the predictable fact that the sun would explode which was bad, nor even the knowledge of this fact by certain human beings. It was the action, even if it was involuntary, that was, in a remote sense, a use of knowledge.

But I am digressing. The previous chapter dealt with science, or the acquisition of knowledge about life. This chapter is concerned with how that knowledge can be or is being used, endeavors which certainly reflect the values of the human beings directing the application of that knowledge. The final chapter of this book is concerned with values and the ethical principles that govern the use of knowledge, or the ethics of technology. This discussion however, is primarily an exposition of current technologies based on our knowledge of living mechanisms and the techniques we have devised to manipulate them.

Medicine

There is no question that the recent advances in cell biology and the development of techniques for isolating and cloning genes are already affecting the practice of medicine in significant ways. In addition to the insight into many aspects of disease, discussed in the previous chapter, these studies have led to greatly improved methods of diagnosis; the large-scale production of rare and expensive biological substances needed for the detection, treatment, and prevention of many diseases (including hormones and vaccines); and a new route to the production of pharmaceuticals. These studies have also brought the direct treatment of genetic diseases, both of the afflicted individuals and of their descendants, within the realm of reality. And it appears that this is only the beginning of the exploitation of the gains of basic biological research.

When it first became apparent that it was possible to propagate "foreign" genes in bacteria, utilizing the cells' own machinery for transcribing the inserted DNA and translating the messenger RNA (mRNA) into protein gene products, the use of the method for producing hard-to-come-by biological substances for medical applications immediately became a selling point. When the controversy raged over the potential hazards of gene splicing, many scientists seemed to think that the use of recombinant DNA methods *needed* to be sold. Perhaps they were right. But this emphasis on "benefits" to counter the arguments about risks tended to skew the public's perception of the real significance of genetic manipulation techniques and their ultimate scientific value. Thus, public (and congressional) understanding of science was given a setback, with the notion reinforced that the principal function of science was to provide consumer goods.

In any event, the scientists, who in 1976 claimed that the theoretical potential of recombinant DNA technology to produce all manner of rare substance would soon be a reality, have kept their promise. Somatostatin, a small peptide hormone involved in the regulation of cell growth, was the first human gene product to be manufactured in *E. coli* cells. This success was soon followed by human growth hormone and insulin. The methods used do not, of course, duplicate events in mammalian cells. The mammalian genes for these substances are interrupted by long regions of silent DNA. In nature, the mRNA must undergo a complex processing procedure before it is fit to serve as a template for protein synthesis. In the hands of the genetic engineers, however, only the DNA sequence corresponding to the expressed protein, plus start and stop signals, is spliced into a universal expression plasmid, which is then incorporated into a bacterial host. Furthermore, insulin is made not as the 84-amino-acid proinsulin, but as two separate chains of 30 and 21 amino acids, respectively, which are then linked after synthesis.

The products so made must be tested extensively to make sure they are free of impurities. For example, *E. coli* endotoxin, an apparently essential component of bacterial cell walls, is a common contaminant of products made in *E. coli*. Small amounts in the human bloodstream produce a high fever and other severe toxic symptoms. Thus endotoxin must be completely removed before the injection of a cloned product into humans. These substances must also undergo clinical trials to demonstrate that they are as biologically effective as the compounds produced by other methods. That is, all of the Food and Drug Administration's rules apply to these materials, as they do to any other pharmaceutical or biological used by humans.

The class of compounds that has perhaps aroused the greatest interest has been the interferons. First discovered in the late 1950s, interferons are proteins that are produced by all mammals and are involved in the natural defense of the organism against invading viruses. Their production, in fact, appears to be triggered by the initial stages of a viral infection. Not only do they seem to help stem the spread of the infection, but they appear to prevent infection by a second virus. This, presumably, is why an individual rarely has two viral diseases at the same time. Therefore, because these substances seemed to "interfere" with the infection process, they were named *interferons*. The genes for three structurally distinct classes of interferons, obtained from different cell types and termed *alpha, beta,* and *gamma,* have been isolated and characterized.

Interferon has been a subject of both intense political and commercial interest because of its suggested value as an anticancer therapeutic. But although its antiviral properties are well established, its value as the magic bullet for cancer is in doubt. That is, it seems to arrest tumor growth in animals under certain conditions, as well as cultures of transformed (cancerlike) cells. In some limited human trials, it appears to have been effective in arresting the growth of certain cancers. But there have also been unexpected toxic side effects. Although it may prove to be of some value in human cancer therapy, most probably in conjunction with conventional therapies, interferon does not appear likely to be the ultimate victory in the war on cancer. However, the interferons are under intensive clinical investigation and are widely used in research, so there is substantial demand for their production. Before gene cloning in bacteria made the large-scale synthesis of interferons possible as well as cheap, the limited supply of interferon was isolated from cultures of human leukocytes (white blood cells) and was prohibitively expensive.

Given the promise suggested by the properties of some of the interferons studied, gene engineers are experimenting with modifications in the structure of interferons to see if they can increase biological activity. This can be done by making hybrids between different parts of the genes for the three types of interferon, or by chemically altering portions of the interferon DNA coding sequence. At present, the precise way that interferons work is not well understood, so attempts to improve interferons by deliberate modification are largely empirical.

There is a large class of proteins that serve important functions in the regulation of the immune system. These natural *immunomodulators,* as they are called, are produced by the T cells of the immune system but lend themselves readily to production by cloning of their genes in a bacterial host. The lymphokines and the thymic hormones are now receiving a great deal of attention, not only for their importance in mediating the immune response, but, like the interferons, as possible therapeutic agents. These agents may prove useful in treating infections, cancer and tumors, and autoimmune diseases, and in organ transplantation, where the prevention of tissue rejection of the transplant remains an unsolved problem.

Because some of these compounds seem to stimulate natural-killer T cells, which in turn appear to attack certain types of cancer cells or at least to stem their spread by preventing metastases, there exists a rational basis of exploring these agents as cancer therapeutics. If this mechanism is indeed nature's way of fighting and preventing cancer, perhaps a bit of a boost of the natural system would be of general benefit to all cancer patients. Of course, like all approaches in this field so far, it is unlikely to be so simple. But given the dismal state of current cancer therapies, even small gains would be welcome.

One approach to cancer therapy that may be of great value in treating at least certain types of cancer is the search for tumor-specific antigens. If tumor or cancer cells contain a specific antigen on their surface that is found nowhere else in the body, then a monoclonal antibody against that antigen may provide a unique therapeutic agent. If the antigen-specific portion of the antibody molecule is then bound to the active part of a cellular toxin molecule (such as diphtheria toxin, ricin from castor beans, or a snake or insect venom component) or a short-range radioisotope, then a means may be at hand for selectively killing *only* the cancer cells and leaving the normal cells untouched. But here, too, what looked very promising in theory has had its shortcomings in practice. For some tumors, antibodies by themselves seem to be just as effective as the immunotoxin. The compounds apparently have trouble delivering the toxin part of the complex to its intended cellular target. But this is the type of problem that might be overcome by some clever molecular engineering.

Current cancer therapeutics (chemotherapeutic agents or radiation) do extensive damage to normal tissue, achieving their limited effectiveness against cancer because of the higher rates of cell division and metabolism in cancer cells. A rapidly dividing cell is somewhat more sensitive to a general antimetabolite than a slowly dividing one. It is not yet known if the tumor-specific antigens detected in cultured cells indicate a general property of cancer cells in living mammals. However, sensitive detection methods using monoclonal antibodies linked to a color-producing substance are able to distinguish human breast-cancer cells from normal cells in tissue samples. Similar diagnostic approaches seem to be effective for a number of other cancers.

There is, however, one rather perverse quality of cancer cells that renders them innately difficult to fight by any mode of therapy. A malignant tumor undergoes metastasis; that is, cells from the original tumor site spread throughout the body, starting tumors in other organs and tissues. Moreover, these rapidly dividing cells undergo their own microevolution, where the fittest—those most able to proliferate and overcome the body's own natural defenses—survive.[6] By the time cancer is diagnosed, it is likely that there are metastases at several sites. It is, in fact, metastatic disease that is usually the cause of death from cancer.

The supreme challenge in developing an effective therapy is the fact that there is generally considerable diversity, both genetic and immunologic, in the population of cancer cells in a single patient at the time of diagnosis. Thus, it may not be possible to find any single antigen that is common to all of the malignant cells and to none of the normal ones. If specific immunotoxin molecules had to be tailor-made for each patient in order to fight each diverse type of tumor cell, the therapist would be working against extreme odds of finding them all in time.

Even if immunomodulator therapy is able to greatly enhance the body's general immunologic capacity, which normally includes a scavenging mechanism for destroying at least some tumor cells when they appear, and to gobble up metastasizing cells before they can get a foothold in vital organs where they don't belong, it may be too late by the time the disease is detected. Nevertheless, although cancer remains perhaps the most cantankerous of human diseases, the methods of modern immunology offer greater promise for an effective treatment than any other approach to date.

Vaccines

The production of vaccines against viral diseases is now largely carried out by growing an "attenuated" virus, one that has lost its high degree of virulence, in cell cultures, chick embryos, or live animals; purifying the virus; and using it directly as a vaccine. The weakened virus must still cause a mild infection in order to produce enough of the viral antigen to confer immunity (i.e., when a smallpox vaccination "takes"). Other vaccines are prepared by treating an active virus in a way that renders it nonvirulent (e.g., by osmotic shock, which causes the DNA to be released from its coat protein). But this once-empirical science is now a perfect candidate for the application of DNA cloning methods in bacteria. A vaccine achieves its effectiveness through the antigenic properties of the coat protein. Generally, several types of antibodies that respond to different antigens in the coat protein are formed against a single virus. But a vaccine that contains its nucleic acid portion is potentially dangerous if, in the case of a "live" virus, there is a reversion to a virulent form, or if the weakening process has not been effective. There have been a few notable cases in which people have been infected with a serious disease in the process of trying to prevent it.

By isolating the viral coat protein genes and propagating them in bacterial plasmids containing the genes required for the expression of the inserted regions, safe vaccines can, in principle, be produced easily and cheaply. Of course, the choice of organism and cloning vehicle will determine the ease of isolation and purification. In general, however, it should completely replace the costly conventional methods of vaccine production and produce a completely safe product. Although conceptually a more complex procedure, vaccines for bacterial diseases could be constructed in a similar manner.

The first vaccines to be produced by recombinant DNA techniques and offered commercially have actually been for animal diseases, such as hoof-and-mouth disease, rabies, and scours, a severe diarrheal disease in piglets and calves. Much of the reason why companies prefer to develop animal vaccines instead of human vaccines is because the regulatory requirements for veterinary products are far simpler and quicker to meet than those for human health products. There are many human diseases for which research has been carried out by means of gene-cloning methods to produce a vaccine. These include hepatitis; herpes simplex virus Type II, perhaps the most widespread sexually transmitted pathogen; and gonorrhea, another venereal disease which is becoming more difficult to treat because of the spread of a strain that is resistant to penicillin. However, because the regulatory delays are long and the economic incentives are relatively small for private firms to develop vaccines with their own funds, the new generation of specific and effective vaccines may yet need federal support before being developed for general use.[7]

Diagnosis of Disease

The accurate diagnosis of disease, particularly in screening individuals before the presentation of overt symptoms, is an aspect of medical practice that is being greatly improved by several of the developments discussed earlier. Because of the elucidation of the many components of the immune system, and the possibility of obtaining large quantities of almost any molecular component in high yield, it is, in principle, possible to develop highly sensitive and specific assays for numerous indicators of pathology, including the early detection of cancer.

It is for this clinical purpose that pure antigen-specific (monoclonal) antibodies are of great value. An assay utilizing specific antibodies can be developed for virtually any substance that will serve as an antigen. Thus, any disease process that alters the usual pattern of circulating antigenic substances should, in principle, be amenable to detection with the use of pure antibody. At present, this technique is used to develop definitive assays for parasitic diseases, such as malaria, schistosomiasis, and sleeping sickness; a number of infectious microbial diseases; and possibly some types of cancer.

The ability to select or synthesize specific genes or portions thereof has led to a novel approach to diagnostics. All that is needed is a novel DNA base sequence in the pathogen sought that is not shared by any other organism, including those less virulent strains of the same group. That is, there are many types of *E. coli,* but only a small subset of these cause disease. The DNA "probe" consists of one or more radioactively labeled specific fragments of DNA that will recognize and hybridize with the unique base sequences in the pathogen's DNA. The test can be easily carried out on specially treated biological samples, giving a highly accurate indication of the presence of the infectious organism. Definitive diagnostic methods now in use require one to identify the organism through culture techniques that are often lengthy, tedious, and expensive.

Other methods are also receiving attention. *Molecular fingerprinting* refers to assays where a large number of soluble protein components are separated quickly in such a manner that all the components are visible at once, forming a unique pattern. A method was developed in 1974[8] for separating proteins in two dimensions using electric fields, a technique that is suitable for automation and electronic pattern recognition. Literally hundreds of proteins can be separated at a time, showing up as a pattern of spots, each with a characteristic position with respect to the others. One abnormal protein will show up as an unexpected spot; a missing protein will leave a blank where a spot was to be expected.

This method has already been applied to the children of the Japanese atom-bomb survivors in an attempt to detect possible genetic damage through altered protein gene products which may not present any clinical symptoms.[9] This method has an advantage over a monoclonal antibody assay in which a specific antigen is sought, in that it is possible to view a large number of proteins simultaneously, but the method is more subject to artifacts and to errors of interpretation.

It is believed that a great many disorders may be revealed by the presence of an abnormal antigen, including atherosclerosis, cancer, autoimmune diseases, and many infectious diseases. If routine screening of apparently healthy individuals were to become a part of normal physical examinations— as they could if, through the automation of molecular fingerprinting assays, antibody or other immunoassays, the costs became low and the reliability high—there could be a revolution in the early diagnosis of most of the major life-threatening diseases. The technology will take several more years to perfect, but it most assuredly will be available for the next generation.

The human leukocyte antigen (HLA) system should probably be given specific mention here. As discussed earlier, there is an apparent linkage between certain HLA proteins and several human disorders, possibly autoimmune diseases. The antigens are readily detected in a blood sample by immunoassay. However, the DNA for this region, coding for the different antigens, exhibits characteristic patterns when digested with specific restriction enzymes, subjected to electrophoresis, and then hybridized to a radioactive complementary DNA (cDNA) probe. This assay for HLA genes should, when perfected, be considerably less costly and much more accurate than conventional assays using serum from an animal immunized against a single purified antigen. As more regions of human DNA are characterized and correlated with the expression of a protein or other trait, analysis of restriction enzyme digests by the correct cDNA probes should provide the basis for assays for most known genetic diseases.

Human Gene Therapy

Gene therapy, or the correction of genetic disorders by direct intervention in the genetic constitution of an individual, is a much-discussed topic but has yet to be successfully carried out. Because so much is known about the human beta-globin gene family, both the beta-thalassemias and sickle-cell anemia are prime candidates for gene therapy.[10] The problem, however, in attempting to correct a genetic defect in an individual, all of whose cells are afflicted, is how to get the corrected gene copies into enough of the person's cells to do any good. In the case of these hemoglobin disorders, it may perhaps be a little easier than if all the cells of the body had to be altered. The red blood cells are produced by the hemopoietic stem cells of the bone marrow. These are rather specialized, actively dividing cells with only one function in life.

Several possible means are being explored of introducing functional globin genes into the defective cells. One is simply the direct injection of normal globin DNA into the patient's own defective bone marrow cells, which can be readily cultured in the laboratory. Those in which the normal gene becomes incorporated and are shown to produce normal globin could be selected, grown in quantity, and then transplanted into the patient's bone marrow. Another method that is receiving much attention is to incubate cells with DNA precipitated in calcium phosphate. Although the efficiency of DNA uptake is low, the inclusion of a marker gene makes it possible to select for cells containing inserted DNA. A third possible method for introducing genes is to hybridize two cell types, with the use of either Sendai virus or polyethylene glycol to facilitate the merging of the cell membranes; one of the cell types would ultimately donate a chromosome containing a normal gene to the cell which originally had an abnormal one. However, engineering such a specific selection would probably be more complicated than the direct introduction of the desired gene. A fourth method would employ a viral cloning vector, such as a disabled SV-40 virus, into which the globin DNA has been inserted.

Although all of the above methods have been successfully used to insert DNA into mammalian cells, attempts to achieve efficient expression of the globin genes have been unsuccessful so far. A much smaller gene, on the other hand—that coding for human herpes-simplex thymidine kinase (TK)—has been expressed in several cell systems.[11] The reasons for this difference are not clear at present. However, the TK-gene–containing fragment was only around 3,500 base pairs in length, whereas the globin gene fragment was about 16,000 base pairs long. Moreover, and perhaps here is where the trouble lies, this is only a fraction of the entire human globin DNA region, which is more than 65,000 base pairs in length. It is entirely possible that the control regions for the beta-globins are located in this region rather than in the smaller fragment used in the experiments to date. In any case, the entire globin region has not been successfully cloned in human cells as a single entity.

One individual so far has actually attempted gene therapy on human subjects. Martin Cline, of UCLA, acquired a measure of notoriety when he attempted to cure two thalassemia patients, after the UCLA review board that was supposed to approve the experiment denied him permission to do it at UCLA on ethical grounds, recommending further animal studies before it should be attempted in humans.[12] More than a year after his application to conduct the experiments, and anticipating that he would be turned down, Cline tried the procedure on a patient in Italy and on another in Israel. Neither were cured of their affliction.

What Cline did was to use the calcium phosphate method of introducing globin genes into the patients' own stem cells. He then established a population of cells containing the genes and put them back into the bone marrow of his patients. Scientists roundly criticized Cline for subjecting patients to risk when the chances of success were believed to be virtually zero. Not only did Cline not demonstrate that his transplanted cells were expressing the proper globin genes, but the odds that these cells could compete successfully with the bone marrow cells of the patients, present in vastly greater numbers, were considered to be exceedingly low.

Although this first long shot at curing a genetic disease apparently failed, it is certain to be only the first of many to come. Conceptually, the globin gene system may be one of the more accessible gene clusters. Some refinements will be required in order to construct a means to introduce the globin genes into a cell in a way that puts them under the normal mechanism for the control of gene expression. I expect that it is only a question of time before the attendant problems are solved.

Other genetic diseases, however, in which a deficiency has resulted in abnormal development or mental retardation, are not likely to be cured by such procedures, even if a viral-like vehicle is constructed that can successfully introduce the correct genes into most cells in the body. But timing may be important. That is, if sophisticated diagnostic procedures can be developed that indicate the presence of a genetic defect long before its symptoms are observed, as, for example, in Huntingdon's disease, then a form of systemic gene therapy may be of value.

Although the correction of genetic defects in any multicelled, differentiated organism presents certain obvious inherent problems, gene therapy on a single cell is quite a different matter. Thus, it has been suggested, the correction of genetic defects, and even perhaps the removal of a carried trait, may be possible if genetic surgery is performed on a fertilized egg. With the perfection of the techniques of *in vitro* fertilization and the subsequent transplantation of the zygote into the uterus, working with fertilized eggs may become a common practice. The problem will be to integrate the correct gene success-fully into the proper chromosome under the control of the regulatory machine-ry of the cell. As we continue to learn more about the position of human genes on chromosomes and the details of their structure, making genetic Band-Aids should become easier. However, the class of human congenital disorders (e.g., Down's syndrome and Kleinfelter's syndrome) resulting from extra chromosomes are not amenable to gene therapy, for they are not genetic in origin. They arise from the incorrect assortment of chromosomes during the formation of gametes, and apparently only in the female gametes, or ova. There is a correlation with the incidence of such disorders and the age of the mother, but the mechanism of this type of error is not known. Correction of an unfertilized egg to the proper chromosome number would undoubtedly be far more difficult than the selection of a normal egg.

Agriculture

Since Mendel demonstrated the segregation of genetic traits in peas, applied genetics has been an important part of the practice of agriculture. Long before the molecular basis of inheritance was understood, the seeds of the hardiest plants were selected for the next crop. The asexual propagation of selected plants has given us the navel orange. And selective plant breeding is continually used to construct hybrids with desired properties surpassing those of either parent, such as higher growth rates, higher yields of fruit or vegeta-bles, resistance to plant disease, and shorter maturation time. In many ways, the seed crops and the horticultural varieties in use today are very different from those common 100 or even 50 years ago. In fact, there is some concern that the practice of selective genetics, and the use by the majority of farms of relatively few varieties, will result in a loss of genetic diversity, to the ulti-mate detriment of agriculture.

Most of the techniques developed for the genetic manipulation of mi-crobes and animals may also be applied to plants. In fact, plants offer certain advantages. For all of the flap about whether or not animals can be cloned, it is commonplace among plants. The propagation of a plant by rooting a cutting or by grafting is one way to form a genetic clone. Thus, most seedless oranges sold today come from clones of a small number of aberrant individual plants, as do the grapes for most wines and numerous other horticultural varieties.

The cells of many species of plants may be made to revert to an un-differentiated state if the cell walls are first digested with the appropriate enzymes to form protoplasts. The dispersed protoplasts are in a form amenable to genetic manipulations. Protoplasts, in the right growth medium, will then divide and grow, either to form callous tissue or, in the presence of the proper combination of plant growth factors, to differentiate and form new plants. It may even be possible to construct artificial "seeds" from bits of callous tissue. Thus, once the desired properties are introduced into even a single cell, it should eventually become a relatively straightforward procedure to create clones of identical cells which could then generate an unlimited number of identical genetically modified plants.

As with other organisms, there are viruses that infect plant cells. These can, in principal, be genetically modified so as to introduce genetic material into plant cells, but without the usual destructive properties of the virus. Most common plant viruses, however, contain RNA, rather than DNA. Even though the RNA directs the synthesis of a corresponding DNA molecule once it is inside the plant cell, it is, at present, more difficult to construct a specifically spliced RNA molecule in the laboratory than it is a DNA molecule. Moreover, the nucleic acid sequences of plant viruses are not integrated into the plant's nuclear DNA; the entire viral life cycle takes place in the plant cytoplasm.

The most promising plant-cloning vector of all of those investigated thus far is the crown gall tumor plasmid. Carried by the bacterium *Agrobacterium tumefaciens,* the tumor-inducing (Ti) plasmid enters the plant cells, where it becomes integrated into the plant chromosomes and directs tumor formation. The plasmid may be readily modified and "foreign" genes introduced. The stability of the integrated Ti DNA through subsequent generations, as well as the expression of gene inserts, is currently receiving considerable attention.[13]

Nitrogen fixation is a property of the bacteria forming the root nodules of leguminous plants (e.g., soybeans and alfalfa). The symbiotic relationship between *Rhizobium* and the plant provides legumes with a source of nitrogen in addition to that which is taken up by the roots from the soil. Plant genetic engineers are currently challenged by the problem of inserting nitrogen-fixing genes directly into a plant, so as to reduce or eliminate the need for nitrogen-containing fertilizers. Certain crops, such as corn, require large amounts of soil nitrogen and quickly deplete soils of this essential nutrient.

There are, however, some enormous problems to be overcome before nitrogen fixation will be a useful genetic modification of plants. Not only must the enzymatic machinery be in place within the cell to perform the conversion of molecular nitrogen (N_2) to the form utilized by the plant (NH_3^+), but it must be located in a suitable place within the plant for the efficient absorption of the gas. The stomata, the pores on the undersides of leaves, are the openings through which oxygen (O_2) and carbon dioxide

(CO_2) are exchanged during photosynthesis. But photosynthesis takes place in very specialized structures called *chloroplasts*, which are well adapted for efficient gas exchange. Although it may be possible to insert nitrogen-fixing genes into plants and to achieve gene expression, the likelihood of achieving high efficiency of nitrogen incorporation seems remote without additional structural modifications.

A more promising way of reducing the need for fertilizers is to increase the efficiency of nitrogen fixation in the varieties of soil bacteria known to carry out the process already, or to add nitrogen fixation to varieties that do not now carry out the process. It should be pointed out that the ecology of soils is highly complex, with literally thousands of varieties of microorganisms living in balance. Maintaining this balance is of critical importance in sustaining the ability of soils to support crops. That is, the soil flora and fauna reduce dead organic matter and process inorganic substances into forms which may then be utilized by plants. They also help give the soil the proper texture, important to the growth and function of roots. Thus, care must be taken to assess the consequences to the soil ecology of introducing a bacterium that has been engineered not only with a survival advantage over other forms, but one with the potential of altering soil chemistry.

There are other important applications of genetic engineering to agriculture. Increasing the yields and changing the composition of nutrients in food crops should be well within the capability of current genetic technology. Another goal of this research is to build disease or predator (usually insect) resistance into the genes of the plant. Depending on the disease or the parasite, the solution to the problem of resistance could take many forms, including the synthesis of a substance in the plant that is specifically toxic to the predator but not to the human consumer. Where there is an invading virus, plasmid, or microorganism, only a small genetic modification may be necessary to prevent the interloper from getting a molecular foothold in the plant cell.

The development of specific biological pesticides is also a subject receiving intense study. The goal of such research is to construct agents that will selectively kill only specific target organisms (for example, the medfly or the gypsy moth), leaving other organisms unharmed and causing little or no disturbance of the environment and the natural food chains. The problem, however, is not a simple one, even with the available arsenal of monoclonal antibodies which can certainly be made specific for insect antigens. Insects are perhaps the best protected of all creatures, which possibly accounts for the fact that ants and cockroaches have had no need to evolve further for literally millions of years. Of course, it is possible to kill insects with general poisons that can enter through either the gut or the respiratory apparatus in the abdomen, but to design a species-specific toxin that can enter an insect in low concentrations and kill it is very problematic. Those molecules that are highly specific for an antigen or other species-specific molecule tend to be proteins. Proteins are broken down readily in the gut, and they are too large to be effective respiratory poisons. Quite possibly, the solution will lie in the specific sex attractants, the pheromones, which might one day be the key to large-scale contraception in insect populations.

A problem that is becoming serious in parts of the world with little rainfall is the concentration of salts in the soil that inhibit the growth of plants. Some desert regions are naturally high in salts and are thus inhospitable to most crops. Other regions have had their productivity lowered considerably because of the application of chemical fertilizers for many years. If the salts are not leached by rain, proper irrigation, or flooding, they continue to build up and cause trouble.

Although such techniques as drip irrigation have been successful in the farming of arid regions, there are efforts to develop salt-tolerant varieties of plants, which either grow in high salt or have an efficient plumbing mechanism that keeps the internal salt concentration at a low level. There are some suggestions that microorganisms containing high levels of certain amino acids are salt-tolerant, although there is no evidence to suggest that transferring these genes to plants will confer salt resistance on the plants. There are, however, a number of plant varieties that grow naturally in salt water, such as the salt marshes all along the shores of the Eastern United States. It is possible that the transfer of certain genes from these varieties to crop plants, or perhaps even entire chromosomes or sections of chromosomes transferred through protoplast fusion, will provide the means to create new strains of plants especially suited to desert conditions. Even the classic methods of creating the desired high-salt environment and then selecting for plant protoplats or clones of tissue derived from single cells that can grow under these conditions will perhaps prove to be simplest way to create crop varieties which will flourish under high stress. So-called osmotolerance is of interest not only to the United States, where many parts of the southwestern states are becoming unsuitable for farming, but to many of the developing nations of the world that have little or no rainfall.

The Environment

The microbial ecology of this planet has left *no* naturally occurring chemical substance containing carbon, nitrogen, or hydrogen that is immune from attack by at least one microorganism. Microbes have adapted to live on virtually every available source of energy and carbon, and over temperature ranges from subzero to nearly boiling.

Perhaps the most inspiring teacher with whom I was privileged to study during my days in graduate school at Stanford was the brilliant microbiologist, Cornelis B. van Niel. Professor van Neil shunned the technology of the modern laboratory and the intense—and to many, nerve-wracking—existence of an establishment faculty member. Instead, he preferred the quiet and beautiful surroundings of Stanford's Hopkins Marine Station, situated on the rocks overlooking Monterey Bay, 100 miles south of San Francisco, where he maintained his (by contemporary standards) primitive laboratory. On rare occasions, but only rarely, he would be persuaded to climb into his 1949 Packard convertible and drive the two hours to the main campus in Palo Alto, his long white mane flying in the wind.

During the summer, the normally tranquil Hopkins Marine Station was alive with students and visiting scientists. van Niel's intensive summer course in microbiology was world-famous. Half of the 12 "students" he accepted were senior investigators. The other 6 were, like myself, young graduate students. So, at the age of 23, having just transferred from the Stanford physics department to join the new graduate program in biophysics, I was anxious to learn all the biology I could absorb. Besides, van Niel was slated for retirement, at least in the eyes of the university bureaucracy. This was perhaps the last time that the course was to be given.

We had to be in the lab by eight o'clock in the morning. At that hour, Pacific Grove is normally encased in the blanket of fog that hangs off and on the Monterey Peninsula throughout the summer. But, charged with caffeine, we would drag ourselves through the cold dampness and into our seats, to remain mesmerized for the next four hours. Normally, it would be considered cruel and unusual punishment to expect anyone to sit still for even a two-hour class. My attention span usually deteriorates badly after that time, under the best of conditions. I fidget, daydream, draw pictures, and finally have to stand up and leave. But this was different.

C. B. van Niel had grown up with twentieth-century biochemistry and microbiology. His firsthand account of this chronicle was full of information and of revelations about how science is actually done, including the blind alleys that were followed for years before they were abanadoned—along with a great deal of science. I had never seen most of it in print before taking the class, nor have I seen it since.

For lunch, we would sit on the rocks watching the cormorants and sea lions, and if we were lucky, the sun would make an appearance for an hour or two. Then it was back to the laboratory for the next five or six or seven hours, to conduct experiments. It was impossible to study microbiology with van Niel without developing an intense appreciation of the human species' intimate and highly dependent relationship with the world of microbes. Before refrigeration, human beings relied totally on microbial action for the preservation of foods. Thus, we cultured, isolated, and characterized yeast and bacteria from cheese, yogurt, beer (but not this "terrible American stuff full of preservatives"), and fruits (the original wine yeasts occur as natural residents of fruit skins).

Whenever it was time to study a new class or type of bacteria or other microorganism, we always had to find and isolate our own. Not once were we given a prepared culture of anything. But because much of the classification of bacteria depends on their biochemistry, it was rather easy to set up elective cultures. That is, we simply started with a medium of tap water, and perhaps some other salts, and whatever compound the desired microbe was to use as an energy source. Into the flask, we then dropped a bit of dirt, or some sewage, or some other likely source. The flask either had access to the air, or if we were looking for anaerobes, or those organisms for which oxygen is toxic, it was tightly sealed. We could also select the incubation temperature, but room temperature usually sufficed.

In this way, it is possible to find an organism that will thrive under virtually any conditions you wish to create. Upon a little reflection, it is really the only way nature could have it. If this were not so, we would have a rather unstable environment. That is, if a particular chemical compound were to exist that had no natural microbial predators, it could get out of hand. Thus, at least for all *naturally* occurring organic substances, there appears to be at least one type of living thing that can eat it.

But man, in all his cleverness with chemistry, has, in a few cases, been able to stay a bit ahead of microbial evolution. And, sadly, he has done a rather effective job of poisoning parts of his environment with highly stable organic compounds that have no natural enemies. Perhaps, in time, a creature with an appetite for DDT, toxaphene, or teflon will evolve. Actually, one has already been found that utilizes the herbicide 2,4-D. And another was reported recently that degrades polychlorinated biphenyls (PCB's) to carbon dioxide and water.[14] So here, then, is a challenge for microbiologists. Given that we have already made a mess of our surroundings, what can we now do to clean them up?

Microbial engineering is one potentially useful solution. The subject of the U.S. Supreme Court's decision to permit a living organism to receive patent protection was a strain of *Pseudomonas* to which a combination of naturally occurring plasmids had been added to permit it to break down petroleum. It was suggested that it might be useful in cleaning up oil spills. Although this particular bacteria cannot readily chew up massive amounts of crude oil, the type of research that led to its development could be quite useful in eliminating or reducing the environmental residues of many toxic agents.[15] Thus, the same scientist who developed the oil-eating strain, Ananda Chakrabarty, has also succeeded in engineering a microbe to break down the herbicide 2,4,5-T. However, no organism has yet been found for which the very toxic contaminant of 2,4,5-T, dioxin (2,3,7,8-tetrachlorodibenzoparadioxin), which is now widespread throughout Indochina, Times Beach (Missouri), and in a number of other areas where massive spills have occurred, can serve as a substrate. Dioxin is so toxic that scientists won't work with it.

Perhaps the greatest boon which biotechnology can provide for the environment is the prevention of the contamination and poisoning that results from our manufacturing and chemical technologies. These industries are energy-intensive, require extensive natural resources to be obtained forcibly from the environment, and produce toxic waste products. Further, the products themselves become environmental contaminants after their useful lifetime. At least a portion of these environmentally disruptive and polluting technologies will very likely be replaced by their biotechnological counterparts, which use neither much energy nor precious expendable resources, and which like biological pesticides, will not contaminate the environment.

Better Living through Biochemistry

The use of large-scale cultures of bacteria or fungi to produce useful products has been common practice for decades. Penicillin and other antibiotics are produced in this way, as are many vitamins, enzymes, and biochemicals for which a demand exists. In some cases, the material of interest is secreted from the cells into the medium, making the recovery much easier than if it had to be purified from cell extracts. The construction of specially engineered organisms to accomplish specific purposes efficiently and economically is now being actively pursued in the growing biotechnology industry. Many of the products discussed above, for use in medicine particularly, are made by large-scale fermentations.

Not only are such microbial factories useful for the production of normally rare and esoteric substances, but they are providing the means of producing rather ordinary chemicals cheaply by the efficient conversion of ordinary materials. There is particular promise for the utilization of materials once regarded as waste products. Potentially, any material containing substantial quantities of organic or carbon-containing matter can serve as a microbial substrate to produce useful chemicals. The chemical by-products of the paper industry, sawdust, grain, and even sewage are all being investigated for their capacity to be converted into such materials as hydrocarbon fuels or other organic chemicals useful to the chemical and plastics industry; food products such as sugars, polysaccharides, and polyalcohols used in food processing; and ethanol.

Many of these materials will probably not require sophisticated genetic engineering methods. That is, the van Niel approach of first finding out what nature can do for you is always an appropriate first step. Then, it may require some tinkering to increase the efficiency of conversion into the desired product. Of course, human intervention will very likely be necessary if we are to develop a microbial process for the conversion of sewage into gasoline. In most cases, the limiting factors on whether or not the multitudes of possible "biomass" conversions will be pursued will be economic rather than technical considerations. In principle, it is possible to develop a system to carry out almost any imagined conversion, but the process must be economically competitive with the alternatives. That is, in spite of all the concerns about the Middle East and the dwindling oil reserves, petroleum is still relatively cheap.

One area that has received little attention thus far is the use of photosynthetic bacteria or algae for large-scale fermentations. Unicellular algae are as susceptible to genetic manipulation as many other microorganisms. The obvious advantage is that they may usually be grown on a solution of simple salts, deriving their carbon from carbon dioxide and their energy from the sun. In the laboratory, carbon dioxide is usually bubbled through cultures of algae to increase the growth rate. However, large-scale algae cultures, in parts of the world where sunlight is plentiful, can probably be developed for the very inexpensive production of many substances. That is, algae create their own biomass.[16]

Enzymes, the catalysts of living organisms, are the determinants of every biochemical pathway. Of the many possible ways in which a complex organic molecule may react with other substances in its immediate environment, specific enzymes lower the energy barrier that impedes a particular reaction. In the presence of an enzyme, one particular reaction is favored over all others.

Everyone is familiar with the grammar-school science epxeriment of holding a bit of saltine in one's mouth for a minute. The taste becomes sweeter as the starch in the cracker is broken down into sugar under the action of an enzyme common in saliva. The digestion of food is dependent on a number of different enzymes being secreted into the stomach and into various other parts of the digestive tract. The ripening of fruit is an enzymatic process. And enzymes in yeast make wine from grape juice. In fact, most of the different protein gene products in every living organism are enzymes.

Enzymes are used commercially in many ways and are common tools in research. The common method of gene splicing depends, in fact, on the use of several isolated enzymes. Thus, the production of enzymes is one common use of microbial fermentation. However, the feasibility of altering the structure of genes at will now makes it possible to alter the properties of enzymes by changing the structure of the active site, as well as other parts of the molecule that have a bearing on the stability and other properties of the enzyme. As we learn more about the physics and the chemistry of enzymatic catalysis, we will someday be able to design and build our own enzymes. That is, through the synthesis of a desired base sequence of DNA, the entire structure of a protein with specific enzymatic properties could be made to order. Not only should it then be possible to make an isolated enzyme catalyst for *any* desired chemical conversion that one wishes, but some of the problems discussed earlier might also be solved by the construction of artificial genes. It may not be enough simply to put existing life together in unique ways; it may be necessary to add to the store of the components with which one works. Thus, it is, in principle, reasonable to expect to be able to construct bacteria someday that will break down dioxin and PCBs or algae that will synthesize gasoline.

In order to accomplish these goals, and, generally, to be able to design a protein molecule for *any* purpose, we will need to be able to predict the precise conformation and the dynamical behavior of a protein molecule from its sequence of amino acids. A number of very bright people are attempting to do this, with the help of powerful, high-speed computers, but the problems are formidable. However, as our understanding of molecular interactions gets better and better, the models of molecular structure will be refined to the point where they are useful in accurately predicting actual conformation in solution. The converse problem, predicting the amino acid sequence from a desired spatial conformation, will be the approach actually used to design molecules for specific purposes. Enzymes are the obvious place to start, simply because we have more structural information about certain enzymes than about other molecules of biological interest. However, in time, we should be able to apply these techniques to the molecular solution of a vast array of problems in medicine and agriculture, as well as to industrial enzymology and the degradation of man-made toxic substances.

Bioelectronics

One of the most revolutionary technologies to be proposed is the marriage of microelectronics and biotechnology. Integrated-circuit chips have undergone rapid evolution during the past decade, giving us a dazzling array of sophisticated electronic tools, including low-cost home computers like the word processor on which this book is being composed. However, many believe that the limit of miniaturization in solid-state electronics using inorganic materials has been reached. But polypeptides are also capable of conducting electrical currents. Thus, there is now a surge of interest in making supertiny integrated circuit chips with a protein as the essential ingredient.

Some of the possible applications that have been suggested seem to border on fantasy. A current research project is attempting to develop implantable electronic aids to the blind, perhaps even replacing parts of the network of nerves that links the retina and the visual cortex. The U.S. Defense Department is supporting research on solid-state/protein-detection devices that can be made not only highly sensitive but specific for a given chemical substance.

Some have even suggested that the DNA of a cell could be engineered to lay down a three-dimensional polypeptide network within a cell, to make intracellular, self-replicating microcomputers that might be programmed to serve a variety of biological functions, particularly to replace damaged or diseased parts of the nervous system. So it seems that the concept of the bionic man may not be so farfetched after all.

Still, I am highly skeptical about the feasibility of intracellular computers, where the hardware and maybe even the software is programmed in the DNA. There are monumental technical problems to be overcome in constructing anything like conventional solid-state circuitry on the scale of molecular dimensions, where even thermal vibrations could seriously disrupt the most ingeneous microchip. Nature has evolved ways to accomplish the same functions far more efficiently and effectively than our best man-made electronics can mimic. Wouldn't our efforts be better spent to first understand how nature has solved the problems of information storage and retrieval, the rapid switching between multiple circuits, sensory perception and analysis, consciousness and creativity? Why go to the trouble of putting a man-designed device inside a cell, when we have scarcely begun to figure out the best way to design a computer? But I shall resist the temptation to say this is impossible, or that work on biochips should not continue. Any research on any subject, if it is properly carried out by intelligent and imaginative individuals, always teaches us something—and frequently things that we did not expect to learn.

Biological Warfare

Up to this point, all of the applications discussed in this chapter have a constructive purpose. All might well be considered to improve the lot of humankind, even if some might be viewed as unnecessary. But the deliberate creation of nasty germs or lethal toxins is something very different. The twentieth century is full of examples of the dark side of microbiology. The Japanese, during World War II, had an extensive biological warfare program and conducted a number of grisly experiments on human populations.[17] The Germans, the Americans, and the Russians have also engaged in such research. Although a moratorium on the development and the use of *any* biological weapons is supposedly in effect, a serious outbreak of anthrax in Sverdlovsk in the Ural Mountains of the Soviet Union occurred in April 1979 and resulted in the deaths of many people and livestock. Some contend that it resulted from an accident at a biological-warfare research installation. The United States currently denies that it has engaged in biological warfare research since it closed the facility at Fort Detrick and converted it into a cancer research laboratory. But there are rumors to the effect that the United States *is* again interested in the design and the manufacture of biological weapons.

Aside from what is actually going on, if one wanted to make a very virulent disease organism, how would one do it? Is there any advantage to using gene-splicing techniques? At a forum at the National Academy of Sciences in 1977, Matthew Meselson, a Harvard microbiologist and an expert on the subject, stated that the techniques of conventional microbiology would be the easiest way to generate new infectious agents.[18] In general, he stated, adding genetic material only weakens the organism.

However, the techniques of genetic manipulation have become very sophisticated since then. It is certainly possible to program an infectious bacterium to produce potent toxins and antibiotic resistance. But if an organism is *too* virulent, its spread into the environment could easily backfire. Thus, one challenge to those who attempt to create these diabolical agents would be to find a way to make a disease germ tell the good guys from the bad guys. To do this, it would have to exploit some genetic trait that was common to the enemy population, but not your own. This might be difficult to do if your enemy was genetically similar to you, but the possibility of selective genocide is, nevertheless, real. There *are* readily observable genetic differences among Orientals, blacks, and Caucasians, and very many more less obvious genetic differences among all human population groups, perhaps different enough so that someone might be tempted to try it. One could, for example, try to construct an immunotoxin of the type being developed for cancer therapy, only against one or a set of cell surface antigens common to those individuals who comprise "the enemy" and not one's own population. Furthermore, it would be possible to immunize your own troops and your own population against such agents, in the likely event that the separation of *any* set of antigens between you and them was not complete. However, in view of the genetic mixing that has gone on in the United States, which is populated with people from all over the world, the pursuit of such lines of weaponry might well be viewed as foolhardy, even if one could possibly rationalize to oneself that there were no ethical problems in creating such a weapon.

The Brave New World

In spite of the many advances that have ensued or will ensue from the new biology, it is often equated with the bogeyman because many feel that it is fundamentally wrong to tamper with nature. At least, it is not considered permissible to violate the presumed genetic sanctity of the human race and to attempt to change the course of its evolution. Nevertheless, particularly in the last century of technological development, the sophisticated propagation of agricultural varieties, the extinction of many species, wars, and modern medicine, we have altered the gene pool of virtually all species, including man. With the development of the methods discussed in these pages, the ability of mankind to alter its own biological destiny with precision is rapidly becoming a reality.

In what ways might it be possible to do this? The notion of human cloning has been discussed, and even if it someday turns out to be possible, it would seem to me far less useful or desirable than many of the other things that might be done. Somehow, I can't see why even an evil dictator would choose to grow in glass bottles hordes of identical, mentally deficient, obedient slaves, even if he could. It would be costly, and one would have to feed and educate (indoctrinate) and train them, not to mention waiting for them to grow up. How absurd! These scenarios are best left to the Saturday morning cartoons. But the possibility of deliberate intervention in the total genetic makeup of human beings must be faced sooner or later, not to mention the possibility of completing the entire process of human development outside the womb.

The fertilized human egg is probably the ideal candidate for altering the genetic makeup of a human being for any purpose. The means to insert specific segments of DNA into specified places on particular human chromosomes is being perfected. But other than the correction of genetic diseases, what would we choose to change?

It is known that many prospective parents would choose the sex of their child if they could. But suppose that they could also select the child's hair color or eye color? Well, that may hardly seem worth the trouble, especially if it had to be done by altering the genes of a fertilized egg, rather than by the selection of sperm or eggs. But now, suppose that in our studies of fundamental genetic mechanisms, we learn the precise genetic determination not only of *physical* traits like height, physical build, strength, or beauty, but of mental and behavioral characteristics as well. Many might well choose to have highly intelligent children, with tractable personalities. The macho father may order a son who is tough and aggressive. And how many parents would elect to have obedient kids? But in tomorrow's society, who is to say that the choice will be the parents'? Perhaps the state will wish to establish soldier farms, where the storm trooper of the future is designed and built, although in the era of guided missiles, smart bombs, and lasers in space, storm troopers are obsolete. Nevertheless, whatever people or governments may *want* to do, it is a certainty that it is only a matter of time before they will be *able* to do it.

The Corporation Biologist

The concept of a corporation scientist is nothing new to twentieth-century history. That is, there have been corporation chemists and corporation physicists around for decades. The development of the pharmaceutical industry—drugs, biologicals, antibiotics, and vaccines—has, of course, required a certain contribution from basic biological research. But the methods have most often been those of chemistry, borrowed from the chemical industries. Nevertheless, large-scale fermentation—biotechnology's principal means of production—has been used to make many biological products for many years, from beer to antibiotics to enzymes.

The difference between what have become the traditional science-based industries and biotechnology lies in the rapidity with which certain areas of research, which in 1970 had little obvious potential for commercial use, have become the basis of expectations of high profits. It has been difficult for many, both in and out of science, to adjust to the fact that the most promising areas of commercial exploitation are those that have traditionally been regarded as lying within the domain of pure research. The disciplines of biochemistry, embryology, microbiology, immunology, and genetics have given rise to molecular and cell biology, which in turn gave us recombinant DNA and monoclonal antibodies, and these are what all the commercial excitement is about.

Early on, in the controversy over the safety of recombinant DNA techniques, many scientists seemed to be on the defensive. There were fears that research would be slowed or even stopped because some scientists were calling for a voluntary moratorium on certain experiments until safety guidelines could be developed. These fears were due not to the partial moratorium itself but to the triggering of more strident voices that sounded a general alarm. In many elements of the scientific community, there arose a cold-sweat fear of repressive government action.

In order to counteract the dark side of recombinant DNA, which was receiving most of the attention in the press for a time, a number of individuals felt that they had to make the case for "benefits"—that is, all of the *practical* applications of recombinant DNA. In speaking speculatively about these ultimate payoffs of basic science (in the first congressional hearings, at the NIH director's advisory committee meeting in February 1976, and at the National Academy of Sciences forum in 1977), the implication was, of course, that a commercial biotechnology industry would soon have to be established in order for these applications to become realities.

Simultaneously with the recombinant DNA debate, the seeds of biotechnology were being sown. The first independent biotechnology research and development firm was Cetus Corporation, established in 1971, long before gene splicing had even occurred to any but a few pioneering scientists. Cetus was established to exploit the ideas of Donald Glaser, a University of California physicist turned biologist. Glaser, who had been awarded the Nobel Prize in physics in 1960 for his development of the bubble chamber for studying the paths of fundamental particles, had been trying to develop rapid screening methods for examining microbial cultures for mutations, or particular enzymatic or metabolic capabilities. So Ronald Cape, Peter Farley and Glaser managed to raise some capital and began their enterprise on a rather modest scale with a single laboratory room near San Francisco Bay. For the next several years, it concentrated on the improvement of microbial strains that produced antibiotics and, eventually, on the development of new industrial processes using newly discovered enzymes.

By 1976, however, everyone was talking about recombinant DNA and the amazing way it would revolutionize the pharmaceutical industry and produce all sorts of rare medicinal substances at low cost. Many of the major drug companies, Cetus and numerous scientists with entrepreneurial instincts all wanted to get in on the commercial recombinant DNA boom and bandwagon. The Eli Lilly Company, one of the major pharmaceutical houses, was there from the beginning, and represented at every step of the deliberations in Washington. So was Hoffman-LaRoche. Genentech was the first of the independents to be formed specifically to apply recombinant DNA techniques to the production of commercially profitable substances, being founded by Herbert Boyer, one of the first plasmid engineers, and Robert Swanson, an ambitious young man not long out of business school. Like Cetus, Genentech's founders chose to locate in the San Francisco Bay area, traditionally more accepting of breaks with tradition than any other part of the United States.

So more and more investors became interested, and more and more companies began to form. Biogen was founded in Switzerland and later added a component in Cambridge, Massachusetts. Bethesda Research Laboratories (BRL), an "older" company, dating from 1975, began getting into the recombinant DNA act about 1978 and later became one of the first casualties of the shakeout which began in the early 1980s. Genex was founded in Rockville, Maryland, a Washington suburb by Leslie Glick in 1978. Then a veritable deluge of other new companies appeared. Calgene, was established by Ray Valentine, a plant geneticist at the University of California at Davis, to explore agricultural applications. Engenics is a consortium with backing from several major corporations. Dnax, even with the strength of Nobel laureates Paul Berg and Arthur Kornberg from Stanford behind it, couldn't survive as an independent. It was bought by Schering-Plough in 1982 for $19 million. But this is not intended to be a detailed historical discussion of how each of the biotechnology companies came to pass. Rather it is to examine the nature of the enterprise, its promise, and its problems.

I was impressed by the differences in the character of the different elements and components of what was biotechnology when, starting in early 1977, I had the responsibility of devising rational recombinant DNA legislation for the U.S. House of Representatives. I found myself the object of lobbying by everyone with an interest in Federal recombinant DNA policy. But that was a perfect vantage point from which to learn rather quickly how diverse the biotechnology industry had become in such a short time. The "new" companies seemed to have an edge over the large, established and, therefore, more conservative organizations, in that they came into existence purely to take advantage of the new biology and had no existing establishment to protect. Although the research directors of the big drug companies may have been excited by the prospects for the new techniques, to implement such programs would require complex managerial decisions. Thus, in spite of their financial power, they have tended to follow rather than to lead the industry, perhaps contracting to manufacture products developed by the small independents. For example, Eli Lilly is making and selling Humulin, a synthetic human insulin developed by Genentech.

When all of the companies, new and old, showed up in Washington to express their concerns over the NIH recombinant DNA safety guidelines and impending Federal legislation designed to extend them to private industry, there was little common ground in the positions they took. The more established companies, used to the requirements for survival in the pharmaceutical industry, seemed more concerned about the protection of proprietary information. They accepted the probability of regulatory legislation that would very likely make the NIH Guidelines mandatory for industry. They were used to that type of regulation. On the other hand, the new and smaller companies, devoted exclusively to biotechnology, were inexperienced in the ways of Washington. Genentech was the only one of these companies to actively oppose federal legislation, arguing that requiring laboratories to be equipped with the expensive containment facilities specified by the NIH Guidelines would put the smaller companies at a disadvantage.

It was possible to tell a certain amount about a company and the philosophy of its management by where they took me to lunch. Eli Lilly took me to the Capitol Hill Club, strictly a Republican organization; Ron Cape of Cetus treated me to dinner once at the Bethesda Holiday Inn; and Genentech didn't take me to lunch at all. For comparison, Harvard University's lobbyists preferred the Democratic Club near the U.S. Capitol when they were in a hurry, and the Lion D'Or, one of Washington's finest French restaurants, when they weren't. The Association of American Medical Colleges (AAMC) liked the exclusive Cosmos Club. Most of the other scientific and academic professional associations also preferred a setting in one of Washington's classier establishments when pleading their cases, a reflection of their savvy of the political environment peculiar to the nation's capital city. But the new biotechnology companies were clearly amateurs. In fact, they would rather not have had to deal with the government at all. They had more important concerns on their minds, such as survival in the world of business.

At first, after a small investment by the various scientist/founders, all capital was raised privately, and most of it still is. Based entirely on the promise of several years hence, it was possible to obtain investment from financial institutions or, more the usual case, from larger, more established companies who wished to enter into cooperative ventures to develop a specific product or class of products. With the few initial reports of success, puffed to the limit of credibility, more capital was attracted and both Genentech and Cetus decided that the time was ripe to go public. It was, and both had highly successful public stock sales. The industry had at last established a foothold.

The continuing challenge to these companies is to construct all of the steps from a research finding or a demonstrated technique on a laboratory scale to a finished product, ready for market. Most of the problems, assuming that you have enough money and competent scientist/engineers, are technical. There is, in fact, an emerging new category of technologist—the bio-engineer—concerned with the development of processes and products rather than basic research. In the early days, success in even cloning the rat insulin gene was treated as a major news event. But what one really needs is a plasmid that contains the necessary control genes to *express,* through the translation of the RNA transcript into a protein, the genetic information in a gene insert. Moreover, expression, *per se* is not enough for an efficient process. It is desirable to construct generalized, high-yield, stable expression vectors that can be used for *any* gene insert.

If a human protein is to be made through microbial synthesis in the quantity and the purity required for market, the desired gene product should represent a significant fraction of the cell's total protein. There are various tricks that can be used to accomplish this end. Multiple gene copies in either plasmids or bacteriophage vectors, as well as repression or deletion mutants that reduce or stop the synthesis of unwanted proteins, have been used, boosting yields to as high as 20%–30% in some cases. Even 5% is considered quite good for most purposes.

Then, the form in which the protein is synthesized is also important. If it needs to be in a particular conformational state, it must be deposited in the bacteria in that state, with little degradation or denaturation occurring before it is harvested. Thus, the lowered biological activity of some human proteins made from cloned human DNA in bacterial hosts may reflect undesired structural or conformational alterations. For example, human interferon can be obtained in nearly pure form by cloning methods, but it generally has a somewhat lower specific activity (units of activity per unit of weight) than that obtained directly from cultured human cells. Activity can be improved if one specific amino acid is replaced by another to make sure that the intramolecular cross-link (disulfide bond) is put in the right place. However, the interferon so made now differs from native interferon, a fact which could have clinical implications.

Insulin consists of two separate polypeptide chains that must be linked by the proper disulfide bridges after the purification of each component. Other proteins require direct modification of the amino acids themselves, such as the addition of sugar molecules (glycosylation). These steps pose additional problems, in that the material must again be handled and subjected to chemical reactions that are generally not 100% efficient. The protein product then must be made free of impurities. Although protein obtained by the engineered high-yield expression of genes cloned in bacteria is generally easier to purify than that obtained from its natural source, the possibility of trace bacterial contaminants is always something to worry about. *E. coli,* the common cloning vehicle, contains a substance called *endotoxin,* which, when present in the human blood stream in even minute quantities, is highly toxic, causing high fever and other serious symptoms. It is the principal culprit in *E. coli* septicemia, infections of the blood stream usually acquired in hospitals and particularly in surgery patients. But the endotoxin problem is known, and special measures can be taken to remove it.

If possible, the cloning vehicles are engineered to excrete the desired gene product into the medium, so that its removal from the cells themselves is not required. Strains of *Bacillus subtilis* and other bacteria are being developed as generalized excretion hosts for cloned DNA products. However, the possibility of unknown contaminants remains a concern; these may ride along with the desired protein and may produce untoward immunological responses in a small fraction of patients following injection. Thus, very stringent tests for purity must be applied to all substances to be used for human innoculation.

The extension of laboratory procedures, where cultures rarely exceed a few liters at a time, to large-scale processes poses special problems. Although large scale fermentation—the growth of bacteria in greater than 1000-liter batches for the production of enzymes, antibiotics, etc.—is not new to industrial technology, the greater delicacy of genetically engineered organisms, the stability of their plasmid inserts, the stringency (and expense) of their growth requirements and yields of the desired products are all challenges to be met. That is why, even if a process is shown to work in the laboratory, the strain used may not be the most suitable for large scale continuous procedures, and the gene engineering may have to be done over again in a hardier strain.

Not all of the processes used in biotechnology entail the production of a gene product from a living organism. Sometimes it is the organism itself which is of commercial value. In other cases, the gene product of interest is an enzyme, that is then purified and used to catalyze a commercially important chemical conversion. Like any other chemical synthesis, the efficiency of the process is key. Thus high yields and simplicity in the purification of the product are necessary requirements. Whether or not a process, either biological or enzymatic, is to be profitable is strictly dependent upon the economics of the entire procedure from start to finish. The difference between a 90% yield and an 80% yield can, for example, represent the difference between profit and loss.

The solution of these problems is generally not in the domain of the exciting research one imagines that brilliant investigators deal with. But those scientists who accept positions with these companies have made the choice to work, not ultimately for the advancement of knowledge, even though that might be their personal choice, but for the success of their company. Thus they may have to spend a great deal of their efforts, not in exploring the more intriguing frontiers of genetic control and expression, but in rendering a proven phenomenon suitable for mass production.

Not unrelated to the perturbations biotechnology has wrought on the traditional life of a scientist is the entire matter of corporate strategy. It is here that we find the new companies often groping in the darkness for a formula that works. Some don't have a strategy and others are in a state of flux attempting to formulate an effective one.

The concept of a "mixed portfolio," in terms of the level of risk associated with each venture, is a basic element of traditional business, and will, no doubt, be valid when applied to biotechnology. That is, a company should have some projects which are safe and for which a profit is certain to ensue after a given investment of time and money. These may include such things as a novel, inexpensive method for manufacturing a common commodity chemical with a known market. Thus biotechnology has been applied to the production of ethanol from sources such as cornstarch and sawdust. However, the prices of commodity chemicals tend to be unstable, making a large investment in processes with already marginal economics somewhat risky. Current efforts are aimed at further reducing costs and increasing the efficiency of the processes. Few biotechnology companies, however, are willing to risk their own capital to develop such processes. Instead, partners are sought from a variety of interested large corporate investors including those specializing in petroleum products, foods, alcoholic beverages, lumber, chemicals, and pharmaceuticals, to foot the bill for this unspectacular but potentially important line of research in return for a piece of the action.

Because it is so hard to find sure things, there is a sizable investment in moderate risk projects, endeavors for which the technology is not worked out, or for which the usefulness or effectiveness of the product is uncertain, or for which the market potential is unknown. The theory is that the laws of statistics will prevail and that at least one of these efforts will ultimately pay off handsomely. It is expected, however, that most will not, even though the best data available may have gone into the selection of even these projects.

A third and essential category of the mixed portfolio is that where any new idea may be explored, as long as there is even a remote chance of a payoff at the end of the road. It is the basic research end of biotechnology, and absolutely essential that it receive continuing support. The smart people within the industry know that a certain amount of research freedom is necessary to keep a good scientist happy, and to attract the best scientists. Serendipity must be exploited at every opportunity. Since many "useful" results of research were never planned or even expected to begin with, the scientist with the wild imagination who can explore hunches and occasionally waste money is an asset not to be underestimated.

While the above mixture may sound entirely reasonable, deciding upon how much of each, and which projects to support is an agonizing task. It is a function of many things, many of them not scientific. First, how much money do you have to spend? Are there venture partners who are willing to fund specific projects of mutual interest? What are your competitors doing (this is often not easy to know)? How good is your proprietary position for each venture? What is the market potential of each? What are the regulatory requirements, costs and delays that will affect each product?

The companies are learning. However, in an arena with so many unknowns, one sees much more muddling along by trial and error rather than enlightened strategic planning. The older companies have all experienced growing pains. The newer ones are attempting to learn from the mistakes of their antecedents. But everyone's perceptions are changing constantly. Genentech, for example, once made the choice to stay entirely within the area of pharmaceuticals and to "vertically integrate," a business term that means to cover all aspects of research, development, manufacture and sales. Yet in 1982, Genentech and Corning Glass formed a partnership (Genecor) to explore the engineering of industrial enzymes. The scope of Genentech's endeavors is now among the broadest in the industry.

Cetus, on the other hand, had made a practice of conducting research and development in almost every aspect of the broad definition of biotechnology. By early 1982, Cetus had programs in industrial enzymes and commodity chemicals, interferon, animal vaccines, and a wide variety of other areas. At the urging of some illustrious Stanford professors, Cetus had formed two subsidiaries in Palo Alto, one devoted to infectious diseases and the other to immunological applications, including monoclonal antibodies. It soon formed another in Madison, Wisconsin, specializing in plant genetic engineering and agricultural applications. However, this diversity earned Cetus the reputation of being "unfocused," an image attractive to scientists but condemned by financial analysts, who saw this structure at odds with what are presumably sound business practices.

In response to these criticisms, along with pressure from the Board of

Directors, falling stock prices, and excessive and undirected expenditures from Cetus' large cash assets following its public offering, a reaction ensued which pushed the pendulum in the opposite direction. Programs were cut drastically in an attempt to prove to the business world that Cetus was indeed focused after all. Ironically, the microbial screening technology that had gotten Cetus off the ground in the early years was scrapped entirely, except for a few vestiges funded by outside investors. Truly exploratory research in all areas was virtually eliminated, in keeping with a conservative business strategy traditional to the pharmaceutical industry, which emphasizes product development, manufacture and, above all, sales.

What we are seeing then, is an industry in flux, with most companies experiencing some degree of internal turbulence as they try to find the correct point of equilibrium between science and business. In order to meet the expectations of their backers, the companies who are realistic about the nature of the business world are taking a hard look at their own insides and addressing head on the problems of defining a long term strategy for both research and development and the nature of their business.

It has not been easy for the biotechnology corporations, populated with a large number of scientist captives from universities, to grapple with the transition from the research institute mentality to the corporate way of thinking. Many hope that the former won't be lost altogether. Personally, I believe that the intimate association between discovery and application in most areas of biotechnology make it imperative to allow industrial scientists a measure of research freedom. The concept of "directed" research, except to solve a very well-defined practical problem, is continually proved wrong. The most useful discoveries often come from where one least expects to find them. Of course, scientists in the universities and the real research institutes will continue to explore the frontiers. Who will get to exploit their results is a question of some concern. Thus some companies are planning for the more distant future. Genex, for example, formed a partnership with Bendix to explore protein engineering in a comprehensive program which includes some very basic research on the conformation of proteins and the development of theoretical methods to aid in the design of new molecules. This program is exciting from a scientific point of view, and one which can be expected to lead to endless commercial applications—eventually. The conventional business wisdom, however, finds such a $16.5 million venture without a well-defined business target difficult to comprehend.

The cold reality that must be faced is that unless the leaders of biotechnology think more like businesspeople and less like philosophers, the investors may go home and leave biotechnology stranded. As this hard-learned lesson sinks in, the original scientist/entrepreneurs are now realizing their own limitations. Experienced senior business executives are now being sought to bring an expertise to the industry that had been lacking in the early days. But this has only produced a painful awareness that scientists and business people do not generally think in the same ways nor are they motivated by the same values. Resolving the science–business dichotomy will require time and care; we may expect to see the tensions and clashes persist a bit longer.

There are perhaps as many models as there are companies. One which bears close watch is Biogen. Walter Gilbert, a Nobel laureate in 1980 and recognized as a scientist of exceptional talent is now its chairman of the board and chief executive officer. He has made it clear that he believes that the best solution is to evaluate the scientific and business considerations simultaneously, and that he can do both.

It should be emphasized that biotechnology does not represent a concept fundamentally different than any of the other "high tech" industries in the world. It is only the most recent. But, the rapid transition of molecular biology from the relative peace and freedom of the university research laboratory to the entirely new set of constraints imposed by a corporate enterprise still has many of our heads spinning.

Investing in the Future: The View from Wall Street

Proctor and Ruth Page, both in their early 60s, live in a sprawling suburban house on the shores of Lake Champlain, near Burlington, Vermont. Proctor, in business for himself, isn't doing badly and is always looking for something good to invest in. One afternoon, around Labor Day 1980, as Proctor was scrutinizing the day's mail on the kitchen table, always cluttered at that time of year with piles of fresh vegetables just picked from the garden, a provocative item caught his eye. It was in the financial weekly called *New Issues*. Its four pages were full of hot inside dope on stocks about to be released for public sale.

This particular issue was devoted to two up-and-coming companies that were about to go public. One was Apple Computer, a young organization which seemed to be doing everything right in leading the wave of small, relatively inexpensive personal computers. The other was a California company by the name of Genentech, the first of the new biotechnology companies that had decided to go public to raise capital. It was offering 1 million shares at $30 per share.

Proctor Page, who followed the financial news regularly, was quite excited about these issues. But he was especially taken with Genentech. It seems that he had read a number of recent items in the paper that said Genentech had made some significant research breakthroughs and would soon be revolutionizing the pharmaceutical industry. As soon as he heard about the stock offering, he ordered a large block of shares from his broker. But even then, he was told that he might not be able to get any, at least at the offered price. Brokerage houses were deluged with Genentech orders, even, it seems, in early September, before *New Issues* had announced the offering.

About six weeks later, on October 14, when the sale finally took place in the over-the-counter market, the brokers scrambled to get a piece of the 1.1 million shares for the thousands of Proctor Pages looking for a good thing, and they drove the price from the offered $35 to $89 per share in the first 20 minutes of trading. By the day's end, the price was falling, and within a few days, it was only slightly higher than its offered value. A few shrewd and lucky speculators made money that day. Many had bought a piece of a company whose only product so far had been great expectations. Incidentally, Proctor Page along with thousands of other disappointed prospective investors, never did get his Genentech stock.

This "event" had been building up for months. It reflected the effectiveness of two activities which conspired to create the public perception that the long-promised dividends of years of research were finally here. First, some well-calculated press releases by a few of the new companies had accomplished their intended purpose. It was important to build the confidence of investors, whether they be the venture capitalists, prospective corporate investors, or the large number of individuals who invest in the stock market on a small scale.

But a second strong force which enabled this to happen was the press. (Here, alas, we are stuck with a vestigal word from an earlier era, before radio and television. Of course, *press* must include the electronic media as well.) Science reporters suffer from the very difficult task of making the esoteric new discoveries of modern science not only understandable to the newspaper-reading public, but they have to make them interesting as well. To a degree, this is the special challenge of reporting generally. But in science, there are usually fewer news stories worth writing, in that there has to be some element of general audience appeal to begin with.

So, when a story comes along that spills over the boundaries of the domain of science and into the realms of public hazards, miraculous cures to dread diseases, hypothetical monsters, war, taxes, or even the business world, then it is far easier to make news out of it. Anything with an emotional or melodramatic appeal is always better copy than even unlocking the innermost secrets of the structure of time, matter, and the universe. Unless the latter can be obviously connected to some immediate, direct application affecting human beings, like superbombs and time travel, it is simply too abstract to generate much interest.

As with the quality and responsibility of newspapers overall, there is a broad spectrum of competence, honesty, and commitment to accuracy among science journalists. Thus, we have the *National Enquirer* and even worse at one end, and *The New York Times* and better (according to some) at the other. But even the best science reporters have to have complete and accurate information to begin with. The press releases and occasional press conferences of a few of the new companies and some university-based scientists with an interest in cashing in on the fruits of their efforts were often lacking in key information. A naive and inexperienced press corps did not necessarily know the right questions to ask regarding the problems of accurate gene expression, scale-up, yield, purity, mass production, human testing, and so on. Often by innuendo, the discovery announced was made to sound more spectacular and much closer to marketing than it actually was.

Still, the way such a report is rephrased by the writer and the headlines used to announce it have a great deal to do with the impression it creates with the reader. In many cases, the science writer doesn't invent the headings for his column but is always at the mercy of an editor with perhaps different motives. Accordingly, *breakthrough* is a catchy word with which to start off. If it is coupled with *cancer,* a lot of people are likely to start reading. Then they encounter the words *biotechnology company,* preceded by the company name, and all the necessary associations are made. If it sounds exciting enough, many will seek a piece of the action.

On the other hand, some papers prefer to create an aura of something ominous or creepy, rather than emphasizing the positive aspects of a development or of an industry. During the 1970s, when the fires raged out of control over whether or not recombinant DNA was safe, and how strict the federal safety standards should be, the press often did its part to keep them burning. And when the first biotechnology companies were getting organized, many of the papers cast them in this same dim light.

For example, the *Boston Sunday Globe,* on June 25, 1978, carried a lead article[19] (front page, upper left corner) with the heading, "Cloning Business: Growing Fast—Growing Fast." It should be remembered that this date was only a few months after one of the more irresponsible acts of the publishing business took place, Lippincott's publication and promotion of David Rorvik's *In His Image: The Cloning of a Man.*[20] The book was considered a phony immediately by the scientists who read it, but the cloning jokes, cloning movies, and stir created by the book had many convinced that you really could duplicate an adult human being. It was nearly four years later that the courts ruled that the book was indeed a fraud, and Lippincott admitted the error of its ways.

The *Globe* article was, of course, about *DNA* cloning, not human cloning. But just to obfuscate the truth, the article was accompanied by a front-page drawing depicting a man holding an identical but smaller copy of himself over his head. It wasn't until the seventh paragraph that the reader was told that the cloning referred to "has nothing to do with making multiple copies of Albert Einstein or Idi Amin Dada," and paragraph eight before recombinant DNA cloning was explained. Now they didn't actually lie, did they?

I am digressing. But not very much. For the kind of reporting that led to the Genentech stock-sale explosion was not so different from that in the article described above. Spectacular advances were touted. Perhaps the pitfalls were discussed somewhere near the end of the article, but the ploy of equating yesterday's science fiction with today's reality worked. And it is still going on, particularly with the introduction of a group of glossy, expensive popular-science magazines of the *OMNI* family. Biotechnology hype still seems to be a formula that works on the public, but the time has passed for that crucial, initial come-on to the investors. You get only one chance. After that, the investors are onto you and will demand something more tangible than promises and delusions of commercial grandeur.

But I do not wish to create the impression that all of those with money to invest are ignorant fools, susceptible to being led astray by the inflated or skewed prose that they happen to find in a newspaper, including even the *Wall Street Journal*. Initially, during the mid and late 1970s, when the first group of biotechnology companies (Cetus, Genentech, Bethesda Research Laboratories, Genex, and Biogen) were seeking capital, they sought primarily corporate investors. Thus, buying substantial blocks of equity in the companies were the oil companies, the chemical companies, some pharmaceutical houses, and such unlikely entities as the Campbell Soup Company, National Distillers, Emerson Electric, and Corning Glass.

These equity sales and partnerships were negotiated by the new organizations in need of capital that could promise a unique brand of research and development. For backers with substantial resources to risk, it seemed like a reasonable gamble, even though the payoff would probably be years away. Usually, the interest of the investing company was based on a specific commodity, product, or process to be developed. The corporate partners have often expected to play an active role in the course of the company's activities in the funded project area, particularly with respect to production and marketing. Thus, Shell Oil is involved in Cetus's interferon project, just as Lubrizol is in Genentech's.

But a second wave of investment followed these initial liaisons, from different sources with different expectations. There were first the venture capital firms, which have a record of being able, overall, to stay well ahead of inflation, occasionally returning their money 10 and 20 times over on a single venture (although these instances are offset somewhat by the times when there is no return at all). The venture capitalists, unlike the original corporate investors, seemed more susceptible to the promises that they read in press reports and were less careful to scrutinize realistically the problems that would always have to be solved before the production of any marketable product.

One of the first experiments was DNA Sciences, established with E. F. Hutton capital. Dr. Zsolt Harsanyi, former project director of the first Office of Technology Assessment biotechnology report,[21] was recruited to provide technical advice for the venture. There was talk of an original commitment of $100 million, that is, before E. F. Hutton began to look more closely and to reevaluate its prospects of a short-term cash turnover. That was when they got cold feet and came (partially) out of the water, shrinking their investment down to represent only the brave and daring who were willing to wait for their money.[22] At the same time, other firms were also going after the bait, money in hand, with varying degrees of shrewdness, expectations and experience with new corporate ventures.

Biotechnology companies, however, pose special difficulties to the investor because no one can predict how an unproven new approach to cancer therapeutics will turn out, or whether it is really possible to make a trouble-free insecticide that will kill only fire ants, medflies, or gypsy moths. So the firms and their underwriters draw up a schedule. If a company can keep reasonably close to its predictions, then it probably won't lose its backing. But, of course, the probability that the timetable can't be met increases as one gets further from the laboratory and into production.

The sum of all of these activities comprises the financial "mood" or the character of an investment activity. Overall, Wall Street tends to go in ups and downs about everything. Thus, it was in a bullish mood in 1979 and increasingly so in 1980. There was a bandwagon effect, reflecting partially the rosy press reports and partially the fact that substantial sums had already been invested by some major firms; the rest didn't want to be left behind. Sensing the growing wave in early 1980, Genentech decided that now was the time to go public. Timing was of the essence. In fact, Genentech greatly underestimated the revenue that it *could* have raised and may have kicked itself a bit afterward. However, stock offerings should not greatly exceed the expected performance of the company, or the value of a share will eventually drop to well below the sale price. Most experts view the size of the Genentech offering as about right.

There were obviously a lot of disappointed Proctor Pages with money to spend. Cetus was not about to miss its chance. In one of the boldest moves in the history of stock sales, Cetus offered 5 million shares at $23 per share. By the time Cetus stock went on sale on March 6, 1981, the event that could only happen once had happened, and the wave had definitely crested. But it followed a sufficiently short time after Genentech's spectular sale to succeed. Cetus raised its $110 million, and that was what counted. It was hard money, with no strings attached, and no oil or chemical corporations breathing down their necks. Cetus did what no one else could do again—that is, until a genetically engineered product is actually brought to market with high profits for its producers, at last fulfilling the promises.

Within just a few months after the Cetus stock was sold, there was definitely a shift in mood. It came about in large part because a number of the less realistic investors expected to start getting a return on their money, when, in fact, nobody was anywhere near coming out with a product. The grumbling was picked up by the financial press, followed by the popular press. And so it became the thing to do to write articles knocking the biotechnology industry for overpromising and not delivering. The conservative *Economist* from Great Britain, in a June 1981 article, put it this way:

> There are going to be many disappointments. The market forecasts are all guesses.
> To turn the base metal of biology into big profits will need not only a lot more
> basic research but also a lot more practical experience, a lot of process engineering
> and much bigger investments than most people are contemplating today. Risks
> will be high, patents hard to enforce, competition frenetic and most products
> (when they come) rapidly obsolescent.[23]

The article did go on, however, to say that biotechnology's "potential is enormous" and to analyze rather accurately the current status of a number of the major products being readied for market. But some of the publications were not so kind. The financial writers seemed to delight in making snide remarks about the biotechnology industry's having lured investors under false pretenses, and in being quick to point out any extravagances that they could find in the profitless companies or their leaders. Downright distortion, not uncommon to the press overall, reared its ugly head in the financial magazines as well, as the bearish trend continued and the price of Cetus stock fell to half and then one third of its offered value. *Time,* in its usual vernacular, published an article entitled "Faded Genes."[24]

The other companies that subsequently dared to go public during the rest of 1981 and 1982 did not fare nearly as well as Cetus and Genentech, at least in their initial offerings. But in spite of the inhospitable financial climate, some were forced by the need for cash to go public anyway. Molecular Genetics raised substantially less than it wanted. After the stock market began its rapid rise in the last half of 1982, Genex decided to risk a public offering on September 19, managing to sell 2 million shares at $9.50 each, not great but better than some had expected. Hybridtech went public early in 1983, and Biogen followed a few months later. By mid 1983, even though the first real products trickling out of the biotechnology industry had yet to include any big winners, the stock prices of at least some of the companies began to rise. Genentech rose to over $60 per share and announced a three-for-two stock split. Genex was up to $17.

What has happened is primarily the oscillation of *perceptions*. In reality, the progress of biotechnology is going pretty much as expected by the realists within the industry: they knew all along what the *Economist*'s readers seemed to be discovering for the first time. Biotechnology is, to be sure, having its growing pains and many companies staked with precious venture capital will not survive. But the settling out of a new industry with nearly 200 starters is nothing unusual and should be of no surprise to the investment community. There will continue to be collapses, consolidations, acquisitions, and an ultimate shrinkage in the number of major competitors to perhaps no more than a dozen companies. So the financial magazines tend to be ignored by the board chairmen of the biotechnology corporations, after a brief period of mild outrage over each snide article. They know that after the first major product is sold, the financial pundits will change their tune abruptly.

Patents and Trade Secrets

The concept of a patent to protect the rights of an inventor never seemed to trouble anyone until it was suggested that the patent laws should apply equally well to the inventions resulting from genetic manipulation. Instantly, in the minds of some, the patenting of a living organism (or a part thereof) that had arisen through the ingenuity of a scientist became a moral issue, and the real purpose of patent protection and the meaning of "proprietary" rights somehow became muddled. Again, some of the contributions of the press did not help to clarify matters and contributed to the public misunderstanding of what patents really mean. This was especially true of the accounts of the U.S. Supreme Court's decision on June 16, 1980, to permit a genetically engineered bacterium to be patented.[25] The 5–4 decision, the culmination of a seesaw confrontation between the U.S. Patent and Trademark Office and the U.S. Court of Customs and Patent Appeals, concerned a strain of bacteria to which Dr. Ananda Chakrabarty, then of the General Electric Company, had added a combination of naturally occurring plasmids containing the genetic information for enzymes that catalyze the degradation of petroleum.

The organism was not, as some reports would have us believe, the answer to oil spills. Dr. Chakrabarty was (and still is) exploring the possibilities of solving problems in environmental pollution through creative microbiology, and he never claimed that this strain would be a suitable survivor in the waters of the North Sea. As a test case in the world of patent law, however, this one did have some interesting implications.

First of all, the purpose for which a patent is issued must be appreciated. Then, we must look at the patent laws themselves to see just how a living microorganism, or a part thereof, fits into the scheme of things and consider just how to deal with matters that Congress never thought of when it last overhauled the patent laws (1952). Is there anything fundamentally different in affording patent protection to the invention of a novel sequence of DNA in order to accomplish a particular purpose? Is there anything *really* unique about patent protection for an invention just because it happens to be alive? Finally, is there a moral issue entangled with the question of patents involving living organisms, as some of the briefs filed during the Supreme Court's deliberations would have us believe?

The U.S. Constitution is very clear on the purpose for which patent protection is granted, and it sets forth the powers of the Congress to enact such laws as appropriate:

> The Congress shall have Power . . . (8) To promote the Progress of Science and useful Arts, by securing for limited Times to Authors and Inventors the exclusive Right to their respective Writings and Discoveries. . . . And . . . (18) To make all Laws which shall be necessary and proper for carrying into Execution the foregoing Powers.

There has been some confusion surrounding the Supreme Court decision, at least in some quarters, between the concept of proprietary rights and "ownership." In one sense, these may be considered equivalent terms, but the proprietary right of a patent holder or an inventor is, as stated explicitly in the U.S. Constitution, a guarantee to exploit one's creations commercially, whereas ownership implies the possession of, or at least the rights over, a particular object. Presumably, such goods are "owned" by the manufacturer (the patent holder or someone licensed by the patent holder) prior to sale. If we buy it, we become the owner. Thus, we may own a wide variety of patented appliances, drugs, cosmetics, and even computer programs. But we do not have the right to copy the unique features of any of these and sell them for profit.

In writing the patent laws, Congress has tried to include the range of subject matter to which patents might apply. However, this section has required expansion over the years. Section 101 of Title 35 of the U.S. Code now allows patents to be issued for "any new and useful process, machine, manufacture or composition of matter, or any new improvement thereof." Although these terms would seem to be fairly comprehensive—and could be argued to be so—what is and is not allowed is dependent on their precise interpretation. Because the legislative histories accompanying the patent laws provide little enlightenment concerning the intent of Congress, the interpretation of these laws is then a prerogative of the courts.

In 1930, Congress apparently felt that the patent laws did not really include living material, for it passed the Plant Patent Act.[26] The purpose of the act, as stated in the identical House and Senate reports accompanying the legislation, was to "remove the existing discrimination between plant developers and industrial inventors." The report went on to argue most convincingly that the invention of a novel composition of inanimate matter and the development of new varieties of plants are conceptually equivalent.

This law, however, was restricted to plants that reproduce asexually, that is, by grafting, tubers, bulbs, and so on. Those that are sexually reproduced, perhaps because the random assortment of genes cannot be controlled by an inventor, were excluded from coverage. To date, the Plant Patent Act of 1930 has been the basis of nearly 5,000 patents, about 40% of which are for roses. Seedless oranges, seedless grapefruit, and other horticultural varieties, as well as recently isolated strains of fungi and algae, have also received protection under this act.

In 1970, the Plant Variety Protection Act[27] was passed to confer patentlike protection (through the U.S. Department of Agriculture) on certain sexually reproducing plants, including hybrid seeds. This law still reflects the criterion that man's intervention has created something that would not have occurred naturally.

Clearly, however, the criteria for originality applied in both of these acts break down under some circumstances, depending on how one looks at them. For example, a seedless orange could arise spontaneously through a rare mutation, without any help from man. It did, in fact. Does the fact that an enterprising individual went to the trouble to propagate cuttings from that single tree to make seedless oranges available generally entitle him to patent protection for his trouble? If the spirit of the patent laws is to encourage innovation—or applied serendipity, as the case may be—then yes, of course, the individual should receive protection. If there were no such incentive to follow up on such useful "sports," then many desirable goods would not have been developed and available for public consumption.

There are two aspects of patents for living organisms that do make them intrinsically different from mechanical or chemical inventions. First, a living organism is a complex entity, containing a multitude of properties, only one of which may be of interest commercially or may reflect man's ingenuity. Does that mean all of the other possible uses of that organism should also receive patent protection. Under the Plant Patent Act of 1930, it does. For anyone to propagate a protected plant without a license from the patent holder is committing a criminal offense. Thus, if you happen to find that the wood from the trees that grow seedless grapefruit is ideally suited for constructing saunas, too bad. You will either have to find your own variety or pay for a license. However, patents under the traditional patent laws are now generally issued for a particular use. Therefore, if you can think of a novel use for an existing substance, even one for which someone else holds a patent, you can obtain a "use" patent.

The second difficulty with patents covering living organisms is that the powerful new methods in genetic manipulation make it possible to readily transform one strain of a microorganism into something a bit different. If the microbe has been patented and is described according to the requirements of the patent office, then relatively minor alterations will bring it outside the scope of the patent. Presumably, genetic alteration might also be used to get around patents issued under the Plant Patent Act.

Under existing patent laws, the interpretations over the years have actually allowed patents for many "products of nature," although it is generally agreed that something that is truly the invention of nature and not man should not receive patent protection. It is argued, however, that a natural product such as an antibiotic would not be available for the benefit of mankind if someone had not gone to the trouble to isolate the organism that produces it and to purify the substance itself. Thus, penicillin and all antibiotics since have received patents. The argument is just like the one above for seedless oranges. Only here, it is only the question of finding something that was already out there. Similarly, enzymes isolated from living material, including microorganisms, can be patented.

The U.S. Supreme Court reviewed a court battle in which the Board of Appeals of the U.S. Patent and Trademark Office had argued that, in view of the existence of the Plant Patent Act of 1930 and the Plant Variety Protection Act of 1970, Congress had never intended that living organisms should be included in the patent laws. That may well be. But the argument that this meant that Congress intended to *exclude* them is not so obvious. That conclusion does not necessarily follow from the fact that two subsequent acts were passed specifically dealing with plants. The Court of Customs and Patent Appeals (CCPA) argued that "composition of matter" could certainly include a living microorganism. The Supreme Court, then, in *Sidney A. Diamond, Commissioner of Patents and Trademarks,* v. *Ananda M. Chakrabarty,*[25] viewed the case from the legal perspective only, reaffirming that a true product of nature should not receive a patent, but that there is no fundamental difference between combining matter in unique ways in a chemical, inanimate substance or in a living microorganism.

The 5–4 decision reflected the previous division in this case, namely, what Congress did or did not intend back when the patent laws were written. That dilemma is, of course, not capable of resolution. It is clear that even in the revisions of the patent laws in 1952, Congress never considered living organisms. Legally, I would have to agree with the majority opinion that there is no indication that Congress intended to exclude living organisms from the patent laws. The high court was careful not to assume the role of the legislative branch of the government and state what it believed the law *should* cover; only what it *did* cover.

The decision, although viewed as precedent-setting by some, was really, then, a narrow legal clarification of existing patent law. Now that it was clear that patents for genetically engineered microorganisms would be allowed, the door was opened for patent claims on scores of genetically engineered microbes. But the Supreme Court's decision, had it been negative, really would not have made a great difference in the course of biotechnology. What the decision did do, however, was generate a wave of publicity. It changed the public's and the investors' impression of the legal acceptability of gene-spliced microorganisms and created the perception that this somehow solved the entire problem of the protection of proprietary rights in biotechnology.

The patent protection sought for any new invention in the production of a pharmaceutical by a genetically modified bacterium is complex, including claims on not only the organism, but the plasmid containing the inserted gene, perhaps even specifying the exact nucleotide sequence in certain regions, and the process used to grow the cells, isolate the product, and any other feature that can be considered original. Thus, if a patent were not allowed on the organism, there would still be enough other routes to ensure protection.

The fact that microorganisms can be readily altered also reduces the effectiveness of a patent on the organism itself. The courts will undoubtedly have to resolve at some point just how general the patent protection afforded a novel organism can be. That is, if one specified the entire genetic makeup of a bacterium exactly, then the patent would afford little protection, for a single, irrelevant mutation could technically result in a different organism. If patents could be issued to cover, say, *all* strains of *E. coli* containing a particular plasmid for a particular purpose, then the protection would be much better. But someone else may already have put that plasmid in a strain of *E. coli* different from the one you have used. Thus, your patent would have to be narrower. Of course, people would like to be able to patent the production of a substance from *any* microbe containing the genetic sequences necessary for its synthesis. But here, the scope of organisms might cover many strains and species, and the chances are much higher that someone would have done it in *some* organism. But if you happen to be the first, then it would not be inconsistent with the patent laws to receive such a patent, even though it would not be simply for a *specific* organism. To offset these ambiguities, however, many companies, although seeking patent protection to the broadest extent possible, rely on trade secrets to prevent someone else from capitalizing on their ingenuity.

It would be helpful to have a clarification of the patent laws to deal with just how living things should be patented, including the scope of organisms, the degree of genetic specificity required, the specified use of the genetically engineered living invention, a way of dealing with the mutability of microbes, and so on. It is not likely, however, that Congress will take such action in the near future. One may expect a great deal of activity in the courts before Congress will be compelled to act. A report issued by the National Science Foundation in 1982[28] recommended that an interdisciplinary committee be formed to review the patent laws with respect to the inventions made possible by recombinant DNA methods and to recommend revisions as appropriate.

What are some of the legal issues that may be anticipated? The first may concern a very general patent[29] issued to Stanford University covering virtually the entire process of cloning DNA in bacterial plasmids, that is, recombinant DNA technology as applied to bacterial hosts. The request for a patent was filled in 1975 by Stanley Cohen and Herbert Boyer, who claimed to be the sole inventors of the techniques. The decision to award a patent has drawn considerable criticism from those who contend that many of the claims made in the patent were, in fact, common knowledge and reflected techniques that had been developed by many individuals. Had Stanford chosen not to issue licenses under this patent, or had it charged dearly for them, it is certain that the case would have gone to court long ago. However, at $10,000 per year for licensing privileges, it is simply not worth the trouble of the biotechnology companies to fight it—yet.

The Stanford patent application contained a second part, covering the products of recombinant DNA technology, rather than the methods themselves. The U.S. Patent and Trade Mark Office, however, now wiser and more experienced than it was when it approved the first part of the Stanford patent, and alerted by a detailed analysis of the claims provided by some concerned individuals in the Washington, D.C., area, has delayed approval indefinitely, pending a thorough review, during which Stanford's attorneys have been allowed to revise their claims. The grounds for the delay are precisely the concerns that are listed above. In addition, the Patent Office cited a letter from Stanley Cohen to Donald Fredrickson, in which Cohen stated:

> Our data provide compelling evidence to support the view that recombinant DNA molecules constructed *in vitro* . . . simply represent selected instances of a process that occurs by natural means.[30]

This assertion, which most scientists believe greatly overstates the implications of the results of one of Cohen's experiments,[31] was made by Cohen for political propaganda when he was fighting proposed federal legislation that would have extended the coverage of the NIH guidelines to all parties engaged in recombinant DNA activities. His often-repeated argument was that DNA recombination between species was a naturally occurring event and therefore could not pose any unique hazards. But, questioned the Patent Office, if it the process is naturally occurring, how can you claim to be its inventor?

The Patent Office is still learning and continues to vacillate about its objections, including those given above. When the question of the issuance of the Stanford product patent is finally resolved, then the U.S. Patent Office will be free to reexamine the original Stanford patent on methods. All it needs to initiate a formal review is a request to do so from any outside party, stating the reasons for doubting the patent's validity. It is certain that such a request will be submitted.

I will have to admit that I was quite surprised when the patent was awarded, with all of the claims made by Cohen and Boyer being accepted by the Patent Office. At the time, it was perhaps a bit outside the technical skills of the patent examiners to judge just how novel and original the claims actually were. On the other hand, when discussing the Plant Patent Act with someone at the Patent Office for an article I was writing on this subject,[32] I sensed a pride among the examiners in seeing on just how many things they could get away with issuing patents. Thus, newly isolated strains of algae and fungi have been patented without the benefit of genetic engineering. It occurred to me that perhaps the Stanford patent application posed a similar challenge. Issue a patent and see if the courts give you trouble. If they don't, the patent must be all right. It is possible that this philosophy might sometimes prevail in certain quarters of the U.S. Patent and Trademark Office, particularly when there is no legal precedent to serve as a guideline for a patent application in a completely new area.

There is an important difference between U.S. patent laws and those in the rest of the world. In the United States, one has a one-year grace period from the time an invention is disclosed in which to file for patent protection. But if you want worldwide protection, there is a danger in *any* prior disclosure. For in Europe and elsewhere, protection extends only from the day of filing. Thus, if someone publicly describes an invention in the United States, someone else may file for patent protection in most other countries. The legal mechanisms for challenging such piracy are costly and are grossly inadequate to permit one to readily recapture one's proprietary rights. Therefore, it is common practice *not* to disclose anything until patents are filed both in the United States and abroad.

Although the patent laws in the United States are designed to bring an invention into the public domain as quickly as possible, while protecting the proprietary rights of the inventor, the inconsistency in patent law worldwide only encourages secrecy in the biotechnology industry (and in others as well). Because of the necessity of filing patents abroad, scientists are often frustrated by not being able to discuss recent research findings at meetings. Such matters must remain trade secrets until all patents are filed, and frequently, in order to ensure one's proprietary position in the future, they are kept as trade secrets until the patent issues. However desirable uniformity may be, there seems to be little hope of bringing it about in the international patent laws.

After a patent issues, usually 12–18 months from the date of application, the invention becomes public information. For this reason, some inventors, particularly in highly competitive industries such as biotechnology or microelectronics, delay the filing of patents, both in the United States and elsewhere, because they feel that, even in a year and a half from the time of filing, the project will still be in development, and perhaps years from marketing. It is feared that even the information contained in the original patent might help competitors catch up. (Of course, if one delays in filing for patent protection, there is a risk that someone else will make the same discovery and file first.) Thus, trade secrets are protected with a fervor in the biotechnology industry that some scientists, used to the openness that once characterized the university research labs, find alarming. This dilemma is discussed further in the following section.

Is there a moral issue in the patenting of living organisms? Some, such as the People's Business Commission, opposed the granting of patents in *Diamond* v. *Chakrabarty* on the grounds that it represented a violation of the "sanctity of life." Jeremy Rifkin's arguments[33] appeared to be grounded on religion. But whether or not patents are granted for inventions involving novel modifications or uses of microorganisms begs the question of just what *is* the sanctity of life.

Certainly there is ample precedent for the exploitation of living organisms by man. He derives most of his food supply from living plants, animals, and even microbes. There are few aspects of man's technological endeavors that do not exploit life in some way, either directly or indirectly. Throughout history, one may observe that most religions have usually held *human* life to be sacred to varying degrees, although few cultures ever considered such status as applying to *all* humans. Our contemporary Western culture, religion or no, generally regards human life as inviolable. Some would extend such esteem to their pets. In America, cats and dogs, although not as sacrosanct as humans, are accorded more rights than cattle, which are viewed almost entirely as an economic commodity. In parts of Asia, the order is reversed.

There is, then, a hierarchy of perception of just how sacred every life form is, defined purely by each culture at any given time in its history. Generally, the closer a living thing is to man, the higher on the scale it is perceived as being. Thus, animals clearly are valued over plants, except perhaps for the rare and cherished ornamentals of a few plant fanciers. Then, within the animal kingdom, there is a general correlation between the sanctity index and the phylum, as one gets closer to humans. That is, we humans seldom have any compunction about swatting a fly or even a spider (see, even here, there is a distinction to some).

Engaging in a recreation that involves luring fish onto a mouth-maiming hook bothers few. Some have no qualms about the so-called sport of hunting, which entails the murder of defenseless animals with high-powered firearms. However, this activity bothers many more than are offended by fishing. Bashing the heads of baby harp seals evokes horror, perhaps not only because they are warm-blooded animals, but because they are babies (don't underestimate the power of motherhood) and because they are "cute." Apes and monkeys, humanlike in many ways, are on a loftier level than most other animals. Medical research practices that are tolerated readily when used on rats and mice have evoked public outrage when the subjects are monkeys.

The conferring of legal rights on living organisms clearly parallels the degree to which life is considered sacred. Thus, the protection of human rights is a current international political issue. There is also a series of laws that grant certain rights to animals, and large groups of activists lobby to enlarge such protection. Most of the existing laws guarantee that at least certain classes of higher animals will be free of abuse by humans. Even trees have some rights, as afforded them by the National Parks and National Forests, although the latter protection is justified on the basis of preserving an economic resource. The Endangered Species Act does, however, recognize the "right" of all species to share the planet Earth with human beings.

From this viewpoint, then, are patents relevant to any moral issue? There is certainly nothing inconsistent in the patenting of a living invention or discovery and the currently acceptable views on the exploitation of life generally. As long as an organism can be owned and possessed, then presumably it can be exploited and developed for commercial purposes, including patentable modifications through genetic engineering.

As long as microbes and agricultural plants are the sole subjects of patents, there is certainly no departure from the way we have traditionally regarded the rights of living things. If, as we may expect before too long, genetically engineered stocks of cattle, horses, and other traditional farm animals are patented, there again should be no real conceptual difference from the way in which breeds of livestock are now handled. Whether the strains are developed by genetic engineering or the best methods of eugenic selection, the results are basically the same. When it is possible to produce thousands of genetically engineered chickens, identical in their ability to produce three times the usual annual egg yield, then it is certain that patents will be sought and awarded, but there would still seem to be no new moral issue.

The real moral difficulty, if there is to be one, will not occur until and if genetically modified humans are to be "invented." One might imagine that a living creature could be created that is almost but not quite "human." Or perhaps it might even be better than humans: stronger, more intelligent, and therefore, threatening to ordinary mortals. Because we humans control the legal system and the patent rights, what would be the legal standing of such an organism? Would it be afforded legal rights to the extent that it exhibited "humanness?" Would it be permissible to own one? If so, how would such ownership fit with the now-archaic concept of human slavery? These questions are not ones that we shall need to deal with for a time. Perhaps we never will. But it is possible that as the methods of genetic and cellular manipulation become more sophisticated, man may indeed have to reckon with ethical and legal problems of extraordinary difficulty.

The Search for the Truth and the Profit Motive: Can They Coexist?

In the eyes of some, the intense level of research and development that now exists in the new biotechnology industry is destroying scientific research—at least, in the biological sciences—in the traditional, pure, idealistic form in which it was imagined to exist in the days preceding recombinant DNA. It is claimed that free inquiry, once the rallying cry of scientists fighting legislation to extend the NIH guidelines to the private sector, is now being stifled by ugly commercialism. It is further argued that the narrow gap between science and technology generates tremendous pressure to protect even a scientist's *ideas* as trade secrets, squelching the free communication that is such an essential component of the creative process. Even scientists who remain at universities, it is said, are driven by the scarcity of federal research funds to accept tempting consultantships and contracts from corporations, which are only after specific useful results. Thus, the argument goes, the old days, when one could explore any problem that seemed interesting, without the requirement that there be a product to sell in five years at the most, are quickly disappearing.

Is the level of gloom of the preceding paragraph justified? Have we really come to the end of the golden age of research? Must we now let private enterprise have its turn to exploit the knowledge brought about by the past three decades of publicly supported basic research in the life sciences? The question, of course, is not quite that simple. It seldom is. But there *has* been a shift, an inevitable one that has followed from years of productive research which have finally given us the tools to apply the methods of molecular and cell biology to the solution of a great many medical, pharmaceutical, chemical, and agricultural problems.

Simply put, there has been a diversion of talent from basic to applied biological research. The total number of research scientists, or even that fraction who could be expected to contribute creatively to basic knowledge, has risen only slightly over the past 15 years. But the fraction of that pool in molecular biology who are now either employees of, consultants to, or scientific advisers of some commercial concern has risen enormously. Particularly significant is the fact that most of the leading figures—Nobel laureates and those recognized as among the most creative individuals in their fields—have such ties. I do not mean to suggest that these scientists have stopped addressing fundamental scientific problems, but this circumstance certainly predicts a shift in the emphasis of research overall.

The matter of keeping even ideas in their most formative stages as trade secrets is also very unsettling to many scientists. The free exchange of ideas among colleagues—that is, in a disciplinary rather than a geographical sense—has always been a cornerstone of the creative process. The steady critique of each other's ideas, the marriage of expertise in different areas, and the synthesis of hypotheses by collective thought—these can take place only when communication is free at all stages of research.

If there were a clearly separable space between basic research findings and commercial applications, then there might not be any problem. In the case of applied molecular and cell biology, the distinction between basic and applied research, although conceptually valid, is considerably fuzzed over in practice. For example, the understanding of the elements of control over gene expression has *immediate* application to the engineering of bacterial cloning vehicles for the production of commercially valuable proteins, such as hormones, enzymes, and immunoregulators (a class of proteins that controls the immune response). And any monoclonal antibody, however interesting its structure or normal function may be, is *per se* of potential commercial value.

As discussed in the previous section, the patent system, because of the inconsistency between U.S. patent laws and those of other countries, as well as the intensely competitive nature of biotechnology, has not really helped to get research findings into the public domain quickly. Moreover, those scientists who have resisted becoming affiliated with commercial ventures on the basis of principle are under considerable pressure from their colleagues, both direct and indirect. The feeling that they are missing out on the real action, to which they are not privy, as well as on the financial rewards, which may be considerable, constitutes a coercion not to be underestimated. The prestige lent to having corporate ties simply by the number of Nobel laureates who do may even suggest that those who do not are somehow unworthy or inferior.

Indeed, corporate affliliation may even be a matter of survival. In the current university system, many good scientists are denied tenure, and those who receive it may still have a difficult time obtaining research funding from either the federal government (research funds from both the National Institutes of Health and the National Science Foundation, in terms of noninflated dollars, have been shrinking) or the few private foundations that fund research.

When viewed over a period of a decade or more, the current perturbations in the biological research community may not be as significant as they seem to those who think in terms of immediate crises. That is, the bright side of the argument goes as follows: The best scientists will be creative, no matter where they work or who supports them. The collegial networks within any given academic or corporate sphere are large enough so that the creative exchange and critique of ideas will take place productively. Therefore, basic knowledge will still be forthcoming. Even if the patent system or the keeping of trade secrets slows somewhat the dissemination of new information, the worst that can happen will be a delay, and probably not a very long one at that. Besides, the incentive for solving problems in commercial biotechnology is every bit as strong as the direct search for the Truth. Because basic and applied research are so intimately intertwined in biotechnology, fundamental knowledge will continue to advance as a result of solving everyday research problems. This "applied" research is bound to lead serendipitously to many unexpected findings of basic importance. Furthermore, university-based scientists have been subsisting on substandard faculty salaries long enough. It is high time that they were paid what they are worth.

It is, of course, not possible to do a controlled experiment. We will never know whether the advent of biotechnology has accelerated, slowed, or had no effect on the rate of discovery overall. And perhaps it doesn't matter anyway, particularly if, as many believe, good research will go ahead no matter what the circumstances. Nevertheless, we can still be alert to problems that attend the biotechnology enterprise and attempt to solve them.

In early 1980, Lewis Thomas, in one of his "Notes of a Biology Watcher" columns in the *New England Journal of Medicine*,[34] expressed concern over the possible reduction of support for truly basic research. He argued that, because biotechnology is essentially reaping the fruits of decades of research supported by the government, the industry is obligated to see that it is still supported. In fact, he argued, a continuing, strong, basic research enterprise is ultimately essential to a strong biotechnology industry. He proposed that "some new mechanisms for a partnership be worked out between the corporate world and the world of academic science, and specifically designed for the very long term."

At the time he wrote this suggestion, Dr. Thomas could not have known that precisely these kinds of arrangements would be proposed—and would generate heated controversy. Hoechst, Inc., offered to fund research at Massachusetts General Hospital to the tune of $50 million in exchange for a say in what got done and exclusive licensing for any patents that were forthcoming from such research. In fact, Hoechst has essentially bought the hospital's new Department of Molecular Biology. Any faculty member who joins the department has to accept the terms of the contract. The scientists in the Department of Molecular Biology are not free to seek their own funds for research, and most of what they work on has to have Hoechst's blessings.

Predictably, the cries of protest were raised over commercial interests messing around in academic research in such a grand manner and presumably compromising the innocence of the scientists who accepted such funds. But for Massachusetts General/Harvard Medical School, it was an offer they couldn't refuse.

Then there was the abortive Harvard affair. A proposal for establishing a cooperative industrial arrangement[35] that would involve some of the university's faculty and an equity interest for the university drew such a reaction from the faculty that President Derek Bok abandoned the whole idea. To be sure, not all of the press accounts were accurate; many people believed that Harvard's entanglement in the world of business would be much deeper than it was actually to be. Such concerns did not, of course, prevent the deep involvement of Harvard's molecular biologists in commercial interests. Professor Walter Gilbert, awarded the Nobel Prize in chemistry in 1980 for his contributions to the development of a method for the rapid determination of nucleotide sequences in DNA, took a leave of absence from Harvard to become the chief executive officer of the Biogen Corporation.

A more recent venture, also in Boston, and perhaps more of the type that Lewis Thomas had in mind, was the establishment of the Whitehead Institute at the Massachusetts Institute of Technology (MIT). The Whitehead Foundation provided $20 million to the university to establish a new institute for research in molecular biology. In addition, the university is to receive $5 million per year in operating expenses. Multimillionaire Edwin Whitehead has also promised to bequeath $100 million to MIT. The institute has positions for 20 research scientists, who also hold faculty positions at the university. The incumbents in these positions require university approval. The institute's director, MIT Professor of Biology and Nobel laureate David Baltimore, has, on paper at least, control over the type of research to be carried out.

Although this arrangement is unlike that proposed at Harvard, it has also brought cries of protest from some quarters of the university faculty. However, MIT decided that it was in its best interests to accept the Whitehead money. The strings? The institute, not MIT, would hold the patents. But the commercial potential of the institute is unclear. Whitehead founded the highly successful Technicon Corporation, which was ultimately sold to Revlon. Few doubt that Whitehead expects his new institute to be a source of potentially profitable science. Presumably, the institute will be autonomous and thus free to negotiate arrangements with commercial establishments independently of the university. Some critics have charged that this arrangement will upset the academic norms, creating essentially two classes of faculty in the MIT biology department.

It is one thing for faculty members to accept research funds from a private concern. In return, the corporate sponsor receives licensing privileges for any patentable inventions which result. Why, then, is doing it on a grander scale so different? Most likely, it is the appearance of concentrated corporate power threatening the independence of the university. Nevertheless, arrangements like the ones described above are being pursued at many campuses. Universities have been struggling to survive the onslaught of inflation and reduction in federal funding. Thus, cooperative arrangements with commercial organizations may become, again, instruments of survival, without which the academic institutions would be in a much weaker position. As Bernard Davis put it:

> We may all regret the loss of the more Arcadian atmosphere of the past. However, if universities are to protect their financial base in order to advance their academic goals, nostalgia will be no substitute for imaginative adaptations and a tough-minded attitude. There are surely risks in developing industrial connections, but they must be balanced against the increasing financial insecurity of universities today and against a monolithic dependence on an often unsympathetic government.[36]

It is perhaps important at this point to examine the motives of the scientist and the extent to which these may be either corruptible or in conflict with one another, for much of what we have heard in criticism of the commercial intrusions into the ivied halls of academia is based on an ideal. The ideal is that academic scholars—practitioners of natural philosophy, as science was once called—are motivated only by their insatiable curiosity to understand the nature of things, or at least the desire to meet the challenge of a difficult problem posed by nature.

The very best, most creative scientists are undoubtedly driven by this intimate involvement with the concepts on which the natural order is based. Some are, to be sure, driven more by the challenge of using their ingenuity to unravel a complex problem than they are by the philosophical implications of their work. Most of these, although they may appreciate money, will probably continue to be creative in any environment. Walter Gilbert's decision to become the chief executive officer of Biogen may well reflect his desire to apply his proven ability to solve difficult problems to the world of business, having reached the top, at least in the eyes of his peers, in science.

I must say, however, that in general less idealistic motives also come into play. Most university-based scientists are concerned to some degree about their survival and their material security. Thus, obtaining research support and promotions receives high priority. The pursuit of these particular goals can certainly involve personal compromises. For example, in the early years of the "War on Cancer," many scientists attempted to relate their work to cancer in some way, often far-fetched, simply in order to partake of the windfall of research funds appropriated specifically for cancer research. Getting a grant was more important for many than being able to work on the problems they preferred to investigate.

Truly creative research is rare. Most so-called research does not really contribute any new concepts or understanding to the world in which we live, whether it is done at universities or in commercial laboratories, although the goals of those two types of institutions are admittedly different. However, for a moderately creative scientist to be in a position where he is told what to do by management, rather than following his own desires, can lead only to frustration. Thus, depending on the amount of research freedom permitted by commercial organizations, a selection process is inevitable. The most creative people will seek to be at those places that afford them the most freedom, regardless of the financial rewards.

Prestige and recognition also enter into the equation. Arrogance has been known to be endemic to some degree in most of the best scientists. Thus, being in a position where one can receive the widest possible recognition for one's achievements is important for the establishment of a career in science. This means that one has to publish research findings, give presentations at important meetings, and generally be seen and heard—all much easier to do from a university environment than from the corporate world, where companies tend to be relatively isolated and are continually concerned about the leakage of proprietary information. Hence, this factor may also be a source of selective pressure.

But what of those who have the best of both worlds? This would include a tenured faculty position and a consulting role at a company, providing both personal compensation and research support. This is, in fact, the current situation of a number of established scientists. The motives of such individuals may be complex, but I must conclude that the determinants of the creative potential of any scientist are primarily internal. There may be external constraints, of course. One has to have a job, and one that will support a research program. Few get everything they want, whether they depend on federal funds or corporate resources. I have yet to be convinced, however, that the human drives that result in original science are controlled by whether the hand that feeds the scientist is also feeding the stockholders, or whether it is taking from the taxpayers.

This does not mean, however, that there are not difficulties and conflicts of interest for those who must exist schizophrenically in both the corporate and the academic worlds. From some of the universities whose faculties have extensive corporate connections come grumblings of many sorts. Graduate students and postdoctoral fellows complain that their mentor is never in his lab, spending more time with his corporation than doing what the university is paying him for. Then, there are charges that university technicians are "stolen" by such professors and are offered jobs at much higher salaries at the professor's affiliate. The charges that research developments arising from federally funded work are taken directly to the company, where they disappear down the black hole of trade secrets, are rather serious.

In early 1982, although few of these charges had been well documented or had taken the form of formal grievances with the universities, the rancor created did cause some preemptive action. Donald Kennedy, President of Stanford University, called a private meeting at Pajaro Dunes, California, in April 1982, with the presidents of Harvard, MIT, the California Institute of Technology, and the University of California. Also invited were a number of corporate leaders, particularly in the biotechnology area. The meeting was the first major attempt to deal with the apparent clash of values that was creating heat on several campuses. A statement of principles emerged, setting forth the general goals of academic–corporate ties. Nevertheless, the meeting was seen by some as an attempt by Kennedy to show the world that he was aware of the problems, and that he was basically a good guy who was not in collusion with any company. The press wanted to come, but was told that its presence would inhibit open discussion. By the time the meeting took place, everyone was sensitized to the public scrutiny that it was getting and to the suspicions of some observers about its real purpose. It was said that an inordinate amount of time was spent on the press release, relative to the time devoted to discussing the real issues.

The corporate view tends to see the above type of difficulties as essentially the university's problem, not the corporation's. In fact, consulting arrangements are governed by explicit rules set forth by every university, usually permitting one working day per week for outside paid work. It is the faculty member's responsibility to obey these rules, and the university's to enforce them. Nonetheless, the abuse of consulting agreements *does* reflect badly on the corporations, as well as on the universities. It is therefore in the company's best interests to exert some pressure on its consultants to toe the line. The Industrial Biotechnology Association, a relatively new trade association of some of the biotechnology companies, held a workshop in May 1982 to address these matters. At this meeting, however, it was apparent that most of the corporate participants were more interested in seeing that the details of their individual research contracts with universities protected their interests than they were in philosophical problems or the funding of basic research in universities.

Other forums have been held to try to resolve these issues. The American Chemical Society had a session on corporate/academic relations at its annual meeting. The University of Pennsylvania sponsored a large gathering of university and corporate officials in December 1982. Numerous articles have been written addressing the real and the apparent conflicts of values. Although not resolving the practical matters with which universities and individuals must contend, these meetings have at least forced people to become aware of the values that govern both corporate and academic interests. For example, some have been concerned that taxpayers' dollars support basic research in universities and that corporations are then permitted to exploit these findings and make a profit on the technology that ensues. But is this really a conflict of values or a failure of justice? In the United States, at least, it is a tradition that private industry develops most of the technology which ultimately benefits society. The federal government supports research, not for the motives that drive the scientist, but for the practical applications that will presumably flow from such research. In order that research results will become useful, then, is it not consistent with the values of the American economic system to license the inventions of biological research for private commercial development? Perhaps in other economic systems based upon other values, it would indeed be inappropriate to permit the private exploitation of public knowledge. In any case, the so-called value conflicts which biotechnology has been accused of fostering are no different from those in any other area of technology. Why should biotechnology be singled out as engaging in some unique injustice?

Still, there are some basic value conflicts that are perhaps most acute for the younger investigator, who has yet to obtain his first professional position or his first research grant. As a graduate student and a postdoc, one is exposed to the mentor-professor role-model. And, in going to meetings and interacting with both academic and corporate scientists, one gets a pretty good idea of any conflicts that may exist between one's ideals and the real world in which he must work. The most common complaint is not so much the professor's having extracurricular corporate activities as the reluctance of people to talk openly about their work. For a young person trying to learn as much as possible about a particular subject, trade secrets can be a most frustrating impediment. Open discussion is as much a part of the learning process as of the creative process. By the time a scientist has reached the postdoctoral stage in the top schools, he knows this well.

With the competition for university faculty positions being rather great, many will take corporate jobs, not because it is their first choice, but because it is the best they can do. This does not mean that those who take corporate jobs are second-rate scientists. The number of positions in the best university research departments that need to be filled each year is rather small. The prestige value of working for a leading biotechnology corporation is now somewhat higher than working for "industry" used to be, at least as viewed from academia. Certainly, for many, a corporate position is much better for doing research than a junior faculty position, where there is neither enough ready money to set up a laboratory nor enough time for research because of a large teaching load.

Those starting out with a company face the problem of trying to build a reputation in science within the constraints of corporate isolation, trade secrets, and a business strategy that impinges on their freedom of inquiry. Job security in the rapidly changing corporate world may be even less than it is in academia. Morale is sometimes a problem, but most will make the most of their situations. Still, like depriving a child of an education and stimuli during his most formative years, it would be sad indeed if those in their scientific youth were to be demoralized by the restrictions that corporate science places on freedom and learning at a time when every creative instinct should be encouraged.

So I return to the question posed at the outset of this discussion: Is the search for the truth compatible with the profit motive? There is clearly no simple answer. There are many qualified answers. In the same society, both can exist, but not necessarily in the same place. There are many limitations on the pursuit of the truth, including the internal limitations on the ability and the imagination of the scientist. The profit motive can certainly force one to direct his attention away from the merely interesting to what will pay off. If the correct selection is made, however, the research interests of some may indeed coincide with the research strategy of a corporation. In general, however, the scientist who wishes to do unrestricted science should not work for a biotechnology company. On the other hand, such an individual may well be frustrated in trying to obtain such unlimited freedom within the academic world. Teaching and applying for research grants may take up just as much time as directed corporate research. Only a fortunate few will have the opportunity to exercise the unfettered freedom of inquiry that is often incorrectly touted as a universal privilege of scientists.

Biotechnology around the World

Most of the discussions of the enterprise of biotechnology up to this point have been concerned with the commercial biotechnology industry as it has developed in the United States. Of course, biotechnology has been of great interest to most of the rest of the world, but often for different reasons than in the United States. It is also clear that a even a truly international commercial industry cannot respond to some of the most important applications of biotechnology, especially the needs of the developing nations of the world.

The entrepreneurial approach to biotechnology seems to have been nearly confined to the United States. While there was, of course, a great deal of interest in Europe in applying the advances in biological sciences to the solution of practical problems, the emergence of a coherent biotechnology industry has been slow. Different countries have followed different models.

Biogen, which was formed in 1977 at the instigation of Swiss scientist Charles Weissman, is perhaps an exception to the European rule. In most countries, there was simply not the same level of activity as there was in the United States, of scientists teaming up with the business and financial communities. When it became apparent that a home biotechnology industry was not developing rapidly enough, several countries sought to develop national policies to promote biotechnology. In France and Great Britain, government funds were set aside for this purpose.

In most of the northern European countries, the large companies with money to invest have become the leaders in developing significant efforts to make gene-spliced products. In Germany it is the large chemical and pharmaceutical companies, such as Hoechst and Bayer, which have dominated the industry. NOVO, in Denmark, a leading producer of enzymes, was a natural to begin more imaginative applications of such methods. In Sweden and Finland, it has also been large companies which have begun to achieve success. For example, Alko, the state owned Finnish National Alcohol Monopoly, is one of the most profitable companies in Europe, with a profit margin of around 27% each year. Alko now has a research department devoted to improving the enzymes in cellulose, starch and sugar fermentation, and is currently setting up its own recombinant DNA laboratory. Alko has been instrumental in establishing a funding institution, to which several Finnish industrial organizations contribute, that sponsors industrially relevant gene-splicing projects in universities and research institutes.

In the United States, there seems to be an obsessive concern with the success of the Japanese biotechnology industry. Reeling from the failure of American electronics, optics, and automobiles to compete successfully with high-quality competition from Japan, many Americans fear that the same will happen in biotechnology, even though the commercial enterprise began in the United States. Japan already has a well-developed fermentation industry. With slight modifications, this existing technology could be adapted to produce a wide variety of microbial products.

There have been numerous studies of why the Japanese have been so successful in beating the Americans at their own game. Some charge that Japan plays by a different set of rules. That is, Japan's Ministry of International Trade and Industry (MITI) has played the role of planner, coordinator, and promoter of the Japanese biotechnology industry. Open communication among competing industries and economic incentives from the government have resulted in less wasted effort, which can result when several domestic companies compete in the same area. Some accuse the Japanese companies of collusion which, under the American antitrust laws, is illegal.

In America, the so-called free enterprise model is operating in biotechnology as much as in any industry. The government has done nothing either to promote the industry or to impede its progress. In fact, the Reagan Administration has made a point of not having an industrial policy in general, or a biotechnology policy in particular, assuming free enterprise will take care of itself. A policy options paper prepared by an interagency working group reporting to the President's science advisor, in which a national biotechnology policy was recommended, at least in part to meet the perceived Japanese challenge, was unceremoniously suppressed by the administration.

Partnerships and cooperative ventures in biotechnology are being formed world-wide, including all sorts of arrangements among Japanese, American, and European companies. Unlike the beleagured American electronics industry, biotechnology has not pleaded for special favors or trade restrictions from the government, at least not yet. But when products finally begin to be produced and sold, the tune may change.

Much of the difference between American and Japanese business must be attributed to culture. In the first place, the Japanese are nationalistic, and are very aware of the Japanese position, as a national entity, in world economics. This is much less true in the United States, where national boundaries are of secondary importance, in spite of the "buy America" propaganda. But perhaps more important is the relationship between workers and management in Japan and their sense of community. Workers join a company with the intention that it will be for life. Companies are sensitive to the morale of the employees and the importance to business success of people taking pride in their work and their company. Productivity of the Japanese worker has been steadily improving over the past ten years, where it has remained relatively constant in the United States. And quality control is a different concept in Japan. There, the goal is *no* defects. In America, quality control is calculated according to some economic formula whereby a certain percentage of defective products is considered acceptable. It is clear, however, that many Americans buy Japanese automobiles and electronic products for the reason that they are less likely to have a defective product on their hands, one that they will have to take back to get fixed.

What the so-called Japanese challenge means in the biotechnology industry is not clear. It could mean, however, that the struggling entrepreneurial companies in America, which are now attempting to function as successful businesses will not be able to compete with the economic efficiency of the Japanese industry. The American companies are now trying, sometimes painfully, to define effective corporate strategies, the proper mix of short- and long-range projects, and the development of effective management. In the face of such uncertainty, morale is a continuing problem. Nevertheless, as long as the American biotechnology industry can maintain its presumed lead in the development of technology, spurred by a high degree of innovation, it should be able to survive its own adolescence and emerge a mature world leader. Some business leaders take comfort in the prevailing view that the Japanese are excellent at developing sophisticated technology and efficient mass production methods, but are short on originality, the sort of innovation essential for the success of a modern biotechnology industry. However, in view of some of the superb work reported in recent months from a number of Japanese research laboratories, there may well be good reason to doubt the validity of the notion that the Japanese are less creative than Americans. If good, new ideas are not limiting, then the large, established companies, and particularly the efficient, well-managed and highly skilled Japanese companies, may have the edge over the American entrepreneurial companies, even though the latter appeared to be far ahead at first.

The way in which the world commercial biotechnology industry will eventually sort itself out remains to be seen. But simple economics dictates that it will continue to develop those products that can be sold most profitably. Thus the markets will be in the wealthier nations, and for those products that people in the economically developed world want and will pay for. Therefore, were all biotechnology to remain subject to free market economic forces, the potential of the powerful new techniques of genetic engineering and cell biology to solve the most pressing of the world's problems would scarcely be realized. For there is little economic incentive to develop vaccines for tropical diseases, or to increase the protein content of taro. No matter how much people may need and want these things, they cannot pay for them.

In the biotechnology companies of the developed countries, one of the most lucrative targets is an effective and safe cancer therapeutic. The business managers dream of projected markets of $10 billion by the year 1993, assuming of course, that efforts to prevent cancer do not succeed and that, somehow, cancer patients will be able to spend ten times the amount that they now spend on therapeutics. But, regardless of how flimsy the foundations of these dreams of riches may be, it is a fact that cancer is a terrible disease, and the pursuit of a cure is indeed noble. There are an estimated ten million people in the world afflicted with cancer at any given time.

We should not forget, however, that cancer is the nemesis of the aging populations of the wealthier, industrially developed nations. There are 300 million people in the world with malaria, 600 million with hookworm, and 200 million with schistosomiasis.[37] But even government supported research in the United States reflects the diseases common to the developed world. The annual budget of the National Cancer Institute is about one billion dollars a year, whereas only about $5 million are spent on research on malaria. For a while, Genentech sponsored a program to develop a vaccine for malaria, but abandoned it in April, 1983, because the initial research was funded by the World Health Organization, a fact which Genentech felt would jeopardize their exclusive rights to the product.

What then is the solution to this dilemma? There have of course been a number of agencies of the United Nations, and of various national governments of the developed countries, which have attempted to bring new technologies to bear on the problems of the lesser developed countries. The National Research Council of the National Academy of Sciences has its Board on Science and Technology for International Development, which, while not in a position to initiate and fund projects directly, is attempting to increase awareness of the third world's problems and provide a forum in which solutions can be pursued. A Conference held in July, 1982, on "Priorities in Biotechnology Research for International Development" defined many of the discrepancies between the advanced countries and the developing nations where biotechnology, if applied properly, could bring tremendous gains. The scientists in the various working groups were able to define priorities in many areas of agriculture, human and animal diseases, and energy.[38]

The International Rice Research Institute in Los Banos, the Philippines, in existence since 1962, has accomplished a great deal in the development of high yielding strains of rice, which now comprise a quarter of the rice grown in the world today. In December, 1982, it sponsored, along with the International Union of Pure and Applied Chemistry, an international conference in Manila on Chemistry and World Food Supplies. This meeting was followed by another, sponsored again by the National Research Council, and by the United States Agency for International Development, also in Manila and following up on the same topics. These and other meetings that address the needs of developing countries are useful in identifying areas in which the methods of biotechnology would be the logical approach to meeting those needs. However, what is missing is the means to implement the consensus which is always reached. From each of these gatherings, a fine volume of proceedings is published, usually with a set of recommendations. But then what? Who or what will initiate the desired activities and create the means to carry out research and technological development where there is no private capital?

Since 1981, the United Nations Industrial Development Organization (UNIDO) has been trying to establish the International Centre for Genetic Engineering and Biotechnology, UNIDO's most ambitious project ever. The proposal for the ICGEB (the acronym now pervades the vocabulary of the UNIDO Secretariat) imagines a core of world class scientists who would conduct research in all of the areas of concern for the Third World, at a place where scientists from developing countries could come for training in the methods of modern biotechnology, then taking what they have learned back to their home countries. It is envisioned as a center of "high excellence," in the redundant prose of the UN bureaucracy, to be as good as any research and training institution in the world. The concept, if a bit idealistic is basically sound. It is at least a concrete step on which to build Third World capabilities in biotechnology. But there are a number of impediments to the success of the Centre, both conceptual and real.

First, perhaps because most of the expert consultants retained by UNIDO to help develop the early planning documents for the ICGEB were scientists engaged in basic research, the early emphasis was on science and research. Relatively little attention was paid to the fact that research only provides the foundation upon which biotechnology rests. Biotechnology is much more than science. The establishment of a research laboratory, and the conduct of high quality science, is far different from establishing the means to carry the findings of the research laboratory to practical fruition. An institution engaged in promoting a biotechnology industry would also have to consider scale-up and process development, manufacturing, quality control, regulatory matters, international patents, and the fact that the benefits would accrue to the prospective consumers primarily through commercialization. These elements would be a particularly important part of a training program. But the 1981 proposal setting forth the structure and work program of the Centre concentrated on science and scientists, scarcely mentioning the practical side of biotechnology.[39]

Second, and perhaps related to the difficulties mentioned above, there seems to be a reluctance on the part of the UNIDO planners to admit that a world-wide commercial industry exists. Why this is so is not entirely clear, but the image of multi-national corporations is anathema in some parts of the world. At the organizational meeting for the ICGEB held in Belgrade in December, 1982, the perception of the commercial biotechnology industry revealed by many of the delegates was that it is enshrouded in secrecy, is innately uncooperative, and only out to satisfy its thirst for profits. While this image certainly contains some elements of truth, there are many reasons why the establishment of an international center would be hurt by not recognizing the existence of commercial biotechnology. The commercial industry has by now amassed a large body of experience in what it actually takes to set up and build an entity capable of carrying out high-quality research and development. For this reason alone, it is hard to believe that in their preliminary visits to the many interested countries, the UNIDO staff and expert consultants did not pay a single visit to a commercial organization, even though the expert panel included several scientists working in America, most of whom have commercial ties of their own. Even though the motives and the sources of funding may be different for an international research and training center than for a corporation, the actual objectives are very similar. The Land-of-Oz idealism that captured the spirits of the entrepreneurs of the 1970s had to give way to a realistic and practical view of what it actually would take to build an effective organization. The learning curve has been and still is long, difficult, and sometimes painful. The ICGEB cannot afford to repeat it.

Yet many of the views expressed by the delegates at Belgrade, especially those from the developing nations, were full of the naive idealism one often heard in the early days of the excitement over the possible applications of recombinant DNA. Genetic engineering and biotechnology were seen as instant panaceas to problems of enormous size and complexity, that could somehow be solved at very low cost without industrial organizations operating according to the rules of international commerce. In perhaps wishing to avoid a confrontation with the strident views on commercialism one encounters in some developing countries, UNIDO allowed a skewed and unrealistic concept to prevail concerning how the ICGEB could function in reality. In so perpetuating such myths, UNIDO fell short of its responsibility to educate the majority of the interested countries in how the Centre might actually succeed in furthering the goal of fostering a biotechnology industry in developing countries. Fortunately, in response to such criticism, UNIDO's more recent documents[40] present a much more practical view of what the International Centre would need.

Ultimately, whether or not we may like it, international commerce is a fact of life which governs the manufacture, distribution, prices and availability of goods in all countries, whether they are capitalist or socialist, industrially developed or still bound by an agrarian subsistence economy. It is through commercialization that the developing countries will ultimately benefit from a new technology fostered by the International Centre for Genetic Engineering and Biotechnology. To attempt to maintain a kind of moralistic apartheid between commercial interests and public endeavors can only subvert the purposes to which both aspire, and this is especially true on an international level. It may turn out that some specific objectives of an international center or of specific countries could be best achieved through cooperative arrangements with private industry, and perhaps vice versa.

The eventual success of a truly international effort to establish a new institution of the attributes of the ICGEB requires both genuine cooperation between nations and the commitment of substantial financial resources. At present, there does not seem to be enough of either. The meeting in Belgrade became somewhat mired down in UN-style politics over the issue of where the Centre would be located. Before the meeting, only sites in developed countries had received serious attention, and it seemd a foregone conclusion that the Centre would indeed be located in an industrially developed nation. The UNIDO expert consultants had recommended that rather stringent criteria be satisfied in order to make the center attractive to the world's best scientists, including such practical amenities as having supplies and equipment readily available, trained service personnel able to respond to emergency calls, and even being sure the power was on all the time. Adding the need to be near other major academic centers would make it difficult to meet such standards in any developing nation. However, in spite of a very attractive offer from Belgium, there was a great deal of lobbying to put the Centre in a developing nation. Before the meeting was over, offers were received from India, Pakistan, Thailand and Cuba. A committee was then established to visit the proposed centers and make recommendations to a ministerial meeting scheduled for July, 1983. The critical matter of funding was not even touched in Belgrade.

The Selected Committee, composed mostly of scientists, spent two months considering the above offers plus one from Italy. It evaluated the sites according to their ability to meet the criteria of excellence as originally set forth. Thus, to no one's surprise, the Committee's report[41] gave top marks to the offers from Italy and Belgium. In part because they felt it important to acknowledge a developing country, the Committee also found many good things to say about the offer from Thailand, going so far as to say that it also met the criteria set forth in the original proposal, although not necessarily to the same degree as the Italian and Belgian proposals. At the bottom of the list was the offer from India, which the Selected Committee felt fell far short of what was needed for a center of excellence in the service of the needs of developing nations.

If the 35 countries assembled at Belgrade could have abided by the process they established to resolve the siting question, then the matter might have proceeded in a smooth, gentlemanly manner. But those experienced in international political proceedings know well that for that to have happened would have been nothing short of a miracle. In fact, India was not pleased by the report, so much so that it began an intense campaign on behalf of its own candidacy. There were attempts to discredit members of the Selected Committee, as well as the report itself. Pressure was applied at the level of heads of state to ensure that when the ministers assembled to establish the ICGEB and choose a site, India would be the winner.

The crucial meeting took place in Madrid in September, 1983. From the beginning, it degenerated into a power struggle between India and its supporters on one side and Thailand, who liked the Selected Committee's Report, and those who saw the ICGEB headed for disaster if it were to go to India, on the other. Invitations to the members of the Selected Committee to attend the Madrid meeting were suddenly withdrawn by UNIDO days before the meeting was to begin. "Lack of funds" was the reason given, but most believe it was really because of political pressure exerted by India. Unlike the Belgrade meeting, where many of the countries were represented by scientists, it was pure politics in Madrid. Nobody wanted to hear the scientific consultants talk of technical excellence. The scientists attached to the delegations, whether from developed or developing countries, watched in dismay as the dream of an international center of excellence in biotechnology seemed to be slipping into a morass of political posturing and expressions of national pride.

Several working committees could not resolve the matter of siting, at last suggesting that maybe having the Centre in more than one location might be a way out. In the meantime, another committee dealing with the statutes, the legal instrument by which the Centre would be brought into existence, amended the provision on assessments to specify that contributions of member nations of the ICGEB during the first five years would be voluntary. Thus neither of the important issues on the Madrid agenda were resolved. But, at midnight on the last day, 25 countries signed the statutes. Four more countries signed in the next two months. Legally, it meant that the ICGEB was created on paper, although the statutes specify that the parliaments of 24 countries must ratify the statutes in order for the International Centre to *really* come into existence.

The signatories of the statutes were then faced with the task of coming to terms with the question of siting, and whether or not a multi-sited ICGEB makes any practical sense. Most of those with experience in establishing or administering research institutions believe that it doesn't, from an administrative, financial or technical point of view. The concept of the Centre was thus also open for discussion. There were no guaranteed funds, except from the individual host country offers; support and interest of the developed countries, upon which the success of a center of excellence depends, was all but gone. Italy and Spain, both with offers to host the ICGEB, were the only Western European countries to sign the statutes. Bulgaria, Hungary, Jugoslavia, and Greece signed. But the major industrial nations were nowhere to be found. Belgium withdrew its offer, and Sweden and Canada, active participants in the proceedings through the Madrid meeting, both announced that they would concentrate on their own national programs and deal with developing countries on a bilateral basis. France, Great Britain, the Netherlands, Finland, and the Soviet Union, all present in Belgrade, ignored the Madrid meeting. West Germany, Austria, Poland, and Switzerland sent only observers. And Japan and the United States had never chosen to become involved. As of late 1983, no further resolution of the ICGEB has transpired, but the outlook is not optimistic.

The attitude of the United States in the matter of the International Centre is especially noteworthy. Prior to the Belgrade meeting, a federal interagency committee decided that the ICGEB would have a difficult time getting off the ground, and none of the federal agencies were willing to contribute materially to the Centre. But somewhere in the cloistered sanctums of the Reagan administration, the decision was made not only not to send even an observer to the meeting, but to boycott it entirely. The putative American delegate was in Paris the week before the meeting but was told to stay away from Belgrade. The U.S. Embassy in Belgrade was forbidden to send an observer. Why was the action so extreme?

Some speculate that it is a reflection of the notion rampant in some quarters of the Reagan administration that the United States should not share its science with anyone else, either its economic rivals or ideological and potential military adversaries. Some of the more reactionary even went so far as to suggest government censorship of all scientific publications, producing a shriek of outrage from the scientific community. But the intelligence agencies, particularly those in the Defense Department, are well known for seeing things differently than those who understand the value of free communication.

Whatever the ultimate reasons, the effect of this extreme behavior was a loss for the United States in world diplomacy. Many of the delegates in Belgrade were angry and contemptuous when speaking of the United States. This move was seen by many Europeans as being consistent with the mentality that was insisting on the deployment of Cruise and Pershing missiles in Western Europe. However, even if it is purely national interest which determines any country's foreign policy, the move to ignore an International Biotechnology Centre and to wish it to fail can be seen to be reactive and short sighted. The crisis mentality that fostered an escalating military debacle in

Vietnam (and which seems to be repeating itself in El Salvador and Lebanon) cannot understand any perspective except that of American power and, thus, will ultimately fail. Similarly, it cannot understand that increasing the economic independence of the developing nations will make them less prone to corruption and imperialism. That certainly would be in the national interest of the United States.

Although the support of the United States could still help to ensure the success of the International Centre, the oscillations of American politics (or for that matter, those of any other country) make it clear that no international institution should become dependent upon any one country for survival. Nor can it allow itself to become a political pawn of any country for any reason. That is why great care must be given to both the funding mechanism and the location, and no doubt why many were wary of locating the ICGEB in India.

The need for bringing the advantages of biotechnology to the developing countries is great. In the scheme of national defense budgets, a superb institution would require only a miniscule fraction of the funds now used for even one piece of sophisticated military hardware. Abdus Salam, Nobel laureate and Director of the International Centre for Theoretical Physics in Trieste, in his keynote address at the Belgrade meeting, drew the comparison with the $3.7 billion it costs for one nuclear submarine. The proposed budget for the International Centre was less than $50 million for five years, plus buildings and land, which are expected to be donated by the host country. While I view this sum as too low for the ambitious scope of the proposal (a biotechnology company of 500 employees requires an annual operating budget of more than $40 million), even a five year investment of $200 million is low next to the cost of most items in the United States' Defense budget.

There is, then, an acute need for the sound planning of mechanisms to bring biotechnology to the Third World. UNIDO launched a heroic effort, against tremendous odds. Wafa Kamel, the dedicated UNIDO staff officer in charge of the ICGEB project, performed a yeoman's task. Whatever the ultimate fate of the ICGEB, he deserves the kind of recognition given to brave soldiers who gallantly rush into a battlefield full of hidden mines, booby traps, and snipers. But heroism may not be enough. Looking back, the tactical errors made by UNIDO seem obvious, although perhaps the constraints of the United Nations procedures made them difficult to avoid. If at all possible, however, the major decisions of funding and location should never have been thrown open to a United Nations forum, where experience shows us that democracy often works against the best interests of the participants. The site, funding and the organization of the ICGEB should have been worked out in detail by UNIDO in private negotiations, and only *then* presented to prospective members for approval. Debate could have been confined to such matters as networks of affiliated centers, the selection of trainees, and so on, rather than leaving the important decisions to the unpredictable whims of international politics. In doing so, UNIDO lost control of the process and, therefore, greatly reduced its chances for success. Once it is recognized that any international proceeding involving national governments will be primarily a forum for the expression and furthering of each country's foreign policy, the difficulty and inappropriateness of trying to resolve any matter according to scientific and technical or even economic criteria can be appreciated.

This was a lesson taught rather poignantly in Madrid. In fact, the degenerating proceedings prompted many of the delegates and UNIDO consultants to begin talking privately about other mechanisms to establish initiatives in biotechnology for the benefit of developing countries. It was agreed that it was very important to avoid politics whenever possible. A number of independent efforts are currently being explored as a direct result of informal contacts made during the course of the UNIDO proceedings. Thus, even if the efforts to establish the International Centre for Genetic Engineering and Biotechnology ultimately fail, the process has had a strong stimulating effect on many countries at all levels of economic development and has clearly greatly elevated interest in the promise biotechnology holds for solving the problems of developing countries.

The next decade will witness many efforts to extend biotechnology to all corners of the world. Idealism, however, must be coupled with a keen sense of the real problems which now confront developing countries, whether economic, educational, political or ideological. Some countries are torn by war at present; many others are in the midst of severe economic crises. It would be too much to expect these endeavors to proceed smoothly and logically, governed by vision. Instead, biotechnology is likely to come slowly to the areas of the world which need it most, through trial, error, and muddling along, through the sustained efforts of dedicated men and women, but, in time, changing the way the world lives.

CHAPTER 3

The Fear and Trembling

Is Gene Splicing Hazardous to Your Health?

Among the controversial issues that arose as soon as it became feasible to put the genes of one kind of bacterium into a completely unrelated species, the question of "biohazards" became dominant almost immediately. The possibility of risks associated with recombinant DNA research must be distinguished here from other important questions having to do with the application of these new techniques, such as the ethics of human genetic intervention and the possible development of gene-spliced biological weapons. Although they are perhaps of much greater ultimate importance than the possibility of biological accidents, it was realized that these less tangible, value-dependent questions would not have to be faced for some years to come. However, if there were actually hazards associated with research activities, they were deemed to be much more imminent. So it was here that attention was focused.

Unexpectedly, the initial query about whether or not gene splicing carried a risk to the scientist, and perhaps to the general public, led to the most bitter controversy that the scientific community had witnessed in many decades. It was called the recombinant DNA *debate* by those who wished to cast it in respectable light. However, the controversy could be called a debate in only a very general sense. *Debate,* to me, has always meant something well ordered and ostensibly rational, where all parties strive to be well informed, logical, and, with luck, unemotional. But the highly contentious melodrama about the use of gene-splicing methods, at its peak during 1976–1978, was anything but that. Norton Zinder, a professor at Rockefeller University and an often-heard voice during the most intense years of the controversy, called it the "Recombinant DNA War." His was an apt appellation. But what was it really all about?

It began with the misgivings of some of the most able molecular biologists when they succeeded in joining unrelated DNA molecules and putting them back into living cells. It was the legitimate concern of responsible scientists, who asked whether or not gene-splicing experiments, even with microorganisms known to be relatively harmless to humans, might inadvertently produce a strain more virulent or infectious than the sum of its genetic parts. Also of concern was the accidental spreading of antibiotic resistance to known pathogens, already a public health problem because of the exchange of genetic information between species by natural processes. Further speculation led to the question of whether or not putting the genes of a tumor-producing animal virus into a common bacterium would produce infectious cancer.

At that time, in the early 1970s, the expression of such concerns was not the call to alarm. Rather, it was the calm voice of prudence asking that the matter of risk be further assessed before certain types of experiments were undertaken. Microbiologists have been working with lethal microbes for decades. Knowing the properties of a dangerous virus or bacterium enables the scientist to take precautions accordingly and thus to work in relative safety. One difficulty with the new biology was that even with extensive knowledge of molecular genetics at hand, most of it involving the human colon bacterium *Escherichia coli,* no one really knew for certain what the risks of recombining the genetic material of unrelated organisms might be. This was particularly true for so-called shotgun experiments, in which thousands of random recombinants might be created at once, or in which very little detailed genetic knowledge was available concerning the host organism. Most scientists, including those calling for initial caution, believed that the chances of a genetic accident were vanishingly small. However, when one suspects that the organisms one has constructed are quite harmless, but there remains a germ of doubt because the microbes never existed in nature in quite the same form, then it is difficult to know just how to proceed. No one wants to go to the excessive time, expense, and bother of heroic safety precautions unless they are warranted. Yet few would wish to take foolish chances either. As in most things, having to live with uncertainty is perplexing and unsettling, and most scientists wishing to splice genes would rather not have dealt with the issue at all. It was, nevertheless, a matter that had to be faced squarely.

Another very real difficulty was the fact that most of the scientists exploiting recombinant DNA techniques were biochemists and molecular biologists, not microbiologists, for whom the well-established procedures of sterile technique had become habit. Good microbiological technique, particularly the more stringent measures used by those doing animal cell culture, is necessary to keep one's cells from becoming contaminated. It is also necessary to prevent contaminants from growing in the laboratory and spreading their invisible spores about where they inevitably cause trouble. A by-product of such good practices is that not only is the worker's risk small, but all living material that is not needed in research is destroyed before leaving the laboratory and entering a public waste-disposal system. This kind of "containment" is very effective, even when known hazardous or infectious materials are being studied. The experienced microbiologists knew that even if something hazardous should arise inadvertently, the probability of spreading it to the general population would be exceedingly small, as long as good laboratory techniques were practiced.

However, many individuals with very little training in microbial methods wanted to become "cloners." Sloppiness in the laboratory about known hazardous materials has always been a matter of concern in every research institution, most of which have a professional safety officer to ensure that proper handling procedures are followed with respect to radioactive materials, toxic chemicals, and high-voltage electricity. Because it is known that even the most brilliant scientists can be deficient in plain common sense, the call for formalized safety precautions for handling genetic recombinant organisms was entirely reasonable, at least until better data on risk were available.

The speculations about possible biological hazards resulting from recombinant organisms are summarized here briefly. It should be mentioned that there has never been a single documented case of accident or injury resulting from a gene-spliced organism. Few people, whether scientists or laypeople, worry much about these anymore. The reasons have as much to do with sociology and psychology as they have with science, perhaps more. They are discussed below. But first, here are the imagined biohazards that generated the most concern.

The vast majority of research in molecular genetics has been carried out on strains of the common colon bacterium, *Escherichia coli* (after the German bacteriologists Escherich, who first described them), the viruses that infect it, and the bits of DNA (plasmids) that allow different strains to exchange genetic information. *E. coli* comes in thousands of species-specific versions in nature, not to mention the countless laboratory strains and substrains. It is a common denizen of the human colon but is pathogenic under only two conditions. The more common is when a colon strain acquires the genes (through the natural exchange of plasmids) for certain virulence factors. These are toxins that, at the worst, produce diarrhea and fever for a short time, but rarely cause serious disease. The second is infection of the blood stream, or septicemia. An infection of the blood by *E. coli,* or any other organism, is very serious, and a significant percentage of such cases are fatal. Nearly all such infections are acquired by hospital patients following surgery, although they can also result from traumatic physical injury.

Of course, because so much was already known about the genetics of *E. coli*, it was logical that most gene-splicing experiments would be carried out using this bacterium as a host organism, and with its plasmids and viruses serving as the ideal vectors into which the "new" genes would be spliced. But because of its intimate association with the human body, concerns were expressed that the presence of alien genes in *E. coli* might provide a direct route for the creation and transmission of new human diseases.

Even though it was argued that the laboratory strains lacked the colonization factors needed for survival in the human gut, even if they contained some other nasty genes, the argument could always be made that, in all experiments where the composition and the function of the genetic inserts were not well characterized, the unexpected could happen. After all, isn't science full of surprising discoveries? How can you be sure that a shotgun experiment, where *all* of the DNA of an organism is fragmented and cloned in different bacterial colonies, will not form, at some finite probability, a highly infectious version of *E. coli?* This outcome might be highly improbable, the argument went, but it only need to happen once. How can you assure me that it won't happen? The best educated scientific estimates could only argue probabilities. Even though such numbers were far better than the odds of surviving almost any human endeavor, it never could be logically argued that they were zero.

The speculation went further when it considered the cloning in *E. coli* of DNA from tumor viruses. If the naked viral DNA itself could be shown to be infectious and possibly tumor-producing, it was suggested that cancer might be rendered an infectious disease if bacteria containing these genes were to die in the colon and release their DNA.

And suppose that plain, ordinary human DNA were cloned in *E. coli* which then produced a plain, ordinary human protein. Could a "normal" gene—if expressed in the wrong place, outside the usual mechanisms for the control of gene expression—perhaps disrupt the regulation of some important biochemical pathway? Or could a new protein that resembled a particular human cell-surface antigen produce an unwanted immune response to a person's own cells?

Antiobotic resistance is already causing serious problems in certain human diseases, such as gonorrhea, which managed to acquire a plasmid a few years ago that carries the genes for penicillin resistance, thus negating the primary means of treatment. We are dependent on antibiotics for the treatment of a number of other serious diseases, such as beta-streptococcus infections ("strep" throat, leading to rheumatic fever) and pneumococcal pneumonia.

Thus, another concern was that recombinant DNA plasmids containing antibiotic resistance genes (which are, in fact, essential in certain selection procedures) would be transferred inadvertently, or added deliberately, to human or animal pathogens.

These, then, were the primary concerns raised by those scientists contemplating the world of gene splicing in the early 1970s and thinking in terms of (1) *E. coli* and (2) human infection. Of course, it doesn't take much imagination to think of many other types of potential biological hazards, especially with the inevitable extension of gene-splicing techniques not only to a vast array of other microorganisms but to plants and animals and even humans. But the focus of the discussion as it was opened originally was much narrower. So it was that minds were set to think, pro or con, within this limited arena. Although other possible biohazards were brought up from time to time, it was over *E. coli* and human infection that the major scientific battles of the Recombinant DNA War were fought and, in the view of most of the scientific community, won.

It turns out that there are many sound reasons to believe that *E. coli* is perhaps one of the safest organisms to use for the study of isolated genes or even to use as a vehicle for the mass production of proteins of pharmaceutical value. But before continuing the discussion of how the matter became a public controversy and how it subsided, I would like to lay out some of the other potential hazards of gene splicing, those that received little early discussion. For it is concern over some of these that lingers even now, years after the war has ended and the combatants have returned to their laboratories, offices, and homes. With *E. coli* now a well-accepted fact of gene-spliced life, discussions about these other possible hazards are proceeding quietly, the concern over biohazards having receded from the public eye to the point of invisibility.

There is the matter of the use of bacteria other than *E. coli*, fungi, and other microorganisms, as well as all higher plants and animals, as recipients for gene transplants. By the mid 1970s, DNA had been cloned in several strains of bacteria and, by 1983, in virtually every general class of organism. Moreover, is it not rather limited to view the universe of possible hazard as consisting entirely of the possibility of human disease or injury? The genetics are understood moderately well for only a few microorganisms other than *E. coli*, such as *Bacillus subtilis* and yeast; relatively little is known about most others, including the manner in which genetic information is exchanged. It is generally assumed that at least some example of all existing mechanisms by which DNA may be transferred from one organism to another in nature has been observed, even though one can expect that there are many variations on the same theme. This is an important assumption, for it is the unwanted transfer of certain laboratory-constructed genetic sequences to organisms other than the original host that one wishes to prevent.

Some have argued that microbes in general are rather promiscuous with respect to which organisms they give their DNA. Therefore, the argument goes, if any dangerous (that term is a tricky one) microbes can be made, they would have arisen naturally after millions of years of evolution. But would they? Presumably, evolution proceeds by small changes and selection for survival in particular environments. A man-made intervention can be of much larger dimensions. Although accidental advantages arising from random recombination may be highly unlikely, very carefully engineered genetic inserts are now being made to accomplish specific purposes, including survival in certain environments. It is here that one is more likely to find trouble. The early definitions of *dangerous* and *harmful* must be expanded to include things other than human injury.

Robert Sinsheimer, for many years a noted molecular biologist at the California Institute of Technology and now Chancellor of the University of California at Santa Cruz, argued that there was a natural barrier between most one-celled microbes (prokaryotes) and higher plants and animals—those containing chromosomes (eukaryotes). He was willing to admit that there was indeed much natural genetic exchange among bacteria (although this does not mean that all such exchanges are without consequence), but he argued that DNA did not normally cross this natural barrier. For this reason, he was concerned about man-made chimeras that violated this principle. That is, how can we really predict what will happen when we put human DNA in a bacterium or the DNA of *E. coli* into tomatoes?

Most other scientists couldn't quite see why he was so concerned. True, there is certainly not very much normal genetic exchange across such biological gulfs, but there are a few examples. The crown gall tumor in plants is produced by the injection of a bacterial plasmid into plant cells. In fact, modified versions of the crown gall plasmid are now being used as vehicles in which to transfer genes into plant cells. This is, of course, a highly evolved, specialized system, and not a general mechanism by which bacterial genes find their way into plant cells.

The mitochondria and chloroplasts of higher organisms are believed to have once been intracellular parasites, resulting in a fortuitous mutually advantageous existence that became refined into the ultimate in a symbiotic relationship. Mitochondria and chloroplasts contain their own DNA, which replicates independently of the DNA of the cell nucleus. Sequence analyses of these DNAs suggest that their relationship to some strains of microorganisms is much closer than that with the nuclear DNA of the cells in which they live.

Some have argued that genetic exchange has occurred since the beginning of life on earth, among all orders of life. This phenomenon is postulated as being an important mechanism in evolution—as well it could be, if the theory of the origin of mitochondria is correct. It is further argued that, whereas the examples mentioned above are the ones that worked out, the vast majority of such exchanges lead nowhere, or possibly add some unexpressed DNA that is carried along by a species for a few thousand years until gradual genetic changes perhaps give it a function.

Yet these arguments and the above examples beg the question of whether or not a deliberate mixing could ever have untoward consequences. Again, this is not an event that anyone believes would have a high probability in any individual case. In fact, it is argued that the further removed, in evolutionary terms, the source of DNA is from the recipient species, the less likely it is to be functional, and therefore, the safer it is. At our present level of knowledge, this argument is persuasive. However, it should not be forgotten that there is still a great deal that we do not know.

Ecological hazards arising from the deliberate construction of crop plants or "beneficial" soil microbes have been suggested but have received little discussion. That is, could a supervigorous strain of soybeans, or turnips, or broccoli spread with such vigor that it would soon choke out every other plant in sight? Triffids[1] may make entertaining reading, but really now! If the inventors of such varieties were to be truly commercially minded, the last thing they would allow is for their creations to reproduce. Otherwise, they couldn't sell a new seed supply to the farmers each year. That, after all, is why hybrid seeds have been so successful for the seed companies. They certainly wouldn't want the genetic engineers to come up with a strain of corn in which hybrid vigor bred true. But accidents do happen.

Soil microbes are another matter. The ecology of soil bacteria has not been studied extensively. Would developing a variety that fixed nitrogen with ease or that produced root-stimulating hormones get along well with the previous residents of the field? Possibly so, but one would hope that it wouldn't displace them and disrupt the important microbial balance that is crucial to the fertility of soils in supporting plant life. It is certainly a matter which needs to be determined before such organisms are generally dispersed into the environment.

One may allow one's imagination to go on forever, imagining all sorts of unfortunate things that might happen if genes are redesigned and reassembled to create organisms that are just a little bit different, as is the case with the usual recombinant-DNA chimera, in which 99+% of the DNA is still that of the host. This simple kind of mixture is just the beginning. As our knowledge increases, so will our ability to design new molecules—and functional sets of new molecules—to serve virtually any biological or biochemical purpose we would wish to see in a living entity. If we are to limit our imagination to the life we see around us, and to the methods available to us today, then we will continue to set ourselves up for one series of surprises after another, as we continue to fail to anticipate the consequences of our ingenuity. Just as we must be careful not to overstate our worries, so must we not allow ourselves to become complacent.

The correct conclusion that the risks of adding recombinant inserts to *E. coli* were overstated in the beginning[2] does not constitute proof of safety for all organisms and viruses containing spliced genes, especially if the added DNA has been designed in the laboratory for a function that never existed in nature. We can state that the methods used to date certainly do not pose a risk of injury significantly greater than that of other laboratory procedures, and that they are probably much safer than many. The absence of any proven injury would indicate that risks of the type imagined in the early days of the recombinant DNA controversy are very small. One cannot, of course, immediately extend this conclusion to future activities involving the manipulation of genes and cells, which may be completely different from anything carried out to date. The nature of the endeavor is changing so rapidly that it would be wise and prudent to maintain continuous scrutiny of activities involving fundamental changes in living organisms in order to improve our chances of anticipating any future problems.

Before closing this discussion, it is important to distinguish between two kinds of risk. The first is the everyday kind, to which we are all exposed in everything we do. There is a risk of injury or death in every human activity, and probabilities are calculated for everything from how much you shorten your life each time you smoke a cigarette, to the probability of getting cancer from exposure to dental X-rays, to the chance of getting squashed by a bus when you cross the street. But although everything in life carries some finite risk of personal demise, this type of risk is in sharp contrast to the risk of disaster. That is, there are certain things that are highly improbable but carry with them consequences of global dimensions. The possibility of the earth's being struck by a giant asteroid, or of another ice age, or of an uncontrollable, virulent infectious disease are examples of this type of risk. Our best modern illustration of the risk of holocaust is the specter of nuclear war.

The paramount question with regard to the possible hazards of gene splicing is whether or not any conceivable activity along these lines could possibly produce disaster. If it could not, but rather carries only some risk of injury to small numbers of people, or of minor ecological disruptions, then the matter of hazard is not qualitatively different from that surrounding any other human endeavor. If that is the case, then the entire matter of genetic and biological risks does not warrant special treatment apart from that ordinarily associated with known infectious organisms or with other types of agents or activities that are potentially harmful to human health or the environment.

Because the numbers can be so large in gene-splicing experiments, especially with microorganisms, even something of exceedingly low probability could take place at least once over a period of years. That, too, may be unimportant unless that one event could wreak disaster. Then even once is too much. As in playing the risk game with a nuclear arms race, *if* there is even a remote possibility of a cataclysmic disruption of human life, some aspect of global ecology, or the environment, then one cannot afford to gamble even with exceedingly low odds. But that is a very large *if*.

It is this kind of thinking that made the discussions of the risk of gene splicing qualitatively different from other kinds of risk discussions, with many of the critics drawing analogies to nuclear weapons. That is, the human health risks of radiation, toxic chemicals, or even cigarette smoking are essentially probabilistic. However severe and undesirable they may be, one is not talking about a single rare event that could kill entire populations or alter the climate or prevent a species from reproducing. The effects of hydrogen bombs have been demonstrated. So we regard them differently from plain, everyday risks.

But unlike the aftermath of a nuclear war, the possibility of a disaster scenario arising through a gene-splicing accident exists only in the minds of a few. Most of the arguments against stringent containment have been based on the conviction that a disaster of global dimensions arising through gene splicing is not only highly unlikely, but impossible. At the worst, there could be some minor tragedies, as there are all the time with all of our other technologies. But, many scientists would state confidently, global pandemics are pure fantasy. Most people are comfortable with this conclusion. That is, it is difficult to imagine how, at worst, some aberrant genetic monster could produce effects even remotely comparable to that of nuclear war. But what if one *tried* to create the ultimate biological weapon?

Perhaps we would do well to consult our books of fables. The boy who cried wolf when there was no wolf lost his credibility and hence was ignored when the real wolf came and ate the sheep. The fact that those who called for caution on gene splicing were not vindicated by genetic disaster from a slightly modified *E. coli* does not mean that the matter of risk is settled once and for all and that there is no further need for prudence. And then there was poor Chicken Little. She mistook an acorn for a piece of the sky and gathered her friends to rush to tell the king that the sky was falling. But they all met an unanticipated disaster. The fox preyed on their fears, and ultimately, they met a grim fate anyway. So those who call for caution must not go rushing to tell the king before they are sure of what they are sounding the alarm about.

Perhaps we all have a need for certainty in our lives, or the assurance of knowing the limits to our lives or the fates that could befall us. Here, however, we cannot allow ourselves that comfort. The knowledge we have gained about living cells in recent years has been vast, but it has also showed us how much more we have yet to learn. We will simply have to accept the fact that there are uncertainties in our lives with which we will have to contend for some time to come. One of those uncertainties is the absolute assurance that there can never be a biological disaster.

The Controversy

The growing outrage over the war in Vietnam, and what to many appeared to be the unconscionable and willful destruction of a country and its people by the U.S. government, had many consequences. By the late 1960s, the reactions to the war produced both increasing political awareness and the hippie phenomenon. A natural outcome of the more sensitive world view that emerged was a very much heightened concern over pollution and the state of the environment—and the untoward consequences of technology. Building on these widespread sentiments, a liberal Congress was able to enact in a relatively short period of time most of the enabling legislation that now forms the basis for many of the rules that, in principle, allow us to protect our environment from further destruction.

It was therefore appropriate and in harmony with the times that the scientists meeting at the Gordon Conference on Nucleic Acids in June of 1973 should take note of the rapid progress being made in DNA-splicing methods and address the question of whether or not biologically hazardous materials could be created by these methods—either deliberately or accidentally. In an open letter to Dr. Philip Handler, President of the National Academy of Sciences, and to Dr. John R. Hogness, President of the Institute of Medicine, published in the September 21 issue of *Science*,[3] Maxine Singer and Dieter Söll expressed the sentiments of the 150 or so scientists present. They asked that certain experiments with known pathogens or the genes coding for human toxins be deferred, calling for the academy to "establish a study committee to consider this problem and to recommend specific actions or guidelines, should that seem appropriate."

During the next year, the National Academy of Sciences did indeed appoint such a committee, chaired by Paul Berg of Stanford University, who had developed a general method of joining DNA molecules in the early 1970s (see Appendix). In July 1974, a letter from Berg was published in *Science*, setting forth the committee's recommendations.[4] It called for a voluntary deferral of experiments that (1) might introduce the genes for antibiotic resistance or bacterial toxin formation into strains that do not contain such genes or (2) might link the DNA from oncogenic (tumor inducing) or other animal viruses to bacterial plasmids or other viral DNAs. It was recommended that plans to link fragments of any animal DNAs to bacterial plasmid DNA or bacterial virus DNA be "carefully weighed."

The committee also recommended specific actions that ultimately led to the involvement of the federal government. It asked the Director of the National Institutes of Health (NIH) to establish an advisory committee to (1) oversee "an experimental program to evaluate the potential biological and ecological hazards of the above types of recombinant DNA molecules"; (2) develop procedures that would minimize the spread of such molecules within human and other populations; and (3) devise safety guidelines to be followed by investigators working with potentially hazardous recombinant DNA molecules.

The latter two requests became a reality. The NIH Recombinant DNA Molecule Program Advisory Committee, usually referred to as the RAC, was established to provide scientific advice "concerning a program for developing procedures which will minimize the spread of such molecules . . . and for devising guidelines to be followed by investigators working with potentially hazardous recombinants." The NIH sidestepped the recommendation to have the committee oversee a risk assessment program, although a few specific experiments were finally conducted at NIH to test the capacity of weakened *E. coli* strains to transfer tumor virus genes to an animal host.

The letter contained a final recommendation. It was for an international meeting in which scientists would review scientific progress and further discuss appropriate ways to deal with the potential biohazards of recombinant DNA molecules.

The proposed international conference was held at the Asilomar Conference Center in Pacific Grove, California, in February 1975, and was a truly historic event in the development of a safety policy concerning research in genetic manipulation. Sponsored by the National Academy of Sciences, with support from both NIH and the National Science Foundation, the meeting's 150 attendees included 52 foreign scientists, 16 journalists, and 4 lawyers.

This conference presented an opportunity to consider all of the pertinent information concerning the present and future uses of gene splicing. But rather than bringing up the global issues of how the techniques might be exploited in the future, the participants focused on what were the experimental details of transplanting DNA, whether any of these activities might pose a threat to health, and what safety measures should be invoked to prevent an accident. As discussed earlier, the focus was primarily on the possibility of human disease and was heavily skewed toward DNA cloning in *E. coli.*

From this conference emerged the concepts of physical and biological containment, which were to be matched with the presumed degree of potential hazard associated with a particular type of experiment (since there were no known or established risks). These "containment levels" were based somewhat on the U.S. Center for Disease Control's procedures for handling infectious microorganisms, and subsequently formed the basis for the safety procedures ultimately promulgated as the NIH Guidelines. The final report to the National Academy also contained recommended prohibitions on certain classes of experiments, but these differed somewhat from the original Berg letter's recommendations, particularly concerning the transfer of antibiotic resistance.

Thus, in early 1975, everything seemed to be proceeding rationally and calmly. Scientists had engaged in unprecedented action—calling for caution in conducting certain types of experiments in genetic manipulation in order to prevent accidents and human injury. At that time, this appeal for prudence was generally regarded as an appropriate, commendable action by the scientific community and certainly one that would not lead to undue restrictions on the freedom of inquiry of the scientist.

The scientists involved in the details of Asilomar, and later, in the proceedings of the NIH Recombinant DNA Advisory Committee, worried over the particulars of their tasks; most other scientists—even most molecular biologists—were very little concerned with these affairs, but those who followed what was going on, through the occasional reports in the pages of *Science,* seemed to be generally supportive. The calm that existed in most university research departments, even those where genes were being recombined in novel ways, was scarcely a forewarning of the furor and the near paranoia over the possibility of a federal law that would simply have extended the jurisdiction of the NIH Guidelines to private, or nonfederal, research.

During 1975, the RAC met several times to draft the NIH Guidelines. The Guidelines under development defined four levels of physical containment, that for the lowest risk experiments designated as P-1, which was little more than a description of good microbiological technique, and that for the potentially highly hazardous work labeled P-4, which was comparable to the most stringent containment procedures required at Fort Detrick during the days of germ warfare research. Three levels of biological containment were also defined, based on the strain of *Escherichia coli* (K-12) that was the vehicle for DNA cloning for most proposed recombinant DNA experiments. The lowest level, EK-1, simply referred to the usual laboratory variety in common use by microbial geneticists (actually there are hundreds of versions of *E. coli* K-12). EK-2, which existed only in concept at the time that it was included in the Guidelines, was a weakened version of an EK-1 strain, which was greatly impaired in its ability to carry out bacterial mating or to survive outside special laboratory conditions. The highest level was denoted as EK-3, which meant an EK-2 strain which had been experimentally verified as not being able to survive or to pass its DNA to other organisms.

Occasionally, the news of disagreements among RAC members would reach the pages of *Science*. The different drafts oscillated in the strictness of their safety procedures, reflecting comparatively wide differences in opinion among the drafters, not so much on the estimates of risk, which most agreed was very small, if essentially unknown, for most experiments, but on the degree of caution that the Guidelines should reflect as a matter of policy. Finally, late in 1975, a compromise draft was developed and submitted to the Director of NIH for approval.

Up to this point, few had paid much attention at all to the legal standing of the RAC or of the NIH Guidelines it was creating. Why indeed should they? What has the law to do with recombinant DNA? Far more than most realized at the time. This is a critically important point, and one that played a major role in dragging the recombinant DNA issue through the halls of the federal bureaucracy and into the chambers of the U.S. Congress. The chain of events and the reasoning behind them went something like this.

At the request of the National Academy of Sciences, the proposed advisory committee which was to become the RAC was housed in the National Institutes of Heath. But this choice was not made because NIH was seen as the overseer and regulator of science, and certainly not because a laboratory safety policy was expected to be developed only applicable to NIH scientists, but because it provided a logical place to handle the logistics and costs of holding meetings, publishing meeting notices, providing secretarial help, and so on. But now, as soon as one involves the federal government, there are legal implications, whether the Berg committee thought of them or not. An advisory committee located in a federal agency and paid for by the taxpayers is, therefore, a federal advisory committee and subject to the rules and procedures governing all federal advisory committees. Furthermore, it must be advisory to someone or something. In this case, the obvious choice was the Director of the National Institutes of Health, then Donald S. Fredrickson, who at that time had been in his new job scarcely six months. Therefore, the RAC's duty was to recommend policy to the Director of NIH. But it was the Director's responsibility to implement it, and also his prerogative to alter the recommendations made to him as he saw fit.

However, it is not the within the authority of NIH or its Director to set policy on any matter beyond the boundaries of NIH matters. Thus the RAC could presume to be setting a set of universal standards for the conduct of recombinant DNA research. But, in fact, the policy as promulgated by the Director would have to pertain directly to research conducted at or sponsored by NIH. Thus, ironically, what began as a process of scientific standard setting soon became something more.

When the idea of a set of safety guidelines was conceived of and endorsed by most scientists, they were regarded to be what the name implies—standards of good practice—which all scientists, whether publicly or privately supported, being rational men and women of good will, would respect and observe without any enforcement provisions, official bureaucratic rules, or, God forbid, federal regulations. In late 1975, then, it was up to Fredrickson to decide what to do with these guidelines, which were bound to make history no matter how they were handled.

But now these guidelines were about to become an official organ of NIH policy, applicable to its scientists and grantees—Guidelines with a captial G. As such, it is inconceivable that they would have simply been published without addressing the matter of how they would be implemented in NIH's research labs and in the numerous projects funded by NIH in universities. Thus, when the draft Guidelines were released for public comment in early 1976, they had a section on "Implementation," designed solely to ensure that any NIH grantee would observe them. This section was short and not particularly oppressive. It called for principal investigators to bear most of the responsibility for assessing the degree of risk of an experiment and where it belonged in the structure of the Guidelines. The institution was to certify that the facilities met the standards as defined in the Guidelines, and NIH study sections were to review the matter of potential biohazards and containment along with the scientific merit of a research proposal.

The important thing, however, was the mere existence of the implementation section, for as soon as NIH decided to make the Guidelines compulsory, even if only to its grantees, the door was opened for questions about how effectively the Guidelines would be enforced in practice. Immediately, this section was criticized for being too loosely defined, with no real checks by NIH or any other body on whether or not the Guidelines were actually being observed. Thus began a process whereby the implementation section grew into something much more elaborate and bureaucratic than it had been in the first edition of the draft Guidelines, eventually to be renamed "Roles and Responsibilities."

The implications of what appeared to be a simple procedural decision to conform the standard setting exercise to the rules of the federal government proved to be far more serious than anyone foresaw. NIH had established a precedent by stating, in effect, that the potential hazards of recombinant DNA experiments were perceived to be great enough to *require* the observance of specified safety procedures by NIH scientists and grantees. Some of the scientists protested this conclusion, claiming that they were only supposed to be guidelines, as the name implies, because the magnitude of possible hazard simply did not warrant enforced regulations. But NIH had made a decision. It then followed logically that if the hazard was serious enough to require NIH scientists to observe safety rules, it was serious enough to require *everyone* engaged in gene splicing to abide by the rules too. It was primarily this corollary that put Fredrickson, who generally opposed comprehensive regulations or legislation, in the awkward position of defending a double standard, and which eventually brought the matter of recombinant DNA before Congress.

Looking back, which is usually much easier than looking forward, one may conclude that in addressing the matter of implementation, even for NIH scientists and grantees, NIH committed a tactical error. Even though NIH cannot officially demand compliance with any of its rules beyond its own jurisdiction, the writing of the Guidelines was clearly a precedent-setting exercise. Perhaps if the section on implementation had been left out of the Guidelines entirely, they would have more properly fulfilled the purpose intended by the Berg committee, serving as a model for appropriate safety procedures to be followed in *any* laboratory. If so, how many people would have raised the question of enforcement? At least, if NIH had not assumed unilaterally that it was imperative that the Guidelines be *enforced* for its grantees, and that it bore the responsibility for implementing this concept, the question of the matter of enforcement would have remained open, and, no doubt, would have been addressed in subsequent forums. Whether or not enforcement of the Guidelines was appropriate at all, and, if so, to whom should they apply, are questions that could and should have been treated as issues separate from the nature of the standards themselves. NIH was the correct forum in which to address the scientific assessment of risk. But it should not have played the role of regulator when it had only limited authority to do so.

Dewitt "Hans" Stetten, the Deputy Director for Science at NIH in the late 1970s and the first Chairman of the RAC, often proclaimed that NIH is not and never was intended to be a regulatory agency. But the advice to Fredrickson from the more conservative, process oriented members of his staff was a bit different. The decision to require observance of the Guidelines for both grant supported and in-house NIH research seemed harmless enough and was, no doubt, viewed as playing it safe. But the implications of this choice could not have been fully appreciated at the time. For, as a direct result of the decision to establish an enforcement mechanism, however innocuous those procedures may have seemed at first, the course was set, from which there could be no turning back. It then became inevitable that NIH would soon become a regulator, in the finest traditions of any element of the federal regulatory bureaucracy.

As 1975 drew to a close, Fredrickson and his staff, draft Guidelines in hand, decided that this was a case where due process needed to be observed. If the Guidelines were to become an official government document, they would of course have to be published in the *Federal Register* for comment. But the growing public sensitivity of the recombinant DNA issue was anticipated. It would be important to allow everyone to have his say *before* a final decision was made, to avoid the repercussions of a sudden change in policy being sprung upon the unsuspecting as a total surprise. Certainly, to impose upon the community of scientists a rigid set of mandatory rules was precisely the kind of issue which required a slow, deliberate, and fair process. It was also anticipated that there might just be members of public interest groups or of the general public who did not understand what was being done, especially if it all happened too fast. Thus, a full airing of the proposed Guidelines before the public and the scientific community was considered an essential, perhaps preemptive, move in order to prevent later complaints and unneeded accusations. The "process" which seemed ideally suited to the purpose was the regularly scheduled meeting of the Director's public advisory committee in February 1976. This, then, was the vehicle that was used to propel recombinant DNA before the eyes of the public with a momentum which, at the time, was surely underestimated.

Special guests were invited to the meeting of the Director's Advisory Committee (DAC), to sit with the members on this unique and historic occasion, the official unveiling of the Guidelines for Research Involving Recombinant DNA Molecules. Of course, such meetings are always open to the public. Appropriate notices were published in the *Federal Register*. But because few people habitually scan the microscopic print announcing all of the proceedings of the executive branch of the federal government, special invitations were sent to all the public interest and environmental groups that the people at NIH could think of.

There was some common ground at this meeting, held in early February 1976. Almost everyone agreed that any risk of human injury from an organism containing foreign genes would necessitate the occurrence of one or more highly improbable events. There were differences of opinion among the members of the RAC with regard to how great these probabilities might be, but rather, great differences in the degree of precaution that was deemed necessary to prevent human risk. The divergence of opinion among the observers present at that historic meeting—invited scientists and concerned citizens—was greater still. And so the great debate began in earnest.

There was a growing undercurrent of concern and a measure of fear about what might happen if one puts genes together in previously unknown ways, especially among those who really didn't understand the science very well. However, the intense and contentious polarization that for the next three years was to characterize the discussions of the safety of the use of recombinant DNA methods in research was perhaps born at this meeting. Although a number of sporadic reports had appeared in the press, and the Boston Area Recombinant DNA Group and Science for the People had both taken rather critical positions with regard to the content of the Guidelines, as well as the procedures under which they had been prepared, this was the first time that *all* the interested parties had confronted one another face to face. This meeting added a dimension of reality to what had previously been only an abstraction, and immediately enlarged the discussion well beyond the bounds of the scientific community.

On this occasion, the breadth of disagreement among scientists over the safety of gene splicing became apparent. Dr. Robert Sinsheimer, one of America's leading molecular biologists and, at the time, chairman of the Department of Biology at the California Institute of Technology, was among those who had been invited to sit with the Director's Advisory Committee and comment on the guidelines. Dr. Sinsheimer's concerns about the consequences of splicing the genes from a mammal into a bacterium were discussed earlier. Because he feared the unpredictable outcome of such experiments, he wondered if such experiments should be done at all, or, if so, at least under the highest degree of containment. This was a direct challenge to the draft guidelines.

As a leading and respectable figure in the scientific community, Sin-

sheimer was at odds with most of his peers. The majority of molecular
biologists, including Paul Berg, who had been among the first to raise questions, had begun to feel, even back then, that what had started as a sincere and
appropriate call for due caution was somehow getting out of hand. Too many
people, especially from outside the scientific community, were getting interested. And now, here was an eminent authority who thought that even the
detailed safety measures prescribed by the RAC might be a bit naive and
would not really give the assurance of safety that they were intended to
achieve. Other eminent scientists testified at the same meeting that the Guidelines were much too strict and ponderous. A member of the RAC stated that
the Guidelines erred on the side of caution, to the degree that they did, partly
to respond to growing political pressure to reassure the public that scientists
were really good and responsible people.

However, Sinsheimer's early questioning did something besides unsettle
his peers. There were a number of individuals in attendance at that meeting
who were worried by the concept of making genetic chimeras, laypeople who
perhaps saw the scientific community in a very different way from the way in
which its members saw themselves. The scientist was and is both worshiped
and feared, in a sense, as a god of the future, a mysterious individual who
knows and understands secrets beyond the comprehension of most mere mortals, the genius who creates the unknown in a laboratory full of strange and
wonderful machines. Although this somewhat exaggerated, stereotyped image may smack of B science-fiction movies, it is not altogether so farfetched.
Some of the concerned citizens at that meeting listened while a parade of the
nation's most renowned scientists, although generally supporting the concept
of the Guidelines, argued that there was really nothing to worry about. This
was confusing. Why go to the trouble of drafting elaborate *mandatory* safety
procedures if there was really nothing to be concerned about? Thus, when
another renowned scientist came forward and disputed his colleagues' views,
the skeptics' worries were given credence. The unrest that they had felt about
this strange and powerful new technique was perhaps not groundless after all.
Sinsheimer's opinions reinforced their fears, even though they really didn't
understand all of his arguments.

At that historic meeting, there were other scientists who raised questions.
They were largely younger and not well known, so their views simply didn't
carry the weight of those of their more prominent colleagues. But there were
enough of them to add to the skeptics' skepticism. They raised many questions concerning the adequacy of the draft Guidelines and the need for universal safety measures, which did not have easy answers.

Thus, the conclusion of the meeting saw many scientists beginning to retreat to a reactive mode of self-protection, from what they saw as a bureaucratic overreaction to what was a new but scarcely a fearsome technique in molecular biology. It also saw the motley collection of dissidents joining forces to mobilize their opposition to what was perceived as an attempt to put one over on the public. From the beginning, the conflict-of-interest charge was made. How could the leading promoter of research in molecular biology involving recombinant DNA methods (NIH) also be its regulator? That question is still being raised. The *fear* of the scientist was given a boost by this open confrontation between scientist and critic, and charges of a conspiracy were even heard.

Many of the attendees had known one another for years, as professional colleagues, students, or teachers; many others had met for the first time, to begin a long association, either as friends and allies, as adversaries, or as neutral (?) observers. The latter group included the journalists and science writers representing the nation's leading newspapers and the widely read journals, *Science* and its British counterpart, *Nature*. It was primarily the relatively small group of people who participated in this historic meeting who were the principal figures in the public debate that was to ensue. These individuals came to know one another well; some subset of this group appeared often on the same platform. The positions that each one held on the issues generally became known to his colleagues, although these positions underwent change over time in all but the most stubborn.

In any event, a number of ideas surfaced for the first time at this meeting which were to be major elements in the discussions that followed. One which did not sit right with many was, of course, the legal inconsistency. The NIH rules were to be mandatory for NIH grantees. But it was clear that the opportunities for commercial exploitation were to be vast. What about the private sector? Recent experience with the pharmaceutical industry regarding compliance with the testing requirements of the Food and Drug Administration (FDA) led many to question whether or not a profit-making corporation could be trusted to observe the recommended safety procedures when these might slow research or add additional costs to the research and development of new drugs or biologicals.

One solution that arose for the first time, during a coffee break at that meeting, came from Peter Hutt, once the general counsel of the FDA and an active member of the Director's Advisory Committee. He believed that an obscure section of the U.S. Public Health Service Act (§361) contained enough authority to cover the promulgation of the Guidelines as a general requirement, rather than their being limited to NIH research activities. Thus, with the precedent set by NIH that the safety measures in the Guidelines were important enough to be a requirement for their grantees and employees, the search began for an appropriate legal authority to broaden the scope of coverage. It was also an obvious corollary that if the law were inadequate, then it needed to be changed in order to apply safety rules uniformly in such an important area.

This exercise in bringing before the public what had been an internal and primarily scientific issue clearly raised questions that were not only anticipated by the RAC, which was immersed in the specific details of containment for the expected uses of recombinant DNA techniques, but also surprised the NIH administrators who had decided to take this step in "due process." What had been designed to anticipate and soothe the possible fears of the public created instead new suspicions, and questions without answers. The regulation of research that was not under the NIH umbrella was only one of many. What about the willful application of these methods to biological warfare? Would the CIA and the Defense Department respect the Guidelines and the spirit of openness in which NIH conducted its business? What about the rest of the world? Could the United States set a precedent that would be followed uniformly? What of the ethics of tampering with nature? Were we on the threshhold of a Brave New World of genetically modified humans and clones of mindless slaves or storm troopers? Wasn't this revolution in science and technology taking place too fast for the public to find out what was happening and give its consent? Was science really about to cure cancer, arrest the aging process, and feed the starving people of the world? Should experiments to measure risk be done *before* research using gene-splicing techniques proliferated? Thus, a new issue in science had come to a historical branch point. This meeting had pointed out the road that was to be followed.

Fear

In reflecting on the glowing embers of what raged as perhaps the hottest controversy in modern science, it is clear that there was one predominant driving force: fear. Of course, the subject is complex, and the reasons and motives of the participants in this affair were many. But those whose voices rang with a strident persistence, who dogmatically proclaimed that the way was clear if only others would see the light and follow, shared in common the fear response so characteristic of all members of the animal kingdom when a threat is perceived.

But what was it that they were afraid of? Many things. Science. Monsters and plagues. The federal government. Local governments. Each other. Everyone, it seemed, represented a threat to someone's interests. Everyone, apparently, felt threatened by something or someone. How much of the collective fear was based on reality and how much on fantasy, false perceptions, or simply misinformation? Now, in the calmer days that have followed the storm, we can hope to understand what actually happened, although I expect the differences in opinion among the many witnesses and participants in the spectacle will persist for some time to come.

The scientists who raised the initial concerns and sent letters to *Science* and *Nature* were appealing to their colleagues for prudence and caution. As such, it was an entirely reasonable and appropriate action. But it was scarcely an appeal for either mandatory safety regulations (for the NIH Guidelines were ultimately to be administered as though they were bona fida regulations) or for a public debate. *Especially* a public debate. Some had begun to feel uneasy about the degree of intricacy in the developing guidelines, but it was still an exercise that seemed well within the domain of the scientific community and hardly a cause for alarm.

But the Director's Advisory Committee meeting in February 1976 immediately broadened the scope of the process to encompass far more than participating scientists and the NIH bureaucracy. The Singer/Söll letter had set in motion a stochastic process, a chain of events that was leading the initial act of responsibility and conscience in directions which had not been foreseen. Could the course of the recombinant DNA affair have been predicted in advance? Did it depend on chance occurrences here and there? Or did it unfold according to the rules of human behavior? These are terribly important questions to answer if we are to explain why history took the course that it did.

There were certain critical points, such as the decision to make the NIH Guidelines mandatory for NIH personnel and grantees, that determined which among the available paths would be followed. Other events seemed to be obediently following the course that one or another natural law would predict. It is a fact, however, that no one to my knowledge foresaw in 1973, or even much later, that what had begun as a simple act of good judgment would lead to years of bitter contention both within the scientific community and outside it.

Although I have identified the NIH Director's Advisory Committee meeting as the point at which the major enlargement of the discussions of the safety of gene splicing took place, and at which a hardening of the already-contentious nature of the debate occurred, some of the seeds that were later to grow out of control had already been sown by that time. Several journalists were present at Asilomar; accounts of that conference appeared in the major newspapers. Senator Edward Kennedy, then the Chairman of the Senate Subcommittee on Health and Scientific Research, thought the subject deserved to be looked into, and held a hearing on genetic manipulation in April 1975. Although congressional intervention was not directly threatened at that time, some feared that it would eventually happen, and that the initiative would come from Kennedy. A few observers believe that even this level of public exposure seriously perturbed what was intended to be a purely objective exercise among the members of the Recombinant Advisory Committee in estimating the risks of using recombinant DNA methods; the RAC members found themselves thinking more and more in terms of politics and appearances, rather than science, at least according to one member of the RAC.[5] And as soon as the subject began to be discussed outside of NIH, it was predictable that more and more people would become interested in the proceedings. A number of concerned citizens showed up at the February 1976 Director's Advisory Committee meeting at the NIH.

The rancor that was to characterize much of the controversy over gene splicing during the next several years was openly displayed at that meeting. Many critics focused on the process and the proceedings of the RAC. There were suggestions that it represented a conspiracy of self-serving scientists who wanted to gloss over the dangerous nature of gene splicing just so that they could get on with their research unimpeded. There were other charges that the RAC was caving in to unreasonable demands from the ignorant and the worrisome, in posing an unreasonable burden on scientific research to guard against undemonstrated and farfetched imaginary hazards. Thus, everyone, it seems, regardless of his position, was demanding that the process be made more objective.

Personal bias is an interesting human quality. Highly opinionated people, such as most of those who came forward to comment on recombinant DNA in the early days, have great difficulty in seeing, or at least admitting, that they are not completely objective. And when individuals are asked to recommend objective candidates for service in such important bodies as the RAC or the NIH Director's Advisory Committee, they generally suggest people whose views are in accordance with their own.

I would view as hopeless any attempt to achieve true objectivity in any controversial proceeding, unless a tested method exists to allow one to make purely rational judgments of fact. This is a lesson that we should surely have learned by now. It is particularly painful to see the rationalization of bias masquerading as objectivity, as one often sees in attempts to assess the hazards associated with an environmental carcinogen, supply-side economics, or the risks associated with novel genetic combinations.

Just as it seems to be a cultural trait of Western civilization to be unable to tolerate a tie in a sporting event, uncertainty in other matters seems to sit equally uncomfortably. Thus, although the actual risks due to most known hazardous agents simply cannot be determined with accuracy, Congressmen and public-interest advocates alike continue to call on the scientific community to squeeze blood out of turnips. And so it has been with the potential hazards of gene splicing. Because it is hard for a scientist to admit, ''I don't know,'' he usually feels compelled to put forth an opinion. In the absence of sufficient facts, what can that opinion be based on? The only realistic approach, after the best educated guesses have been made regarding risk, is to accept uncertainty and learn to live with it. Once this necessity is recognized, then problems of control and a correct safety policy are far easier to deal with.

The conclusion seems obvious that those on all sides of the question, although calling for an objective process in assessing the risks of genetic manipulation and for appropriate safety measures, were really concerned because their personal views might not be taken into account by the RAC. To broaden any controversial discussion, as many on all sides of the question demanded for the recombinant DNA issue, either by finding committee members with a wider divergence of viewpoint, or by bringing the matter to additional forums, is to make it more adversarial in nature. And, certainly, this is never the way to increase the level of objectivity.

There are many opinions about what constitutes the most effective process. The American system of representative democracy, as well as our courts, are essentially adversarial systems. The criteria for selecting juries, committee members, or public representatives in every decision-making process have been constant subjects of discussion and debate, So it is no wonder that the decision making process became an issue with regard to recombinant DNA policy. In short, *who* decides?

As it became clear that most were more interested in seeing their own opinions enshrined in official policy than they were in listening to anyone else's arguments, emotions began to rise, and as in the escalation that precedes most real wars, the failure to convince only led to perceptions of threat. The NIH Director's Advisory Committee witnessed the deadly serious intonation of many voices, and the curled lips of contempt. Because a number of scientists, some of them quite prominent, had sided with those urging extreme caution, the concerned but untrained lay critics felt a measure of vindication for their worries and a reinforcement of their perception that they were up against a conspiracy of hubris and arrogance, endemic in most of the scientific community. Hand in hand with mistrust and the polarization of the discussions came the fear. When that rather fundamental property of human emotion becomes dominant in any kind of controversy, then constructive, rational proceedings become impossible. At best, one can hope to muddle through without leaving too much carnage and lingering bitterness.

These, then, were the beginnings. The RAC and the NIH continued, more or less, in the planned direction, making a few rather minor changes in the Guidelines prior to their becoming official government policy on June 23, 1976.[6] Many of those concerned combined forces and began to plan further action. The major public-interest groups got involved, having found a new and exciting cause to champion. Some university communities called meetings of citizens and concerned faculty. Senators Kennedy and Javits wrote to President Ford asking him to find a way to extend enforcement of the Guidelines beyond NIH. The number of articles and commentaries increased. Molecular biologists who had initially believed that calling for prudence was the right thing to do began to regret their actions.

One occurrence deserves special mention. Of the several communities that chose to look into gene splicing on their own, the most prominent and most contentious event was in Cambridge, Massachusetts.[7] The colorful mayor of Cambridge, Alfred Vellucci, and his ally and adviser, Harvard Professor George Wald, were concerned about Harvard's planned recombinant DNA experiments. Wald, who had been awarded a Nobel Prize for his pioneering work in vision, became the charismatic guru of the young innocents in need of a cause and a leader. He played the part well, with long flowing gray hair, a turtleneck shirt, and a medallion on a chain (his Nobel Prize?) around his neck. His wife, Ruth Hubbard, also a Harvard scientist, joined him. Boston was also the home of most of the other, younger scientist-critics, acting through the Boston Area Recombinant DNA Group, not to mention the more radical Science for the People.

The Cambridge hearings received national attention. The Cambridge Experimentation Review Board was a committee of citizens appointed to review the entire matter and to recommend policy to the city fathers. After heated testimony about whether genetically modified microorganisms would escape from Harvard laboratories and cause plague and pestilence in the city of Cambridge and throughout the countryside, the review panel determined that it was not qualified to resolve such a complex scientific matter, especially when there had been sharp disagreement among the parade of scientists whom they had heard. Instead, the panel concluded that the NIH Guidelines were probably the best attempt to assess risks and to construct appropriate safety measures that we were going to get. The Board endorsed the Guidelines but did add a few provisions of its own, requiring that certain experiments be done under stricter containment than the Guidelines specified, establishing a city biohazards committee and requiring workers to be monitored for organisms that might contain added genes from laboratory experiments. This last provision was a good example of how well-intentioned laymen can make policy that makes no sense at all. That is, how would a microbiologist ever tell whether or not a fecal sample contained recombinant genes? One would expect to find very many colonies of bacteria. But only if the spliced DNA contained a specific antibiotic resistance marker not usually found in nature could anyone tell if it came from someone's experiment.

The Cambridge affair was significant for two reasons. First, it showed that a citizens' proceeding on such a controversial subject could work, without wreaking the mindless disaster and overregulation which many scientists feared if the safety rules for science were not made by knowledgeable scientists. If Mayor Vellucci had had his way, gene-splicing work would have been banned in Cambridge. But the process, even at this local level, was able to prevent the extreme views from prevailing. On the other hand, many scientists believed that if the issue had stayed out of the hands of the public, which did not and could not really understand the complexities of the science and the factors that might really produce hazard, then those extraneous provisions— viewed as needless, burdensome, and expensive—would not have been added on top of the Guidelines.

The imposition of local requirements, then, led to the second major consequence of the Cambridge affair, which was to raise a question that finally become even more contentious than the matter of safety itself: Should there be a uniform federal standard for gene splicing, or should state and local governments have the right to enact their own, perhaps stricter, rules, as they saw fit? The NIH Guidelines did not, of course, have the force of law and had no binding authority outside NIH. Harvard was to spend a small fortune lobbying for a federal law that would extend the Guidelines as uniform federal standards, preempting any local ordinances.

The proceedings in Cambridge must be considered a singular event which helped to determine the future direction of the policy debate that was shaping up. But perhaps the most significant single event in escalating the controversy was an article by Liebe Cavalieri appearing in the *New York Times Magazine* on Sunday, August 22, 1976, entitled "New Strains of Life—or Death."[8] It represented an extraordinary fear reaction to the imagined horrors that were to occur if this new method in molecular genetics were permitted to be used. Many of the nonscientist activists who were working for very stringent controls believed that they had found another champion from within the scientific community. Everything he said, which was far stronger than anything that their other scientific allies had said to date, only strengthened the fears already residing in the pits of their stomachs. Friends of the Earth had the article reprinted and circulated to all of their members as part of their regular publication, *Not Man Apart*.

Cavalieri presented a number of hair-raising scenarios, mixing demonstrated fact with wild speculation and fantasy in a completely indistinguishable manner. The following excerpt is typical:

> Consider, for example, the fact that DNA from cancer viruses has already been introduced into a weakened form of *E. coli* (the ability of this form to survive in the human intestine is disputed at present). Suppose a laboratory technician accidentially pours a culture of these bacteria into a sink—not an unlikely occurrence. In the trap of the sink, or farther on in the sewage system, malignant properties are transferred from the laboratory bacteria to normal *E. coli*. The sewage, with the bacteria containing cancer genes, is eventually discharged into the sea near a shellfish bed. People in distant places eat the shellfish and the bacteria take up residence in their intestines and are spread from person to person. In the individual the bacteria can transfer recombinant DNA containing cancer genes to human cells. The result—cancer, normally not infectious, is spread in epidemic proportions by normally harmless bacteria.

Would this passage scare *you?* No? What can you find that is wrong with it? It reminds me of the pictures in the children's activity books with the caption "What's wrong with this picture?" You are then supposed to look carefully and observe that the clock has only one hand, the chair is missing a leg, and the poor bloke has his shoes on backwards, among other things. As I think of it, an excerpt like the one above would make a good examination question for a graduate student in molecular biology: "What's wrong with this paragraph?"

But such an article cannot be readily evaluated by the nonscientist reader. If it reinforces one's preconceived notions, it will probably be believed. If it does not, it won't. If the reader doesn't have preformed biases on the subject or simply doesn't know about it, then the decision about whether to believe it must be based on something else. Then, it makes a difference who wrote it. Chances are, the reader will never have heard of the author, even if he has a Nobel Prize. But if it's a scientific article, "Ph.D." or "M.D." helps, as does the author's professional affiliation. Sloan-Kettering Institute for Cancer Research and Professor of Biochemistry at Cornell University Graduate School of Medical Sciences was Cavalieri's—not bad. But the greatest determinant of all regarding the believability of an article is probably *where* it appears. If it is published in a prestigious journal, or one with a reputation for honesty and integrity and quality, then you will probably take it seriously.

As everyone knows, the *New York Times* enjoys a sound reputation. Only the news that's fit to print. Also, its readers include a great many members of Congress, business leaders, and educators. If the article had appeared in the *National Enquirer*, it would have gone unnoticed and certainly would not have been believed by the great bulk of educated Americans, most of whom had scarcely heard of DNA, let alone anything to do with gene splicing. That's right; it was still an esoteric issue in August 1976. It never did really become a public issue, in the sense of taxes, inflation, unemployment, who would win the Super Bowl, or, more to the point, Three Mile Island. Of course, the *National Enquirer* has millions of readers who perhaps believe the spate of nonsense that embellishes every issue. Or perhaps they just enjoy it. But then, predictions of doom are commonplace in the *National Enquirer*, and its regular readers are inured to them. But if something appears in the good old reliable *New York Times*, the policymakers who read it are apt to take it very seriously. In this instance, many of them did.

The article was immediately condemned by many scientists. It contained numerous errors of fact, and in many places, Cavalieri described his fantasies, like the one quoted above, as likely possibilities. But the distinction was not made by the *Times* readers in Congress. Senator Kennedy was worried and scheduled another hearing, this time for September.

This incident clearly illustrates the power of the media. Cavalieri's fears were instantly transmitted to numerous others, including many in responsible positions in government. The editorial and review policy of the *New York Times Magazine* was roundly criticized for publishing such an article. In fact the *Magazine* has a completely different editorial staff from that of the news part of *The Times*, so it did not necessarily follow that the high-quality science writing that we had come to take for granted in *The Times* would also apply to its Sunday *Magazine* section. And besides, how were the editors to judge the accuracy of the article? *The New York Times* is not a refereed journal.

Senator Kennedy's hearing was held on September 22.[9] Fredrickson came and defended the NIH Guidelines. Scientists came to discuss the risks. Nobel laureate David Baltimore quietly but firmly tried to convince Kennedy that the risks, if they were real at all, were not likely to be greater than those from the host organisms into which the recombinant DNA was added. But other scientists weren't so sure it was that simple.

The hearing showed that already the "establishment" participants were getting weary of defending the safety of a technique—and the wisdom of the NIH Guidelines. Already, because of articles like Cavalieri's and the hard questions from political pros like Kennedy, the tone of testimony was becoming increasingly defensive. And the questions over procedure would not go away. There was a need to be able to enforce the Guidelines in private industry if indeed the risks demanded that they be inforced for NIH scientists, as Kennedy was quick to observe. NIH, in taking the action it had, *had* created a double standard, and NIH, as Dewitt Stetten proclaimed continually during his tenure as the chairman of the RAC, was not a regulatory agency.

Having received no reply to his letter to Ford after three months, there were rumors that Senator Kennedy might introduce legislation to regulate recombinant DNA research. That prospect sent shivers down the spines of some. Kennedy was not known as a legislative genius. His regulatory proposals in the past had tended to be ponderous, excessively bureaucratic, and unrealistic. He especially liked the concept of presidential commissions, but he seemed to want to give them powers that were probably not legal under the Constitution. And he usually associated himself with popular, rather than establishment, causes. In this case, the scientists who wished to pursue research relatively unhindered were definitely the establishment.

The fears of those who were worried about legislation were shared by Donald Fredrickson. The Director's Office at NIH was also sensitive to the jurisdictional problem that had been created by the promulgation of the Guidelines. Of course, Fredrickson was always consistent in his assertion that he *hoped* that all recombinant DNA research, whether public or private, would be conducted according to the Guidelines. The Cambridge episode had also been disconcerting. There were fears that what had happened there would serve as an example to other communities, and that the result would be a "patchwork quilt" of disparate local regulations. Kennedy's hearing finally prompted a response from the White House, which recommended that the subject be studied by an interagency committee, that would include all federal agencies with any interest in the subject. Fredrickson chaired the Federal Interagency Committee on Recombinant DNA Research. It was to consider the inconsistencies that arose when NIH took the lead and recommend a solution. Most assumed, correctly, that it would propose legislation which would extend the Guidelines to everyone and override local ordinances like the one in Cambridge. If Fredrickson's committee could act quickly enough, it would take the lead in setting policy and would provide an alternative to anything that might be proposed by Senator Kennedy or his colleagues.

With Fredrickson in control of the Interagency Committee it was possible to influence it along the lines on NIH's already established policy. If anything, the other agencies had little appetite for jumping into the recombinant DNA issue. They had enough problems of their own, especially with a new administration taking over. On the other hand, what could be better for NIH than to have an administration-wide consensus on policy? In addition, it would be embarrassing for the NIH if the other agencies that supported research, such as the National Science Foundation and the Department of Agriculture, did not voluntarily adopt the Guidelines as rules for their own grantees. With an interagency committee in place, these agencies would be forced to deal with the question.

Anyone who has ever worked within the federal bureaucracy—or any other, for that matter—knows that nothing ever gets done very efficiently. The more interests that are represented on a committee, the harder it is to accomplish anything, especially if those interests are federal agencies and departments. The Interagency Recombinant DNA Committee, in fact, performed in record time for a federal committee. But it was still no match for Congress, where bills are written and introduced overnight—literally. By the time it had reviewed the existing statutes and determined that none really provided adequate authority to extend the Guidelines uniformly, had drafted a bill, and had it cleared by the White House, the new Ninety-Fifth Congress had been busy reviewing recombinant DNA legislation for months.

The U.S. Congress Meets Recombinant DNA

As 1976 drew to a close, the Federal Interagency Committee on Recombinant DNA Research was hard at work, watching Capitol Hill constantly for signs of activity. But the politically astute Kennedy was still not sure what he was going to do. The first legislative activity came, in fact, not from Kennedy but from one of his colleagues, Dale Bumpers of Arkansas. In the past summer, Bumpers had read Cavalieri's article in *The New York Times* and had been alarmed. He concluded that the Congress must act now to protect the public from possible disaster.

That fall, his staff reviewed possible legislative alternatives, and Bumpers tried to interest Ted Kennedy in cosponsoring a bill. After a long silence, Kennedy sent a curt reply to Bumpers, saying that he wasn't interested in a legislative venture at that time. Bumpers was said to be a trifle miffed and decided to go it alone.

After the hoopla over the inauguration of a new president had subsided, the action began. Richard Ottinger, a liberal Congressman from New York and a trustee of the Environmental Defense Fund, introduced a resolution[10] that began, "Whereas unregulated research involving recombinant DNA is potentially devastating to the health and safety of the American people, . . ."

The Bumpers Bill[11] was introduced on February 4, 1977, in the Senate.

Three days later, Ottinger introduced the same bill in the House of Representatives.[12] This bill wasn't as horrible as some anticipated. Nor was it particularly competently drafted from a legal point of view, for it left many loose ends. It called for the Secretary of Health, Education, and Welfare to promulgate safety guidelines for recombinant DNA research (presumably, the NIH Guidelines), but it contained a worrisome clause: It specified that anyone conducting such research would be held "strictly liable without regard to fault" for any injury resulting from the conduct of recombinant DNA experiments. In the law of torts, this means that the mere fact that such research is being conducted would be sufficient cause for one to be held liable. Negligence would not have to be shown, as is normally required in order to collect damages from someone as a result of injury. As the molecular biologists slowly began to realize what was happening and read the proposed legislation, the reaction was not calm, for the strict liability clause implied that spliced genes were intrinsically dangerous, an implication that ran counter to everything most of the scientific community was contending. The bill also allowed local governments to enact stricter rules than those specified by federal law. This also was cause for deep concern.

There was still only silence from Kennedy. But Senator Howard Metzenbaum of Ohio introduced a bill,[13] another amateurish attempt to extend the NIH Guidelines (by name, this time). This bill also created a study commission to examine gene splicing in some depth. Congressman Steven Solarz of New York introduced legislation proposing another study commission.[14]

In early March, the National Academy of Sciences scheduled a three-day forum in Washington to discuss all aspects of recombinant DNA research. In view of the accelerating pace of activity, Paul Rogers of Florida, Chairman of the House Subcommittee on Health and the Environment, decided that he could wait no longer. He chaired the committee that had jurisdiction over all biomedical research matters in the House. It was, after all, the chairman's responsibility to be the leader for any important health-related regulatory legislation emerging from the House. Dick Ottinger was a member of this subcommittee, but none of the bills introduced thus far were particularly well done. Rogers scheduled three days of hearings a week hence and ordered his staff to have a bill ready the next day.

The National Academy Forum, held March 7–9, 1977,[15] was timely but, again, managed only to enlarge the debate and to generate more press coverage. Criticisms of gene splicing from participants and attendees alike were harsh; the battle lines were drawn along the old issues and several new ones were brought up. A few contended that, for certain moral reasons, genes shouldn't be spliced at all. Some scientists felt that it was necessary to go beyond justifying science for science's sake and to defend genetic manipulation on the basis of the promised benefits to mankind that would soon ensue. A demonstration by the People's Business Commission, an organization espousing its own ideology, which resembles a curious recombinant between Marxism and the Moral Majority, disrupted the meeting for a time amid chants of "We shall not be cloned."

The National Academy Forum did not settle any of the controversial issues, for by that time, neither the participants nor the observers were approaching the issues with particularly open minds. The general emotional level displayed and the intransigence of a relatively large fraction of those present suggested that we were in for a rather long and wearying confrontation.

The Rogers bill[16] emerged, containing a number of experimental provisions, such as licensing of projects and federally supported high-containment research centers. Part of the legislative process often not appreciated by anyone not on Capitol Hill is the fact that, in the early stages of prospective legislation, bills are introduced initially as discussion vehicles, serving as a basis on which to hold a hearing to air all of the policy alternatives (the Rogers recombinant DNA bill was such a draft). From the hearing record, plus the subsequent subcommitte debates, a committee bill is drafted reflecting the consensus of the subcommittee with jurisdiction over the issue. But this fundamental process was apparently not understood at this time, either by the scientific community or by the Carter administration and its minions at HEW and NIH.

The long-awaited administration bill[17] was slow in coming. Around the end of March, it had finally slogged its way through "channels" and was sent to Congress, but with an unexpected twist. It was bad enough for Fredrickson and the Interagency Committee to have lost the initiative. However, from Jimmy Carter's White House had come the ultimate irony. The preemptive legislative strike that the Fredrickson committee was planning included a provision that the federal standards (the NIH Guidelines) would override any state and local rules. This was something that Fredrickson personally believed to be an essential provision of legislation, and considered to be a large part of the justification for a law in the first place. But the new Carter Administration had courted the environmental and public interest community. A number of individuals from such organizations were appointed to high positions within the administration. One happened to be a young lawyer on the domestic council who was given the Interagency Committee's draft DNA bill to review. True to his populist commitments, he reversed the provision on federal preemption of state and local laws. When the officially approved administration bill was finally sent to Congress, it overrode local laws unless they were "no less stringent" than the federal bill.

Both Rogers and Kennedy, the chairmen of the House and Senate subcommittees that had jurisdiction over such matters, introduced the administration bill as a courtesy. That was last that was to be heard of it. Its disappearance again underscores the impotence of the administration in influencing federal legislation. If there is a matter of overwhelming immediate importance, then the White House *can* generate legislation that has an effect, but it must act with the full cooperation of and constant consultation with congressional leaders. If there is disagreement between the president and Congress, then the president must lobby personally for his bill, if he hopes it ever to become law. This was a lesson that Jimmy Carter never really learned. His proposed legislative packages on all sorts of issues, representing thousands of hours of work by dedicated bureaucrats, were sent to Congress and never followed up. Given the ways of Washington, it is not surprising that nothing ever came of these proposals. In the case of recombinant DNA, it is unlikely that Jimmy Carter (or Ronald Reagan, for that matter) ever knew or particularly cared what it was all about. It was never a major or even a significant political issue. No one's reelection ever depended on recombinant DNA.

Thus, only those who cared, like Donald Fredrickson, followed the issue and tried to influence the outcome. But Fredrickson was expected to endorse the "administration position." Thus when he testified at Rogers's legislative hearings, he could officially endorse only the White House position. Only in private conversations with members of Congress could he express his real convictions, and this he did, running the risk of being reprimanded by his superiors within the administration for acting independently. Both Kennedy and Rogers knew the NIH position, but that was only one parochial view among the many that were being brought to bear on federal recombinant DNA legislation.

Kennedy's solution to the recombinant DNA problem finally emerged, using the same bill number as the administration bill but with the entire text crossed out and Kennedy's own version written in. It was patterned after the Atomic Energy Act of 1947, except that everywhere that the original act said *atomic energy*, the words *recombinant DNA* were substituted. It created an omnipotent regulatory commission to oversee, control, and regulate all recombinant DNA activities in the United States. It was clear that the safety standards to be promulgated were intended to reflect the NIH Guidelines, but the administrative apparatus proposed sent a shudder throughout the scientific community. The result was an immediate fear-of-Congress reaction, which greatly intensified interest in legislation among scientists, as well as lobbying efforts to kill *any* bills that focused on recombinant DNA and imposed the law of the land on research laboratories.

In the months that followed, the legislative process ground forward in both the House and the Senate. The Congress, then, had become the focus of the controversy, for it was here that a universal policy, if any were to be forthcoming, would be formulated. The lobbying was intense, by concerned individuals, by the scientific professional organizations, and by the public-interest groups. In general, the scientists who had been alerted, who had no experience in the ways of legislation nor even any understanding of what a bill was intended to do, were fighting almost desperately against what they perceived as bureaucratic oppression. But their Washington-based organizations, such as the American Association of Microbiology and the Federation of Societies for Experimental Biology, knew better. There were some good reasons for a federal law. And it was nonsense to believe that the majority of Congress really wanted to suppress and oppress scientific research and the freedom of inquiry, as some of the more paranoid complained. One cannot leave anything to chance, however.

The focus of the organized scientific lobbying efforts was the Kennedy bill. These efforts did manage to convince most of the Senate that the Kennedy proposal was an extreme overreaction to the degree of risk actually posed by spliced genes. Although Kennedy controlled his subcommittee (Health and Scientific Research), there was virtually no support for his proposal in the rest of the Senate. In addition, Kennedy insisted on legislation that permitted local laws to prevail over federal standards. It was, in fact, the fear of oppressive local ordinances that prompted many scientific groups to believe in the necessity of federal legislation and to endorse the more moderate legislation that was emerging from the House.

The synthesis that occurred through a series of committee debates and votes (markups) in the House resulted in a proposal designed to extend the NIH Guidelines uniformly and to prevent communities from enacting stricter rules unless they could prove that these were really warranted on the basis of hazard. Only a few scientists had complained that the Guidelines themselves were burdensome; most were already subject to them anyway because of the nearly universal support of research by NIH. A law extending them to privately supported research wouldn't have been noticed, except that in a few communities, such as Cambridge, Massachusetts, there would have been relief from the imposition of additional rules. Still, perhaps because of the ominous legalese that appears in most regulatory bills ("penalty, fine, inspection, imminent hazard"), the prospect of a law was feared. There was also concern of enshrining the somewhat fluid Guidelines as a stone monument to bureaucratic regulation that would be difficult to modify, even if and when it became clear that the standards therein were too strict and needed to be relaxed.

By the end of the summer of 1977, the Kennedy bill was all but finished. A conference held to evaluate the risks of recombinant DNA propagated in *E. coli*[2] concluded that such manipulations were really quite safe. Although these conclusions could not really be extended to the use of other vehicles for spliced genes, they provided ammunition for scientists to argue that the guidelines were unnecessarily strict and that a law would be going too far: What ever happened to the notion that they were supposed to be only guidelines anyway? The action by NIH to make them a requirement for grantees had led far beyond what was anticipated.

In the House, the legislation was undergoing its own unique history.[18] The casual reader of federal statutes may wonder why any law is constructed in such an illogical way, but it must be kept in mind that any bill which proceeds down every step of the legislative process undergoes an evolution which can take it in several possible directions. As in the evolution of an organism, the result is not likely to be the same as if some great, wise, omnipotent one had designed it as the optimum solution to a problem. Generally, the longer a bill is debated and considered by Congress, the more embellished and grotesque it becomes, until, in some cases, its original purpose is lost. Like a dinosaur overspecialized for a specific ecological niche, it loses its flexibility and adaptability, becoming a ponderous version of what it once was. Usually, such bills are beyond redemption. Although they may contain everyone's pet provisions, they are no longer workable legislative solutions and are best forgotten.

Unfortunately, the House recombinant DNA bill, originally rather simple in its intent, had fallen victim to the Christmas Tree effect. It had acquired so many new ornaments over the months that its original intent was difficult to discern. In its scheduled review by the House Committee on Interstate and Foreign Commerce (now Energy and Commerce), the parent committee of Rogers's subcommittee, it promised to gather even more. By this time, the central issue had become federal preemption of state and local laws and regulations. Who would have believed that recombinant DNA would become the arena in which a states' rights battle would be fought? But there was little talk about risks anymore, or at least, there was no debate over the desirability of everyone's observing the NIH Guidelines. Still, a couple of the more militant scientists[19] managed to prevail on Harley Staggers, Chairman of the Commerce Committee, to delay consideration of the recombinant DNA bill long enough so that action could not be completed in the first session of the

Ninety-Fifth Congress. Ironically, those two scientists could not have succeeded in preventing the bill from continuing on its course to the House floor without the help of their ideological foes in Congress. Their insistence on offering so many more amendments, particularly those pertaining to the rights of communities to enact their own rules, took so long that there was simply not time to complete the markup of the bill.

The ensuing winter recess allowed Rogers and his staff to start over. This time, following private consultation with Donald Fredrickson and Gilbert Omenn, then with White House Office of Science and Technology Policy, a far simpler bill was drafted, establishing the safety standards of NIH Guidelines as federal law, but leaving administrative provisions up to the Secretary of Health, Education, and Welfare.[20] The bill again overrode local rules and thus lost the support of the public-interest lobbyists and their champions in Congress. It contained the flexibility to respond quickly to new knowledge concerning risks, so as not to impose needlessly strict rules if they were shown to be unnecessary, and it allowed for the exemption of those experiments known to be safe.

Cosponsored by Paul Rogers and Harley Staggers, thus avoiding any internal disputes, the bill sailed easily through all of the necessary committees. But by mid-1978, the mood had quieted considerably. Kennedy had gotten burned with his legislative fiasco and was not about to risk losing another one. Congress was busy preparing for the fall elections and clearing out the necessary legislation so that the members could go home and campaign. That year there was, in fact, a huge log jam of bills, far more than could ever be considered by Congress before adjournment. Debate over Carter's energy bill had used up an inordinate amount of time, delaying even the routine reauthorization of many bread-and-butter programs.

Recombinant DNA simply got lost in the shuffle. The fact is that nobody really cared enough about gene splicing as a political issue to be bothered. When there were taxes and inflation and energy crises and nuclear missiles and reelection to worry about, Congress could give little attention to something that not only seemed irrelevant, but which most people still didn't know anything about. The attention span had run its course, as it does in most imagined crises when nothing occurs to keep them going. There were no genetic disasters, nor was there even a documented case of a runny nose or a stomach ache. There is a natural limit on how long one can prepare for the sky to fall, even if one starts out believing that it really is falling.

Some of the scientist-lobbyists like to pat themselves on the back and boast that *they* killed the dragon of impending legislation. Not so. They did help to accelerate the demise of the Kennedy bill, but it is unlikely that, given the dynamics of Congress, particularly in view of the very different approach in the House of Representatives, the Kennedy bill would have survived anyway. As for legislation *per se*, however, it was never more than a minor congressional issue and never could have become anything more than that without a tangible crisis—a *real* genetic accident. In the end, the major scientific organizations were supporting the House bill, if only to suppress local activity, but even that fear turned out to be a nonissue. As interest faded in Washington, it receded just as surely in Cambridge, Massachusetts; Princeton, New Jersey; and Ann Arbor, Michigan. The Cavalieri article in *The New York Times* that had aroused so much concern was forgotten. There had been no cancer epidemic. In spite of a few local ordinances and even a state law (Maryland), none have been enforced, and the major issue of the recombinant DNA controversy—at least, as it emerged in Congress and among community activists and public-interest groups—faded into oblivion.

Since that time, there has been only decreasing concern over the potential hazards arising from the conduct of research or even from the large-scale application of gene-splicing methods by biotechnology firms, which all claim to abide by the NIH Guidelines. Occasionally, attempts at local legislation still arise. A politically inspired bill, of innocuous provisions, passed the California Assembly and Senate in 1982 but was vetoed by Jerry Brown.[21] The RAC continues to reduce containment standards for many classes of organisms. In fact, the Guidelines now exempt large classes of experiments from any rules at all. There is still a watchful eye kept on the deliberate release of genetically modified organisms into the environment, especially important as genetically engineered agricultural varieties become ready for field testing. The RAC must also approve of any experiments involving the splicing of genes for potent toxin molecules. But these events are proceeding in an orderly and quiet manner now.

In looking back, it would be hard to insist that a law was necessary, or, perhaps, that even guidelines were necessary. But a law of the type finally considered in the House wouldn't really have hurt anything either. In fact, it would have expired long ago, even if it had been enacted in 1978. Legislation would have accomplished one good thing. It would have relieved NIH of a burden that it should never have been saddled with in the first place. For many years, and even to this day, it has not only been the home and the curator of the Guidelines, but it has administered them like real regulations.

The current level of activity is nevertheless important, for the RAC continues to provide a permanent forum in which to consider all matters of safety, including, now, the safety of large-scale operations as practiced by industrial concerns. Every week, there is a notable scientific advance. As the power of the techniques continues to increase, new questions of safety and hazard will continue to arise. Many will be difficult to assess. Now we can say with confidence that the focus of all the fuss in the mid-1970s was really not much to be concerned about. On the other hand, if there is a real risk related to the unforeseen consequences of gene splicing, it is no doubt far more likely to occur from the use of the highly developed methods in use today, and those that will be in use tomorrow, than from the almost trivial modifications of the genetic makeup of *Escherichia coli*.

CHAPTER 4

Encounter with Tomorrow

Foretelling the Future

Up to this point, I have dealt with the past and the present. I have tried to present all aspects of the status quo, not necessarily in detail, but in concept, particularly with regard to the current state of our understanding of living systems and with regard to the technology based on this knowledge. While this book has already touched upon some of the problems that the New Biology has created for our own and future generations to solve, much of what we shall encounter ahead cannot be predicted accurately. Indeed, if the past teaches us any lessons, much of the future cannot even be imagined.

There is no reliable oracle to consult. The powers of tarot cards, the I Ching, and the entrails of freshly slaughtered goats are of little help, especially to rank amateurs like myself. And I can't seem to trust my own powers of clairvoyance, which can't even be depended on to tell me where I parked my car in the morning. Nevertheless, certain directions have been established from which, we may predict with assurance that there will be relatively little deviation. Of course, the farther ahead we attempt to see, the more our errors become compounded, and the more likely we are to be wrong. Perhaps out of a stubborn belief that it *is* possible to anticipate at least certain elements of our future, rather than because there is any evidence that a careful examination of the present and the past somehow allow us to know the future, I embark on this journey of the mind.

It is a certainty that in the absence of nuclear war or some unforeseen natural catastrophe, our knowledge and understanding of all living systems, including man, will continue to increase rapidly. This increase will take place no matter what policy the federal government takes with respect to the funding of basic research, or what the ratio of public to private sector scientists might be, or even what political or economic systems are in vogue at any particular time in any particular place on earth. The time scale may be slightly affected, but not much, in terms of the present rates of change among contemporary civilizations. But beyond that almost trivial statement, what can we *really* know about the future?

The history of scientific discovery reveals a great deal about how the human mind thinks and creates. It also reveals the mind's limitations. Let us then examine our ability to see what lies ahead, and to anticipate the future of scientific understanding and technological invention.

Why is it important to look ahead? Why should we try to imagine any of the unknowns in our scientific and technological future? They will come when they are are ready, when we have assembled enough of the pieces in the understanding of a phenomenon to move ahead to the next level of generalization. But there is one very practical reason for trying to imagine what will come next, aside from the fact that doing so may aid in the act of discovery itself. And that is that society must prepare itself for its own social adjustment to the perturbations which science, and the technology it spawns, will necessarily produce.

I have referred to a gap between the state of our technical knowledge concerning natural phenomena and our collective social immaturity. We have managed to survive and even flourish in spite of this discrepancy, although not unscathed. However, as the power of knowledge and its applications becomes forever greater, its capacity to alter significantly the ways in which people, and nations, interact becomes a major social and political determinant. Thus, the Industrial Revolution of the nineteenth century, the railroad, the automobile, the airplane, and advances in organic chemistry and solid-state physics have produced major social and political shifts.

But these forces cannot compare with the potential effects of nuclear weapons, which have certainly shaped international politics. Should even one such weapon ever be used for military purposes in the future, the effects on society can be expected to be far greater than the dropping of two atomic bombs on Japan in the context of a prolonged war and the American practice of saturation bombing of civilian populations in many Japanese cities. That is, an increment of horror on top of existing horror somehow does not seem to shock the senses as much as does an isolated incident against a more serene background.

The advances in biology are enabling the development of many beneficial technologies, perhaps reversing many of the undesirable effects of the chemical and pharmaceutical practices of the previous decades. But because these same technologies also have the capability of altering the genetic balance in all species, including ourselves, the potential effects on society are no less profound than those of nuclear weapons. I do not mean to imply that the changes to be brought about by these powerful new technologies are necessarily destructive or undesirable, but that they will present us with many new kinds of problems, with which we and our political and social institutions are simply not now prepared to grapple.

Thus, the more advance warning we have of what is to come, the greater will be our chances of anticipating the possible ways in which society will be affected. Any prior knowledge will give us time to create mechanisms to keep the transitions smooth and constructive, and perhaps even to decide that there are certain kinds of technology which we simply don't want to develop. The problem is, *can* we imagine which aspects of today's speculations and science fiction will become realities. Are there "experts" who can correctly anticipate the discoveries and the developments of the next 10 or the next 50 years? If so, are our societal means of decision making and planning sufficiently mature and foresighted so that those responsible will listen to the soothsayers? And how can political bodies composed of laymen or the "public" tell the experts from the dreamers or those with a penchant for predicting doomsday? And can anyone really believe the experts? Who can tell who is a real expert and who is defending a vested interest or a bias?

Before any attempt to use such information is relevant, we must first try to see if it is possible for us even to see into the scientific crystal ball. If not, why not? And can we get better at it? What qualities of mind are important to seeing ahead, and are these different from those necessary for scientific creativity?

Even the best scientists have not been particularly good at anticipating the next conceptual advance. Often, even when the data are at hand and it is necessary only to put them in order, it can take years before someone sees the essential relationships required to formulate a new theory. When they attempt to look several levels ahead of the present, contemporary experts have not been particularly successful, and few even dare to try.

Usually, in order for something to be thought of at all, there seems to have to be a precedent in human experience to imagine it. However, it seems that the more removed from everyday human experience a branch of inquiry is, and the less experienced the investigator, the more imaginative and innovative such an investigation is likely to be. Abstract endeavors such as music and mathematics, and even theoretical physics, have seen the highest degrees of creativity in the young and sometimes in the very young. The value of prodigious talent must not be discounted, nor must the fact that the aging brain loses, never gains, capacity. Experience also seems to have a dulling effect. The older and more experienced one becomes, the more conservative he gets, and the harder it is to break away from the bonds of convention, whether they be in a style of dress or an intellectual dogma. Ironically, the young are trained by the older and more experienced. This arrangement is appropriate when they are being taught the tools of the trade, but it is not correct if the student, in order to be successful, must master his mentor's world view of nature. The best teachers, therefore, encourage their students to question everything, including the teacher's own cherished theories and the semisacred building blocks of their illustrious careers.

Still, even when constraints have been kept to a minimum, there have been many things that were never imagined until they were experienced. That is, sound hypothesis formation depends on clues or observations within the realm of experience. Further, the validity of a theory requires conformation by experiment. The existence of microorganisms is a case in point. No one had postulated them *a priori* nor imagined that such creatures were responsible for the centuries-old processes of making wine and cheese or for causing human disease. Contagion and fermentation were known long before the discovery of the microscope, but it required many years after the description of protozoa, yeast, and bacteria as living creatures before the connection was made between microbes and these common experiences of life. Could anyone have imagined that minute creatures existed at all? When we look back, such an idea would seem to have been an obvious extension of the fact that animals had been described down to the resolving power of the unaided human eye. Then why wouldn't there be even smaller ones? Even now, most people have difficulty in accepting the existence of those things that do not impinge on one of the senses or on our instruments (such as a television set) for extending our sensory powers. Even when people are told that certain foods they like might be laden with toxic chemicals, they are likely to eat them anyway, as long as they can't smell or taste the offending substances.

Neither radio transmission nor other forms of electromagnetic radiation other than visible light were appreciated until they were demonstrated many years after Maxwell's theoretical prediction of their existence. Neither the source nor the properties of all of the forms of ionizing radiation had been predicted by the time Henri Becquerel[1] discovered these mysterious invisible rays in 1896 in the course of his studies on uranium compounds. Radium was such an intense source of gamma radiation (very high-energy electromagnetic radiation) that its properties could be characterized.[2] But this was long before the atomic nucleus had been described, from which the nature of ionizing radiation might have been predicted. In fact, it was the subsequent description of the forms of ionizing radiation that provided many of the data which led to an understanding of the atomic nucleus and its components.

Could anyone, then, have predicted the existence of ionizing radiation in 1875, Maxwell notwithstanding? At that time, it was very far outside of human experience, and there was no obvious evidence of the presence of the natural radiation in the environment. It is highly unlikely, then, that anyone *could* have predicted the existence of these forms of radiation, let alone the events in the atomic nucleus that are their source. No one did, in fact, foresee the existence of ionizing radiation. There simply wasn't enough to go on.

Genetics, on the other hand, long before it became a science, was known through anecdotal experience. Sexual intercourse was associated with having babies, eventually. It was further observed that children could resemble either the mother or the father, or both. Selective animal breeding had been practiced for centuries. Moreover, after Gregor Mendel demonstrated the independent assortment of inherited traits in peas,[3] the concept of determinants of phenotype transmitted through the structures of reproduction (pollen and ovules) seemed to be on a firm footing. But could the nature of deoxyribonucleic acid (DNA) have been predicted in 1900? That is extremely doubtful, given the state then of our knowledge of chemistry and the properties of molecular interactions.

By the time it was determined that chromosomes were the site of mammalian inheritance, it was also known that living matter was composed of complex organic molecules. Thus, the requirements for the fundamental unit of heredity could be set forth: The molecule, or the complex of molecules, would have to be able to direct its own replication. The unit would also have to be able to contain, probably in coded form, the information specifying every aspect of an entire organism. It is conceivable that, with these essential needs, a mechanism might have been imagined that would function very much as we now know DNA works. Furthermore, it would probably not have been necessary to know about chromosomes to be able to predict the existence of a molecular unit with the correct properties. But, to my knowledge, no one did.

Could the nature of the motion of planets and the sun's central role in the solar system have been predicted without detailed astronomical observations? Again, perhaps they could have been. But here, too, the data were available long before a coherent picture of the solar system was constructed. Newton's formalism of mechanics[4] was needed to put the description of the motion of celestial bodies on a firm quantitative footing.

It is an instructive thought experiment to pick the date of the first recorded instance of a new conceptual advance in science and to go back 50 years, to what was known at the time, and then to try to imagine if you could have predicted what was to come in half a century. Of course, it is not a fair test of predictability, except that when I try to do it, and try to put out of my mind what I know about such things, I must conclude that it would have been an extraordinary feat for anyone to have predicted any of the major achievements in physics, chemistry, astronomy, or medicine so far in advance of their actual occurrence. There was simply too little experience, and what there was was too fragmented to be related to a coherent theory.

There are some exceptions to this rule in the history of science, and these may be accidental. Epicurus[5] described matter as consisting of "atoms" 19 centuries before the beginnings of modern atomic theory. Was his intuition simply good? Or was he just lucky? Of course, his atoms didn't exactly fit the Bohr model. But it was a good try for his time.

A few writers of fantasies of the future, unconstrained by too much scientific knowledge, have predicted some advances that either have come to pass or for which the theoretical basis now exists. H. G. Wells wrote of death rays[6] well ahead of ionizing radiation or lasers. He also wrote of time travel.[7] The theory of relativity predicts that at least forward time travel should be possible. (Moving backward in time poses certain philosophical difficulties, and no theory predicts that it is possible.) Aldous Huxley foresaw *in vitro* fertilization in *Brave New World*,[8] as well as human embryogenesis taking place completely outside the womb. The former has been fact for several years now. Many believe that the latter is well within the realm of technical feasibility. Flying machines were envisioned by many, well ahead of their construction, and Jules Verne wrote of a voyage to the moon[9] before the turn of the century.

Where, then, does this all leave us when we try to contemplate what may lie ahead in the biological sciences. Do we now have enough awareness of all of the fundamental principles of life to be able to make a reasonable prediction or at least a first approximation of all of the discoveries we are about to experience in the next 50 or 100 years? Or are there entire realms of phenomena that still lie completely outside our personal experience and the capabilities of our instruments? Or are there some of which we have an inkling, without concrete data (such as mental telepathy)?

There could well be areas of knowledge that we have not begun to touch. If the history of science teaches us anything, it is this. However, there are very many that we have recently been able to begin to explore. On the basis of these alone, I have suggested the possibility of many achievements in the relatively near future that, to me, hardly seem remote. Just as Huxley was on relatively safe ground in predicting *in vitro* fertilization 50 years before its time, on the basis of what was known about embryology when he wrote *Brave New World*, I don't consider it farfetched at all to suggest that, within the foreseeable future, we will achieve the ability to alter the human genome in any desired way.

The Future and Determinism

One question that has always perplexed philosophers is whether our future is determined. Some have argued that, because everything in the universe is reducible to matter and energy, would not a truly complete description of the universe allow one to predict how it would unfold with time? That is, does the present *completely* determine the future? Or, viewed incrementally, does the total physical state of the universe at time t determine the physical universe at $t + 1$ nanosecond? Or $t = 1 + \delta$ where δ is an infinitesimally small interval of time?

The answer according to Newtonian physics would be yes. Classical physics describes the behavior of large populations of particles statistically— for example, the molecules in a gas. Such properties as temperature and pressure can each be defined as a function of the distribution of velocities and energies of the individual particles, which are assumed to be following random paths and colliding with one another. However, if one could specify the position and the velocity of each particle in a gas, and if ones assumes collisions between molecules to be elastic, it is possible, in principle, according to Newtonian mechanics, to describe the exact path of any of those particles at any time in the future. The distribution of the positions and energies of molecules in a gas calculated in this way should agree with the results of much simpler statistical computations. That is, the future in the Newtonian world must be completely determined by its configuration at the present.

In other words, if complete knowledge of the present would allow us to determine the future totally at some time interval, however small the interval, then it follows that the future is determined totally, including the nature of all creatures and people who will inhabit the earth a thousand or a million years from now. For the process of going from one minuscule time interval to the next will still result in a completely determined future, no matter how many times the process is repeated. The classical model of the universe described by Isaac Newton does, in fact, suggest a completely determined future.

If, however, this concept seems intuitively untenable, contemporary physicists would agree with you. Quantum physics would give a different answer to the question of whether the future is determined. Usually the answer is simply no, but for large objects, it might be "almost, but not quite." According to the rules of quantum physics, no event in the future is completely determinable. This statement derives from a law of quantum physics which states that the parameters necessary to describe the present cannot all be specified at the same time. The principle of uncertainty, first formulated by Werner Heisenberg in 1926,[10] states that certain physical quantities, which exist in pairs of so-called conjugate variables, cannot be completely specified at the same time. That is, if the position of a particle is exactly specified, its momentum is completely indeterminate. If one arbitrarily imposes a range of possible positions on a particle, this determines the range of uncertainty in the particle's momentum. For example, if there is a marble on my desk and I can specify that its center is between 20.00 and 20.05 centimeters from the edge, this tells me within just what limits I can determine the momentum of the marble's motion simultaneously with the measurement of its position. A similar relationship exists between the energy of an object and the time when that energy is measured.

Thus, if the position of every particle in the universe is specified precisely at any given time, then other physical parameters necessary to predict the course that it will follow through time cannot be determined at all. Hence, it follows that chance is itself a universal operating principle. In fact, the laws of physics are described statistically, rather than exactly. Within the limits of measurement, a large object, such as a baseball, does indeed obey the exact rules of Newtonian mechanics. However, if our measurements were fine enough, we would see that its behavior in space and time follows the same statistical behavior that we can expect to see in a single electron. In fact, if one does the right experiment, the effects of quantum mechanics even on "large" objects can be made quite visible.

A classic homework problem that I first encountered in my student days at Harvard is to calculate how long it would take a "perfectly" balanced ice pick on an ideally hard surface to fall over. A Newtonian ice pick could presumably be placed in a precisely vertical position, and at the same time, its angular velocity about its point of balance could be zero. That, after all, constitutes the definition of perfect balance. The Newtonian ice pick would therefore remain balanced forever in an ideal world. Not so, however, with an ice pick governed by the laws of quantum mechanics. If you can place it so that it is really perfectly vertical, then its angular momentum will be indeterminate, and it will soon fall over. Similarly, if you specify that its velocity in any direction is zero, then its deflection from the vertical will be undefinable, and gravity will quickly pull it down. But somewhere in between, there is an optimum set of conditions that will allow the ice pick to keep from falling down for the longest possible period of time. This is, in fact, how one must define "balance" in order to solve the problem. At best, this time is not as long as you might think. A typical ice pick will stay up for about six seconds. Even if you have a very odd ice pick, your best time will still be within a few seconds of this number.

At the atomic or molecular level, the lack of determinism is an important and intrinsic part of the mathematical descriptions of these systems; they cannot be described at all without quantum mechanics. There are, of course, many properties of matter at the level of atoms that require the quantum formalization to be described, such as discrete energy levels, as first observed, from the light emission spectra of the elements. The uncertainty principle is simply one way of stating that the course through time and space of any object cannot be determined precisely.

Large objects are, practically speaking, Newtonian. Thus, the orbits of the planets may be described with precision without our worrying about the minute perturbations injected into their behavior by the uncertainty principle. Does this mean, then, that for any object big enough to really count, the future of the universe *is* determined? No, not completely. The future paths of the stars and the planets may be predicted accurately for millions of years to come, but only because they are huge objects. Quantum fluctuations are important for the atomic events going on inside those objects, but not for the motion of the center of mass, at least over very long periods of time. A human being is also a large object compared to an electron. However, the workings of the human brain are at the level of molecules, atoms, and even electrons. DNA, the determinant of heredity, may also be sensitive to the change of a single atom. Thus, it is not unlikely that quantum effects do play a role in the workings of the brain and the mind. To what degree, then, do these effects add an element of randomness to the human future? That is, if our planet could be exactly duplicated once, or a hundred or a thousand times (cloned?), how would all of these once-identical planets differ in a year, or a hundred years or a thousand? For example, can we say that there is a statistical probability of being obliterated by nuclear war within the next 100 years? If we started with 100 identical earths today, would 10 or 40 or the entire 100 blow themselves up in 100 years? Or would they all be nearly the same? Or would they be different in detail, but statistically the same in all important parameters?

We cannot, of course, know the answers to these questions—at least not now. But the answer does have bearing on the degree to which human free will *really* exists and the extent to which we have control over our own destiny. Thus, to return to a question posed earlier, should we try to predict the future? And if we think we can foresee problems ahead, should we try to invent solutions? If so, how do we define "solution"? Isn't any course on which we attempt to direct our future dependent on a set of arbitrary values (human, social, economic, cultural, and political)? If we recognize a disparity of values not only among but within our contemporary cultures, then how must these values be taken into account in making decisions affecting our future? Who decides what course to take? Who selects the decision makers, and how?

It is obvious that the future of mankind will be affected in profound ways by the continuing advances in our understanding of life and our ability to direct our own biological evolution. But I am assuming that humans, however uncertain the internal workings of their brains may be at times, do have a degree of control over their future. I am further assuming that the greater the effect of a potential problem, or the natural consequence of a particular technological advance—and here I mean those events that, according to most value systems, would be considered undesirable—the more important it is to anticipate the future well in advance and to take steps to direct it early on. That is, of course, the optimistic view. There is no evidence that the human race will ever learn to anticipate tomorrow and to take appropriate steps before it is too late. Our current anguish over a world laden with nuclear weapons should be a lesson for us all, if we are capable of learning one.

Improving Human Life

The object of medical practice is to improve the life of the individual, by healing his maladies and by helping him to prevent acquiring new ones. It is probably safe to state that nearly everyone agrees that physicians should save lives and help people to live as long as they can, free from illness. Consistent with this value, therefore, it follows that every improvement in man's physical and mental well-being that medical technology is capable of achieving should be put into practice and be made available to all.

The value placed on human life, as expressed in the first paragraph, is held nearly universally. Although it may not rank as high as national security (the object of war is a bit different from that of medicine), the fact that a significant fraction of the civilized world's economic resources go toward the end of enhancing and prolonging human life reflects the high esteem that we afford it. (It may seem trivially obvious to state explicitly, but when viewed in the context of world history, human life and its length and quality were not always valued so highly.)

It would seem to follow, then, that the remarkable recent advances in molecular and cell biology should be exploited in every way possible to improve the human condition. In fact, a large fraction of the activities of commercial biotechnology is directed toward the large-scale production of rare and costly pharmaceuticals and biologicals, and toward exploring the entire field of new diagnostic and therapeutic agents. It was the promise of many wondrous things that would improve human health that offset some of the concerns over the possible dangers of gene-splicing technology.

But the goals of this part of the biotechnology industry are the same ones pursued by the pharmaceutical industry for decades. Only the technology is different. Few question the ethics of making new drugs and antibiotics by cloning the appropriate genes in bacteria. Of greater concern is the direct application of the methods of the new genetics and cell biology to human beings. At present, the object of such activity is the correction of human pathology. Thus, the first targets of direct genetic intervention in humans are the hereditary diseases (see Chapter 2).

Aside from the ethical concerns that accompany any new medical research or practice, there are few who would claim that an object of medicine should not be to treat and cure individuals afflicted with genetic diseases. Mechanisms are in place for determining when it is appropriate to try a new procedure on a patient, with the object of protecting the patient's right of informed consent, and ensuring, to the extent possible, that the risk to the patient from the procedure will be offset by its value in treating his affliction. In some cases, the use of new procedures cannot be expected to benefit the patient at all, but it will advance medical knowledge. Some patients agree to be the subjects of these experiments, and they are entitled to be fully informed regarding all pertinent information. The degree to which medical practice is conducted in an ethical manner and the rights of the patients are respected is a matter apart from the laws designed to ensure the protection of patients' rights. However, there appear to be relatively few instances in which patients have been harmed because of violations of these codes of ethics.

Many hereditary diseases are not readily amenable to treatment in an individual exhibiting the symptoms, even with the most advanced techniques available. A number of the most severe disorders are not detected until well after birth, some not even until adulthood. Frequently, developmental problems and mental retardation are manifest by the time the cause of the symptoms is identified. Aminocentesis[11] now allows many genetic defects, even rather subtle ones, to be detected by the third month of gestation, permitting the proper treatment to be instituted as early as possible—if, indeed, there is a proper treatment—or the option of abortion if there is not.

If a genetic defect is expressed by the lack of a circulating substance, then treatment is relatively easy. One merely has to supply the missing substance. Thus, the treatment of sickle-cell disease now consists of periodically replacing the blood containing the defective red cells with normal blood, through transfusions. Patients with hereditary blood disorders may also soon be the recipients of gene therapy, by having their bone marrow cells cultured in the laboratory and the genetic defect in these cells corrected by gene-splicing methods. These cells, now producing normal hemoglobin, can then be returned to the patient's bone marrow, where presumably they will produce normal red blood cells, without the risk of the rejection that can occur when one receives a bone marrow transplant from another person.

If the lack of a hormone required for growth is detected early enough, injections of the missing substance can restore the normal pattern of growth.[12] Failure to metabolize a particular substance, which then builds to toxic levels, is also a common type of genetic disease. For example, infants in the United States are now routinely screened for phenylketonuria (PKU), the failure to break down the amino acid phenylalanine, a common constituent in nearly all proteins. If detected at birth, PKU can be treated successfully by adjustment of the diet.

However, if a metabolite or an enzyme *inside* the cells is defective, there may be no way to influence the altered biochemistry of the patient. Thus, such diseases as muscular dystrophy, cystic fibrosis, Altzehimer's disease, and Huntington's chorea can be treated only symptomatically. The same considerations may also apply to psychiatric disorders, such as schizophrenia, depression, and drug and alcohol addictions, all of which exhibit at least some degree of genetic determinism. There is no way at present to replace the missing molecule in a structure that has already formed incorrectly. Although some disorders may be amenable to some limited direct genetic therapy, there is little promise that these diseases can be cured in this manner, particularly after the extent of development and differentiation that has occurred by the third month of gestation, let alone birth or later. Cost is also a consideration. Is it worth spending vast sums of money to develop a treatment that will never be satisfactory, at the expense of putting those resources into more potentially fruitful endeavors? That is another question of ethics which we shall return to in due course.

Although our methods of detecting genetic anomalies continue to become more sensitive, there still may be no satisfactory way to treat most diseases, and abortion may be the only practical preventive measure. But let us not dwell on the ethics of abortion. I would argue that abortion of a genetically defective fetus *is* ethical. It is perhaps far less ethical to permit the development to term of an infant who is destined to be physically and mentally handicapped throughout his life. Still, is early detection and abortion the best we can do?

It is believed by many that, for a large number of such hereditary diseases, our hope lies not in improving the treatment of afflicted individuals but in preventing pregnancies where the fetus would be genetically defective or that would even carry the genes for the disorder. In other words, is there a way to intervene selectively in the reproductive process early enough so that neither anmiocentesis nor abortion will be necessary, but which will still allow prospective parents who carry a disorder to have normal children? In order to accomplish this end, one or both of two possible approaches is required. A detailed knowledge of each parents' genetic constitution, as it relates to the disorder, would of course be desirable, but it is not necessarily essential.

The first approach would entail the selective removal or destruction of those sperm or egg cells that carry the defect; fertilization would then proceed either normally or perhaps *in vitro*. Or, possibly, a means could be found to determine if the fertilized egg is genetically intact. If the genes in question are not normally expressed at that early stage, as they would probably not be for most human genetic disorders, then it is highly unlikely that a simple satisfactory method could be found to answer the question, particularly if the genetic defect involves only a single DNA base-pair change. Current gene-detection methods using complementary DNA probes are, in principle, sensitive enough to detect the presence (or the absence) of any specific genetic region in a single cell, but they cannot detect most single base-pair mutations or those that do not alter the base-pairing efficiency of the probe. Although potentially useful for the accurate genetic screening of prospective parents for the presence of virtually any DNA sequence, this type of test entails the destruction of the test material and therefore does not allow one to determine if a specific human ovum or sperm, or a fertilized combination, thereof, is free of defects. The only way in which this type of approach might be of value would be to sacrifice one cell of a zygote at the third or fourth cleavage for DNA analysis.

The second method would entail the correction of the defective gene either before or immediately after fertilization. There has already been some success in inserting DNA fragments into fertilized mammalian eggs. Presumably, if the right type of cloning vector were used so that the defective gene could be not only replaced but also placed under the normal control mechanisms, which would determine its proper expression, the egg would develop normally, and the individual would then pass the corrected gene on to his children and subsequent generations. If and when gene insertion techniques are perfected, it should not be necessary to know whether a defective gene is present in either the sperm or the egg, as long as the added gene is functional. It is this latter approach that offers the greatest promise for corrective human genetics.

There are, however, some who view this type of preemptive therapy as getting too close to tampering with the nature of human life. It would be difficult to argue that the correction of a genetic defect is anything but good. But one frequently hears the argument that if we do X, it will soon "lead to" Y. Do-gooders have always used this argument to prevent sin. Sure, they may admit, pot may not be that bad, but it will "lead to" the use of heroin. As adolescents, our parents may have warned us that kissing and petting should be avoided but were often evasive and embarrassed about just what it would "lead to." And it took me years to figure out why card playing was, in the eyes of certain religious orders, forbidden. The sin it is supposed to "lead to" is compulsive gambling. This is the so-called slippery slope argument. That is, once you start down a particular direction, you cannot stop.

Is it an appropriate argument to contend that those who would alter human genes to correct terrible afflictions will become so taken with their success that they can't stop, changing all manner of human genes willy-nilly? This is perhaps too simplified a way of viewing research, although there is also some truth in this view. That is, once the techniques are developed for modifying the human genome, they can be used just as easily to alter genes that control traits with regard to which societal values are completely subjective, as they can to correct what everyone agrees is undesirable. I think it can be predicted with some certainty that it is only a matter of time before such techniques are perfected. Just how much time it will take is almost of no importance, but it probably won't be as much as 50 years and could be as short as 10.

In order to alter "normal" genetic regions, a great deal will have to be learned about how such traits as physique, pigmentation, personality, intelligence (however one chooses to define it), temperament, and the shape of one's features are determined genetically. There are, of course, many who would contend that not all of the above characteristics *are* controlled genetically. I would argue, however, that, although all of the evidence is not yet at hand, as we learn more and more about human genetics more, and more correlations are being established between genes and almost every observable human characteristic.[13] Certainly, we must have proof. But I would assert that the influence of genetics will ultimately turn out to be far more important than ever imagined by the sociologists and psychologists of 20 years ago. By this assertion, I do not mean to minimize the importance of a stimulating and healthy environment for proper human development. Learning is a concept that applies to much more than mastering languages, academic training, and manual skills. However, one's basic personality, musical and artistic ability, the capacity to learn and create, and perhaps character are limited by one's endowment of particular DNA sequences. In any case, I ask for the skeptical readers' indulgence while I, for the sake of argument, assume that most human traits do indeed have a genetic basis.

If it becomes possible to alter human phenotypes, the important question is then, *should* we? If so, what traits should we change? Should there be any efforts on the part of governments to control the use of such technology? Should it be left in the hands of private entrepreneurs? What is the potential, for good and for harm, that could result from the application of such methods? Can we even define a set of criteria that will help us to proceed over a relatively short period? Or should we take the easy way out and not deal with the problems at all, declaring, as some have done, that human life is sacred and should not be tampered with in any way?

These are questions that I often pose to the students in my classes and seminars on ethics and science. There is always a wide spread of opinion, and classes in different institutions may respond in very different ways. Few argue that human life is sacrosanct, but the class discussions of the degree to which modifying human gene lines are acceptable never fail to be highly spirited.

Most readily accept the concept of genetic intervention as long as it is limited to achieving the ideal of the total absence of pathology. But when it is suggested that perhaps there are innate "human" traits that are not in the best interests of the survival of the species, then it is difficult to achieve any form of agreement, at least among university students. Nevertheless, there is often value in the contemplation of a thought experiment, which, although completely outside of the context of the present world, can force us to view ourselves in a completely new perspective that *is* relevant to our ultimate existence. I ask here for the reader's indulgence and open-mindedness in reading the next few pages.

Suppose that it could be shown beyond any reasonable doubt that certain genetically determined human traits which at one time were important to our survival—such as aggression, selfishness, and competitiveness—remain in our gene pool only as vestiges of our animal ancestry. And assume that it could be further shown that these traits could be clearly correlated with the common practice among nations of settling their disputes by force, and with the intransigent posture of the major powers in perpetuating the nuclear arms race. (Certainly, if you were to ask most people what they thought of selfishness, even in themselves, they would very likely repudiate the concept.)

Would such knowledge provide sufficient justification for attempting to eliminate these traits from the human population? First of all, to accomplish such an undertaking would probably require doing genetic surgery on *all* fertilized human eggs. And that would entail, at least for a time, the end of the usual mode of sexual reproduction. Eggs would have to be obtained from each prospective mother (a process now requiring a surgical procedure) and fertilized *in vitro,* and the genetic modification would have to be performed on the fertilized egg. The resulting zygote would then have to be transplanted back into the mother's uterus, where, presumably, it would develop normally. It would require at least two or three generations—perhaps 60 or 70 years—before the selected "undesirable" traits would be effectively eliminated from the human gene pool.

Even to think of this kind of program on such a grand scale, even if one assumes that each stage of the procedure would be successful in 100% of the subjects, is preposterous, at least in terms of the global human and societal values of the 1980s. Even more absurd is the notion that normal sexual reproduction, as a means of procreation, would be forsaken by the world's population. (Remember, this is only a *thought* experiment!)

But let us suppose—again, for the sake of argument—that the human genome may be modified easily and in a way posing no significant risk or inconvenience to the parents (the reader may imagine what such a procedure might entail). Should, then, direct genetic intervention be pursued at all? In order to deal with such a question, one must first attempt to order one's values. First, is the prevention of human conflict, and possibly, then, human survival, to be ranked above all other values? Clearly, if it were guaranteed that society would not survive if these innate human traits were perpetuated, then the choice is, at least, simple. To be weighed against obliteration and nonexistence, would be human existence without the traits, say, of aggression, selfishness, and competitiveness that now obviously underlie many societal institutions (e.g., competitive sports and capitalist economics).

Most people probably hold the perpetuation of the species, not to mention themselves, above virtually any other consideration (i.e., the "better Red than dead" philosophy). The desire to survive as a species is one of the strongest genetically determined drives, although it probably does not involve higher levels of problem solving, which occur in the outer layers of the human cerebral cortex. But could it ever be determined that we absolutely would *not* survive if we did not submit to a change in our "humanness"? Probably not. So we are back to the indeterminate nature of the world. Then, should we take the chance? Should we come to a collective decision to make our children innately different from ourselves in order to greatly increase the odds for their survival? Obviously, any action to accomplish something this drastic would have to involve everybody. If it included all but the Brezhnevs and the Reagans, or the Hitlers and the Nixons, we would probably be worse off.

Perhaps even more indeterminable than societal self-destruction is the effect that removing these one-time survival traits would have on future societies. How important are aggression, selfishness, and competitiveness to social structure, or even to our success as individuals? Although people vary greatly in the expression of these characteristics, we probably all have some measure of each, whether we like it or not. We don't know what it would be like not to have these traits. Perhaps, by eliminating them, we would do something else which would ultimately be destructive to human life. For example, is directed aggression responsible for the drive that makes people want to work and build and learn? One might presume that if we were at a level of knowledge where we could pinpoint the genetic determinants of aggression, then we would also know what determines drive and curiosity. But, as in any scientific investigation, you can't be sure until you do the experiment. And even if you did try it on a small test population (I am assuming that such an experiment would be considered ethically justified by the society performing it because of the importance of the consequences), could you predict the results in a large population over a period of generations? No matter how one tries, with the most well-controlled thought experiments, the conclusion is the same: Nothing is *really* certain. For that reason, decisions to alter our genetic makeup will forever be extraordinarily difficult to make with wisdom, even if the means to do so were easy and the population of the world would cooperate (which, of course, it never would do).

But let us now consider the alteration of human genetics on a much more personal level and return the discussion to the probable realities of our own lifetime. The techniques of *in vitro* fertilization are becoming perfected to the point where the probability of pregnancy is nearly as good as it is with natural methods. Unfertilized eggs must be removed surgically from the mother, fertilized with sperm in the laboratory, and then transplanted to the mother's uterus. This procedure does result in some discomfort and risk to the mother, but it permits women to become pregnant who could not otherwise do so. As dicussed earlier, it will probably provide the means for performing genetic alterations on prospective human beings at a stage of development where all the cells of the resulting child will contain the modified DNA. It is at this stage that genetic defects could be corrected, or other traits added, deleted, or modified.

Suppose that performing genetic surgery on a fertilized human egg is a relatively complex and expensive procedure, available only to a few, as surely it will be when it first becomes feasible. Should the prospective parents have the option of selecting their child's hair and eye color, stature, build, intelligence, personality, temperament, disposition, and any other trait than can be associated with a genetic determinant? Such a choice would be an extension of the present capability (through amniocentesis and selective abortion) of allowing parents to select the sex of their children. Given the choice, particularly if the procedure were costly and posed some risks to the mother, as *in vitro* fertilization methods now do, it is clear that the overwhelming majority of people would prefer to play the odds. Even the availability of a bit of applied eugenics through Shockley's Nobel sperm bank[14] has scarcely attracted a stampede of women trying to have genius babies. People are proud of their genes, even the ordinary ones, simply because they are theirs. As the number of people affected by such a procedure will very likely be too small to have any appreciable effect on society as a whole, why shouldn't it be permissible?

If and when such a made-to-order baby clinic opens its doors, it is certain that there will be cries of protest. It would not be primarily the matter of tampering with the sanctity of human life that would be the cause of concern, but the matter of equity. Few would contend that everyone is born with the same genetic endowments or has the same opportunities to achieve success in life, even though legal equality is supposedly guaranteed in many societies. At present, all prospective parents must play the game of genetic roulette. Of course, it is legitimate to try to beat the odds. Many parents encourage their children to be very particular when choosing their mates. Everyone wants smart kids. Thus, those who are fortunate enough to be smart are often advised to practice a little applied eugenics and to pick someone to marry and have children by who is similarly gifted. But this is all right, for we must all ultimately play by the rules of chance.

However, if it were possible for one to cheat at this game, by allowing one's gametes to be doctored, someone would be sure to cry foul. It would not be fair for one family to raise a brood of beautiful and handsome athletic geniuses, destined to become world leaders in science, law, music, business, government, or whatever they chose, while those who couldn't find the $20,000 fee would be the victims of statistical fluctuations and stuck with the genes their parents gave them. That is where we all are now. But as soon as someone has an edge, as defined by the values of his particular culture, there is an issue of justice to be reckoned with.

This is not unlike existing issues in health care, which we all know is anything but uniform.[15] If someone develops a miracle drug and there is only enough to treat a very small number of patients, what factors and which individuals determine who will benefit from it? This was the case in the early days of kidney dialysis as a means of treating the thousands of cases of kidney failure. At first, there was no justice, and those who could afford it received it, whereas those who could not died. The U.S. Congress then intervened (with the help of the dialysis machine lobby). Institutional dialysis, which maintains but does not cure kidney patients, is now provided free for anyone who needs it, costing taxpayers around $1.3 billion in 1982. The result has not necessarily been in the best interests of the patients. Whenever the government appropriates large sums of money for any purpose, there are many hungry wolves who try to get some of it. In this case, the dialysis machine establishment discourages patients from using less costly home dialysis, which is much less traumatic for the patient, and from receiving kidney transplants. Transplants offer the hope of cure to those who don't reject them and greatly improve the quality of life even for those who ultimately do reject the transplants. In addition, the funds for research on end-stage renal disease are only a small fraction of those spent for providing dialysis. The lesson to be learned is that attempts to bring justice to any new procedure that may benefit some, but not all, can be beset with difficulties.

There is another thought experiment that I now ask the reader to contemplate. It concerns the possibility of extending, perhaps indefinitely, the traditional human life span of four score and ten years. It is only begrudgingly that man has accepted his destiny to grow old and die. I would assert that man's preoccupation with his own mortality forms the foundations of most of the world's religions. Throughout recorded history, there has always been the quest for the Fountain of Youth, or its equivalent. Gods, always endowed with the traits that men value the most, are immortal.

Should we try to stop or slow the aging process? Most certainly, with continued research in human development, genetics, and cell biology, we will one day understand *why* cells age. That is certain. What is not certain at this time is whether it is possible to engineer the genes is such a way that the intrinsic human life span is extended significantly (see the discussion of this problem in Chapter 1 of this book). But let us assume that eventually it will be possible to design a human cell that does not age and that also has no undesirable side effects because of the changes made—not an unreasonable assumption. What, then, would be the consequences of intervention in the human aging process?

If, as in the case of altering human traits in fertilized human eggs, performing the genetic manipulations necessary for the extension of life span were a complex and expensive procedure that could affect only a limited number of people, then the net effect on society would be negligible. In fact, the same techniques that will probably be used to modify other traits will also very likely be those used to modify the genes that control aging.

However, if an easy, cheap, and readily available method were developed, the social consequences could be disastrous, particularly if there were a way to arrest the aging process in adults. Our entire social structure is geared to the human life span. People are perceived and placed within that structure according to their age. Whether one is applying for college or a job, looking for a mate or companion or just choosing friends, age is all-important. When people are described in newspapers or journals, whether they be those who have committed murder, appointees to high office, winners of international awards, or the subjects of obituaries, the first statistic given most often is the person's age. If the age distribution and the rate of aging were to change suddenly, the economic disruptions, not to mention the psychological and social adjustments demanded, could be overwhelming.

There is little question that of all the human desires recorded in the history of mankind, immortality would probably come out ahead of wealth and power. As long as it is only a dream, or the subject of great literature, people accept death as an inevitable part of life. But if it were available, almost everyone, I would venture to guess, would want immortality. The number of potential Fausts among us is probably greater than we would like to admit.

As an equity issue, it is similar to the case discussed above concerning the selection of traits in one's children. If living and staying "young" for greatly extended periods were available only to a few, the disparity between the immortals and the rest would produce extraordinarily intractable social problems. The haves would be greatly resented. As long as we are relatively equal, we manage to survive, although any individual or group that is "different" has always had difficulties. Unless such people were confined to an isolated elite, separated from society, like the royalty of Europe, such a discrepancy would probably not be tolerated. And we all know that however fortunate or unfortunate we may be, death is the final equalizer. That knowledge somehow makes the inequities of life more tolerable. The larger the age-arrested group became, the worse the problems would become.

If the procedure could be performed only on the unborn, then the problems would be delayed, but they would come nonetheless. Only if it were readily available to *all* newborns would there be a chance that society could adjust. Even then, the economic upheavals could be more than we could deal with.

It would seem that with all of the problems which could surround modifying humans genetically, society might be better off to leave well enough alone. Certainly, there is no valid *social* argument for extending the human life span, just as there may be no compelling reasons to alter any other traits. But what is best for society is not necessarily reflected in personal values. As any successful politician who is capable of winning an election knows well, people put their selfish desires and needs well above any abstract notion of a common good. It is these the politician must appeal to, not the salvation of society at some point in the distant future. Perhaps it is the recognition of this human quality that has given us governments and mechanisms for making decisions that presumably transcend immediate personal desires.

How will our social and political institutions deal with a technology that is capable of altering human life, and perhaps of creating a "superior" life form in terms of accepted human definitions and values? It is now that we should contemplate this question, for it will be a reality sooner than we think.

Forbidden Knowledge

The history of science contains many examples of the fear of knowledge. This is almost certain to be a corollary of the fear of the unknown in general, for it is scientists who dare to probe the unknown, looking where man has no business. In Western society, the most frequent grounds for the mistrust and the occasional condemnation of scientists have reflected the traditional premises that the provinces of both God and Satan are territories forbidden to man.

But even in the late twentieth century, when the powers of the Christian church and its ability to hold sway over entire countries exist as mere shadows of the glory that was Christianity in its prime, there are still those who perceive that knowledge is dangerous, and particularly inquiry that will provide new knowledge. It should therefore come as no surprise that the notion that there should be some things better left unknown has been revived along with the introduction of recombinant DNA techniques. The people who hold the view that research into the innermost workings of the living cell should not be carried out are in a rather small minority. Nevertheless, the concept that there is perhaps some knowledge which should remain unlearned deserves to be examined critically, particularly with respect to the new biology. Can the suppression of knowledge *ever* be justified?

There has always existed a tension within human societies between the comfort of tradition and the complusion to explore uncharted territory. These are both fundamental, intrinsic components of human nature, and they are forever in conflict. These two drives may exist not only within the same society but within a single individual, where the competition between these opposing forces can lead to neuroses or worse. Usually, in either a social entity or a single person, one of these drives must ultimately dominate, for they are, to a very large degree, mutually exclusive, at least with respect to any given subject.

It is the timeless dilemma of having one's cake and eating it too, or the essence of the difference between conservatives and liberals in the truest sense. You can't have it both ways. You can't be both a conservative and a liberal, nor can you really be neither. You can't be a stay-at-home and an adventurer at the same time. And you can't believe in God and be an atheist.

But it is not a matter of simple choice. Well, perhaps sometimes it is.

One may be faced with the choice between going on a dangerous white-water canoe trip in a wilderness area or staying safely at home, where all is familiar and predictable. The reasons for making the choice, however, will ultimately reflect one or the other of these two basic needs, and the process of deciding which course to follow will have to resolve the tension between them.

The unknown has always been troublesome to man. Whether it was the land outside the village walls and the creatures that inhabited it, or what lay beyond the sea, or the nature of life and death, it has always been necessary to resolve such matters, one way or another, for human nature traditionally has dealt very poorly with uncertainty.

Thus, depending on the resolution of the fundamental conflict referred to above, societies or individuals have two ways of eliminating uncertainty. The first is to construct a belief system to account for all of the troubling elements of the unknown. The other is to explore the unknown, in order to determine its nature. Religion is the manifestation of the first approach. Science (that is, exploration and inquiry) is the embodiment of the second. The first is based on assumptions, disguised as ''revealed'' truth by its leaders, which must be accepted on faith. To question the dogma so derived is unacceptable. The second, in addition to the gathering of raw data, is also based on assumptions, but these must be tested by observation and experiments carefully designed to reveal any errors in the hypotheses.

The first category, of course, includes much more than religion *per se*. Political, economic, and pseudoscientific dogma differ very little from religious dogma, and the minds of their proponents are no less closed to alternative models. Similarly, the second category includes not only those trained in the sciences who wear white lab coats and think esoteric thoughts, but explorers and inventors and anyone else who is not content with the currently accepted state of knowledge or the prevailing explanations of observed phenomena, or events in any area. Or to look at it another way, the external labels attached to categories of people (physicist, economist, historian, philosopher, psychologist, machinist, teacher, garbage collector, housewife, dancer, ballplayer) do not reveal whether they are engaged in a search to understand the truth behind some set of data or whether they have accepted a particular dogma and have closed their minds to further conceptual changes. One is likely to find both sorts within the same academic departments in most universities, and in every field of study.

I do not mean to suggest that there are only two, basically opposite kinds of people, forever in conflict, although to a crude first approximation it does seem to be true. People's capacities for dealing with uncertainty vary considerably. I have known some fine scholars who were devout believers in a personal god. For many, the concept of death is too difficult to deal with through any form of scientific objectivity. Thus, only a religious or a postulated concept of what happens when a person dies suffices to give such people the peace and comfort that they need in order to accept death at all. At the same time, they can be brilliantly creative when it comes to the abstractions of the structure of the atomic nucleus or the motion of galaxies. The only requirement is that they keep thesc two sides of their nature and their needs completely separate, applying them to different aspects of their personal universe.

Trouble arises when one person's or group's manner of dealing with the unknown is perceived as a threat to the power or the security of those who determine the way in which a society handles such matters. Thus, traditionally, life has generally been difficult for the innovators and explorers who refused to accept the prevailing explanations of the nature of the sun, the shape of the earth, the origins of man, or the laws of inheritance. Even a single individual who challenges dogma can be viewed as dangerous to those whose position in society may depend on a universal belief in that dogma. One sees examples at all levels. The bright student who challenges his professor's pet concepts may be put down for his failure to accept the "way it is." The political dissident who is seen as a threat to the power of the state may be persecuted, arrested, imprisoned, exiled, or executed.

The concept of tolerance is an interesting one. If some poor, misguided individual had gone around in 1400 A.D. proclaiming that the world was round, wouldn't he have been laughed off as being a screwball and a nut? Why, indeed, was Galileo forced to publicly recant his objectively determined conclusions about the motion of the planets around the sun? Couldn't he simply have been ignored?

I think it rather unlikely that he would have been ignored. For every new idea, there are receptive ears that will listen. If the basis of the new idea is not only logical but based on observation, then it is even more appealing. One does not have to have heard of the scientific method or to have been taught the rules of formal logic to accept a basically reasonable explanation of something. So the fear that a new dogma will replace the old one, along with its priests, is a compelling reason for the suppression of knowledge. At least, it is for the priests.

It would seem, however, that there must also be at least a seed of doubt in the minds of those who would suppress, for them to react to such "heresy" as they did to Galileo and Darwin, and as they have reacted more recently to the sociobiologists who contend that there is a strong genetic component in observed behavioral differences. It is possible that the discomfort alone, produced by the jarring of one's faith by the exercise of scientific inquiry, might be sufficient grounds for trying to silence the intellectual heretics.

I do not contend, then, that the reasons for suppressing knowledge throughout history are significantly different from those resulting in the discrimination against any minority by the majority. That is, religious and racial intolerance is based first on a group identity and then on the perception that the minority somehow threatens the power of the majority, if even only majority status itself. The minority may be tolerated as long as it clearly keeps to itself and makes no claim to being the "superior" group. That is, the black slaves in the United States were happily integrated into southern white culture as an inferior, subservient caste which could never challenge the power of the whites. But as soon as they gained a measure of independence and dared to presume that they were on an equal plane with their former masters, they were despised.

Differing beliefs and cultures may be sought out and destroyed, at great expense and effort to the suppressor. The crusades of the eleventh through the fourteenth centuries A.D. testify to the fervor that can be generated over a belief, so that any degree of brutality may be rationalized in the name of God. Not dissimilar to the Crusades were the Nazis' efforts to rid the world of Jews, or the systematic attempt of the United States to destroy Vietnam in the name of the godly American Way vis-à-vis the total evil of the Communist ogre.

Science, or the quest for knowledge, gets in trouble when it helps to provide the basis for differing beliefs. If there is a new belief system or world view that becomes established and challenges an existing order, it really doesn't matter to the challenged whether the threatening ideas come from scientific inquiry or a belief in pagan gods. There will be an attempt to put them down in either case, along with their proponents.

There is, however, an important difference. Pagan gods and belief systems may come and go. But a scientifically determined fact, if it is indeed valid, will continue to emerge from more and more sources, until, ultimately, it must be accepted, subject of course to the accuracy of measurements and the conditions under which the observations were made. That is, early intuitive theories of gravity stated than heavier objects fall to the ground faster than lighter ones. Newton challenged this notion, his view of gravity predicting that the rate of acceleration of an object due to gravity at the earth's surface should be independent of the mass of the object. Countless measurements confirmed that, to a high degree of accuracy, that was indeed the case. Within the limits of measurement, then, a "fact" had been established. Now, with relativistic corrections, gravity waves, highly accurate measurements, we know that the gravitational "constant" isn't as a simple concept as that envisaged by Newton. But these refinements of the gravitational model may also be incorporated into what we may consider a "fact."

The suppression either of the act of acquiring knowledge or of the knowledge itself can, therefore, be only temporary. Galileo recanted. However, the facts and Galileo's compelling interpretation of them could not be ignored. In time, even the church had to settle for the earth's less-than-central role in the scheme of the structure of the universe.

Darwin challenged the fundamentalists, who prefer a literal interpretation of the Bible. He, in turn, is still being challenged by them. But he seems to be winning. Lysenko conformed genetic theory to the dogma of dialectical materialism. The USSR could not permit its geneticists to contradict, through scientific inquiry, the concept that acquired characteristics could be inherited, until the elucidation of the structure of DNA and the mechanism of inheritance made such a notion blatantly preposterous.

A similar phenomenon has occurred in the United States within the last 20 years and is still not settled. This is the matter of the inheritability of intellectual and behavioral traits. A century ago, part of the prevailing mind set was that indeed all human qualities, good and bad, were inherited. Although there were few attempts at controlled or properly conducted observational studies, the overhwelming body of anecdotal experience suggested that there were born criminals as well as born geniuses; temperament, musical talent, moral fiber—all were assumed to lie in whatever it was that was passed from generation to generation. The class structure in Britain and elsewhere, as well as the eugenics movement in the United States,[16] was certainly based on the premise that proper breeding is as important in people as it is in farm animals. Indeed, *a priori,* if one can cast off one's social and political visions of human equality, it is an entirely rational assumption.

But stepping outside of one's mind set is difficult to do. Class elitism always raises the hackles of all but those in the top stratum. And Hitler's promotion of breeding a master race, along with his concepts of Nazism, led to the quiet end of discussions of the practice of eugenics. Still, in spite of entirely justified pressure to obtain legal and social equality among all racial and ethnic groups and between the sexes, most geneticists and people in general believe that traits other than those that may be observed physically have at least a partial genetic basis. Certainly, anyone in the education profession is aware of a great spread of intellectual abilities among students, differences that persist from early life and that are relatively immutable, regardless of the environment. Such variation of abilities is common among siblings in the same family, who receive, more or less, the same stimulation and opportunities.

The study and measurement of mental and behavioral qualities, and even their genetic basis, were considered a legitimate branch of scientific inquiry until Arthur Jensen drew a conclusion that ran head-on into the civil rights movement. The hypothesis that blacks, *on the average,* are less intelligent than whites is supported by a number of studies comparing test scores from rather large samples, intelligence or IQ being defined here by whatever it is that these tests measure.[17] Presumably, these tests present an individual profile of a number of distinct mental qualities indicating the ability to reason and to learn. Jensen, Eysenck, and the outspoken physicist-turned-sociologist, William Shockley, the principal proponents of this theory, were summarily denounced as racists, even by many scientists. The timing was unfortunate. The past two decades have been a crucial period in the struggle for legal equality between blacks and whites. The efforts of the civil rights movement to gain for blacks everyone's respect as worthy human beings required that there be no shred of evidence that any bigot could use to argue that blacks were somehow inferior. Logically, of course, the possibility that there may be a difference in the *mean* test scores of two populations, has no connection with the intelligence, worth, or social standing of an individual. In fact, the spread of abilities within either the white or the black population far exceeds the maximum difference in mean population IQ claimed by anyone. If one accepts that the behavioral differences, including intellectual ability, that one observes among individuals have a genetic component, and couples that with the fact that there are differences in the distribution of all readily observable genetically determined traits (hair color, skin color, blood group factors, hair patterns, etc.) among human population groups, then it follows that there are likely to be differences in the distribution of behavioral genes as well. But there was fear that such studies would provide ammunition to the real racists, and so there were attempts to denounce and suppress such studies without subjecting their claims to the test of critical and objective scientific evaluation.

The data were undeniable, but the critics argued that the differences in intelligence, however it may be defined or measured—in individuals or in group averages—were primarily if not entirely sociological in origin, and not genetic. There were attempts to explain away and discount the studies showing the remarkable similarity in test scores between identical twins reared in different environments. There were other studies purporting to show that IQ could be increased by as much as 30 points through intensive education, although criticism of the bias in these studies is every bit as valid as the criticism of the validity of IQ tests. No one would deny that an enriched environment at an early age is important in developing interests and the desire to learn, which certainly could affect performance on certain types of scholastic aptitude tests. Nevertheless, there is a strong argument that tests may be designed to measure innate abilities, and that these can be made relatively immune from the effect of environmental enhancement or bias. In fact, the principal study purporting to show the most dramatic gains in IQ has never been published, and the raw data have never been revealed for validation by other scientists. Only the conclusions drawn by the investigator, Richard Heber, have appeared, and those only in the popular press. (Heber is now in prison for pocketing a substantial portion of the federal grants given him to study IQ improvement.) This case is discussed in a recent article by Richard Herrenstein,[18] who blamed much of the popular bias against the legitimate scientific investigation of innate behavioral and intellectual differences among populations on grossly slanted press coverage, by journalists who confuse social and political equality with biological equivalence.

Even many geneticists seem wary of the topic, or else they seem to be bending over backward to avoid the conclusion that the role of genetics is the predominant one in determining intellectual and behavioral qualities. Dobzhansky *et al.*[19] went to great lengths to point out that these qualities have a highly complex genetic basis, with many interdependent phenotypic interactions. To be sure, there are very many genes that must be involved in influencing in some way one or more of the numerous phenotypic qualities that comprise what we call intelligence. And, certainly, there are many ways in which environment could interact with these genetically determined factors. Nevertheless, there seems to be an extreme reluctance to argue what I believe is the simpler premise, that however complex they may be, the genetic determinants are more important than environmental ones.

One should not, of course, assume that the explanation of the ultimate expression of all genetic and environmental factors in an adult human being will be simple. I would suggest, however, that it is erroneus to view the issue as one in which environmental and hereditary determinants are somehow acting as equivalent types of influences in an additive manner. Rather, our entire *physical* being, including the structure of our brains and levels of the many substances which regulate its function, certainly must be specified in our genes. Therefore genetic determinants undoubtedly dictate the manner and degree to which all creatures including humans respond to and can learn from their environment and experiences. Thus, on top of perhaps innate personality traits, the degree to which one is capable of abstract thought, logic, memory, concentration, spatial visualization, auditory resolution and musical sensitivity, hand-eye coordination, and so on, will determine how an individual will be able to benefit from or be influenced by his environmental stimuli, including parental attention, exposure to problem-solving situations, and formal education. That is, genes determine the nature of the environmental response of a particular individual. But obviously, the amount one learns or the extent of the skills one acquires could be limited either by the innate ability to respond to stimuli or by the degree of environmental exposure to those stimuli. Thus the net result in a mature individual will be a function of both. However, this view stipulates that the degree to which one can compensate for the lack of genetically determined abilities by increasing the extent and intensity of the environmental stimulus is definitely rather limited.

I was surprised to find in a textbook on molecular genetics,[20] a lengthy and somewhat polemical critique of the notion that intelligence and, particularly the mean intelligence between racial and population groups, could possibly be genetically determined. One of the authors is well known for his activities in attempting to discredit the work of Jensen and those who share Jensen's opinions. While this individual is entitled to his opinions, he would appear to be using the vehicle of a textbook to indoctrinate the readers with his point of view. For a scientist to foster a belief in dogma of any sort, rather than the spirit of an open mind and the free inquiry into any question, regardless of how much at odds the possible conclusion may be with a social or political ideology, is a serious and dangerous business. Whether by innuendo or direct denunciation, such activities can be harmful to scientists attempting the legitimate investigation of unpopular questions, or at least questions that may have unpopular answers.

But Jensen and Shockley were just the beginning. Edward O. Wilson published a scholarly work entitled *Sociobiology*,[21] in which the final chapter extended the biological principles apparently governing animal societies to human sociology. Because Wilson's theory postulated a genetic basis for behavioral differences between males and females, it soon became the center of controversy. Although it may seem obvious to many that there are, of course, behavioral differences between males and females, not only in humans but certainly between cows and bulls, male and female cats, and males and females of just about every other species, the notion flew in the face of the tenets of the women's movement.

Julian Stanley's studies on mathematically gifted children,[22] showing that virtually all of them were boys, only continued to unsettle those to whom the *belief* in innate, substantive equality between the sexes is a necessity. Lumsden and Wilson have published another work[23] contending that cultural differences also have a genetic bias. New studies relate the behavioral differences between men and women to the levels of androgens during development.[24] And a report on differences in intelligence between populations indicates a marked difference in the mean test scores between the Japanese and the Americans, the Japanese having been consistently around 11 IQ points higher than Americans since World War II.[25] (The difference was only about 4 or 5 points prior to 1942.) The breakdown of the data from the 1983 Scholastic Aptitude Test (SAT), administered to most prospective American college students, is consistent with the hypothesis that there are fundamental differences in the mean scholastic abilities between different racial groups and do not contradict any of the controversial studies cited above.

What we are witnessing, then, is the same old story. Cherished beliefs are being challenged by data that, in spite of the flaws in some of the studies, all seem to be pointing to the same general conclusion: There *are* clear behavioral and intellectual differences not only between individuals but among different racial or geographical populations and between the sexes. At least some significant fraction of these differences would appear to be embedded in the genes. Even though there have been numerous attempts to discredit much of the research in sociobiology and behavioral genetics, to impugn the motives of the investigators, and to explain away the results in terms of environmental differences, cultural bias in test methods, and so on, the message that is emerging is clear, even if it is at odds with the view of reality preferred by those who must believe that social and political equality requires biological equality. Sadly, even some scientists among this group would contend that there can be no rational inquiry on the question of genetics and behavior or intelligence, declaring in advance that the premise is absolutely false.

Thus, the Biophysical Society, of which I have been a long-time member, passed a resolution in 1972 (offered by the same geneticist whose textbook was cited above) saying that the work of Jensen and others had no rational or scientific basis. I must say that I was astounded at the time that presumably competent scientists could allow their concepts of social equality to cloud rational scientific judgment totally and could become part of a move to suppress free inquiry.

Jonathan Beckwith, a molecular biologist at Harvard Medical School and representing an organization known as Science for the People, chose the 1977 National Academy of Sciences forum on recombinant DNA to put down all research indicating that behavioral characteristics might have a genetic basis.[26] This stance comprised part of his case for proscribing research involving genetic manipulation. However, Science for the People espouses an ideology having much in common with Marxism, with the status of the worker being paramount and the intrinsic equality of all people a necessary component. This ideology *must* attribute all differences in behavior between men and women, criminals and the law-abiding, or the working class and the bourgeoisie to circumstances, never to innate, genetically determined traits. It is precisely elucidation of the details of genetic determinism, greatly facilitated by gene-splicing technologies, that could expose and refute the premises on which this ideology rests.

It is also not surprising that *Sociobiology* and Edward Wilson have been and still are under scathing attack.[27] At the 1978 annual meeting of the American Association for the Advancement of Science, during what appeared to have been a premeditated protest, someone, in a flurry of unconstrained self-expression, rushed onto the platform where Wilson was speaking and dumped a pitcher of ice water on his head. (At that moment, I was on a panel discussing recombinant DNA legislation in the adjacent room. When the roar of voices exploded following the incident, we quickly lost our audience to the melodrama next door.)

Now that man's control over the genetic makeup of living organisms has increased to the point where it is easy to imagine the day when it will be possible to alter the course of human genetic destiny, Jon Beckwith is only one of a large number of people who are uneasy. In one respect, it is unsettling to the very religious, who take comfort in believing that life has a spiritual quality that lies outside the realm of scientific explanation. But perhaps "very religious" is too strong. The hippie era of the late 1960s and early 1970s had a strong quasi-religious component. This came, in part, from the renewed interest in Eastern religions, meditation, yoga, and the occult. I know many who, although not religious in the traditional sense, prefer to believe in a quality in life which not only has been out of the reach of scientists so far, but that is forever immune to the probing of the scientific method. There is loose talk of "energy fields" that somehow cannot be examined rationally. One holding this viewpoint doesn't need to answer the critics, for there is a ready answer in the hypothesis that these all important life forces and energies lie safely outside scientific inquiry and cannot be verified experimentally. These models of life and causation and the universe tend to be rather elaborate and mystical, whereas the models of validated scientifc inquiry tend toward greater simplicity, confirming the principle of Occam's razor (the simplest of competing theories is the most likely to be correct). Most of these belief systems, like the Judeo-Christian religions, elevate man far above other life forms. Their construction certainly reflects the universal need to explain man's existence and life generally in terms that can be understood. As the biologist's explanations of life become more mechanistic and molecular, there is an increasing reluctance on the part of many to accept that something as complex and extraordinary as a human being could possibly be only a reflection of the laws of physics and chemistry. This retreat to mysticism, or to revealed or experiential truth, is an unfortunate reaction to the complexities of present-day knowledge and the technology it has spawned. It is really a form of intellectual cowardice, which carries with it an unwritten antirational, antiscience element. Even some scientists, frustrated by the inability to explain, for example, the phenomenon of morphogenesis during embryonic development, resort to elaborate, unprovable theories. Rupert Sheldrake postulated intricate "morphogenic fields" that span time and space and are altered by existing life, and that control the details of the life cycles of all organisms and perhaps the properties of inanimate matter.[28]

By whatever name is currently acceptable, religion continues to satisfy the same basic need to deal with the complexities of human life and the finality of death. Thus, those who look closely into the workings of life and find rational, scientific explanations are tampering in the province of God. Or Yaweh. Or Buddha. But even this tampering may be acceptable as long as no one tries to alter the course of life. Look, but don't touch. If you do, you are guilty of "playing God."

It is not surprising that two of the first books on gene splicing used that very phrase in the title. June Goodfield published *Playing God*[29] in 1977. This work, however, although taking note of the power of the new genetics, was not antiscience. Ted Howard and Jeremy Rifkin's book, *Who Should Play God?*,[30] published only in paperback in 1977 is, on the other hand, definitely opposed to inquiry in certain areas, but the message is really more antitechnology than antiscience. There is an important distinction, which deserves further clarification.

In the late 1970s, much of the objection to the support and the conduct of research using recombinant DNA methods—that is, objection that was not based on the presumed hazards of the technique—was directed at the misuse of knowledge. Slogans such as "slippery slope" and "whatever can be done, will be done" were heard as reasons not to obtain certain kinds of knowledge in the first place. Just as concerned parents have perennially tried to maintain the innocence of their children as long as possible to save them from being led down the self-destructive paths of temptation into sex, alcohol, drugs, and general debauchery, we were warned by the nay-sayers that this forbidden knowledge of the secrets of life will lead to all manner of evils. Of course, the development of atomic weapons from the fundamental relationship between matter and energy is cited as proof that we should *not* learn how life can be modified.

Hence, a new ground was found for opposing research, or the acquisition of knowledge, that was *not* the traditional challenge to an ideology, as is the case with sociobiology. Rather, it was the fear of how knowledge of awesome power could and, the argument went, *would* be used for nefarious purposes. This fear of how new knowledge might be used is only another form of the fear of the unknown. In principle, it is still the conservative world view. It is again the preference for the comfort of staying at home, even if it gets a bit dull, to exploring a place where you have never been. It is choosing to live all your life in Baltimore, instead of disrupting your life to change jobs and move to Boston. Or Paris. Or Peking. It is an unwillingness to take risk.

I do not mean to suggest that there is not a valid issue concerning the use of knowledge, as well as the responsibility of society and its institutions to use it wisely. The development of an ethic for technology has now become a necessity for contemporary society. But there is a very basic difference between achieving this control through curtailing inquiry, in which case society is deprived of any of the *benefits* of knowledge as well, and controlling the applications themselves. The question of the societal control of technology is explored later in greater detail.

The fallacy in any proposed policy of suppressing the acquisition of knowledge is the false assumption that it is possible. The curious and adventuresome side of human nature is the part that cannot rest until it knows what is on the other side of the mountain. This is a part of humanity that will always survive, no matter what attempts are made to chain the mind or the spirit, unless some future world tyrant decides that it is too threatening and genetically engineers the trait out of the human race. It is this quality that will render impossible any attempt to limit the acquisition of knowledge.

It may be possible, in one country, at a particular time, to squelch absolutely the pursuit of knowledge in a given area, but it cannot be stopped everywhere, forever. Accordingly, the suppression of inquiry during the Lysenko era in the Soviet Union merely served to put Russian genetics far behind the state of the science in the rest of the world. I am certain that no attempt to suppress research in the United States, Western Europe, and most of the remainder of the technologically advanced world could ever gain enough support to prevail—now. However, there are areas of research which the U.S. government will not fund, such as human *in vitro* fertilization, because of political pressure from the right-to-life lobby. In the unlikely event that a political force to the right of the moral majority should come to power, who can say what might suddenly become fair game? There were those of us who once thought it highly improbable that Richard Nixon could ever get elected to national office, especially after his defeat by Pat Brown for the governorship of California in 1962. There were probably even more who once laughed at the thought that an aging right-wing extremist movie actor named Ronald Reagan would ever be considered seriously for any public office. But research, like politics, is unpredictable. The findings from a line of inquiry may have absolutely no bearing on the original problem investigated. Science is an adventure in the unexpected. And the mind cannot be controlled. At least, not yet. Could Einstein have been prevented from thinking? Much of his early learning and speculations about time and matter were done in his spare time while working in the Swiss Patent Office, the only job he could get after being unable to obtain an academic post. And even if Einstein had met an untimely fate and had not contributed the theory of general relativity to physics, sooner or later someone else would have done it. The phenomenon of simultaneity of discovery is continually being confirmed. That is, advances in science are not, as it sometimes seems, only the singular contributions of an occasional rare and brilliant intellect, without whom science would not progress. This is not to say that there have not been individuals whose achievements have been monumental. There will always be such geniuses, and someone has to get there first. More often than not, however, the new and startling discoveries are made independently by two or more different investigators, sometimes without the knowledge of the work of the others. Each is dependent on the accumulated knowledge up to that point, the contributions of many over a long period of time. When most of the pieces of a new puzzle finally emerge, there are usually several who can and will put them together.

A classic example of simultaneous discovery occurred in 1925, when both Werner Heisenberg and Erwin Schrödinger published formalizations of quantum mechanics, each explaining the observations on atomic spectra and the Bohr model of the atom. The mathematical form of the two theories, at first glance, appeared to be totally different. There was intense discussion for several months over the validity of either theory until Schrödinger proved, in 1926, that Heisenberg's matrix mechanics and his own wave mechanics were equivalent.[31]

One may view the progress of knowledge as proceeding forward with a relentless pressure. Although political or religious forces may momentarily retard it, none of them is capable of resisting it ultimately. It is an intrinsic element of the human spirit. It is the yang of the human psyche, which will always pursue its curiosity about the unknown, even though it must coexist with the yin of security, stability, and comfort. Therefore, whatever reasons people or governments may put forward for stopping certain lines of inquiry, or for keeping scientific results a secret (usually for political reasons), the concept is totally at odds with an essential component of humanity. Curtailing inquiry cannot work. Suppressing knowledge cannot work. In whatever form it is presented, whether in ideological indoctrination, the burning of books, classified research, or a proscription on dangerous thinking, all are ultimately folly.

Thus, the fears that a latter-day Hitler will order thousands of genetically engineered, mindless, brutal storm troopers are not going to be assuaged by the prohibition of research in genetics. If such an outcome is within the realm of technological reality, and someone mad enough to want to do it could again rise to power, then it will probably happen. If this is a fear people have about the *use* of knowledge, then that is where it must be dealt with. Just as the decision to build nuclear weapons received a strong political impetus by the timing of the first fission reaction with World War II, the use—or misuse—of biological knowledge will no doubt be similarly influenced by political and social forces rather than scientific ones.

Military and industrial secrecy are perhaps two topics that should be mentioned here. In weapons research, it is assumed that our scientists and engineers may be able to think of a way to construct a diabolical weapon that somehow theirs can't or won't, and that it is necessary to keep everything secret. There is perhaps some truth to the concept of buying time—a little. But it won't get you much more. The recent story of a college student writing a report on how to construct a hydrogen bomb,[32] thoroughly upsetting the Pentagon, is perhaps a lesson in the absurdity of the concept of classifying everything. The basic principles of physics on which the hydrogen bomb is based are well known to every advanced student of physics. Given the task of applying this knowledge to the technical problems to be solved in actually building a working bomb, it strikes me that any reasonably competent group of physicists and nuclear chemists could, starting from scratch, design a functional weapon within a reasonable period of time. Therefore, it is nonsense to assume that any country in the world that has a reasonably advanced technology and that really wants a bomb doesn't know how to do it. They may not have the resources to obtain and refine the necessary materials to make a bomb, so there are both economic and geographic constraints on whether or not they can actually make one. But the limitation is not the knowledge.

In the case of industrial secrecy, or the protection of proprietary information (trade secrets), the primary purpose is simply to give your company enough of an edge to apply for the patents first. This is usually a relatively short period of time. In the intensely competitive biotechnology industry, people are especially sensitive about revealing trade secrets, and every original idea automatically becomes a trade secret. Yet no one is under the delusion that a trade secret is any more than temporary protection. With more than 200 companies striving to be first in reaching many of the same goals, trade secrets—and a little luck—may determine who is first to the patent office. And that is enough.

Even though it is certain that *any* scientific discovery will be made more than once, and that keeping secrets is ultimately useless, how is a scientist to proceed if he discovers something for which the undesirable applications, or even those that are wanted by society, are those which he would personally prefer not to take place? Or worse, suppose that he foresees disastrous social consequences as a direct result of his findings. Should he publish his results anyway, disclaiming any responsibility for someone else's use of the knowledge that he has provided? It is not an easy question.

Returning for a moment to our discussion of the implications of the control of aging, let us suppose that you are a scientist and you discover, perhaps by accident, the key to the aging process. Moreover, you find that it is so simple that the process can be arrested in adults from a concoction of common ingredients to be found in the average household. No, don't laugh. The science may be farfetched, but the ethical dilemma facing you, the scientist, is quite serious. Would you tell anyone? Would you publish it? I won't ask you if you would apply for a patent, for it would be impossible to prevent people from mixing their own potion of nutmeg, garlic, vitamin E, and Br'er Rabbit Brand molasses.

But keep in mind what would happen if you did tell the world. The disruption in society would be an utter disaster. Even though you have found the way to save and prolong lives (isn't that the goal of medicine after all?), your little discovery could quickly disrupt the world economy, not to mention the destruction of the funeral industry. Agriculture would pick up for a while, until it couldn't keep up with the demand any longer. Sooner or later, political solutions would have to be sought, and I leave it to your imagination what these might be. No doubt some of you have seen the films *Logan's Run* or *Soylent Green*. There may be better answers than these. And there may be worse.

Now, suppose that you make the same discovery. However, instead of the magic youth potion being cheap and easy to make, it's complicated and expensive. Then, I would pose the same questions. You could, of course, ask *how* complicated and *how* expensive. It does make a difference. If it were so difficult to make that no one could benefit, you have no problem. But that is unlikely. What if its concoction were easy for a trained scientist and required a clinical procedure, but impossible for a layman to perform on himself. Would you patent the process and open a clinic, letting economics dictate who will stay young and who will get old and die? Or would you relinquish all rights to the federal government and let the bureaucracy take care of the problem with its characteristic wisdom? Or would you just treat yourself and your family and not tell anyone else? The solution to this thought experiment is left as an exercise for the reader. Remember that whatever your choice, if you were able to find a cure for the aging process, so will someone else.

Toward an Ethic for Technology

I would defend the support of scientific research with public funds as being among the more worthwhile and valid activities of government. Science, along with the arts and the humanities, contributes to the cultural plane of any society and so is in its best interests. Of course, a corollary of the broad support of science is the many practical benefits that will ultimately ensue from the knowledge gained. Another corollary is that many of the presumed benefits of certain of these technologies will have undesirable and probably unforeseen consequences. Some of these may possibly be of disastrous proportions. Witness the precariously metastable confrontation of two posturing superpowers laden with nuclear weapons, the ultimate fruits of science and of technological development promoted in the interests of national security.

Although some of us would rank the cultural value of knowledge well above the value of any of its practical, tangible expressions, probably most taxpayers and certainly most governments have a different order of priorities. The debates in the congressional authorizing and appropriations committees are centered primarily on the practical utility that science will give us: the cures for disease and the better airplanes, cars, televisions, and computers—a better life, defined in material terms. And in much of the world, where the average person's life is one of poverty, inadequate diet, and diseases unknown in the United States, science and the pursuit of knowledge as cultural endeavors are luxuries in which only a privileged elite can afford to engage. In these countries, any humanistic world view would demand that science be pursued purely as a means to the solution of pressing problems plaguing their countries. To explore science without the goal of developing technology to improve the human condition is seen as immoral.

Not long ago, the discussions in the congressional appropriations committees were focused on space, and on the worry that perhaps the largest political rival of the United States would win the race to the moon and the planets. Sputnik, marking the dawn of the space age in 1957, did more for American science than any amount of lobbying by scientists could ever have accomplished. The logic is simple: To build space vehicles requires advanced technology. Advanced technology can come only from basic science. There-fore, in order to become a world leader in science, the United States must increase the support for both basic research and the training of new scientists. The primary motive for the public support of science in the United States in 1957 became competition with the Soviet Union, ultimately in the name of national security, just as the Manhattan Project had a primarily military objective.

Today, a quick glance at the 1984 federal budget for research and devel-opment reveals the traditional priorities of the government of the United States. First is national security, or whatever that phrase may be a euphemism for. Second come projects that are expected to yield tangible public benefits. A small third is anything of purely cultural value. But federal research and development are only half of the story.

The "private sector," or corporate enterprise, conducts research and development where a salable product or service will follow. Profit is the only governing value, at least until aging and wealthy tycoons who have had their success in business see fit to become philanthropists before they die. Perhaps the returning of their personal fortunes to the public in this way is the ultimate act of atonement for the sin of avarice. Nevertheless, it is a poignant irony of our society that most of the support of activities and institutions of true cultural worth—private universities, art collections and museums, research institutes, concert halls, fellowships for study in the arts and sciences, and prizes for scholarly excellence—have come from the donation of funds once amassed purely in the name of profit, and often ruthlessly so. Even the conveted Nobel prizes, the epitome of recognition for achievements in the arts and sciences, exist because of Alfred Nobel's success in the manufacture and sale of explosives.

Aside from direct governmental support of applied science for military applications and the space program, private enterprise has historically been the primary seat of the application of scientific knowledge. At least, this is the model followed in most of the economically developed world. Presumably, a natural process takes place, called economics, which determines that only products will be produced which people want, and are willing and able to pay for.

But what if what people want isn't really good for them? Who, if any-one, is to protect them? And what if nobody knows at first that something might do more harm than good? As an example, DDT was sprayed indis-criminately until the persistence of the chemical began to be appreciated, and the disruptions in the food chain and the near demise of the peregrine falcon began to suggest that something was wrong. Our wondrous technology has introduced not only the age of chemistry but the age of carcinogens. The products of the combustion of our fossil fuels have seriously perturbed the acid–base balance of the lakes and soils. The Aswân High Dam in Egypt is turning into a major ecological debacle. Who would have guessed that giving premature infants elevated oxygen would make them blind, or that Valium (diazepam), the real opiate of the masses, would be addictive?

So, relatively recently, on the heels of the Industrial Revolution, came the concept of regulation. In the United States, we now have a multitude of regulatory laws and the agencies to administer them, much of the apparatus being there to protect the public from the side effects of technology. The Food and Drug Administration has the responsibility for ensuring the safety and the efficacy of drugs, and that the foods we eat are free from harmful substances. The Environmental Protection Agency administers laws concerned with toxic chemicals, pollutants in air and water, pesticides, and radiation. The Nuclear Regulatory Commission is charged with overseeing the safety of nuclear power plants and with regulating the use of radioactive materials. The Consumer Products Safety Commission is supposed to protect the public from injury from consumer products. The Occupational Safety and Health Administration looks out (in principle) for the safety of workers. And there are numerous additional regulatory authorities that are concerned in some way with the control of technology for the ultimate protection of the health and safety of the people.

In practice, the effectiveness of the entire system is, of course, highly subject to the strength and the direction of the prevailing political winds. Thus, what was established in large part as a by-product of the age of flower children and outrage over the war in Vietnam—that is, the passage in the early 1970s of broader and greatly strengthened environmental legislation—is now suffering from deliberate neglect because of the political shift toward the right in the early 1980s. Eventually, times will change, and protecting human health and the environment will again take priority over policies favorable primarily to big business and a giant military establishment.

But that is another matter. At least, the legal apparatus was put in place by Congress to control some of the harmful consequences of technology. Other countries, to varying degrees, have a similar awareness of the necessity to keep a measure of ethical scrutiny imposed on technological development, in the event that the moral choices are not made spontaneously. If the people really decide, through their representatives in their respective political institutions, that technology needs to be controlled, then it is possible to control it, except where technology is entirely under the direction of a totalitarian elite or its equivalent, as it is perceived to be in many parts of the globe.

There remain certain areas of the applied science where regulation is still an anathema. Medicine is a case in point. The medical profession in the United States has generally opposed all forms of regulation, even when it is designed to ensure a high level of professional standards. The medical professional associations in the United States have maintained that they can do a better job of regulating their own profession than the government. They may be right.

Medical ethics is full of difficult problems, but it is generally accepted that even with untried methods of treatment, there should always be the promise of a net benefit to the patient. There has also been subscription to the concept of informed consent. That is, a patient must be fully informed of the nature of the procedure and the known or possible risks, as well as the prospective benefits. A national study commission[33] examined the ethics of research on human subjects and recommended policies governing research involving prisoners, children, the mentally infirm, psychosurgery, and other issues of concern. Human subjects of research, it is generally agreed, should never be subjected to a net risk, either from the procedure itself, or, if they belong to a control group of a clinical trial, from being deprived of treatment from which they may expect a net benefit, once the treatment is shown to be effective.

The same principles apply generally to any patients being treated for an illness. Of course, if it is a new procedure, perhaps being tried for the first time, the patient is *de facto* a research subject and is subject to whatever rules or precedents exist for the protection of his rights. But even in a routine procedure, such as an appendectomy, the patient is still entitled to the right of informed consent and should expect the treatment to benefit him or, at least, not to make him worse.

As is true of environmental and health regulations, there is sometimes a difference between medical ethics in theory and in practice. In some cases, there are review boards appointed to oversee the progress of human subject research, as in the case of clinical trials for the testing of new drugs, but patients can still be the victims of abuse, neglect, or incompetence.

With this somewhat inconsistent history, how do we now stand with respect to the new technology, which is being developed from the findings of basic biological research at an extraordinary rate and which may create a completely new set of ethical dilemmas? Do we have mechanisms by which the applications of the new biology to human beings or to other life forms can be regulated or controlled by society? And what of the question of equity? If, indeed, there are to be highly desirable or beneficial results of applied biological research, are there mechanisms for guaranteeing that they will be available to all? Should there be?

Thus far, we have one example on which to draw. The fertilization of a human ovum outside the body was achieved in the 1970s, with the first successful birth from a fertilized egg transplanted to the mother's uterus occurring in 1978. Since Steptoe and Edwards assisted in the creation of Louise Brown, the procedure has become refined and is now practiced in a number of clinics in the United States and abroad. However, the procedure was, from the beginning, controversial, primarily on religious grounds. As a result, the politically sensitive U.S. government would not even approve of research on human *in vitro* fertilization, lest the right-to-lifers make a fuss. Consequently, all work in this area has taken place in private clinics and is now, for some, a lucrative practice. Even though the use of the procedure has come to be widely accepted with time, so that it has practically become a routine, if somewhat expensive, procedure, the U.S. government and the Department of Health and Human Services still conspicuously avoid the subject.

The case of Martin Cline at UCLA is not directly comparable. He attempted genetic therapy on two thalassemia patients abroad, anticipating, correctly, that his university's institutional Review Board (IRB) would tell him that because the method had not been shown to work in animals and was unlikely to on theoretical grounds, his procedure would subject patients to unnecessary risk. A great deal of trouble for Dr. Cline followed, including the loss of some NIH grant funds, for not complying with the established procedures instituted to protect the rights and safety of the patient, and for violating the NIH Guidelines for recombinant DNA research. Subsequently, he was roundly critized by his peers in scientific journals for trying something on a patient that had such a remotely small chance of success.

But suppose that Dr. Cline had been a private physician with his own laboratory and had not been conducting research with federal funds. Then, he would not have been subject to any such constraints, for there is no IRB to review in advance a procedure that a physician wishes to try on a patient. Thus, the *in vitro* fertilization clinic in Norfolk of the Drs. Jones has never required such scrutiny. Many patients with blocked fallopian tubes are willing to pay $3,000 for a chance to get pregnant by this method. But is it ethical? There seem to be no grounds on which to fault the Joneses. They are not encouraging false hopes and appear to be fully informing the patients of the risks involved (which are rather small). All would agree that the Joneses are conducting their clinic in an entirely ethical manner. If they were not, however, adequate legal grounds may not exist to bring action or to protect the health of the patients. Medical fraud is illegal, and so is the broadly nebulous thing called *malpractice*. But there are instances where either of these may be difficult to prove or even to define clearly.

The matter of risk is only one side of ethics. *In vitro* fertilization is an expensive procedure. Because it is not viewed as essential medical treatment, many health insurance companies will not cover such services, and those without insurance are out of luck anyway. In the United States, the matter of equity in health care has been an issue for some time. Where should the line be drawn between necessary services and those that may be a bit new, esoteric, and risky but that offer a great advantage to the patient who can afford to pay for them? The President's Commission for the Study of Ethical Problems in Medicine and Biomedical and Behavioral Research examined the matter of equity in health services,[15] but it did not give much attention to services over and above those needed to assure good health, or to problems in countries other than the United States. Most other economically developed countries have, as an element of policy, some sort of national health program, whereby needed health care is not limited by a person's income and resources. But how does one define *need?* In Finland, for example, working mothers get up to 13 months' maternity leave, the first seven at full pay, and at no risk of losing their jobs. Even the father gets some extra time off. In a culture that places a high value on giving all children every chance at a good beginning in life, this is not viewed as extravagant. Infant health statistics in countries with these types of programs indicate that they do make a difference.

So what of the future? What will happen when the first clinic opens offering genetic surgery on your child-to-be? Especially if the promised methods work, and there is little risk to the mother, and the parents are fully informed of everything that is done, there would at present be no legal or regulatory constraints on such a practice. I do not contend that there should be. At least, there is no inconsistency with the criteria that past presidential commissions and ethics advisory bodies have established for a practice to qualify as ethical. But many would advocate that such practices should be curtailed anyway.

There are really no *new* questions of ethics with regard to the protection of the rights of the patients, or of justice concerning the unequal availability of a service, that do not now already exist with respect to conventional procedures. But the deliberate modification of a new human being raises a completely different issue from the traditional ethical questions.

There are, of course, always the protests that human life is sacrosanct and should never be tampered with directly. To be sure, current medical practices intervene in human life all the time, but somehow, direct genetic meddling is viewed as going too far, especially if it is done for a purpose other than to restore the status quo following the detection of a genetic defect. Such arguments cannot be met logically. If one believes in the santity of human life, this belief will define an ethic for technologies that would directly alter genetic makeup. If one does not, then the ethical principles governing the use of such a technology must be defined on more pragmatic grounds.

In the above example, the effect on society would probably not be significant. However, if it were known who possessed doctored genes, those select few—even if, and especially if, they were exceptionally endowed with desirable attributes—could experience social difficulties with their less fortunate peers. But it would be difficult to assess in advance the degree to which this would be a serious problem.

If, now, one imagines that other procedures, such as the age-arresting techniques discussed earlier, become common clinical practice, the social consequences might be expected to be more severe. However, if someone wished to carry the experimental manipulation of the human genome past the point where the result could be considered "human," the problems confronting society would be most difficult. How would a "super human" or a "sub human" be dealt with? What would its legal standing be? Would it be afforded rights under the Constitution? With the development of facility in altering human genes, the definition of *human* as we now use the word could cease to have meaning. Then what?

Many believe that such uses of applied genetics would be carrying things too far; that even if we could transform humans into something a bit different, we should not.[34] What purpose would be served by doing so? Should we experiment with presumed improvements in the 1990-model human being, designing him to cope better with the twenty-first century? Should the matter be left to individual innovation and discretion? Or should a government decree that we will just leave well enough alone? The fact remains that there is not now any current mechanism for the regulation of such practices, even if the federal government decides to stay completely out of the baby business.

There are other areas to which the new biology might well be applied over which we may wish to have some control. Most of the current activity in biotechnology is directed toward the efficient manufacture of pharmaceuticals and other useful chemicals. However, research on the genetic modification of plants and bacteria, in order to improve agricultural yields, may have untoward environmental consequences. That is, the object of such research is not a chemical substance, but a living organism which not only may be designed to have a survival advantage but is intended to be released into the general environment. For most crop plants, there is probably no particular reason for concern, but suppose a very healthy, highly competive nitrogen-fixing soil bacterium is developed. Its release into soils may so alter the soil flora that the structure and the nutrient value of agricultural soil would inadvertently be rendered poorer rather than richer. Ecological disruptions of this sort could spread well beyond the original site of deposition.

In many ways, this is like dispersing an unknown toxic chemical into the environment. It could be very difficult to return things to normal. There may thus be many new ways in which we could interfere with the ecology of the planet, as we have done so often in the past. But there are no regulatory authorities to deal with such possibilities. Kudzu, that madly vigorous vine brought to the southern United States from Japan, is more a nuisance than a hazard. Nevertheless, we have no guarantee that each new perturbation that we impose on the environment will remain relatively benign. The U.S. Environmental Protection Agency (EPA) announced in 1983 that it intends to regulate the release of genetically modified organisms into the environment, using an authority intended for toxic chemicals.

The employment of the new biology in biological warfare was one of the first suggested uses. At the 1977 National Academy of Sciences forum, it was the consensus that conventional bacteriology and virology would be sufficient to make anything as nasty as you wanted.[35] But this is no longer the case. Specific immunotoxins could perhaps make genocide a cinch. And designing viruses with special new and highly toxic properties is well within the reach of current methods. There are endless possibilities. Given the current attitudes toward chemical and nuclear weapons, there is reason to believe that both the United States and the USSR have taken a fresh look at the development of biological weapons. But if there are currently efforts in either country to develop weapons using genetic manipulation or the recent advances in immunology, it is a well-guarded secret.

The problem as one in international politics is thus not new. We have faced this one before and are facing it again now. If the only institutions at our disposal for controlling the development of biological weapons are the ones perpetrating their existence, then what recourse is there for the citizen? Perhaps, it is the same problem that now exists with nuclear disarmament. National governments cannot be expected to take unilateral action to forfeit *any* perceived advantage that they think they may have over a potential adversary. I was surprised that the RAC (the NIH Recombinant DNA Advisory Committee, in case you have forgotten) avoided taking a position on the use of gene splicing for biological weapons at its June 1982 meeting. It was proposed that the RAC (and NIH) endorse a statement that any use of gene-splicing methods for the design and development of biological weapons should be prohibited. There were only three votes for the resolution, which was replaced by a flaccid reminder to the Director of NIH that the Geneva convention was still in effect. Why was there such reluctance to endorse, in the context of the NIH Guidelines, a policy position that was presumably subscribed to by the U.S. government? The answer would require yet another analysis of human nature, the sociology of groups, and the perceptions of authority. Our history in reaching and enforcing international agreements on any aspect of war is not encouraging. Perhaps the RAC's recent inaction will serve to illustrate why it is so difficult deal with sensitive issues at an international level. Yet, it would appear that the evil side of biotechnology will be prevented from becoming reality only through the development of effective international controls. And these, if they are ever to work, will have to include a large measure of trust, since the verification of the absence of biological weapons development is essentially impossible.

Who Decides?

The previous discussions have presented for your consideration some of the possible directions in which technology based on an intimate knowledge of life's details may take us. But applied science is more malleable than basic science. That is, we shall continue to learn more and more about our universe, continually sharpening the pictures of understanding we have about every aspect of it, from the structure of the basic components of matter to the creation of galaxies. This continual pressure to gain knowledge will be only slightly affected by the cultural, political, or social values that predominate in any particular society at any particular time.

However, the technology developed at any given time and place will be determined very much by these values. It will reflect what people want, or think they want; the state of peace or war among nations; material and educational standards of living; economics; and, as always, a measure of chance. We must therefore examine how the decisions are made to pursue a particular line of technological development, and who makes them or—perhaps more relevant to our look into the future—who *should* make them.

The determinants of technology have been discussed earlier in this book. Economics in a more-or-less free market dictates that there will be technological development in any direction where a demand exists or can be created. A government of an economically developed country initiates new technological development most often to enhance its position internationally, but occasionally, for the benefit of its citizens. For economically undeveloped countries, these priorities may be reversed. For either, however, a conscious decision *not* to proceed with the development of a particular technology that may otherwise be desirable is usually based on its being too costly. Rarely is such a decision based on a concern about undesired consequences. Regulations designed to prevent human injury may be invoked to prohibit a specific class of drugs because of harmful effects, or the use of a pesticide that is toxic to more than its target organism. However, these prohibitions tend to be directed at very specific substances.

There is no instance that I can think of where a conscious decision by a national or a state government was made to stop or to curtail a particular branch of technology because its future was viewed as potentially harmful. However, there have been attempts by some individuals, both in and out of government, to initiate such policies, such as public referenda in some states to stop nuclear power. As the ultimate potential for destructive, undesirable, or simply problematic sides of some types of technology increase, we can expect to see many more attempts to stop or to control some technological endeavors, some of which will, no doubt, be successful.

Nuclear fission, with its awesome destructive power and its creation of lingering radiation, has generated the most concern in recent years. The movement to stop nuclear power continues, based chiefly on concerns about long-term problems, such as the disposal of radioactive wastes and the fear of a serious accident. However, because most people have never been directly affected, as far as they can tell, by the presumed evils of nuclear power, the issue is too abstract to attract large numbers of individuals. Thus, the more clever of the antinuke activists are turning to more tangible grounds on which to appeal directly to individuals to whom radiation is only a word. By citing the delays, the huge cost overruns, and the graft and incompetence in construction, all of which make nuclear power far more expensive than the cheap source of energy it was once promised to be, it has been possible to gain much more citizen support against nuclear power than by appeals based on health, safety, and the quality of the environment, Three Mile Island notwithstanding. When it is pointed out that utility bills in some areas have doubled to pay for some nuclear-power-plant debacle, ordinary, conservative citizens who wouldn't join any kind of "movement" become outraged.

The former governor of New Hampshire, Meldrim Thompson, who personified the stubborn intransigence of the extreme right for many years, was finally done in at the polls by the infamous Seabrook nuclear plant, which he had staunchly supported, not by the numerous demonstrations of the Clamshell Alliance, but because of the 23% surcharge on New Hampshire utility bills. Elsewhere, the overall botchery that has characterized the Diablo Canyon plant in California, or the Moscow, Ohio, plant, which is now at least seven years behind schedule, seems to be characteristic of a technology which simply wasn't destined to make the grade.

This is not to say that there aren't some successful nuclear plants, or that we will soon see the end of nuclear power. This is, however, a case where because of some bad decisions in the choice of reactor design made back when the technology was in its infancy, plus the failure to make accurate economic forecasts and to account for human error, the technology has been far less successful than it might otherwise have been. Moreover, the potential for serious problems is very real, even if the probability of serious human injury is rather low. Unlike in many other types of technologies, human or mechanical errors *can* place a large number of people at risk. These factors have conspired to make the ultimate survival of what once was a highly touted technology of the future seem now to be very much in doubt.

This, then, is a case of what is, in a sense, a decision-making process that is working *against* technology. However, only a small component of that process—as least, as far as it has been effective—involves the conscious decision by human beings, expressed through the political process, that this technology is intrinsically undesirable and should be abandoned, even though there have been well-organized opposition and reports in the media that have frightened many people.

The other side of nuclear fission is, of course, nuclear weapons. Atomic and hydrogen warheads have been a part of United States and Soviet national policies for more than 40 years now. But the concern about whether this is a sane approach to foreign policy or national defense (or offense) has been growing steadily for two decades. President Reagan's return to the simplistic philosophy of the old days of having to keep ahead of the Russians in all things, and especially nuclear armaments, along with propaganda suggesting that survival of a nuclear war is possible, has brought about a public reaction against the nuclear arms race that seems stronger and more unified than at any previous point in our nuclear history.

The pressure of this popularly inspired movement is now becoming a political issue and is showing how the strength of a concern can enter the traditional decision-making mechanisms, and can even penetrate the establishment of government. Propositions on the ballots of several states in the 1982 elections, calling for a bilateral freeze on the manufacture and the deployment of nuclear weapons, passed by overwhelming majorities, a consensus reflected in the freeze resolution passed by the House of Representatives in 1983. Candidates who had previously been afraid to appear ''un-American'' spoke out against the arms race. Even Reagan, although not stopping his sabre rattling, had to respond to the public pressure by pursuing talks with the Soviet Union on nuclear arms reduction.

Here, then, is an example of how concerns about the ultimate consequences of pursuing a technology with a deliberately destructive purpose can possibly lead to its curtailment (although they have not done so yet). In a system where citizens have a voice in selecting their representatives and can speak out freely on the issues, it is more likely that they can comprise an important force in the process of deciding which technologies will be pursued and which will be stopped.

Closer to the subject of technologies based on advances in the biological sciences, there have been some attempts to stop, rather than promote, certain applications of knowledge, the proponents of which believed would greatly benefit the people. These attempts to stop ''progress'' have generally resulted from fear and ignorance of the scientific basis of the principle to be exploited.

In the 1950s, there was much interest in the fluoridation of water to prevent dental caries. Although fluoride is a metabolic poison, low concentrations seem to be harmless and, at the same time, harden tooth enamel. The issue was debated intensely in state and local governments. In a few cases, the opponents garnered enough power to prevent the fluoridation of local water supplies,

I have a clear recollection of the annual town meeting of Durham, New Hampshire, one year in my youth, when the matter of fluoridation of the town water supply was put on the agenda. The arguments were heated and the discussion seemed to be getting nowhere. Finally, my father, a chemical engineer, stood up and made an eloquent plea for reason, stating that the fears of the opponents of adding such minute quantities of fluoride to the water were groundless. Durham then voted to fluoridate its water and has been doing so ever since.

But it was around the same time that my well-intentioned parent wrote and published a book[36] extolling the virtues of DDT. This marvelous chemical was the salvation we had been waiting for, to save our crops and prevent the spread of malaria, sleeping sickness, and other insect-borne diseases. Curiously, there were no citizen's groups in the late 1940s protesting the spraying of poisons not only in our drinking water but over all our food and in the air we breathe. The issue was never a hotly debated issue in New Hampshire town meetings. Perhaps, everyone was just too accustomed to reaching for the Flit every time some uninvited crawling guest was spotted. That, of course, was years before the latent, nasty side of DDT became apparent, and 25 years before it was finally banned by a federal regulatory authority. How, then, could anyone, a professor of chemical engineering included, really be sure that there were no insidious long-term effects of fluoride? They couldn't, of course. It was possible only to make educated guesses, based on what was already known. Because hypothesis formation is based on clues lying within the total body of knowledge at hand, it is generally not possible to predict the existence of a phenomenon or its effects when there is no hint within our experience. Of course, looking back, we can usually see the hidden evidence of those things that we could not foresee. This hindsight may make us feel a bit dumb, and indeed, we should not be so arrogant as to believe that we are smart enough to be able to see the invisible. There is always the possibility of the unforeseen, particularly when the level of knowledge does not even permit one to ask the right questions.

The public debate over the potential hazards of using recombinant DNA methods was analyzed in Chapter 3. This controversy was not unlike the fluoride issue, except that there was some rational basis for believing that there might possibly be a chance of accidentally putting some genes together in a way that would create a virulent disease organism. This was not technology *per se*—the application of knowledge to solve practical problems. It was science—the process of discovery. It was not the knowledge that most people feared; it was the use of a *technique* used to acquire that knowledge. In a strong sense, then, it *was* a concern over technology—the technology of the tools of research.

As an example of a decision-making process, the debate over the safety of the use of recombinant DNA methods was highly interesting, for it was discussed in virtually every available forum, and at all levels of government. Perhaps more because, at the request of a National Academy of Sciences Committee, the NIH had taken the initiative than for any other reason, the NIH Guidelines became the determinant of policy for recombinant DNA. These dealt only with safety procedures that would reduce the human risk that could result from the practice of the techniques. The suggestions of several that these genetic manipulation techniques either not be used at all or only under extreme conditions of containment were given little quarter. The debate centered on the *degree* of containment that was appropriate for any given class of experiments, and which level of government, if any, should administer the controls. However, the ultimate technology that was expected to flow from recombinant DNA methods was very promising, and few opposed it, even though there was a level of mistrust of some of the pharmaceutical companies and the budding biotechnology concerns that were vocal advocates of the exploitation of gene splicing.

As in the cases of fluoride and DDT, the assessment of the relative safety of recombinant DNA techniques was based on educated guesses. As in the case of fluoride (and DDT, in the early days), the best estimates of risk were that the risk was extremely low. But there were few actual safety data, and, of course, no one can guarantee that anything will be absolutely free of risk. There is always the chance that something *could* happen that nobody ever imagined. However, the promise of new, important knowledge was very real and imminent. The practical benefits of exploiting the technique, conjured up in the beginning to respond to the critics, were very likely to be achieved. Thus, the consensus of the collective decision-making process was that the pursuit of knowledge using these methods was well worth the risk.

A corollary debate that comprised a significant part of the discussion generated by recombinant DNA was over who or what was entitled to make decisions concerning the future use of a technique that might have accompanying risks, or the development of a technology that might either be intrinsically dangerous or be misused. What is the role of government, and at what level? Should there be constraints on "free" enterprise? Should the federal government be in the business of promoting a technology (as it has been with nuclear power)? When differences of opinion exist between federal, state, and local governments, which should take precedence? On what criteria should such decisions be based? Is fear sufficient grounds, in a democratic society, to block the pursuit of a branch of technology, even when no scientific basis for the fear exists? If the majority would elect to pursue an obviously harmful technology, even though the wise knew better, should that collective will determine policy? In essence, *who* decides? And *how* should decisions be made? And who decides who decides? [37]

In practice, it is clear that these decisions are not made by one body at one level, such that all other bodies or individuals are ignored. One may ultimately have the authority to make the final choice, but that choice is undoubtedly influenced by many other sources. That is, in our society, a company can presumably produce any product it wishes. If, however, there is a significant body of individuals who object to the production and sale of that product, then the freedom of the company can be greatly curtailed, through litigation, boycotts, or bad publicity.

For example, there is no prohibition on the manufacture of handguns, a technology which many would like to see prohibited or at least highly restricted. But because of the fact that handguns are made primarily to shoot people, their sale and use are restricted, depending on the state or locality where one lives. In some states, it is illegal to possess a pistol unless you have a special reason to own one. Concern about crimes of violence with guns, definitely a case of the misuse of technology, is creating a growing pressure for the regulation and the possible cessation of this specific application of the laws of physics and chemistry.

There is the perennial question of whether such matters should be the focus of national policy or should be left to local determination. This is a fundamental problem in federal law, where the U.S. Constitution sets forth which powers are the province of the whole, and which are reserved for the states. In principle, the justification for local decision-making is based on differences in circumstances among different geographical and political subdivisions. That is, the geography, climate, and population density of certain California urban areas may well justify a different approach to atmospheric pollutants emerging from automobile exhausts than in the plains of Kansas. But something independent of location, such as the destructive potential of an automobile traveling at 100 miles an hour, would seem to warrant uniform constraints, as would the possible creation of an unknown virulent microbe.

Obviously, our laws do not always adhere to this principle, Many issues that are seemingly of universal concern are governed locally, and others, which may seem to be very dependent on local conditions, are handled nationwide. There are many issues too that transcend national boundaries. That is, nuclear war, even though it was alluded to on the California ballot, is a world issue. It cannot be dealt with effectively within any single nation, let alone a state. Similarly, technologies that may result in the modification of human beings must also be considered of universal relevance.

Thus, how shall we approach these technologies of the future? The knowledge will come. That is certain. But who shall decide how it is to be applied? Are our existing political and professional decision-making institutions enough? Can an unregulated biotechnology industry and medical profession be trusted to act with the foresight and the responsibility that we would like? Or must we try now to invent a new international mechanism to review the directions of the applications of biological knowledge, and to determine the biological fate of the human race?

I would argue that there are certain applications which cannot be left to purely selfish or single-minded interests. For some, certainly, it really doesn't matter that much. Does it really matter if the fraction of blue-eyed babies is altered? But just as the 1972 convention on biological warfare[38] was an attempt at the international control of an undesirable technology, there are some possible uses of molecular and cell biology that require international scrutiny and control. Any application for military purposes is one. Any attempt to alter the traits of human beings beyond the range which now exists in the human gene pool is another—that is, the extension of the life span, or the removal or enhancement of genes controlling behavioral traits—for in either case, the future of human society could be affected, and in profound ways.

The report of the President's Commission for the Study of Ethical Problems in Medicine and Biomedical and Behavioral Research, entitled *Splicing Life*,[34] called for the establishment of a permanent oversight body to act as the conscience of the federal government and to recommend policies concerning the control of technologies relating to human genetic intervention. Congressman Albert Gore introduced legislation in the U.S. House of Representatives to accomplish this purpose, modeled after the president's bioethics commission. This has caused some skittishness among scientists and in the biotechnology industry, remembering recombinant DNA and fearing a legislative overreaction. In general, however, most perceive the concept to be relatively benign and not threatening to the business of the day. The concept does, in fact, have a great deal of support in the scientific as well as the lay community. But this is only the beginning of a way to keep track of things in the United States.

There are really no good, effective models for universal decision-making. The United Nations has revealed its impotence on too many crucial occasions. The superpower bullies use the forum to enhance their own national political interests, rather than for the good of the planet. However, the escalating nuclear arms race is forcing us to face the need for the creation of some sort of effective worldwide government that can reflect at least some of the idealism that the utopians have longed for. Time is running out. The technologies of the present and the future are too powerful to be left to single companies, states, or nations. Because they are capable of significantly altering the direction of human destiny, it is imperative that we accept now the formidable task of planning our future with care.

Limits

Human culture has always been concerned in one way or another with the concept of limits. Many instances of those limits have been discussed elsewhere in this book. A limit is a boundary, a line, real or imaginary, that either *cannot* be crossed or *should* not be crossed. Thus, the velocity of light, c, at least according to the theory of special relativity, represents the limiting velocity that any object in the universe can ever attain, *Star Wars* notwithstanding. Although one must entertain the possibility that this feature of physical theory is still not sufficiently general, and that c really isn't the universal speed limit, there is no evidence thus far that this is so. The velocity of light is therefore an absolute limit.

The speed limit signs along the freeway, the Ten Commandments, and attempts to proscribe certain lines of scientific inquiry are, on the other hand, moral limits. One *should* not exceed them, even if one is able to. Here, I shall consider whether there are any absolute limits to how much we may learn about the remaining secrets of nature and of life. Is "the way it is" such that it is only a matter of discovery and ingenuity, to understand completely all of the presumably immutable laws of nature? Or are these laws, after all, not really absolute statements of the ultimate nature of the universe, fixed in time and space? And what are the limitations of the human animal's ability to know?

First of all, one may reason that there is a finite amount of material to be understood. If this were not so, then it would be infinite. That would imply an infinite chain of subdivision, of finer and finer detail, with respect to the structure of matter and the laws of physics. Like the Chinese boxes, where each time you remove the lid of the box, there is another box inside, only slightly smaller, is there a limit to the number of boxes that can be contained within a box of finite size? Mathematically, one could indeed have an infinite number of boxes, each inside the next larger one. In practice, however, I have never found a set of Chinese boxes that goes down to more than 10 or 12 boxes. The walls are of finite thickness, and there are small spaces between the boxes of each incremental size. So, practically speaking, the number is not only finite, it is rather small.

Can one apply a similar analogy to subatomic particles? Perhaps, although it is really not possible to prove whether or not there really is a smallest box, or a truly fundamental particle or subdivision of matter. Protons and neutrons can be subdivided. Can electrons? Are so-called quarks real subunits of these particles? Do they exist at all, or do they simply represent a convenient mathematical construct? That is a problem in natural philosophy that we do not need to attempt to resolve here. Life, as far as we can tell, does not involve the subdivisions of subatomic particles. It does involve interactions not only between individual atoms, but between electrons, protons, and the excited states of atoms.

However, this is essentially chemistry, molecular physics, and perhaps electronics. Are not these phenomena accessible to objective, scientific scrutiny at every level of detail relevant to life? It would seem so. But logically, can we ever prove that a complete description of life down to the level of electrons and protons is sufficient to explain every aspect of life? *A priori*, one might expect this to be the case. However, we cannot be certain until we have, in fact, described every detail of life in terms of understood phenomena.

Lest we get carried away with ecstasy over our successes in molecular genetics and the manipulation of cells, we should remind ourselves of the phenomena yet to be explained. There are still many problems remaining in molecular biology. How are the genetic components that code for antibody molecules recombined uniquely in response to a specific antigen, to produce a clone of cells making only that single type of immunoglobulin? How are animal and plant genes controlled during development from a seed or a fertilized ovum? What manner of control determines that the dividing cells of a zygote (a fertilized animal egg cell) will be slightly different from each other? Why do some cells proliferate up to a point and then die, to help the developing animal assume its functional form? What causes different types of partially differentiated cells to migrate and then to reassociate, to form functional tissues and organs? The structure of skin and bone and cartilage and blood vessels is essentially the same from one individual to the next. The cells in your nose contain all or nearly all of the same enzymes and genetic messages as those in everyone else's nose. Yet, why do I have a big nose, whereas my wife has a small nose? The answer seems to have something to do with the fact that my father had a big nose, too. But just how is it that genes control the sizes of noses?

If the problems of embryogenesis seem to be staggeringly complex, the understanding of the structure and the function of the brain and the nervous system baffle us perhaps even more. I have contended at several points earlier in this book that I believe behavioral traits to be just as influenced by genetics as are physical characteristics. In fact, it seems a bit silly to feel that I have to make this statement at all, and I do so only because of past controversy and lingering dogma to the contrary. Some of the scientific evidence was cited earlier. But all of us can, no doubt, supply many anecdotes to support this thesis. My mother and one of my sisters have the habit of unconsciously twisting their hair during their idle moments. One of my daughters has exactly the same characteristic and has had it since she had enough hair to twist at all. Yet, during her early childhood, she had very little exposure to either my mother or my sister.

If one believes in genetics, there is no reason at all to assume that the explanation would lie elsewhere, although I am sure that some of my readers would argue the point. Behavior is, after all, a function of the intricate workings of the brain, is it not? And the brain and its component cells are physical structures, like bones or muscles or a heart or a pancreas or a nose. If the physical structure is specified by genetically coded information, should not then the function of that structure also depend on genetic determinants? And certainly, as we know that all observal physical traits vary from individual to individual, so then we would expect brains—and hence, behavior— to vary similarly.

How does this complex system work? We know that it has some primitive similarities to electronic circuitry, but there are also many differences. What is there about the brain of one sister that makes her twist her hair, whereas my other sister does not? How can we explain reasoning, and memory, and the concept of consciousness? And how does vision manage to inject into our consciousness such a clear portrayal of the scenes in front of our eyes?

Our conscious perceptions include the curious and genuinely subjective phenomena of color, aesthetic form, and musical pitch and quality, as well as rhythmical form and harmony. That we interpret the detection of minute quantities of different chemical forms as smells and tastes is also a construct of our physiology, not an absolute, physical quality. In fact, the concepts of color, odor, taste, pain, music, and even light, sound, and tactile feelings are purely the creations of consciousness—the internal images sensed in the mind.[39] Although there seem to be certain physical and mathematical relationships that distinguish the beautiful from the ugly, at least to a point, the concepts of beauty and ugliness, or of pleasure, sadness, elation, fear, or fright, are strictly the products of our internal neurophysiology. They are undefined in terms of physical reality.

When one adds to the mysteries of consciousness the ability to dream, either sleeping or awake, and to make creative and original associations among learned facts and concepts as a means of generating new ones, then there can be no doubt that there will be no shortage of challenges to scientists for many years. But we are still left with the question: Is there a limit? Is it indeed going to be possible to understand, in a scientifically satisfactory way, the phenomena discussed above? Or is there an increasing difficulty in understanding those phenomena which get closer and closer to the object that is performing the understanding—that is, the human mind? To be sure, it has always been easier to understand abstract phenomena, totally detached from humanity—for example, the structure of the atom or the nature of electromagnetic radiation—than it has been to understand ourselves. Thus, an understanding of human behavior has been a far more difficult task for us than probably any other, a fact that may well be responsible for a world in which our technical capabilities have far outstripped our capacity to deal with each other.

This is a question I certainly cannot answer with confidence. Yet, I have little doubt that we shall eventually understand the complexities of embryonic development and shall know exactly why my nose is big and why my wife's is not. I am also optimistic enough to believe that we are capable of unraveling the mysteries of the brain and the way it controls our sensory perceptions and the way we think and create and dream, and know why one of my sisters twists her hair. The answers are not obvious. Simple theories that the brain works anything like the way we would design a computer are almost certain to be wrong. But we are continually learning more and more, at a faster and faster rate (although this, admittedly, is a somewhat subjective evaluation). I would be most astonished if, at some point, we should encounter a barrier to further learning, some mystery which we cannot even begin to penetrate.

There are other phenomena that deserve to be mentioned here. The holy men of the East and of some Pacific island tribes also seem to be able to perform remarkable feats: Their skin becomes fireproof or does not bleed when pierced with sharp objccts. Others seem to be able to sleep naked in the snows of the Himalayan mountains without suffering any adverse effects. These are well-documented occurrences. When they are attempted by unholy skeptics, or those who would be holy but have not endured the proper rites of initiation, disaster always follows. I have no doubt that these observations, illustrating remarkable capacities of the human body that few have learned how to master, are well within the grasp of the scientific method.[40]

However, there is another class of supposed human talents that presents more problems. These are the so-called psychic phenomena, which, although they exist in concept, are the object of disagreement about whether or not they are, in fact, real. Many people believe them to be true because their subjective, conscious perceptions of them are no different than any other sensory experience that takes on form and meaning within the conscious mind. Included would be extrasensory perception, Clairvoyance, mental telepathy, psychokinesis, faith healing, and the experiences of those near death who claim to have seen the "afterlife" and whose stories are remarkably consistent with one another.

There are two relevant facts. First, it has been demonstrated repeatedly that if someone *wants* to believe something badly enough, he usually does, even if it means altering his memory of past events to conform to that belief. One disturbing example is the intrinsic unreliability of eyewitness accounts, particularly of those events that involve strong emotions. The feeling invariably colors the memory of the perceived event, including the appearance of people and surroundings, the sequence in which the events occurred, and the nature of the actions that took place. Faith healing may indeed work when the patient believes strongly enough in the cure so that his physiology adjusts to the belief and fights the affliction more effectively. There is evidence that stress and psychological factors definitely affect the level of immune surveillance in the human body. The belief in healers (which no doubt plays an important role in modern medicine) may well be related to the control that holy men can exercise over most of their bodily functions.

The second inescapable fact is that when most mentalists and spoon benders are scrutinized carefully, they turn out to be frauds. Still, that fact does not prove that all such reports are fradulent or are cases of self-deception. Although I am instinctively skeptical, I must remind myself to remain open-minded and to accept any valid demonstration of such supposedly extra-normal abilities. The fact that such reports are universal, and they are certainly part of the folklore of most cultures, tells us at least not to dismiss lightly the possibility of a whole domain of phenomena, with an accompanying physical reality, of which only a few have been able to catch a glimpse.

The resemblance between the belief in psychic phenomena and religious phenomena is, of course, obvious. The devout claim that the latter is beyond the reach of science. And so, it turns out, do most believers in psychic talents contend that human experience is the only valid form of investigation. I disagree. If either are real, then it should be possible to subject them to investigation. However, I am not so smug that I insist that our traditional modes of scientific inquiry will necessarily give us the answers we seek. As in experimental physics, we may need to become considerably more clever than we are now in designing and carrying out the proper experiment. If there is a physical reality to psychic or "paranormal" experience, just as electromagnetic radiation provides the basis for what we see as light, and the propagation of vibrations through matter is perceived as sound, then there must exist a means of exploring psychic experience and detecting it by some means external to the human body and mind.

If there is a physical reality to paranormal phenomena, then we are forced to reexamine an assumption made earlier in this chapter, that life can be described completely in terms of atoms and the interactions among their component parts. Any complete model must, of course, include the properties of electromagnetic radiation, as well as the physical propagation of energy through matter. However, in order for clairvoyance, mental telepathy, or psychokinesis to occur, there would have to be another, as yet undiscovered, means of transmitting energy over distance. If such a form of energy transmission is part of our environment, then it is not surprising that we have evolved a means to utilize it, even if it is very subtle and of low power.

Should this be the case, however, then the physicists, along with the biologists, have some work ahead of them. Physics is, in fact, also at a very exciting point in its development. At present, I feel that the picture of the most fundamental relationships between matter and energy that currently prevails is a bit too chaotic and contains too many loose ends to be in its most general form. It is much like atomic theory in 1920, before Heisenberg and Schrö-dinger tidied things up. Just as no one knew that radio waves existed before a means of detecting them was devised, it is conceivable that there is yet another physical means of transmitting information over a distance.

Thus, of all of the psychic phenomena, telepathic communication would seem to be the most plausible. Although I haven't a clue about how it could work, one could imagine something analagous to a properly tuned transmitter and receiver plus a means of propagating thought patterns, in whatever form they are coded by the brain, from one person to another. In telepathic communication, at least, all events should be nearly simultaneous. However, even if one allows this possibility, there are aspects of other psychic phenomena that would seem to be too difficult to reconcile with what we know, without our having to completely alter our physical world view and the laws of physics.

Clairvoyance, for example, particularly with regard to knowledge of the inanimate or of the future, poses some fundamental philosophical difficulties. If the future can be seen, then at least certain parts must be determined rather precisely, a concept that we have some reason to reject. Furthermore, the means by which information concerning an event in the future could be transmitted to an individual's consciousness in the present would have to be *totally* at odds with our current understanding of time, as well as of life and consciousness. And if one *could* know the future, then would it not be possible for one to alter it, thereby creating a rather basic contradiction? It is hard to believe that our present level of understanding of the universe in which we live is as limited as it would have to be in order to accommodate the concept of seeing into the future. But, again, against my instincts, I must avoid stating categorically that it is impossible. It might just be that we are at a much more primitive level of comprehending the ways of the universe than any of us would care to admit.

And what about extrasensory perception (ESP)? How can someone "know" how many spades or diamonds are on the other side of a playing card lying face down on the table? I certainly don't know how he could. A number of studies have been carried out to determine whether there are individuals who can consistently beat the odds by simply guessing, the most well-known conducted by the Rhine group at Duke University. But there have also been studies of the investigators' objectivity. Most have been found to have a bias in favor of the phenomenon that they were trying to prove. The influence of the investigator in perturbing, say, the results of tests of the effectiveness of a new drug is well known. That is, if the doctor administering the drug knows which is the real drug and which is the placebo, he sends subconscious signals to the test subject, who then responds, also subconsciously, in the direction expected by the investigator. It is for this reason that the double-blind experimental design is essential in such trials. Recently, a magician and two associates succeeded in fooling the investigators of paranormal powers for two years. These facts do not disprove the existence of the phenomena; they only emphasize the difficulty in investigating something that depends so intimately on human experience.

In the event that any or some of these psychic phenomena are genuine, I am sure that they are accessible to analysis, experiment, and, ultimately, understanding. It may be harder to disprove them because such talents, if they occur at all, seem to favor only a privileged few, and then not even all the time. Still, this is an area that merits more definitive, properly controlled experiments. As we finally elucidate the workings of the mind and consciousness, we should be able either to explain psychic phenomenon or to explain why some people think they have psychic abilities. Until there is resolution of the issue, it is permissible to remain an agnostic.

If there are limits to science, one must also consider the possibility that human intelligence is limited in the degree to which it can grasp complex phenomena. Could it be that we are deceiving ourselves in imagining that we are at the pinnacle of intellectual ability? I can imagine intellects, human or otherwise, that would be vastly superior to the earth's best, most creative minds. Is it possible that, just as calculus will remain forever elusive to chimpanzees, so will there be areas of understanding that are simply too difficult for us? Perhaps we have only a highly limited view of space and time, and of energy and matter, and of the dimensions of life. If indeed we are so limited, is there any point in trying to understand everything? For if that is the case, we won't be smart enough to know what it is we don't know.

We could now ask, turning again to the applications of whatever understanding of life we can manage to gain, are there limits to the extent which we can modify life—any life—to suit our purposes. Because it is only a matter of time before we may expect all human genetic information to be completely mapped, with the biochemical and control functions of each region determined, it is difficult to imagine a barrier to the modification of any nucleotide sequence in the human genome.

If, as we expect, general principles emerge that relate DNA base sequences to structure and function, then it should also be possible to alter the human species to express features that never existed before. That is, I do not see a technical limit to the deliberate improvement of the human species, however *improvement* may be defined in terms of our individual and social values at any given time. Presumably, such endeavors would be undertaken only if a society determines that that is a desirable goal. If it does not, or such tampering with the human genome were to be barred on ethical grounds, as defined by the society in place at the time it were feasible to do, there are still thousands of other species that would undoubtedly be fair game. That is, if we can improve any aspects of human ability which we wish, then we should be able to modify other animals to the point where they have capabilities that surpass human talents. Again, *improvement* is a tricky word, for it implies a value that can only be assumed, not derived.

Nevertheless, if it is possible, by genetic design, to increase human intelligence to a great degree (I will not go into the question of how modified a human has to be before it no longer qualifies as "human"), that act should also push back the limits to scientific understanding, if, indeed, they exist. Thus, just as we may "improve" the brains of chimpanzees so that they are at ease with the calculus, we might elevate human intelligence to a plane which it cannot now imagine. Then, we (or they) should have a much better chance of understanding all elements of life and the physical universe than we may have if we remain "unevolved."

But building into humans, or our successors, or other species of living things, such greater capabilities will also enable them to exercise even greater creativity in the ways in which they choose to modify life. Now, we speak of essentially following the human template, or the templates of life forms that we are familiar with, possibly improving traits which already exist. But can we imagine how to create new ones? Can we even imagine what these new traits should be?

It would seem that the possibilities of invention are endless. Just as chemists have been creating more and more new organic molecules over the past few decades, why could we not create more and more new forms of life? Presumably, if we were to understand the underlying principles of enzyme catalysis, of energetics, and of the formation of organic structure, we could do virtually anything. All that we require is a good molecular architect.

In terms of the twentieth century, such speculation can well be considered within the domain of fantasy. However, it is a rational fantasy. At some point, in 100 or maybe 1,000 years, I would imagine that we will be directing our own evolution. Many would argue that Darwinian evolution ceased in the human race some millennia ago, and that, if anything, modern twentieth-century technology is "de-evolving" the human race.[41] That is, advanced social organization has allowed many individuals less well adapted for survival to live and procreate, leading perhaps to less hardy and talented individuals. A strong case can be made for this view.

Practically speaking, then, there may be limits imposed on what living beings are intrinsically capable of doing (e.g., psychic phenomena), but I can see no technological limit to the control that we, and/or our successors, will be able to exert over life. Nor do I see an ultimate limit to the level of understanding and knowledge of life and the nature of the universe that can be attained, but there may well be limits at present that will be removed only after the species has undergone some improvements.

One might also ask if there are limits to our sociological evolution. There is a great risk that, for all our advances in science and technology, remaining in a primitive sociological state will prevent the human race from ever reaching its intellectual potential. Can we, along with designing new, improved models of human beings, also include the capacity to live in peace and harmony in a cooperative, rather than a competitive, society? In principle, probably yes. But that is an inherently more difficult problem to solve than changing tangible physical, or even psychological, traits. Of course, the nature of a society of beings is necessarily a function of their individual attributes. But how can we determine that function in advance? An empirical determination may be risky.

If I may offer an observation and interject an opinion here, it would behoove us as a society to avoid being carried away with our technological prowess and to concentrate as a society on quickly outgrowing our protracted infancy. We are like the lopsided prodigy who may have mastered Beethoven and Hilbert space at the age of 10, but who is socially inept. As a collection of social enclaves, the human race has proved its inability to contend with itself with anything near the level of maturity with which it deals with its intellectual abstractions.

But could it be that, in the course of astronomical time, the brief instant of the evolution of the human race, and its ultimate self-destruction, will be one of those Darwinian branches which simply didn't have the right combinations of traits for survival? Perhaps it was too intelligent for its own good and at the same time too irrational in its behavior to see the importance of self-perpetuation. This could be yet another type of limit that will make all others irrelevant.

Where Do We Go from Here?

A considerable part of this book has dealt with the future. However, up to this point, it has been full of conditional statements. By now, the reader may be growing weary of "if . . . then" clauses and strings of impossible questions. This approach is, of course, one way in which to consider difficult concepts that are both perplexing and real.

Now, however, I shall indulge in the author's prerogative of expressing a series of opinions. Those that I offer here are my own predictions of how the future will unfold in the realm of our understanding of and control over life.

Most of them, I believe, have at least some concrete basis in established knowledge. Some are educated fantasy. A few are pure intuition.

How much will we understand of the basic mechanisms of life in 5 years? Or 10? Or 50? Or 1,000. There now remain numerous problems in genetic function and expression, cellular differentiation and embryonic development, cellular and functional aging, immunology, and neurobiology. The latter area includes such seemingly intractable problems as the organization and function of the brain, the nature of sensory perception, consciousness, language, reasoning, and intelligence.

There is no doubt that techniques involving gene splicing, along with the rapid determination of nucleotide sequences in DNA, have made possible many discoveries concerning the basic organization and control of genetic information, particularly with respect to mammalian DNA. The next decade will continue to witness rapid progress in this area. The function and the evolutionary significance of "intron" DNA will continue to be clarified, with the finding that the three-dimensional conformation of these and perhaps other DNA regions plays an important role in gene regulation. (Keep in mind that the so-called intron regions of DNA—that is, those which occur interspersed within a gene but that do not code for amino acids, or anything else, it seems—were discovered only recently as a direct result of recombinant DNA methods that allow the study and characterization of isolated mammalian genes.) New, and yet unimagined, features of mammalian genetic function will be elucidated. These may include instances of DNA transcribed from an RNA template as a normal part of the function of certain cell types; gene amplification, where large quantities of a particular protein are required; and further clarification of the replication and transmission of extranuclear DNA (such as that contained in the mitochondria).

The folding and packaging of DNA within cells will also be clarified, in a way that demonstrates that some of the intron regions do indeed have a function based on more than coding for amino acids or controlling protein recognition sites. The mechanism by which the chromosomes of higher plants and animals condense and segregate during cell division will be understood. The next decade, then, will continue to be one rich in discovery in molecular genetics, with the further elucidation of the control, function, and structure of genes.

Also within the next 10 years, and perhaps sooner, we may expect to understand completely the recognition mechanism for new antigens and the proliferation of single antibody-producing clones. We shall also clarify the mechanism of action of the immune response modifiers, such as the interferons and the lymphokines. Of particular importance in the control of the immune function will be protein/receptor-site interactions, and the manner in which these are coupled to the regulation of gene expression in the target cells.

These problems in cell biology have some elements in common with the understanding of cellular differentiation and embryonic development. However, elucidation of what makes a freshly fertilized mammalian zygote totipotent (that is, capable of developing into an entire organism), whereas a somewhat differentiated cell is not, will take longer than a decade to understand. But not much longer. By 1995, we will be able to reverse the expression of genes that have been turned off during development and to achieve totipotency from at least some classes of differentiated animal cells or cell nuclei, as may now be done in plant cells. Further studies in plant cell biology will help to clarify the understanding of development in animal cells.

A corollary to the above paragraph is that we shall also be able to produce clones—genetically identical copies—of adult animals. These methods will be used extensively in animal husbandry by no later than the year 2010, and there will be a rising concern about limiting genetic variability in animals, as is now the case with plant varieties.

After a period of learning how to translate laboratory achievements into economical large-scale production, the biotechnology industry will succeed in making many common pharmaceuticals. The manufacture of these substances from cloned DNA in bacterial factories will, in fact, replace conventional methods within two decades. This will be particularly true of vaccines, hormones, antibodies, and immune response modifiers. The result will be safer and cheaper substances, but not before a number of unanticipated technical problems are solved. The industry will revolutionize many areas of industrial chemistry within the next 20 years, including the efficient conversion of cheap or "waste" carbon sources into useful products. The agriculturally oriented companies will make a number of major advances, including the development of insect-resistant crop plants, of specific biological pesticides that will bring the gypsy moth and other serious pests under control, and engineering soil microbes that will greatly reduce the need for chemical fertilizers. However, the uncertainty of agricultural economics will be felt in agricultural biotechnology. The large number (more than 200) of independent biotechnology companies will shrink to about 20, through mergers, acquisitions, and simple failure.

When we look back on the early days of the biotechnology industry, it will be obvious that the headlong rush to make new products and to get them on the market before their utility and function were well understood was naive. This will be the reason for failure of some of the companies that seemed to be doing well initially. Those companies that succeed will be those which promote products of known mode of action and value, even if they are not the more spectacular goals hyped in the press. Monoclonal antibodies and improved enzymes will turn out to have been wise commercial choices. Those companies which ultimately dominate the industry will be those that maintain or support significant exploratory research, and that are sure of their products before trying to get the FDA to approve them for sale. The companies that expected to make it big by curing cancer will lose out to their more pedestrian rivals, for a product of significant value in treating cancer will be much longer in coming than many now expect. The long-dreamed-of El Dorado of huge profits for cancer therapeutics will never materialize. By the time suitable treatments are found, the prevention of cancer will be a realistic goal in much of the world, sponsored through government-supported public-health programs. The big flop will be interferon, the supposed miracle drug of the late 1970s. Although it will have some limited value in treating some viral infections and as an adjunct cancer therapeutic, it will turn out to have little or no net benefit to most cancer patients, especially those with the more intractable types of cancer (lung, liver, pancreas, colon, and brain).

The spectacular glamour of biotechnology, which peaked around 1980–1981 and that has already faded considerably, will soon disappear altogether. Biotechnology will become just another industry, but one whose time has come. In many ways, it will be much like the electronics and computer industries, where competition is intense and technological innovation rapid. I would also predict that, within 10 years, the biotechnology industry in Japan, already experienced in large-scale fermentation, will become a formidable rival to the early success of the American and European endeavors. Moreover, the Japanese will surprise the world commercial industry by being first with the basic science leading to a number of revolutionary and lucrative products, establishing themselves as leaders in innovation.

Most of the successes in understanding basic life processes will continue to come from independent scientists, working primarily in university research laboratories. However, the area, in which the private sector will excel will be in tailoring new compounds—bioactive proteins and enzymes in particular—through site-specific alterations in DNA nucleotide sequences. To do this successfully will require a much more detailed understanding at the molecular level of hormone/receptor and enzyme/substrate interactions. But the promise of making unique substances that are unknown in nature (and therefore on firm ground at the patent office) will spur the more imaginative companies to invest substantially in research that will result in the design of new, useful molecules. This development will require a synergistic group-research effort involving not only expertise in DNA cloning and sequence determination, but theoretical quantum chemistry, physical chemistry, catalysis, and computer modeling, which will in turn require the kind of investment and resources that are generally out of the reach of university-based scientists. For those companies with the perseverance and resources to stick it out in this area (for the payoff will take somewhat longer than finding unique ways to produce natural compounds), the future will be theirs, for it will then be possible to be free of whims of nature. Classical, energy-intensive organic syntheses will be replaced in large part by biocatalysis (including synthetic enzymes), which will give higher specifity and yields at far less cost than today's methods. A byproduct of this technological revolution in the pharmaceutical and chemical industries will be far less industrial pollution and energy consumption.

In medicine, the first achievements in gene therapy will come through partial cures of the hemoglobin diseases in adults, through bone marrow transplants containing genetically healthy cells that will give rise to functional red cells. Thalassemia and sickle-cell disease will be the first and should be readily treatable within a decade. Noninvasive treatment of some genetic diseases will eventually be possible through synthetic virus-like particles, derived from human viruses that inject their DNA into cells, but with the genes producing virulence removed and replaced by the correct DNA messages lacked by the patient. It will first be necessary to add the control and integration sequences so that the inserted DNA will remain with the "infected" cell and function properly, in a normally regulated fashion.

This approach to treatment will again be only partial because methods which correct *all* affected cells will generally not be possible, nor will it be applicable to all genetic anomalies, particularly those undetected until irreversible abnormal development has taken place. However, at the level of the fertilized ovum prior to human embryogenesis, genetic surgery will permit the correction of most genetic diseases, and every cell in a person so treated will contain the correct genetic message. These techniques, however, will not be generally successful for at least 20 years.

Within 50 years, however, any genetic anomaly will be preventable as long as both parents have undergone complete genetic screening. Genetic screening, or genetic "fingerprinting," will undergo great advances during the next 10 years. At present, it is possible to screen for genetic differences in certain regions (such as those coding for human leukocyte antigens). However, with advances in computerized instrumentation, it should be possible to detect differences in any genetic sequence that would indicate trouble, with the sensitivity of the methods improving to where a single base alteration can be detected. Parallel to the development of such diagnostic methods must be the detailed genetic mapping of the entire human genome, including the different alleles that determine differences in "normal" traits among individuals (e.g., hair color, stature, musical talent, and the size of one's nose). Today, this would appear to be a formidable, if not impossible, task. But we already have sequence information for a number of human genes, and the techniques for making these determinations are known and are getting better all the time. Thus, 50 years is perhaps a very conservative estimate, but I shall try not to overpromise science.

Of course, if complete information is at hand to enable the prevention of genetic diseases, then it will also be possible to alter genetic traits at will. But here, where there may be overriding ethical concerns about the use of such technologies, I am far less confident in predicting the attitudes of society in 50 years than I am in forecasting the state of scientific achievement. I would only venture to say that there will be at least some human experiments done at the zygote stage to modify the traits to be expressed following development. I have discussed the many possibilities of what *might* be done previously and shall not reiterate them here.

I should devote at least a few paragraphs specifically to the principal medical fear of the late twentieth century: cancer. Along with an explanation of the control of differentiation, we will also gain an understanding of the mechanism by which cell division and differentiation get out of control, as in cancer. I would predict that by the year 2000 we will understand the basic systems that are altered when a cell becomes cancerous. However, it will turn out that there are many variations on the principal theme, all of which will involve actual somatic mutations, or disruptions in at least one primary genetic sequence, leading to the disruption of control mechanisms. The oncogene model, although explaining the transformation of cells in tissue culture, will turn out to be insufficient to explain all aspects of the induction of cancer in animals and man. Because of the diversity of cancer cells, even within a single patient, an effective cure for cancer will take more time, although immunological approaches will replace chemical and radiation treatments within 10–15 years, and modified genetic therapies will offer hope to patients in 25 years.

There is current interest in attaching a toxic agent to a pure single (monoclonal) antibody, which could seek out at least some subpopulation of the cancerous cells. Thus, a means might be found, of killing some cancer cells selectively and leaving any normal cell unscathed. This approach will be tested on patients in the 1980s and will be of some, but limited, usefulness. A similar approach, using a viruslike particle containing correcting genetic messages, either with a monoclonal antibody or alone, would perhaps be able to reverse the cancerous or precancerous cells to their normal state. This gene therapy approach to cancer is a bit farther in the future, but it will be tested by the year 2010.

The use of immunomodulators may allow the general competence of the immune system to be enhanced to the point where early cancer can be fought by "natural" means, but interferon, the darling of the late 1970s and the early 1980s, will not live up to the expectations that many have had for it. A number of other, more promising compounds will be produced and tested within the next decade, but the early approaches will be too empirical to be generally useful. Not until the overall picture of immune regulation is well understood will it be possible to design effective human therapeutics based on this concept. The most difficult obstacles in the treatment of cancer will continue to be the great diversity of cancer cells and the difficulty of early diagnosis of most types of cancer, even by means of highly sensitive immunological tests. Because a simple cure for cancer will remain elusive for so long, much more attention will be focused on a preventive approach to cancer, but by publicly supported research rather than profit-inspired corporations.

In particular, it will become possible, through appropriate genetic modification, to greatly improve the resistance of individuals to cancer. It is known now that some families have a significantly lower incidence of cancer than others, aside from the differences in exposure to environmental agents. The genetic basis for this resistance will be elucidated and will turn out to be due either to a high degree of immune competence, to genetically determined cellular factors, or to a combination. I would expect, therefore, that one of the first priorities in what we might term *preventive genetics* would be to confer resistance to cancer on the population. Whether this will be done through a semipermanent enhancement of the immune system or by direct genetic intervention, I would predict that the concept of genetic vaccines will be a reality in 50 years and will, of course, be applicable to diseases other than cancer.

Up to this point, I have dealt primarily with predictions of a very positive nature that I expect will transpire within the next half century. But what about the negative side? Will there be accidents of the type feared by the early critics of recombinant DNA experiments? Or recombinant DNA accidents of a kind *not* imagined by the critics? Or will there be some totally unanticipated consequence of some desirable application of the new biology? And what of biological warfare? Aren't the development of such sophisticated methods in altering cells only inviting the invention of a new class of even more diabolical weapons than those we have in our present arsenal? And will the mixed blessing of a "cure" for the aging process become a reality?

I could answer, simply, "probably yes" to all of the above questions, except possibly the first. The early fears of the critics of recombinant DNA methods, as well as the focus of attention of the NIH Recombinant DNA Advisory Committee, concerned the inadvertant creation of a new class of infectious microbe, possibly one carrying cancer genes, or worse. At this stage, unless the sensitivity to the importance of proper laboratory technique deteriorates totally, I would imagine that a *serious* problem concerning a new strain of infectious organism is very unlikely, and I predict that this will not happen. However, there are other possible effects that have not been given much attention. For example, soil bacteria are being engineered to increase the deposition of atmospheric nitrogen as nitrate or ammonia in agricultural soils. To achieve this successfully, the organism must have survival advantage. Thus, the possibility of an ecological accident cannot be ruled out.

Also, it cannot be assumed that new pharmaceutical products will be free of side effects, as is the case now with conventionally produced products, although the problems may be of a different nature. I imagine that it would be rather likely for at least one case to occur before the year 2000 where a product of the biotechnology industry will run into trouble. Because the product is made by cloning DNA, there will be an intense, but rather brief, public outrage over the safety of pharmaceuticals produced in this manner. But it will pass, more scrutiny will be given to potential safety, and a specific new section on genetically engineered pharmaceuticals will be written into the Food, Drug, and Cosmetic Act.

Biological warfare raises some disturbing thoughts. Yes, the United States and a number of other countries will secretly pursue the development of biological weapons over the next two decades. These efforts will focus on two major areas: virulent infectious agents and immunotoxins. A serious international incident will occur when such weapons are used in a "minor" war, causing widespread worldwide pressure to control the manufacture and deployment of such weapons in the United States.

As for aging, we will learn how to control the ultimate human disease, but only by modifying cells at the beginning of life. The magic youth pill will remain elusive, perhaps forever. Within 50 years, there will, however, be experiments on human zygotes to control the eventually destructive aspects of aging, along with attempts to modify other characteristics. Not until the first successes, however, will the applications of this technology become a public issue. And again, I must say that I have absolutely no idea at this point how society will deal with the issue, but it will have to face in earnest the questions I raised earlier, when the first tall, handsome, and highly talented individual fails to exhibit the first signs of wear, usually detectable in people at least by their early 20s.

When will we be at a point where we begin to attempt to improve on the human species? When will we be able even to think of what our ideal creature should have? That will occur some time in the future. And the farther off things seem, the more difficult it is to make even semi-intelligent predictions. Eventually, it will come. In a century? Perhaps. In two. Certainly by then.

Well, I have ventured as far as I dare, at least in this book. In the scheme of things, I really haven't ventured far into the future at all. Some of the predictions may seem shocking and radical to some readers. I must regard them as conservative, if, indeed, I have learned anything from history. However, there is one important qualification I must make before I close.

The tacit assumption in this chapter is that the world will remain a place of relative serenity and prosperity. I do not have a great deal of confidence that the planet Earth can survive another century without a major human catastrophe, and of course, I am referring to nuclear war as the most likely candidate. Science is a thrilling endeavor; discovery of the unknown is perhaps the ultimate high to many. But I cannot say that it is the most important human activity. Survival is essential to everything else. Without it, science and discovery, the much revered technological "progress," life and hope, happiness and sorrow—all become nothing.

We now live in a most precarious era. One false move, and we are dead. If only that we may someday experience the ultimate expressions of what is noble in the human spirit and intellect, we should—we must—transcend the pettiness of our collective social childhood and repudiate once and for all the creation of instruments of massive destruction as national policy. Separately and together, we must devote ourselves to this goal until we prevail. The human race will not get another chance.

Epilogue

I have recounted a tale of the past, the present, and the future. It is my sincere hope that the reader has found it informative, entertaining, and disturbing. Yes, disturbing. For only when one is uncomfortable with the way the world is going will tacit values and assumptions be questioned.

The wonders of science and technology, both in the present and in the future, should be appreciated from a realistic perspective. It has been my intention to give that perspective clearly to the reader, without hype or distortion. On the other hand, the path to enlightenment is not necessarily an unobstructed yellow brick road. With scientific advancement comes the responsibility to use what we have learned wisely. Mankind has not always done so. This book, then, is in part an urgent appeal to society to begin to treat knowledge with the respect it deserves.

This is not a book of answers. If you were expecting to be told all you ever really wanted to know about genetic engineering and related matters, then perhaps you have found some of the answers here. Far more important, it is a book of questions. These are not easy questions with simple answers. Rather, they are questions that need to be pondered and worried over. The pondering and the worrying may be of far more value than believing that answers must be found.

Appendix
A Concise History and Current Status of Molecular and Cell Biology—Or the Truth about Gene Splicing

---

The First Recombinant DNA

Is there some way that one could study the function of mammalian genes in a system as easy and quick to exploit as a bacterium? At least some scientists were asking this question long before *recombinant DNA* became part of household jargon and its meaning became lost. Paul Berg of Stanford University was one of the first.[1] He reasoned that enough enzymes had been described which either synthesized DNA or split apart its components in unique ways so that one should be able to add a kind of "sticky tape" to the ends of any DNA molecule that one wished to use and thus splice different molecules together. Berg solved the problem using an enzyme (terminal nucleotidyl transferase) which simply adds a single-stranded piece of DNA to one of the two chemically different ends of a DNA molecule. If one wished, the DNA one added could contain only one of the four nucleotide bases. Onto the appropriate ends of one type of double-stranded DNA, Berg added a DNA-like polymer containing only the base adenine (polydeoxyadenosine or, simply, poly dA). Onto the corresponding ends of another DNA population, he added a polymer containing only thymine (polydeoxythymidine or poly dT). Because poly dA and poly dT are "complementary"—that is, they have a naturally specific affinity for each other and spontaneously form a double helix in solution—the two types of DNA molecules could be stuck together, end to end. The gaps left could be filled by DNA polymerase I, an enzyme that catalyzes the synthesis of DNA,[2] and the remaining chain breaks could be sealed with another important enzyme, called *DNA ligase*. Well-known separation methods allowed for the selection of a given type of recombinant molecule. If one type of molecule used was a plasmid DNA molecule (a small bit of circular DNA that was found to be capable of transferring genetic information between strains of bacteria) and the other a mammalian gene, then a means was at hand for introducing the mammalian DNA into a bacterial cell. The prospects of this method caused great excitement among molecular biologists, who foresaw endless possibilities for exciting new experiments, and who also began to be concerned about inadvertently and irreversibly altering some existing form of life in undesirable ways, by this unnatural mixing of genes across the boundaries of species.

But the Berg method, although it was ingenious and it worked, was laborious. It required many steps, and when it was first developed, many days were needed to obtain a very small quantity of the desired recombinant DNA molecule. Also, what about the small amounts of poly dA:dT introduced into the recombinants? Would these affect the various control functions and mechanisms that one might wish to study, and if so, how?

The Discovery of Restriction Enzymes—An Exercise in Serendipity

At about the same time that Berg was beginning to think about studying mammalian genes in a bacterium, other scientists were investigating a much more specific problem in the infection of bacteria by bacterial viruses, or bacteriophage. A bacteriophage contains a relatively small piece of DNA—enough for only a few genes—covered by a protein coat. The usual type of bacterial infection by bacteriophage is, by any reckoning, a truly vicious parasitic attack. It proceeds by a phage particle's attaching itself to the bacterial cell wall and then injecting all of its DNA into the cell. The DNA of the virus then takes over complete control of bacterial cell biochemistry, degrading the cellular DNA and reassembling the nucleotides obtained into multiple copies of the viral DNA. New coat protein is synthesized, utilizing the synthetic machinery of the infected cell, producing perhaps 100 or more complete copies of the virus. At this point, the bacterial cell is literally a mere shell of its former self. The last viral gene function to be turned on is the production of a phage-coded lysozyme, an enzyme that breaks down the bacterial cell wall.

——→

FIGURE 17. The Berg method of joining DNA molecules, using terminal transferase to add complementary cohesive ends to DNA molecules. The molecules terminating in poly dA combine with those ending in poly dT. In this manner, fewer types of random recombinants are created than with the restriction enzyme procedure (Figure 13.) (Redrawn from Stanley N. Cohen, "The Manipulation of Genes," *Scientific American*, **233**, 24–33, July, 1975.)

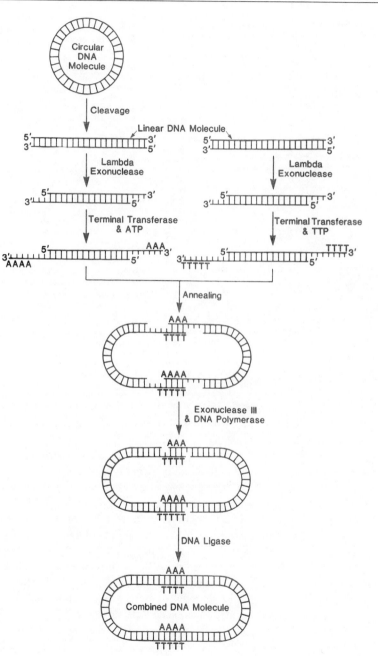

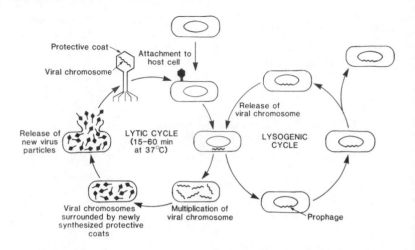

FIGURE 18. A schematic representation of the two kinds of bacteriophage infection. On the left is the typical lytic phase, where the virus particle multiply within the host cell, lysing it with the release of perhaps 100 times as many virus particles with each round of infection. On the right is shown the lysogenic phase, exhibited by certain viruses, such as lambda, in which the viral DNA multiplies along with the host DNA, but none of the genes controlling the virulent lytic phase are expressed. (Redrawn from James D. Watson, *The Molecular Biology of the Gene*, 3rd ed. Menlo Park, Calif. W. A. Benjamin, Inc., 1976.)

The cell wall disintegrates, releasing the hordes of new bacteriophage, which can then go on to attack the new bacterial cells. One generation of phage infection can require only about 20–30 minutes.

What puzzled scientists was the phenomenon of "restriction," one of those obscure bits of scientific jargon that nobody could possibly ever understand the meaning of from the name alone. Restriction refers to the fact that certain strains of bacteria appeared to be resistant to infection by certain bacteriophage. A strain of bacteriophage could infect the cells of *Escherichia coli*, Strain K, but not *E. coli*, Strain B. At least, infection occurred only with about 1 phage particle in 10,000. If the progeny phage particles from such a "plaque" were then used again to infect Strain B, then all were infectious. That is, something mysterious seemed to happen, which appeared to be a single mutational event, that removed the resistance to infection by these phage in certain hosts. Similar phenomena were observed in other species of phage and host bacteria.

For years, however, this phenomenon could not be explained satisfac-

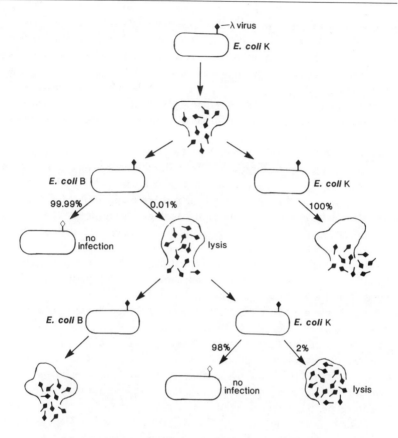

FIGURE 19. Host restriction in bacteria. If a certain strain of bacteriophage that normally infects *E. coli*, Strain K, is used to infect *E. coli*, Strain B, only about 1 phage particle in 10,000 is able to grow on Strain B. The phage produced from this rare event can then infect *E. coli*, Strain B, but only about 2% of the particles are capable of growing on Strain K. This once-baffling observation was explained by the elegant work of Werner Arber (Appendix, Reference 4), which ultimately led to the elucidation of the mechanism of action of restriction enzymes (Appendix, Reference 5).

torily. Then, it was determined that there was an important difference between DNA from the phage that could not infect strain B and the DNA from the mutant form that could. The DNA from the strain that infected Strain B contained methyl ($-CH_3$) groups on certain of the DNA bases, replacing hydrogen, but relatively few of them were present, and certainly not enough to change the molecular weight or the density of the DNA. With the discovery of specific DNA methylases, the enzymes that added these methyl groups to DNA—and by using intensely radioactively labeled methyl donors, the direct methylation of the DNA—could be demonstrated. It turned out that the phage containing DNA that was methylated could infect both Strain B and Strain K. The nonmethylated phage DNA was quickly degraded soon after the virus injected it into a bacterial cell of Strain B, but not so in Strain K. The virus was just as effective in multiplying itself and destroying K host cells, whether or not it had methyl groups attached to its DNA.

Thus, it appeared that the host cells of Strain B contain an enzyme which breaks down DNA (any enzyme which breaks down DNA is called a deoxyribonuclease, or just a *DNAase*) only if it is not methylated. Strain K does not have such an enzyme. The molecular biologists were finally on the track of understanding restriction, and the postulated enzymes were therefore called *restriction endonucleases,* or just *restriction enzymes.*

Before long, the breakdown of nonmethylated DNA was demonstrated in cellular extracts, and the enzymes responsible were soon purified to a high degree. But the way they worked was still a mystery. It was especially baffling because not only did the enzymes appear to break both strands of the DNA in the same place—at least, approximately—thus differing from any known nucleases, but they left rather large pieces of double-stranded DNA, about 1,000 base pairs in length on the average. The long pieces left in a limit digest could not be broken down further, even if reisolated and subjected to fresh enzyme. The conclusion was drawn that there were very few sites on the DNA molecule that were susceptible to attack.

Werner Arber of the Institut de Biologie Moleculaire in Geneva postulated that the enzymes must recognize a specific short sequence of DNA. Based on the number of breaks in a phage molecule, or in other DNA that was susceptible to restriction enzyme breakdown, Arber postulated that this sequence should be approximately six nucleotides long.[3]

Working with enzymes from *Hemophilus influenzae,* a bacterium infectious to humans that has also been shown to exhibit the phenomenon of restriction to certain of its bacteriophage, Thomas Kelly and Hamilton Smith investigated the sequence of DNA at the points that were attacked by the restriction enzyme. What they found was the exceedingly clever and efficient way nature had devised to prevent bacterial cells from being attacked by bacterial viruses. The enzyme, denoted *Hin*dII, did indeed recognize a sequence of six nucleotides, making a break in each strand, as Arber had predicted. But what Kelly and Smith didn't expect to find was that the sequence of six nucleotides on one strand was exactly the same as that on the other, only in the opposite direction. That is, the complementary strand to these particular six nucleotides is the strand itself.[4] This clearly makes sense from an evolutionary point of view, in that the enzyme required to perform the breakage might then need only one type of recognition site, perhaps one for each DNA strand contained in identical enzyme subunits. If a specific nucleotide in the six-nucleotide region has been methylated, then it is resistant to attack by the restriction enzyme.

This first restriction enzyme to be characterized split the DNA chains at the center of symmetry of the recognition sequence. But when the second *H. influenzae* restriction enzyme was studied, a discovery was made that soon led to the novel use of these esoteric restriction enzymes that made them famous. For this enzyme (*Hin*dIII), the breaks were not made at the center of rotational symmetry of the six-nucleotide recognition sequence, but between the first and second nucleotides on each strand, reading in opposite directions. The establishment of the mechanism for this particular *Hemophilus* endonuclease led immediately to similar investigations of other known restriction enzymes, with the finding that a similar mechanism is used by most, although the recognized sequences are generally different. Only occasionally is the break at the center of symmetry, as with *Hin*dII.

After attack by this *H. influenzae* enzyme, DNA is left with a single-stranded piece of four nucleotides on each new end created by an en-

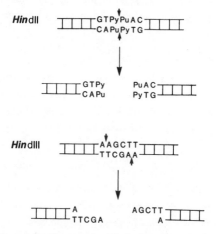

FIGURE 20. The action of the first two restriction enzymes isolated from *Hemophilus influenzae*, *Hin*dII, which makes a cut at the center of the pallindromic recognition site, and *Hin*dIII, which leaves tails of four nucleotides that are self-complementary and thus suitable for DNA recombination. (Pu = either of the purine bases, adenine or guanine; Py = either of the pyrimidine bases, thymine or cytosine.)

zymatically induced break. Moreover, each of these identical pieces is also complementary to itself and every other such piece. Any piece could therefore, under the appropriate conditions, combine with another such four-nucleotide piece of DNA to form a stable double helix. Hence, this restriction endonuclease has provided a means not only of generating pieces of DNA, but of rejoining them, end to end, but in a random fashion. That is, the fragments of digestion can be made to *recombine,* but they are unlikely to reform in the order in which they were originally present, especially if the digest contains many different types of DNA segments. So that the recombined DNA molecules will not come apart, all the needed covalent bonds can be formed with DNA ligase, as in the Berg method, and a stable product created.

Clearly, however, it would not necessarily be of much value to chop up a particular sample of DNA and recombine the fragments at random. However, small viral DNA molecules tend to have relatively few sites that can be recognized by the restriction endonuclease. And tiny plasmid DNAs are often blessed with only one such site, a great boon to the scientist wishing to add a piece of some other DNA to a bacterium. (A plasmid is a very small piece of DNA that can exist apart from a bacterial chromosome and that can be transferred, along with its genetic information, to other bacterial strains.) If plasmid DNA and the DNA from some other source are both treated with the appropriate restriction enzyme and then mixed, a few recombinant DNA molecules are obtained that consist of the original plasmid with a "foreign" DNA insert. One can then use these recombinant DNA plasmids to study that isolated gene in an easily accessible bacterial system.

It was purely fortuitous that the restriction enzymes purified more than a decade ago had exactly the properties that enabled DNA fragments to be put together in unique ways. This fact illustrates only too well how science often leads one down unexpected paths in directions that could not have been foreseen in advance, nor included in a grant proposal.

Daniel Nathans of the Johns Hopkins University School of Medicine (a colleague of Hamilton Smith) and his students were among the first to put the *H. influenzae* restriction enzymes to good use. They were studying the way in which a small DNA virus (called SV-40, where SV = Simian Virus), which produces tumors in animals, infects and transforms animal cells in culture. Nathans asked how a virus that contains only three genes could be capable of producing tumors. It turned out that when the circular DNA of SV-40 was treated with the first *H. influenzae* restriction enzyme to be purified and characterized (*Hind*II), 11 specific fragments could be isolated. This fact alone permitted much to be learned about SV-40 DNA and the way in which it replicates.[5] Once restriction enzymes were found that generate DNA fragments that can be rejoined, it was possible to modify the SV-40 genome by selectively removing certain restriction fragments, or by adding multiple copies of others. These studies permitted a great deal to be learned about the individual genes of the SV-40 virus.[6]

Soon, many people were purifying and using restriction enzymes to put DNA together in novel ways, primarily as a tool for studying precisely how genes function in living cells. The use of restriction enzymes to create spliceable fragments quickly became the method of choice for forming hybrid DNA molecules because of the ease with which it can be carried out. Nevertheless, the Berg method has the advantage of not being limited by the presence and position of restriction sites, and it is especially useful for splicing synthetic DNA fragments into plasmid and phage DNA. It has been of particular value in constructing generalized expression vectors.[7]

Some years later (1978), after recombinant DNA techniques had revolutionized molecular genetics, Arber, Smith, and Nathans shared the Nobel Prize in Physiology and Medicine for their early work on restriction and restriction enzymes. Paul Berg, who had originally intended to find a method to splice DNA into places where nature did not plan to put it, was awarded the Nobel Prize in Chemistry in 1981 for his pioneering work.

Plasmids and Recombinant DNA

As it became apparent that the means were at hand to combine fragments of DNA, almost at will, the quest began to find and develop systems in which to propagate and study isolated genes. Daniel Nathans was one of the first to succeed, using Ham Smith's restriction enzymes to take apart the entire SV-40 DNA molecule or to modify it selectively in ways that would allow him to study the function of individual genes during the process of viral infection and cellular transformation in the line of monkey kidney cells that were usually used to study the properties of the small tumor virus.

But Paul Berg wanted to study the function of animal virus DNA *outside* its normal host cell. That is, why not put animal virus DNA, or a selected part thereof, into a *bacterium*, where individual genes could be studied free of the complexities of the mammalian cells in which they normally propagate? If possible, it would be best to insert the DNA into a bacterium that had been studied extensively, such as *Escherichia coli*, a common bacillus normally found in the human colon. When Berg perfected his own method of joining DNA fragments, he used it to join SV-40 DNA to the DNA of an extensively characterized virus that infects *E. coli*, known as lambda, in order to study the function of the virus in a simple system. This very fruitful line of investigation occupied Berg's attention for several years.[8]

During the early years of gene splicing, *E. coli* was the organism of choice in which to "clone" foreign DNA or even other genes from *E. coli*. Much was known about the genetics of this bacterium, not only about the ways in which genes are turned on and off, but about the viruses (bacteriophage) that infect *E. coli* and about the ways in which DNA is normally transferred between different *E. coli* cells. It was discovered that some strains of *E. coli* contain small bits of circular DNA that, at least at certain times in the life cycle of the cell, exist as an entity apart from the single large bacterial chromosome. These bits of "epigenetic" DNA, called *plasmids*, may contain a few nonessential genes, and only a minute fraction of the cell's normal complement of DNA. Genes coding for antibiotic resistance, so-called colonization factors (cell surface proteins that enable the cells to attach to the surface of the colon), and enterotoxins (substances that produce the symptoms of diarrhea) have been identified as occurring naturally in *E. coli* plasmids. A bacterial plasmid containing one or more genes for antibiotic resistance is called an *R factor* (R for "resistance"). This class of plasmids proved to be of key importance in the development of recombinant DNA techniques.

Thus, many obvious means seemed to exist by which a piece of DNA might be hooked to phage or plasmid DNA, which, in turn, would carry it inside the *E. coli* bacterium. But getting a piece of DNA containing a gene of interest inside a bacterial cell was only part of the problem. Would the inserted gene replicate along with the rest of the plasmid DNA? And would the gene be expressed, utilizing the necessary enzymes, ribosomes, and etc. of the host bacterium? If the correct start and stop code words, which the bacterial RNA polymerase recognized, were present in the right places, there seemed to be no reason why such an experiment shouldn't work.

Several scientists set out to construct a means by which a foreign gene—*any* foreign gene—could be transferred to the laboratory strain in common use, *E. coli* K-12. It is of interest to note that much of the intense activity in the development of techniques for rearranging genes in the early 1970s took place at Stanford University. In the interests of constructing a readable text, I have concentrated on the developments rather than on who did what when, although the important original papers have been cited and may be consulted by those wishing to pursue the history of this era in detail. The laboratories of Paul Berg, Dale Kaiser, David Hogness, Vittorio Sgaramella, Charles Yanofsky, and Stanley Cohen at Stanford, and of Herbert Boyer at the University of California at San Francisco, were the scenes of many of the most notable early achievements. After 1973, however, many laboratories throughout the world were contributing significantly to the perfection of these revolutionary methods.

The base sequence of the DNA recognition site for the first of several *H. influenzae* restriction enzymes (designated as *Hin*dII) was reported in 1970. Soon to follow was another (*Hin*dIII), which had the unique property of creating identical, self-complementary unpaired segments of DNA four nucleotides in length at every break. Daniel Nathans immediately seized the opportunity to take full advantage of the properties of these enzyme to characterize the genetic function of SV-40 DNA. However, the full potential of restriction enzymes as an indispensable tools in DNA cloning was not fully appreciated immediately, as Hamilton Smith now admits. Moreover, it is curious that Stanford scientists did not immediately take advantage of the good news from Johns Hopkins. (At this point, I will resist the temptation to make a bad pun about *Hin*dsight.)

Instead, another restriction enzyme, this from good old *E. coli,* was being studied at Stanford, with the finding in 1972 that it worked in exactly the same way as the enzyme from *H. influenzae.* This enzyme, now designated as *Eco*RI, was immediately exploited in the laboratories of Stanley Cohen and Herbert Boyer to investigate the potential for joining isolated DNA fragments to bacterial plasmids. By this time, a great deal of information was available concerning the R factor plasmids. These were interesting objects in their own right, not only because of their importance in human disease, but because they lent themselves readily to the study of certain aspects of bacterial genetics.

A method had been found for treating *E. coli* cells in a way that would render them capable of taking up isolated plasmid DNA (albeit somewhat inefficiently), thus bypassing the bacterial mating techniques that are the means by which plasmid DNA is transferred between cells in nature. Thus, if a suitable plasmid could be found as a vehicle into which foreign DNA fragments could be incorporated, a means might exist for inserting these genes into a living cell in a state where they could function more-or-less normally.

The ideal candidate was soon found among the many plasmids isolated and studied at Stanford.[9] This was a small plasmid, designated *pSC*101 (p for "plasmid," SC for "Stanley Cohen"), that contained only a gene conferring resistance to the antibiotic tetracycline to its host, in addition to the genes necessary for its own repliction. Moreover, *pSC*101 contained only one recognition site for the *Eco*RI restriction endonuclease, which, fortuitously, did not cleave the molecule in either the region coding for antibiotic resistance or those genes necessary for replication.

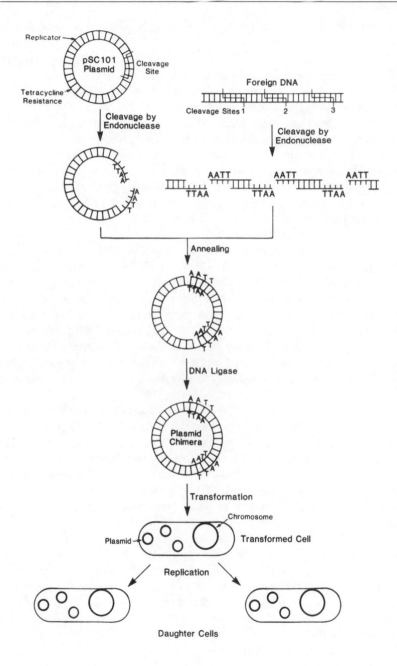

The next step was to see whether *pSC*101 could be used to transfer an isolated gene inside an *E. coli* cell and, if so, whether that gene could function. Thus, another plasmid, containing the gene for resistance to the antibiotic kanamycin, was subjected to *Eco*RI digestion. The fragment containing only the gene for antbiotic resistance, but not replication genes, was then isolated.

This piece of DNA was then mixed with plasmid DNA that had been cleaved with the same restriction enzyme, under conditions that favored the formation of double helices between the identical, complementary single-stranded tails at the end of every piece of DNA present in the mixture, each containing the same sequence of four nucleotides. The remaining single-stranded gaps were then sealed with DNA ligase.

When cells of *E. coli* that had been treated to take up plasmid DNA were mixed with this "recombined" DNA and then allowed to grow to form colonies, a few clones could be isolated that were resistant to both tetracycline and kanamycin. The plasmids isolated from these cells were shown to consist of the DNA from *pSC*101 bound to DNA containing a gene for kanamycin resistance. Because each colony had been derived from a single cell, the experiment showed that the plasmid DNA combined with an additional gene in the laboratory had not only replicated along with the host bacterium, but that both the plasmid genes and the added gene were expressed.

This success then led to a number of experiments to test the generality of the method. First, the above experiment was repeated, only this time with a fragment of a plasmid of a completely unrelated species of bacteria, *Staphylococcus aureus*, containing the genetic information for penicillin resistance. Because these two species do not normally exchange genetic information, a successful means had been found to circumvent nature.

Donald Brown of the Department of Embryology of the Carnegie Institution of Washington, which is located in Baltimore, had been studying the genes of the African clawed frog, *Xenopus laevis*, and had isolated the DNA coding for ribosomal RNA. Some of this DNA, about the only purified animal DNA preparation available at the time that contained only a few genes, was

←——

FIGURE 21. The splicing of foreign DNA into a plasmid (*pSC*101) using a restriction enzyme (*E. coli Eco*RI) and DNA ligase. The plasmids containing a DNA insert may then be used to transform cells of *E. coli* so that they contain and perhaps express the information coded in the inserted genes. (Redrawn from Stanley N. Cohen, "The Manipulation of Genes," *Scientific American*, **233**, 24–33, July, 1975.)

given to Cohen, Boyer, and their co-workers to see if the same method could be used to propagate animal DNA in *E. coli* cells. Sure enough, *Eco*RI digestion fragments of frog DNA, when combined with plasmid DNA, were propagated along with the *E. coli* host and the plasmid DNA.[10]

It appeared, then, that the method was completely general. All that was needed for *any* DNA to be propagated in *E. coli* cells using the *pSC*101 plasmid was that the DNA contain a recognition site for *Eco*RI restriction enzyme on each side of the gene of interest, in order for it to be stably integrated into the plasmid before uptake by the host bacterial cells. The method was clearly applicable to other plasmids, other restriction enzymes, and other host cells. Soon, many such systems had been described in the literature.

Isolating Genes

Suppose that you wished to study the genes coding for a particular function in a particular plant, animal, or microbe, and you hadn't the faintest idea how to isolate that particular region of DNA from all of the rest of the DNA. In a case where little or nothing is known of the genetics of the organism, or the characteristics of the DNA of the region of interest, what would you do?

Well, molecular biologists are becoming increasingly clever in devising ingenious ways to accomplish their purpose. Thus, methods have been developed for isolating the genes of animal or human DNA which codes for virtually *any* gene product of interest. There are, of course, some genes that are easier to find than others, but it is clear that it is now possible, by combining several techniques, to isolate and synthesize multiple copies of essentially any segment of DNA in a suitable host cell. Expression of the DNA to form the appropriate gene product is another matter entirely, and often far more complex than merely incorporating a structural gene. There has been considerable progress in the development of generalized expression vectors that contain the appropriate promoter and control genes, so that any selected polypeptide sequence will be produced in quantity by a suitable bacterial host.

The first method to be used to select a specific piece of DNA from the total DNA of an organism was the so-called shotgun experiment. As implied by this graphic appellation, the shotgun experiment is indeed designed to get everything. First, a suitable host and vector are selected, such as *E. coli* K-12 and the *pSC*101 plasmid. Then, the entire DNA complement of the organism is isolated (that is, DNA that contains all of the DNA sequences present in that organism) and subjected to attack by the same restriction enzyme used to split the plasmid DNA. The plasmid DNA, now consisting of linear rather than circular molecules, is then mixed with the fragmented DNA from the organism, under conditions that permit recombination to take place, and the gaps are again ligated. The resulting mixture, containing a multitude of different DNA recombinants, is then added to bacterial cells treated so that the DNA will be taken inside the cells. The bacteria are then grown on the appropriate solid medium in petri dishes. The resulting colonies, or "clones," of cells may contain many different fragments of the DNA under study. Most, however, will contain none. Therefore, as in the simpler experiments described above, it is important to use a plasmid cloning vehicle containing antibiotic resistance genes. Thus, when grown on medium containing the antibiotic, only those cells containing the plasmid will grow into visible colonies.

Ideally, there should also be a means of selecting for the cells with plasmids containing the particular segment of DNA of interest. If the gene is expressed in the host cells, then there may be some distinguishing feature whereby those cells may be selected. In general, however, without genes specifying the correct control signals and perhaps other information, most genes will not be expressed—especially animal genes—in a shotgun experiment. One may attempt to construct a plasmid containing such signals in order to increase the probability of expression of uncharacterized genes, but for various reasons, this method does not usually work.

Each human cell contains DNA corresponding to approximately 3 billion base pairs. Based on the size of the average protein, the coding portion of a gene corresponds, again on the average, to about 1,000 base pairs. A single gene, therefore, according to this simple view of the world of mammalian DNA, corresponds to one millionth of the DNA of a cell. In practice, it has turned out that the isolation of a single gene is not quite as difficult as this simple calculation would indicate; there are not 1 million separate genes in a human cell. Nevertheless, any procedure based on random screening would entail prohibitive odds of ever finding what one is looking for. Thus, the problem of isolating a single specific segment of human DNA (or, for that matter, DNA from *any* mammal) seemed insurmountable. Shotgun experiments, although sometimes useful for isolating microbial genes, clearly were not going to be the way of the future, at least without the help of methods to simplify the screening process.

However, since the "early" days of pioneering work in the exploration of recombinant DNA methods, a number of discoveries and developments have revolutionized even this revolutionary field, to enable the study of human genes and gene function to proceed at an unprecedented rate. Perhaps the most useful has been the development of techniques for the rapid determination of DNA base sequences. Walter Gilbert of Harvard and Fred Sanger of Cambridge University, who had each been pursuing the problem of DNA sequencing independently, shared the Nobel Prize in Chemistry in 1980 for their achievements.[11] The means of determining DNA base sequences, coupled with knowledge of the genetic code and synthetic methods that allow for the construction of a piece of DNA corresponding to a particular protein gene product, have made it possible to isolate almost any gene of interest.

In order to do this isolation efficiently, it is first necessary to find, or construct, a "probe." A probe is generally a piece of DNA that contains at least some sequences in common with the genetic region to be studied, and it functions much as does the bait of the fisherman. If you wish to catch a particular type of fish, and not others, you try to find something that only that type of fish likes, and that the others in the sea can't stand. Thus, the molecular biologists who construct their DNA probes refer to the process of finding genes as *fishing*. In order to be a good fisherman, you have to have just the right kind of DNA bait.

In finding some genes, the problem is relatively easy. That is, if a particular cell type makes primarily one type of protein, it is usually possible to isolate from that cell the messenger RNA (mRNA) which directs the synthesis of that protein. For example, the cells that give rise to red blood cells synthesize large amounts of globin, the protein portion of hemoglobin. Hence, it was possible to isolate and purify the globin mRNA from these cells. Because the mRNA contains base sequences complementary to DNA, genes can be isolated by forming a DNA/RNA hybrid. Only the DNA coding for globin is complementary to and forms hybrids with globin mRNA, or at least that was the assumption (this led to a surprising finding). Usually, however, an enzyme called *reverse transcriptase,* originally isolated by David Baltimore of the Massachusetts Institute of Technology from animal cells infected with an RNA virus, is used to make a DNA copy of the mRNA template.[12] The RNA may then be digested away, leaving the more stable DNA, called *complementary DNA, or cDNA.*

In order to obtain enough cDNA to conduct a variety of experiments, the cDNA may be "cloned" in a plasmid/bacterium host-vector system in a way similar to that described above. In this case, however, because the ends of the cDNA are generally not complementary to the ends of DNA molecules produced from digestion with any of the 355 known restriction enzymes, the original Berg method is used to insert cDNA into a plasmid. That is, a plasmid is split once with restriction enzyme, and a polymer of a single deoxyribonucleotide is added to each end. The complementary nucleotide base is polymerized onto the end of the cDNA molecule, and the recombinant is formed as described earlier. In this way, a vanishingly small amount of cDNA may be amplified at will to produce whatever quantity is needed.

Now suppose you are not so lucky as to have a cell that makes mostly

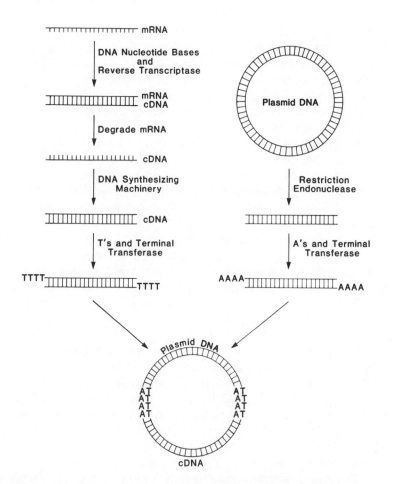

FIGURE 22. A gene-splicing experiment in which complementary DNA (cDNA) is made from isolated messenger RNA coding for a known protein. The cDNA is then spliced into bacterial plasmid DNA using the Berg method. The recombinant plasmids can then be used to generate large quantities of the cDNA in a bacterial host.

one kind of protein, or the protein which interests you is present only as a small fraction of the total protein. In general, the genes you wish to study will *not* make a product that dominates the biochemical output of a cell. Some of the most interesting genes code for specialized proteins which may be present in very small amounts. However, it is now relatively easy to determine the sequence of amino acids in a protein molecule, even if you have only small amounts of material. Because we know the genetic code, it is possible to synthesize a piece of DNA that *might* correspond to the actual sequence present in the gene. I say "might" because there is redundancy in the genetic code, so that, in certain positions, the exact base in the gene cannot be determined from the amino acid sequence. It is therefore necessary to make a synthetic piece of DNA that is large enough to ensure a reasonable degree of complementarity to the original gene, even though there are bound to be a few mistakes in the bases you put in. You might even need to construct several of the possible sequences before you get a probe that will work efficiently.

It may then be desirable to refine your probes before setting out to catch the big one. Thus, the small DNA probe synthesized from the base sequence of a protein may be used, not to find the gene directly, but first to locate the actual messenger RNA for the gene of interest. If that can be done, then specific cDNA can be made and cloned to construct a much longer and more specific piece of probe DNA.

Once you have your probes, the process of fishing often proceeds in several steps. Clearly, if you want flounder, it would be better to fish in waters where there are many flounder relative to other species. Not only are your chances better for catching the fish you want, but the chances that somebody else will steal your bait are also reduced. That is, one usually tries to enrich the population of genes desired before embarking on such a fishing expedition.

Sometimes, then, a shotgun experiment may be performed, to at least divide the DNA of an animal into smaller units within which to work. In such cases, it is common not to use a plasmid cloning vehicle, but a bacteriophage, into which the pieces of animal DNA from a restriction enzyme digest have been spliced. If the phage containing the added DNA retains its functions of producing many copies of itself during the process of infection, then much more of the cloned DNA is produced, relative to the host DNA, than if one uses a plasmid vector.

The phage containing a specific piece of cloned DNA still produces the "plaques" characteristic of normal phage infection. That is, a single phage particle on a sheet of bacterial cells immobilized in agar on a petri dish produces a cleared area, called a *plaque*, where all the surrounding bacteria have been infected by phage, usually several generations, and lysed (broken open). The plaque, however, is covered with phage particles, all containing the cloned DNA. The single recombinant phage particle has now been duplicated about 10,000 times.

The experiment can be conducted so that there may be perhaps 150,000 *different* fragments of human DNA. It may still seem like a formidable task to screen this number of plaques. It would be, too, if it weren't for the DNA probes. If one uses a technique called *replica plating,* whereby two essentially identical petri dishes containing the same phage plaques in the same positions can be prepared, the plaques on one dish may be rapidly tested by means of a radioactively labeled cDNA probe. Methods have been developed whereby the phage DNA can be exposed and hybridized with the cDNA directly on the plate. Exposure to photographic film produces a black spot wherever there is a plaque containing radioactive cDNA. The film can then be compared with the duplicate petri plates, and the virus particles from the corresponding plaque can be used to infect a large culture of bacteria.

Because each phage particle contains a piece of animal DNA that is specifically bound to the cDNA, only somewhat larger, the procedure succeeds in "fishing" out of the total animal DNA, a small (perhaps 25,000-base-pair) piece of the total DNA, presumably containing the gene of interest. This piece of DNA may then be further treated with various restriction enzymes and cloned separately to produce eventually pure DNA coding for the protein under study.

Split Genes, Tandem Genes, and Pseudogenes

When procedures like those above were carried out to examine the structure of animal genes, some unexpected results were obtained. One of the most remarkable findings was that the coding regions within most animal genes studied were discontinuous.[13] That is, perhaps only 15%–20% of the DNA in the region called a gene actually codes for amino acids in a protein. There are coding regions separated by often rather long "silent" regions of DNA. In order for a protein to be synthesized, the entire gene is copied into mRNA. But the silent regions are clipped out of the mRNA, and the remaining pieces are rejoined to form the active template for subsequent protein synthesis.

The significance of these findings remains unclear, although the phenomenon of split genes now seems to be universal in animals. The discovery of Donald Brown, more than a decade ago, that the African-clawed-frog ribosomal DNA contains apparently useless "spacer" DNA regions, was then thought to be a quirk of nature rather than a rule. On the surface, it would appear to be a somewhat inefficient process. Nature, in the slow but deliberate wisdom of evolution, rarely seems wasteful or without purpose. But then, at what intermediate stage have we chosen to look in on her workings? And perhaps, when we finally understand much more than we now do about the internal mechanism of a cell and all of its components, this apparently obtuse way of going about the business of gene transcription and translation may yet be the optimal, most efficient way in which all of the requirements of living animals can be satisfied.

There are (at least) two theories to account for these unexpected findings.[14] Paul Berg has suggested that this curious splicing phenomenon may reflect an important element of gene regulation. Some believe that the presence of split genes may have revealed an essential element in biochemical evolution. But could all this complex processing machinery really be there only because it confers a survival advantage by generating a greater diversity of proteins?

The gene that codes for the protein cytochrome b exhibits an unusual property. Not only is the messenger RNA the result of a cut-and-patch process reflecting about 15% of the gene's DNA sequences, but there is another small protein that is encoded in the first coding regions of the cytochrome gene plus part of the next intron, the name given to the intervening sequences. This protein seems to be necessary for the excision of the next intron region on the cytochrome mRNA. Moreover, the enzyme cytochrome b oxidase, of which cytochrome b is a substrate, contains a subunit that cannot be synthesized unless the cytochrome b mRNA is spliced correctly. Could this be a mechanism whereby genes, in a sense, communicate with each other through their "silent" regions?

The relevance of these findings to evolution, along with the phenomenon of gene duplication, seems to be clear. If all of the DNA in a cell were necessary for the organism to function, then even a small alteration of the DNA, such as a single base-pair change, could greatly decrease that organism's chances of survival and could even be directly lethal. Although evolution could, in principle, proceed in this situation, it is not likely to be very efficient. That is, the chances of a mutational event's actually *improving* the organism's situation in life would be remote indeed.

Another remarkable discovery was that there often seems to be more than one gene that is "fished" out by a cDNA probe. These regions of DNA tend to be located next to each other, both physically and genetically, and are of about the same size. However, they are never identical, even though they often contain considerable homology in their base sequences. For example, there are five genes similar to the one coding for beta globin in humans.[15] The entire region of about 70,000 base pairs has been sequenced. The intensive study that this system has received is unraveling much about the control of the synthesis of human globins during development (newborns have a different type of globin from that of adults, except in certain genetic disorders in which production of the fetal form continues throughout adulthood). These studies have also revealed the precise defects in the class of hereditary blood disorders known as the thalassemias, and in sickle-cell anemia. The knowledge of the exact nature of the defective gene is the first step in any attempts to correct a hereditary disease through "gene therapy."

In the course of the discovery of related genes in tandem, it was found that sometimes the gene products, although bearing structural similarities, had rather different functions, such as enzymes' catalyzing different reactions.

Let us suppose that, through a quirk in DNA replication, or a mismatched recombinational event, a coding gene is doubled or acquires some extra DNA. If the gene were doubled, then there would be two complete copies, only one of which would be essential for survival. Thus, changes in one of the copies might be easily tolerated, with no deleterious effects to the organism. If by chance, after the accumulation of several changes, a useful gene product were made eventually, conferring some advantage on the organism, that gene might then be fixed on a course that could result in a highly refined new function.

The five genes in the human beta-globin region appear to have resulted from gene duplication, with some regions in common but with certain differences. Thus, the globin portion of fetal hemoglobin, which aids in the survival of babies at birth, when they are likely to be deprived of oxygen, as well as of adult hemoglobin, appears to have arisen from a common ancestor gene. Other instances of gene duplication result in an adjacent gene with some sequence homology but a completely different enzymatic function. In still other cases, duplicated genes, detected by the cDNA "fishing" experiments described earlier do not seem to code for anything and are called *pseudogenes*.[16]

Could the intervening regions between coding portions (exons) serve a similar evolutionary function? It would seem logical that they could. But the mRNA editing mechanism would also need to be involved in this evolution. The cytochrome *b* example suggests that two proteins might be coded in the same region of DNA. In addition, there is a region in SV-40 DNA that comprises parts of two separate genes. Moreover, the reading frame for these two overlapping genes is shifted, so that the same base sequences do not code for the same amino acids in the respective proteins. Is it possible, then, that a genetic region, complete with introns and exons that code for a particular protein, might, if processed differently, also code for a *different* protein, with the introns and exons in different places? If so, what might control which function is processed, or at what time? Perhaps the region could code for different proteins in different tissues, under the constraints of other control mechanisms. So far, all intervening sequences of the unedited mRNA that have been studied begin with the bases GU and end with AG. Thus, there are some constraints in the system that seem to be general for all eukaryotes. But this is one of those places where, like the announcers on the old radio serials, I am forced to say, "Tune in again tomorrow for the next exciting episode . . ."

Animal Cloning

The first successful animal clones were created in 1952 by Robert Briggs and Thomas King[17] at Indiana University, and later by John Gurdon[18] at Oxford. Both teams worked with amphibians. The technique involved first carefully removing the cell nuclei from fertilized frog eggs. Then, from a single frog embryo, cell nuclei were removed from cells of a particular type and transplanted individually into the enucleated frog eggs. The cell membranes seemed to be able to reclose after puncture with a tiny pipette through which the new nuclei were transferred. In this manner, a population of frog eggs with precisely identical nuclei, each containing an identical complement of DNA, could be prepared. Generally, the genetic material in each of the thousands of eggs produced by a single frog is different, even if in minor ways. After receiving DNA from the male, the fertilized eggs differ even more.

From the large numbers of frog eggs receiving identical nuclei, many embryos were produced. Most, however, were abnormal, and many apparently normal ones died before hatching. A few, nevertheless, appeared to be completely normal, both during development and subsequently as frogs. These frogs, therefore, constituted a "clone," albeit a rather small one, of genetically identical animals.

It was then asked if a somatic cell nucleus from *any* tissue at *any* stage of development would serve to replace the original nucleus in a fertilized egg successfully. The answer appeared to be no. Although a few embryonic cells could serve as sources of nuclei that would ultimately give rise to a live, healthy, properly developed animal, all would not. Moreover, beyond a certain developmental stage, no cell nucleus seemed to work. The development of an embryo would take place for a while, but the cells failed to mature properly. Nuclei from adult cells were even poorer candidates.

It has been assumed that the DNA complement of all somatic-cell nuclei remains constant throughout the entire life cycle of an animal. However, these experiments showed that something irreversible happened to the nucleus, after a certain time in development, to prevent its DNA from being expressed in the way necessary for complete differentiation and development to take place. At least, that is how the theory goes. Could the DNA of the cell actually be irreversibly altered as a normal part of development? There is as yet no evidence that this is so, but that possibility has not been ruled out.

What about mammals? Can the same type of procedure be carried out successfully? Apparently, it can. The problem with mammals is that the egg cells of all species are much smaller than those of a frog, so that the technical problems in handling them are much more difficult to overcome. Thus, success in obtaining genetically identical mice was first achieved by two other methods. Clement Markert developed a means of causing an unfertilized mouse ovum to undergo a doubling of the number of chromosomes, thus converting it from the so-called haploid germ cell into a diploid cell, like the cell that the egg becomes *after* fertilization. He was then able get these cells to begin to undergo normal development. Now, if he took the embryo at the four- or eight-cell stage and dissociated the individual cells, each one of these could also begin to form an entirely new embryo. In this way, Markert was able to produce genetically identical parthenogenic mice—those having no father—which, because they were produced from a chromosome doubling, were all females. Moreover, this property also rendered every gene in the mouse homozygous, meaning that both members of each pair of chromosomes (and genes) are identical. This method did not quite produce clones genetically identical to the mother, for the offspring had only half of her chromosomes, which were then doubled to produce the normal complement. However, if the same procedure were to be carried out on ova produced by one of the totally homozygous daughters, then her parthenogenic children would indeed be true clones of their mother.

If early mouse-embryo cells obtained in the above manner can be separated and made to form separate embryos, why can't cloned mice be produced from a zygote (jargon for a fertilized egg, and the subsequent cleavage stages) produced by normal fertilization? Well, that seems to work, too. In either application, however, only a limited number of identical mice can be produced, for the probability with which separated embryo cells will go on to start a new organism declines precipitously with the sixteen-cell stage and beyond. This method has been successfully used to produce identical animals of several species, including identical calf twins, each developing in the uterus of a different mother.

Building a Better Mouse

It seems that we owe a great deal to the mouse. That is where the *really* interesting developments are taking place. Beatrice Mintz, who has been studying embryonic development in mice for more that 20 years, wished to find a way to "tag" embryonic cells at a very early stage in order to trace the origin of the various differentiated structures in the adult mouse. Using methods similar to those discussed above, she dissociated mouse embryo cells from each other at the eight-cell stage (that is, one that has undergone three synchronized cell divisions).

Dr. Mintz, however, was not particularly interested in making genetically identical cloned animals. Instead, she mixed the separated cells of two different strains of mice, each with a very different set of genetic markers, including hair color. The cells were very cohesive, quickly forming a new embryo, which then proceeded to undergo cleavage and to differentiate normally. The embryos so formed were transplanted into the uterus of another mouse to produce so-called allophenic mice. These mice, although normal, healthy animals, are said to be genetic *mosaics*. That is, their bodies are mixtures of two genetically different cell types instead of the usual one. In different animals, the patterns of distribution of the two cell types seemed to be somewhat random, depending on their original location in the reassociated embryo after it had acquired an orientation (that is, after which end was to be the head and which was to become the tail were determined).

With the refinement of her experiments, Dr. Mintz was able to establish patterns of which cell "clones" (yes, the term can be applied to cells *within* an organism as well) gave rise to certain structures of regions in the body of the adult. Mice derived from the cells of a strain of white mice mixed with the cells from a black mouse produced some rather interesting color patterns, characteristic of the sequence of developmental events in a mouse. These studies revealed that the fate of an individual cell is not determined as early as scientists had believed. In spite of all of the cellular shuffling that was done in these experiments, the mice they produced always seemed to develop normally.

Once a cell becomes "committed" to a particular function during differentiation, it appears to be irreversibly committed. From that point on, only certain genes are expressed, and not others. The mechanism of how this commitment comes about remains a question, but many believe that it involves the regulation of the production of certain types of messenger RNA, rather than an irreversible change in the DNA itself.[19]

One of Dr. Mintz's goals was to be able to introduce specific genetic traits into mice. The molecular biologists were getting rather sophisticated at modifying the genes of cultured cells. If only there were a way to get cultured cells incorporated into developing mice . . .

It turned out that teratocarcinomas, tumors that are derived from undifferentiated embryonic cells, provided the perfect material. When these tumor cells were mixed with normal embryo cells and transplanted back into a surrogate mother mouse, a normal mouse developed, with part of its cells coming originally from the teratocarcinoma. The tumor cells were "totipotent"—that is, capable of producing any cell type—and their tumor properties were completely reversed in the environment provided by the normal embryo cells.[20]

It has been only recently that scientists have been able to produce stable cell lines of teratocarcinoma cells, on which to perform genetic manipulation experiments. Of the mosaic animals created with this technique, it can be shown that, in some, the germ cells or the ova are derived from the teratocarcinoma. Thus, it should be possible, by adding "new" genes directly into cultured teratocarcinoma cells, to derive a strain of mice perpetuating those genes. This technique has now been used to develop strains of mice containing "new" genes, and it has led to the development of animal models for human genetic diseases.[21]

Adding New Genes to Mammalian Cells

The most direct method of introducing new genetic material into an animal is the direct injection of a segment of DNA into a fertilized egg. Achieving the stable integration of the injected DNA into the chromosomal DNA has been a problem. In a small number of the animals resulting from such experiments, the adult cells contain the DNA insert, and in a few cases, it is also contained by the cells of the offspring of these mice.[22] But more difficult is integration of the DNA insert in such a way that gene expression will also take place. Richard Mulligan and Paul Berg[23] have been able to achieve the expression of a bacterial enzyme in cultured mammalian cells, using a specially constructed SV-40 DNA cloning vehicle containing the necessary control genes, so that presumably *any* gene that is inserted will be transcribed. More spectacular, however, was the finding by Palmiter *et al.*,[24] who fused the gene for rat growth hormone with a mouse promoter DNA fragment and then microinjected it into fertilized mouse eggs, which were then implanted into receptive female mice. Of the 21 mice that were born, 7 contained the fused DNA in their cells, and 6 of these grew to be substantially larger than normal mice, some nearly twice the size of their littermates. Gene expression was demonstrated both by mRNA specific for the injected DNA and by high levels of growth hormone in the blood.

Thus, we would seem to be very close to the achievement of a general method whereby any gene can be inserted into cells, from which an animal may be produced, which would then pass this gene on to its progeny. The teratocarcinoma lines of Mintz offer the advantage of a great deal more selection of the desired cell type containing a particular insert before the introduction of the gene into the animal. Injecting the DNA directly allows the scientist much less control over where it goes, but it has the advantage that the animal so produced has the gene in all of its cells.

The Immune System

The heart of the immune system is comprised of two classes of cells, both produced originally in the bone marrow. One type of cell, the circulating T lymphocyte (T for the thymus, which processes the T cells), recognizes the antigen—almost any antigen. This recognition event then triggers the production of antibodies specific to that antigen in another type of cell, called a B lymphocyte (B for the bursa of the chicken, which produces the fowl's version of B cells). A clone of one specific type of the thousands of kinds of B lymphocytes present proliferates in the spleen, where large quantities of antibody specific for that antigen are produced.

The basic antibody structure consists of four polypeptide (protein) chains (see Figure 16, p. 53), two identical large ("heavy") and two identical small ("light") chains. Five kinds of antibodies are defined, depending on the properties of the heavy chain, and all are designated by the prefix ig (for immunoglobulin), followed by one of the letters G, A, M, D, or E. The antibody molecule contains so-called constant regions and variable regions. The constant regions are more-or-less the same within any class of immunoglobulins, but the variable region differs in amino acid composition, depending on the antigen to which the antibody corresponds. More than one type of antibody may be produced for any "foreign" protein or antigen. Thus, the immune serum prepared from an animal by injecting it with a particular substance, even a purified protein, usually contains a mixture of several, perhaps many, antibody types.

During the 1970s, there was a debate going on among immunologists— molecular immunologists, I should say. (It seems that everything has to be molecular these days to be of any significance.) How could an animal make the incredible variety of antibodies that it was known to produce? Was there a general mechanism whereby the antibodies synthesized conform in some way to the antigen? Or was there enough genetic information contained in each and every cell to code for all possible antibodies? If so, that would require much more DNA than is known to be present in a human cell.

It is now clear that both models are partially true, depending on how the problem is viewed. The information coding for all of the possible different segments of the variable portion of the antibody molecule is stored on three different chromosomes. An antigen-specific recombination takes place that reassembles the DNA corresponding to the correct sequences for specific locations within the variable portion specific for the antigen that triggered the response initially. Once this pattern of DNA reassembly is set, that B cell, or all the members of the clone it generates, can synthesize only that one type of antibody. It is believed that there are a small number of most of the millions of possible antibodies on the surfaces of T lymphocytes, which serve to recognize an invading antigen. The precise way in which this cell-surface antibody–antigen complex tells the particular B lymphocytes to start dividing rapidly and make more of that particular type of antibody is not understood.

Hybridomas and Monoclonal Antibodies

In recent years, a method has been developed whereby large quantities of a single *pure,* specific antibody to any given antigen may be prepared almost at will.[25] This technique depends on a property of certain cultured mammalian cells that has been used for many years to study animal genetics at the molecular level: their ability to form hybrids with each other. The early methods of hybridization combined cells with the help of the Sendai virus, which facilitates the fusion of cell membranes. But the resulting cells have twice the normal complement of chromosomes, and so, over time, they get rid of the extras until they have the right number again. Hybrids may now be formed between many types of cells.

The so-called hybridoma is the result of fusing two types of cells with useful properties that would be desirable in the same cell. First, one needs a cell that makes only one type of antibody. Once the spleen B cells have been turned on to make an antibody, each makes only one specific type. But the B lymphocytes cannot be cultured easily to make clones *in vitro.* What is needed, then, is a B cell with the immortal properties of a cancer cell, or a cell "line."

Such a cell can be constructed by fusing a population of spleen cells with myeloma cells, cells that are derived from a form of cancer of the immune system and that are an abnormal form of lymphocyte. The hybridoma so formed has the desirable features of culturability and immortality of the myeloma cell, plus the antibody-producing ability of the spleen B lymphocyte. The preparation of the cells does take some time, but the results are usually worth the effort. Individual hybrid cells are cultured for about two weeks, after which time there are about 1,000 cells in each clone. Then, the individual hybridoma cultures must be screened for the production of the desired antibody, a tedious process by any reckoning, but not really any worse than the method described earlier for cloning and selecting specific human genes. Once the correct cellular clone has been selected, many more clones are grown and stored. Because the single molecular species of antibody is derived from a clone of a single B-cell hybridoma, the antibodies obtained are said to be *monoclonal.*

Making an antibody, however, is still an inefficient process in culture. Therefore, hybridoma cells are injected into the peritoneal cavities of mice, where they form rapidly growing solid tumors that are around 1,000 times more efficient in antibody production than cells grown in culture flasks. Although *in vitro* cell-culture methods are being improved, many laboratories are now cloning the genes for specific antibodies in bacteria. Thus, what have now become traditional recombinant DNA techniques should greatly facilitate the production of single antigen-specific antibodies.

The Control of Genetic Expression—Prokaryotes

The central problem in biology is now—and has been for several years—the regulation of genetic expression. During the 1960s, considerable attention was devoted to the understanding of the control of gene function in bacteriophage. Their relatively small DNA molecules were readily accessible to genetic studies, and their gene products could be easily found and purified.

During the course of phage infection, the first events entail the usurpation of some of the synthetic machinery of the cell to allow for the transcription of the ''early'' phage genes. These gene products then proceed to direct the degradation of the bacterial DNA and to reassemble the component nucleotides into perhaps 100 or more identical copies of new phage DNA. The last functions to be carried out are the synthesis and the assembly of phage coat protein, and an enzyme called *lysozyme,* which digests the bacterial cell wall, releasing mature phage particles which are then free to attack new cells.

This entire process takes as short a time as 20 minutes, completing the ultimate parasitic attack.

Different phage, even those specific for the same bacterium, carry out these functions differently. Thus, the *E. coli* phage T-4, using the cell's enzymes, first synthesizes a regulatory protein called a *sigma factor,* which becomes part of the host *E. coli* RNA polymerase.[26] This factor serves as a recognition signal that directs the way in which the remainder of the phage DNA is transcribed. Phage T-7, on the other hand, again with the help of the *E. coli* enzymes, proceeds to make its own RNA polymerase.[27]

One of the first specific control systems was demonstrated in another bacteriophage specific for *E. coli,* called *lambda.* It was shown in the late 1960s that a separate control protein, called a *repressor,* is coded in the phage DNA and plays an important role in the regulation of its functions.[28] Normally, phage lambda exists in a so-called lysogenic state, in which its DNA is replicated along with the host DNA. But most of its genes, those necessary for the usual destructive infectious mode, do not function because the repressor molecule is bound to two "operator" regions of DNA, thus preventing the transcription of most of the phage DNA. Another protein, the product of the so-called N gene, is, however, capable of releasing the repression, allowing mRNA synthesis to proceed through the repressor binding sites, or operators.

A similar phenomenon was demonstrated in *E. coli.*[29] The repressor protein for the *lac* region, which contains the gene for the enzyme beta galactosidase, was the first such system to be characterized. In this case, however, repression is released by the binding to the repressor of a molecule of galactose, the sugar that is the substrate of beta galactosidase. Thus, the synthesis of the enzyme is controlled by the presence of the substance on which it would act, an efficient way for nature to conserve its resources. This type of control is common in the world of microbes.

The Control of Genetic Expression—Eukaryotes

The intricacy and precision of control demanded by higher organisms is far greater than that required by bacteriophage or single-celled creatures. First of all, the process of development and cellular differentiation requires a high degree of specificity in the regulation of genetic expression. The differentiated multicelled organism, whether plant or animal, contains many specialized cell types, all of which presumably contain the same complement of DNA, and some of which are organized into tissues and organs. The entire organism must function as an internally harmonious whole. Thus, regulation must occur on every level. Here, we consider briefly the general problems in the development of plants and animals, more to present the complexity of the problems to be solved than to suggest solutions. A large body of data has been accumulated in recent years that bears on the regulation of gene expression in development. It is well beyond the scope of this book to discuss these findings, except to say that no clear picture has yet emerged from which general inferences can be drawn. Most molecular biologists are confident that the complexities of eucaryotic gene expression in development, and otherwise, can ultimately be untangled and understood purely in terms of molecular interactions; a few suggest that entirely new, as-yet-undiscovered principles will have to be elucidated before the picture will be completed. My personal bias is with the former view; we have just begun to appreciate the power of the molecule.

In animals, even the fertilized egg seems to have a preferred orientation. In some animals with rather large eggs, there is an obvious asymmetry to the unfertilized egg, and this seems to have a bearing on how the fertilized egg will develop. At least, it seems to know where the head, the legs, and the tail will go. This polarity becomes more pronounced with each cell division, and the cells become more and more unlike one another. Studies discussed earlier demonstrate that this orientation may be reversible up to a point—perhaps to the 8- or 16-cell stage—after which it seems to become fixed. That is, the increasing irreversibility of animal cells that have begun to differentiate seems to be universal, consistent with the inability to create cloned animals from all but the nuclei of embryonic tissue. In this case, however, the nucleus seems to retain totipotency for a longer period than the cell itself, where many of the irreversible changes may be in the cytoplasm. Some lower forms of animals, such as hydras, starfish, earthworms, and salamanders, will regenerate severed portions of their bodies. This phenomenon has not, however, ever been demonstrated in birds or mammals.

Plants seem to work a bit differently. That is, there are many instances where adult cells, or at least those from the actively growing regions, can be made to revert to an undifferentiated state and can be grown in laboratory cultures. The addition of the correct mixture of plant hormones causes the cells to differentiate and to form a normal plant. Of course, any home gardener knows that a pruned tree will grow new branches, and many types of plant cuttings will grow roots readily. Even a small section of stem is often enough to start a new plant.[30]

But what is actually happening to the DNA and its transcription? There is no doubt that the techniques of isolating and studying individual genes of higher organisms—and advances in our ability to manipulate cells—have given us some very important leads. For example, there seems to be an important relationship between the methylatron of DNA and its capacity to form other stable helical forms (such as the left-handed Z conformation) which appear to play an important role in gene expression.[31] However, we still have only begun to understand the control of gene expression in development and cellular differentiation.

Notes and References

Preface

1. Throughout this book, I have used the masculine pronouns when the sex of the antecedent could be either male or female, or the human race generally. Thus, I have used *he* when the meaning is obviously "he or she," *him* to mean "him or her," and *his* to mean "his or her." I also use "man" to denote the human race collectively, or one of its members. By this usage I intend no sex discrimination whatsoever. The English language, unlike a number of others, is deficient in the absence of a pronoun that means, precisely, "he or she" or simply denotes the human antecedent, regardless of sex.

Introduction

1. *Mutation* is a word that entered everyday vocabulary when scientists reported that radiation could produce genetic changes in living organisms. But the popular conception of the word *mutation* in postwar science-fiction movies meant not a simple, usually deleterious alteration in the DNA, but a genetic change producing a grotesque monster. Thus, when people feared the mutational effects of radiation exposure on, for example, human reproduction, they usually imagined two-headed babies rather than a fetus that would probably not survive the first few days of pregnancy. It is one of those terms, like *clone* or even *recombinant DNA*, that acquires a greatly distorted popular meaning in the absence of a clear definition.
2. Two years after the end of World War II, Congress passed a comprehensive bill establishing federal programs to develop atomic energy for peaceful uses, reflecting the view that this awesome new source of energy should and could bring about technological miracles. The result was the funding of considerable research and development, particularly in the National Laboratories (Oak Ridge, Brookhaven, Los Alamos, and Argonne), which included not only the engineering of reactors for nuclear power generation, but much basic research in physics, chemistry, and biology.
3. That we are indeed disturbing the universe in ways that we may one day regret is discussed in the highly readable, somewhat autobiographical book by physicist Freeman Dyson, *Disturbing the Universe* (New York: Harper and Row, 1979).
4. See particularly, Joseph W. Meeker, *The Comedy of Survival* (New York: Charles Scribner's Sons, 1974).
5. Alvin Toffler, *Future Shock* (New York: Random House, 1971).
6. Paul and Anne Ehrlich, *Extinction* (New York: Random House, 1981).
7. Edward O. Wilson, *On Human Nature* (Cambridge: Harvard University Press, 1978). See also, Reference 10, Chapter 1.
8. J. Brownowski, *The Ascent of Man* (Boston: Little, Brown and Company, 1973), p. 436.

Chapter 1

1. My original choice of a title for this chapter was "Life Itself," as in, for example, "Freedom is more precious than life itself." *Life itself* is a term that is meant to embody the pure essence of life, as distinguished from the inanimate. This expression was, therefore, a fitting title for a recent book by Francis Crick (*Life Itself—Its Origin and Nature;* New York: Simon and Shuster, 1981), in which the origin of life—and its essence—is discussed in terms ranging from the molecular to the cosmological. This highly readable volume, which I would strongly recommend to my readers as a supplement to Chapter 1, came to my attention shortly after I had completed the first few chapters of this book. Of course, everyone wants to be original, and no one wants to be called a copycat, especially if one is *not* a copycat. So, reluctantly, I changed the title to simply "Life," which is less explicit, perhaps, but certainly accurate. Now, however, I suppose that there is always the chance that the publishers of a once-popular pictorial magazine might have grounds to claim that I am a copycat nonetheless.

2. Thomas Kuhn, *The Structure of Scientific Revolutions* (Chicago: University of Chicago Press, 1962, Second edition, 1970).

3. See, for example, the collection of classic papers in the biological sciences, Mordecal Gabriel and Seymour Fogel (eds.), *Great Experiments in Biology* (Englewood Cliffs, N.J.: Prentice-Hall, Inc., 1955).

4. Anthony van Leeuwenhoek, *Philosophical Transactions* (London), **11,** 821 (1677). Reprinted in *Great Experiments in Biology* (Reference 3).

5. Walther Flemming, Contributions to the Knowledge of the Cell and Its Life Phenomena, *Arkiv für Mikroskopische Anatomie,* 16, 302–406 (1879). Reprinted in *Great Experiments in Biology* (Reference 3).

6. Walter S. Sutton, The Chromosomes in Heredity, *Biological Bulletin* of the Marine Biological Laboratory of Woods Hole, Massachusetts, **4,** 231–251 (1902). Reprinted in *Great Experiments in Biology* (Reference 3).

7. For a concise discussion of the different techniques in microscopy, see Arthur C. Giese, *Cell Physiology,* 5th ed. (Philadelphia: W. B. Saunders Company, 1979, 609pp.), pp. 72–84.

8. A readable discussion of the electron microscope can be found in G. A. Meek, *Practical Electron Microscopy for Biologists* (New York: John Wiley and Sons, Inc., 1976).

9. B. H. Hoyer, E. T. Bolton, B. J. McCarthy, and R. B. Roberts, "The Evolution of Polynucleotides," In V. Bryson and H. J. Vogel (eds.), *Evolving Genes, and Proteins: A Symposium.* (New York: Academic Press, 1965), pp. 581–590.

10. Edward O. Wilson, *Sociobiology: The New Synthesis* (Cambridge: Harvard University Press, 1975); Edward O. Wilson, *On Human Nature* (Cambridge: Harvard University Press, 1978); Charles J. Lumsden and Edward O. Wilson, *Genes, Mind, and Culture: The Coevolutionary Process* (Cambridge: Harvard University Press, 1981). See also a review and analysis of the latter work by Roger Lewin in *Science,* **212,** 980–910 (1981).

11. Gregor Mendel, letter to Carl Nageli, April 18, 1867. This historic description of Mendel's experiments on the segration and the independent assortment of genes is reprinted in *Great Experiments in Biology* (Reference 3).

12. James D. Watson and Francis H. C. Crick, "Molecular Structure of Nucleic Acid: A Structure for Deoxyribose Nucleic Acid." *Nature,* **171,** 737–738 (1953); J. D. Watson and F. H. C. Crick, "The Structure of DNA," *Cold Spring Harbor Symposium on Quantitative Biology,* **18,** 123–131 (1953).

13. The terms *base* and *nucleotide* may seem to be used interchangably throughout the text. The

nucleotide is the basic subunit of DNA. It consists of a pentose sugar molecule, deoxyribose (ribose in RNA), to which is linked a phosphate group and one of four "bases": adenine, thymine, cytosine, or guanine. The nucleotides are strung together through a phosphate diester linkage. Because it is the individual bases that determine the specificity of DNA, it is correct to refer to either *base sequence* or *nucleotide sequence*. A nucleoside is a sugar molecule + a base, but without the phosphate. A nucleoside monophosphate is, by definition, a nucleotide. DNA is assembled by the polymerization of deoxynucleoside triphosphates, two of the phosphates being eliminated with the formation of each diester bond. For further details, consult one of the references given in Reference 1 for this chapter.

14. The first and now classic paper on the demonstration of the triplet code is Marshall W. Nirenberg and J. H. Mattaei, "The Dependence of Cell-Free Protein Synthesis in *E. coli* on Naturally Occurring or Synthetic Polynucleotides," *Proc. Natl. Acad. Sci., U.S.A.*, **47,** 1588 (1961). See also "The Genetic Code," *Cold Spring Harbor Symposium on Quantitative Biology,* **31** (1966).

15. Of the many books written on biology and biochemistry at all levels, one of the most lucid and concise discussions of the state of molecular biology as of 1980 for readers with little background in science is James Watson and John Tooze, *The DNA Story* (San Francisco: W. H. Freeman and Company, 1981), "Scientific Background," pp. 529–583. A somewhat more advanced but very thorough and well-written text is James D. Watson, *Molecular Biology of the Gene,* 3rd ed. (Menlo Park, Calif.: W. A. Benjamin, Inc., 1976), although parts of this book are now somewhat dated. The most up-to-date, comprehensive treatise on the subject, somewhat more advanced than the relatively brief discussions in *Biofuture,* is by Bruce Alberts, Dennis Bray, Julian Lewis, Martin Raff, Keith Roberts, and James D. Watson, *Molecular Biology of the Cell* (New York and London: Garland Publishing Co., 1983). A text of equally high quality but concentrating more on the biology and physiology of the cell is Arthur C. Giese, *Cell Physiology,* 5th ed. (Philadelphia: W. B. Saunders, Inc., 1979).

16. Donald D. Brown, Pieter C. Wensink, and Eddie Jordan, "Purification and Some Characteristics of 55 DNA from *Xenopus laevis*," *Proc. Nat. Acad. Sci., U.S.,* **681,** 3175–3179 (1971); Donald D. Brown, Pieter C. Winsink, and Eddie Jordan, "A Comparison of the Ribosomal DNA's of *Xenopus laevis* and *Xenopus mulleri:* The Evolution of Tandem Genes," *J. Mol. Biol.,* **63,** 57–73 (1972). For a less technical discussion of Brown's work, see Donald D. Brown, "The Isolation of Genes," in *Recombinant DNA* (San Francisco: W. H. Freeman and Company, 1978), pp. 81–90, a collection of articles from *Scientific American,* this one having appeared in August 1973.

17. The first live birth of a human child conceived outside the body was Louise Joy Brown, on July 18, 1978. Dr. Steptoe and Mr. Edwards had been experimenting with human *in vitro* (literally, "In glass") fertilization for several years before achieving this milestone. The first such birth in the United States was Elizabeth Jordan Carr, conceived at the Norfolk clinic and born on December 28, 1981.

18. What has a big red nose, orange hair, and long floppy shoes and lives in a test tube?

19. David M. Rorvik, *In His Image: The Cloning of a Man* (New York: J. B. Lippincott Co., 1978).

20. Erica Jong, "Lullaby for a Clone," *The New York Times,* May 15, 1978.

21. André Hellegers, A review of David Rorvik's cloning book, appearing on the op. ed. page, *The Washington Post,* June 4, 1978.

22. Robert Briggs and Thomas J. King, "Transplantation of Living Nuclei from Blastula Cells into Enucleated Frog's Eggs," *Proc. Nat. Acad. Sci., U.S.,* **38,** 455 (1952). See also the review by Robert Briggs, "Genetics of Cell Type Determination," in *Cell Interactions in*

Differentiation, M. Kärkinen-Jääskeläinen, L. Saxen, and L. Weiss, eds. (New York: Academic Press, 1977).

23. Robert McKinnel, *Cloning* (New York: John Wiley and Sons, Inc., 1978). See also Robert McKinnel, *Cloning—A Biologist Reports* (Minneapolis: University of Minnesota Press, 1979), 130pp.

24. Clement L. Markert and R. M. Petters, "Homozygous Mouse Embryos Produced by Microsurgery," *J. Exp. Zool.*, **201**, 295–302 (1977); C. L. Markert and R. M. Petters, "Further Investigations on Homozygous Mouse Embryos Produced by Microsurgery," *Genetics*, **88**, S62–S63 (1978).

25. U.S. House of Representatives, Committee on Interstate and Foreign Commerce, *Developments in Cell Biology and Genetics*, Hearing Record 95–105. U.S. Congress, 1978.

26. Edward Jenner, an English physician, in what would now be viewed as an experiment of questionable ethics, innoculated a boy with pus from a milkmaid's cowpox lesion. A month later, he innoculated the same boy with pus from a smallpox victim. The boy did not contract smallpox. He repeated the experiment many times, establishing in 1798 the rationale for vaccination (after *vacca*, Latin for "cow"). It is curious that this phenomenon lay latent and virtually unused for the next 80 years. Robert Koch showed in 1876 that a microbe was responsible for anthrax, and Louis Pasteur, unaware of Koch's work, began in 1878 to explore again the matter of conferring immunity. He developed vaccines for anthrax, chicken cholera, rabies, and swine erysipelas.

27. Ivan M. Roitt, *Essential Immunobiology* (Oxford: Blackwell Scientific Publications, 1980), 358 pp.; NIAID Study Group Report, *New Initiatives in Immunology*, U.S. Department of Health and Human Services, National Institutes of Health, National Institute of Allergy and Infectious Diseases, 1981; Philip Leder, "The Genetics of Antibody Diversity," *Scientific American*, **246**(5), 102–115 (May 1982).

28. G. Kohler and C. Milstein, "Derivation of Specific Antibody Producing Tissue Culture and Tumor Lines by Cell Fusion," *Eur. J. Immunology*, **6**, 511–519 (1976); C. Milstein, G. Galfre, D. S. Secher, and T. Springer, in *Ciba Foundation Symposia*, No. 66, 1979, pp. 251–276. For a readable review of Milstein's pioneering work, see Cesar Milstein, "Monoclonal Antibodies," *Scientific American*, **243**, 66–74 (October, 1980). See also the popular article by Gina Maranto, "Monoclonal *What?*", *Johns Hopkins Magazine*, August 1981, pp. 26–31.

29. Leonard Hayflick "The Cell Biology of Human Aging," *New England Journal of Medicine*, **295**, 1302–1308 (1976); see also Leonard Hayflick, "Current Theories of Biological Aging," *Federation Proceedings*, **34**, 9–13 (1975). For a good review of Hayflick's work and a discussion of others' research, written for nonscientists, see his article entitled "The Cell Biology of Aging," *Scientific American*, **242**, 58–65 (January, 1980).

30. Leslie E. Orgel, "Aging of Clones of Mammalian Cells," *Nature*, **243**, 441–445 (1973).

31. Beatrice Mintz, *Proc. Nat. Acad. Sci., U.S.*, **58**, 344 (1968); B. Mintz, "Clonal Basis of Mammalian Differentiation," *Symp. Soc. Exp. Biol.*, **25**, 345 (1971). See also the Appendix to this book.

32. For a comprehensive collection of papers covering the entire area of neurotransmitters, see the special issue of the *Journal of Experimental Biology*, E. A. Kravitz and J. E. Treherne, eds., *Neurotransmission, Neurotransmitters and Neuromodulators* (Cambridge: Cambridge University Press, 1981), 250 pp. See also Solomon H. Snyder and R. B. Innes, "Peptide Neurotransmitters," in *Annual Review of Biochemistry*, S. H. Snell, ed., Vol. 48 (Palo Alto, Calif.: Annual Research Reviews, Inc., 1979), pp. 755–782. A good review of the peptide neurotransmitters for those unacquainted with the subject is Floyd E. Bloom, "Neuropeptides," *Scientific American*, **245**(4), 148–168 (October 1981).

33. Solomon H. Snyder, *Madness and the Brain* (New York: McGraw-Hill Book Co., Inc., 1974), 295 pp.; Solomon H. Snyder, *Drugs, Madness and the Brain* (London: Hart-Davis and MacGibbon Co., 1975), 287 pp.

34. See especially Charles J. Lumsden and Edward O. Wilson, *Genes, Mind and Culture: The Coevolutionary Process* (Cambridge: Harvard University Press, 1981), 428 pp.

35. Arthur R. Jensen, "The Current Status of the IQ Controversy," *Australian Psychologist*, **13**, 7–27 (1978); Arthur R. Jensen and Arlene R. Inouye, "Level I and Level II Abilities in Asian, White, and Black Children," *Intelligence*, **4**, 41–49 (1980); William Shockley, "Models, Mathematics, and the Moral Obligation to Diagnose the Origin of Negro IQ Deficits," *Review of Educational Research*, **41**, 369–377 (1971).

36. Richard Lynn, "IQ in Japan and the United States Shows a Growing Disparity," *Nature*, **297**, 222–223 (1982). Figures released in October 1982 by the Educational Testing Service in Princeton, N.J., which administers the Scholastic Aptitude Test taken by almost every prospective college student, showed that blacks achieved scores not only significantly lower than whites, but than every other minority group as well. Asian-Americans, on the other hand, although achieving somewhat lower scores than whites in verbal skills, did significantly better in mathematics. These data have provoked a new round of cries to equalize the quality of public education available to all, based on the assumption that the differences can be erased by improvement of the environment. Again, however, the question of whether or not inherent differences exist has been raised and will ultimately have to be addressed in a rational, scientific manner. Arthur Jensen, in 1969, argued that although poor education can deprive a child of reaching his potential, a superb one cannot elevate one above his innate ablity. See Arthur R. Jensen, "How Much Can We Boost IQ and Scholastic Achievement?", *Harvard Educational Review*, **39**, 1–123 1969).

37. Hugh O. McDevitt, "Immune Response Genes in Relation to Disease," in *The Role of Immunological Factors in Infectious, Allergic and Autoimmune Processes*, Roland F. Beers, Jr., and Edward G. Basset, Eds., Miles International Symposium Series, No. 8 (New York: Raven Press, 1976).

38. R. Marian Hicks, J. Chowaniec, and S. J. Wakefield, "Experimental Induction of Bladder Tumors by a Two Stage System," in *Carconogenesis: A Comprehensive Survey, Vol. 2: Mechanisms of Tumor Promotion and Co-Carcinogenesis*, Thomas J. Salga, Andrew Sivak and Roswell K. Boutwell, eds., Gatlinburg Symposium, 1977 (New York: Raven Press, 1978), pp. 475–489.; R. Marian Hicks and J. Chowaniec, "The Importance of Synergy between Weak Carcinogens in the Induction of Bladder Cancer in Experimental Animals and Humans," *Cancer Research*, **37**, 2943–2949 (1977).

39. A comprehensive review article on oncogenes is by Geoffrey M. Cooper, "Cellular Transforming Genes," *Science*, **218**, 801–806 (1982).

40. Howard M. Temin, "We Still Don't Understand Cancer," *Nature*, **302**, 656 (1983).

41. Robert A. Weinberg, "The Secrets of Cancer Cells," *The Atlantic Monthly*, August 1983, pp. 82–88.

Chapter 2

1. James Clerk Maxwell published a comprehensive unified theory of the electrostatic and magnetic forces in 1864, predicting that electromagnetic waves could transmit energy over large distances, at the velocity of light. For his original writings, see James Clerk Maxwell, *Treatise of Electricity and Magnetism*, 3rd ed. (Oxford, 1873). It was not, however, until

1888 that Heinrich Hertz devised a method for generating and receiving electromagnetic waves of radio frequency, thus confirming Maxwell's theory.

2. In 1895, Guglielmo Marconi developed the wireless telegraph, the first practical means of radio communication, and achieved transmission across the Atlantic in 1901.

3. The brilliant American engineer Lee De Forest contributed many innovations to the development of radio components and circuitry during the first half of the twentieth century. His invention of the grid, the critical third element in a vacuum tube, made possible the amplification of electronic signals, and thus, radio became a practical means of communication.

4. The transistor, developed from an understanding of the electronic structure of metallic crystals, grew out of intensive applied research in electronics during World War II. The first published report of the principles of the transistor was by J. Bardeen and W. H. Brittain, "The Transistor, A Semiconductor Triode," *Physical Review*, **74**, 230 (1948). See also G. L. Pearson and W. H. Brittain, "History of Semiconductor Research," *Proceedings of the IRE*, **43**, 1794–1806 (1955).

5. There are a number of comprehensive accounts of this intense period in American physics. Others, while perhaps not so thorough, are entertaining and give insight into the human motives behind the rush to build an atomic bomb. For a detailed account, see Daniel J. Kevles, *The Physicists* (New York: Vintage Books, 1979; originally published in hardcover by Alfred A. Knopf, Inc., 1978), especially Chapters 19–21. For one of the more revealing accounts of J. Robert Oppenheimer, see Alice Kimball Smith and Charles Weiner, eds., *Robert Oppenheimer: Letters and Recollections* (Cambridge: Harvard University Press, 376 pp.).

6. Isaiah J. Fidler and Ian R. Hart, "Biological Diversity in Metastatic Neoplasms: Origins and Implications," *Science*, **217**, 998–1003 (1982).

7. Judith Randal, "Orphan Drugs," *Science '82*, September 1982, pp. 31–37.

8. Patrick H. O'Farrell, "High Resolution Polyacrylamide Gel Electrophoresis of Proteins," *J. Biol. Chem.*, **250**, 4007–4021 (1975); Patrick H. O'Farrell and P. Z. O'Farrell, "Two Dimensional Polyacrylamide Gel Electrophoretic Fractionation," in *Methods in Cell Biology, Vol. 16: Chromatin and Chromosomal Protein Research. I*, Gary Stein, Janet Stein, and Lewis J. Kleinsmith, eds. (New York: Academic Press, Inc., 1977), pp. 407–420; K. E. Willard, C. S. Giometti, N. L. Anderson, T. E. O'Connor, and Norman G. Anderson, "Analytical Techniques for Cell Fractions 26: A Two Dimensional Electrophoretic Analysis of Basic Proteins Using Phosphatidyl Choline-Urea Solubilization," *Anal. Biochem.*, **100**, 289–298 (1979).

9. William J. Schull, Masanori Otake, and James V. Neel, "Genetic Effects of the Atomic Bombs: A Reappraisal," *Science*, **213**, 1220–1127 (1982).

10. W. French Anderson and Elaine G. Diacumakos, "Genetic Engineering in Mammalian Cells," *Scientific American*, **245**, 106–121 (July 1981); W. French Anderson, Testimony before a hearing of the Subcommittee on investigations and Oversight, Committee on Science and Technology, U.S. House of Representatives, November 16–18, 1982; Martin J. Cline, *Ibid*.

11. A. Pellicer, M. Wigler, R. Axel, and S. Silverstein, "The Transfer and Stable Integration of the HSV Thymidine Kinase Gene into Mouse Cells," *Cell*, **14**, 133–141 (1978); E. F. Wagner, T. A. Stewart, and B. Mintz, "The Human Beta Globin Gene and a Functional Viral Thymidine Kinase Gene in Developing Mice," *Proc. Nat. Acad. Sci., U.S.*, **78**, 5016–5020 (1982); see also the review of Lloyd H. Graf, Jr., "Gene Transformation," *American Scientist*, **70**, 496–505 (1982).

12. Dr. Martin Cline proposed to treat thalassemia patients using recominant DNA methods in a request in May 1979 to the UCLA Human Subject Protection Committee. The request was

formally disapproved on July 16, 1980. Shortly before that decision was announced, Dr. Cline had performed his procedure on patients in Israel and Italy, apparently with local approval, although Israel had not approved the use of recombinant DNA. The UCLA Human Subjects Review Committee concluded that his conduct was in violation of the requirement that any UCLA scientist needed UCLA approval, regardless of where the work was to be performed. Furthermore, the UCLA Biosafety Committee concluded that Dr. Cline had violated the National Institutes of Health Guidelines concerning the use of recombinant DNA by injecting recombinant DNA into human patients. Dr. Cline was reprimanded for his action, resigned his position as chief of the Division of Hematology-Oncology at UCLA Hospital, and had NIH research funds withdrawn.

13. Josef Schell and Marc Van Montagu, "The Ti Plasmids as Natural and as Practical Gene Vectors for Plants," *Bio/Technology*, **1**, 175–180 (1983); Mary-Dell Chilton, "A Vector for Introducing New Genes into Plants," *Scientific American*, **248**(6), 51–59 (June, 1983).

14. Scott T. Kellogg, "Pesticides and Genetic Engineering," *Manufacturing Chemist* (April 1983), pp. 31–32; "Mutated Microorganisms Degrade 'Priority Pollutant,' " *Biotechnology Newswatch* (March 21, 1983).

15. Ananda M. Chakrabarty, "Transposition of Plasmid DNA Segments Specifying Hydrocarbon Degradation and Their Expression in Various Microorganisms," *Proc. Nat. Acad. Sci., U.S.*, **75**, 3109–3112 (1978).

16. Ralph A. Lewin, "Phytotechnology—How Microbial Geneticists Might Help," *BioScience*, **33**, 177–179 (1983).

17. Robert Gomer, John W. Powell, and Bert V. A. Rolling, "Japan's Biological Weapons: 1930–1945," *Bulletin of the Atomic Scientists* (October 1981), pp. 43–53.

18. Matthew W. Meselson and James M. McCullough, The National Academy of Sciences Forum, *Research with Recombinant DNA*, Proceedings, Report of Workshop No. 6, concerning biological warfare, National Academy of Sciences, 1977, pp. 195–198.

19. Robert Cooke, "Cloning Business: Growing Fast—Growing Fast," *Boston Sunday Globe* (June 25, 1978), p. 1.

20. David M. Rorvik, *In His Image: The Cloning of a Man* (New York: J. B. Lippincott Co., 1978).

21. The Office of Technology Assessment had been given more than $600,000 to conduct a study of applied genetics in all areas except human medicine. They needed a project director. When I turned the position down, it went to Dr. Zsolt Harsanyi, a geneticist from Cornell who, after the OTA project was completed, went to work for E. F. Hutton to help organize their biotechnology ventures. The report, *Impacts of Applied Genetics: Micro-Organisms, Plants and Animals* (Washington, D.C.: Congress of the United States, Office of Technology Assessment, April 1981), has been a best-seller.

22. E. F. Hutton disbanded its first venture into biotechnology, DNA Sciences, in August 1982. It is now raising capital for a new attempt to get in on the action called California Biotechnology, Inc., or Cal Biotech, for short, in Mountain View on the San Francisco peninsula.

23. "Biotechnology Becomes a Gold Rush," *The Economist* (June 13, 1981), p. 81.

24. "Faded Genes," *Time*, **119**, 64 (April 19, 1982).

25. Decision of Supreme Court of the United States, No. 79–136, *Sidney A. Diamond, Commissioner of Patents and Trademarks, Petitioner*, v. *Ananda M. Chakrabarty et al.*, June 16, 1980.

26. Plant Patent Act of 1930 (35 U.S.C. 161 *et seq.*).

27. Plant Variety Protection Act of 1970 (Public Law 91–577).

28. *Emerging Issues in Science and Technology*, Report of National Science Foundation, August 1982.

29. *Process for Producing Biologically Functional Chimeras,* United States Patent 4,237,224, issued December 2, 1980. Inventors: Stanley N. Cohen and Herbert W. Boyer; Assignee: The Board of Trustees of the Leland Stanford Jr. University, Stanford, California.

30. Letter from Stanley N. Cohen to Donald S. Fredrickson, September 6, 1977.

31. Shing Chang and Stanley N. Cohen, "*In Vivo* Site Specific Genetic Recombination Promoted by the *Eco*R1 Restriction Endonuclease," *Proc. Nat. Acad. Sci., U.S.,* **74,** 1811–1815 (1977).

32. Burke K. Zimmerman, "The Case against Patents for Living Organisms," *Am. Pat. Law. Assn. Quarterly Journal,* **7,** 278–287 (1979).

33. Jeremy Rifkin, Amicus curiae brief for *Diamond* v. *Chakrabarty,* 1980.

34. Lewis Thomas, "Notes of a Biology Watcher: On Science Business," *New England J. Medicine,* **302,** 157–158 (1980).

35. The most thorough analysis of the Harvard affair is the article by Edward Tenner, "The Laboratory as Profit Center," *Harvard Magazine,* **83,** 15–19 (1981). See also *Science,* **210,** 1104 (1980).

36. Bernard Davis, "Profit Sharing between Professors and the University?", *New England J. Medicine,* **304,** 1232–1235 (1981).

37. Tineke Bodde, "Biotechnology in the Third World," *Bioscience,* **32,** 713–716 (1982).

38. Board on Science and Technology, Office of International Affairs, National Research Council, *Priorities in Biotechnology Research for International Development*—Proceedings of a Workshop (Washington: National Academy Press, 1982).

39. *The Establishment of an International Centre for Genetic Engineering and Biotechnology,* prepared by a Group of Experts. Document No. UNIDO/IS.254, (United Nations Industrial Development Organization, Vienna, Austria, 9 November 1981).

40. Burke K. Zimmerman, *Practical Considerations of the Operation and Work Programme of the International Centre for Genetic Engineering and Biotechnology,* Document No. ID/WG.397/3, (United Nations Industrial Development Organization, Vienna, Austria, 16 August 1983); Burke K. Zimmerman, *The Organization and Operation of the International Centre for Genetic Engineering and Biotechnology,* (United Nations Industrial Development Organization, Vienna, Austria, 29 August 1983).

41. *Report of the Selected Committee,* Report No. ID/WG.397/1, (United Nations Industrial Development Organization, Vienna, Austria, 7 June 1983).

Chapter 3

1. John Wyndham, *The Day of the Triffids* (New York: Doubleday and Co., 1951).

2. Letter to Donald Fredrickson from Sherwood L. Gorbach, dated July 14, 1977, summarizing the results of a conference held in Falmouth, Massachusetts, June 20–21, 1977, to assess the risks of accidentally converting *E. coli* into an epidemic pathogen. This letter became a center of controversy when some of the more militant scientists in the recombinant DNA controversy used this letter to draw the conclusion that the risks of recombinant DNA experiments *in general* had been overstated.

3. Maxine Singer and Dieter Söll, letter of July 17, 1973, to Philip Handler, President of the National Academy of Sciences, and to John R. Hogness, President of the National Academy's Institute of Medicine, published in *Science,* **181,** 1114 (September 21, 1973).

4. Paul Berg *et al.,* "Potential Biohazards of Recombinant DNA Molecules," letter in *Science,* **185,** 303 (1974). This is the well-known "Berg letter," which set forth the conclusions of

the National Academy of Sciences committee, recommending among other things that the National Institutes of Health (NIH) write a set of safety guidelines for the conduct of gene-splicing research.

5. Donald Brown, Testimony before the National Institutes of Health Director's Advisory Committee, February 11–12, 1977.

6. Department of Health, Education, and Welfare, National Institutes of Health, *Guidelines for Research Involving Recombinant DNA Molecules,* June 23, 1976.

7. Sheldon Krimsky, *Genetic Alchemy—The Social History of the Recombinant DNA Controversy* (Cambridge: M.I.T. Press, 1982); see especially Chapter 22.

8. Liebe Cavalieri, "New Strains of Life—Or Death," *New York Times Magazine* (August 22, 1976), p. 8.

9. U.S. Senate, Committee on Labor and Human Resources, *Recombinant DNA Research,* Hearing, September 22, 1976.

10. H. R. 131, introduced by Richard Ottinger on January 19, 1977.

11. S. 621, introduced in the U.S. Senate by Dale Bumpers, February 4, 1977.

12. H.R. 3191, introduced in the House of Representatives by Richard Ottinger, February 7, 1977.

13. S. 945, introduced by Senator Howard Metzenbaum, March 8, 1977.

14. H.R. 4759, introduced by Steven Solarz, March 1, 1977.

15. The National Academy of Sciences Forum, *Research with Recombinant DNA,* was held on March 7–9, 1977, in Washington, D.C. The proceedings of this forum were published in 1977 (Washington: National Academy Press).

16. H.R. 4759, introduced by Paul Rogers on March 9, 1977.

17. H.R. 6158, introduced as a courtesy by Paul Rogers on April 6, 1977; S. 1217, introduced as a courtesy by Edward Kennedy on April 1, 1977.

18. From the first review of all introduced bills plus a 100-page issue paper prepared by the staff, the consensus of the Subcommittee on Health and the Environment, chaired by Paul Rogers, was H.R. 7418, introduced on May 24, 1977. The final subcommittee markup resulted in H.R. 7897, introduced by Rogers on June 20, 1977. Gaylord Nelson introduced a slightly modified version of H.R. 7897 in the Senate (S. 754) on August 2, 1977, as an alternative to Kennedy's bill.

19. Letters were sent to Harley O. Staggers by Stanley Cohen and Norton Zinder urging him to block the markup of H.R. 7897. These letters are reprinted in James D. Watson and John Tooze, *The DNA Story: A Documentary History of Gene Cloning* (San Francisco: W. H. Freeman and Company, 1981).

20. H.R. 11192, introduced by Harley Staggers and Paul Rogers on January 19, 1978.

21. The bill passed by the California Assembly and Senate was originally sponsored by Assemblyman Art Torres. It would have required all recombinant-DNA activities conducted in state institutions to observe the NIH guidelines (as all California universities receive Federal research funds, they are already required to observe the NIH Guidelines), and would have set the Guidelines as a standard against which any cases of injury were to be judged. It is believed by knowledgeable lawyers that the Guidelines would be regarded as a uniform standard even in the absence of a law. Therefore, the California bill would only have endorsed the effective *status quo.* Torres's office had consulted the California biotechnology companies in advance to find out what sort of bill they would not oppose and had thus written legislation against which they expected no opposition from the industry. However, Governor Brown reportedly responded to pressure from Genentech and other companies in vetoing the bill anyway.

Chapter 4

1. Henri Becquerel, *Comptes Rendu,* **122,** 420 (1896).
2. Pierre Curie and Marie Curie, *Comptes Rendu,* **127,** 175, 1215 (1898).
3. Gregor Mendel, letter to Carl Nageli, April 18, 1867. This historic description of Mendel's experiments on the independent segregation of genes is reprinted in Mordecai L. Gabriel and Seymour Fogel, eds., *Great Experiments in Biology* (Englewood Cliffs, N.J.: Prentice-Hall, Inc., 1955).
4. Sir Isaac Newton, *Mathematical Principles of Natural Philosophy,* 1729 translation by Andrew Mottel, revised by Florian Cajori (Berkeley: University of California Press, 1934). This work was originally published as *Philosophiae Naturalis Principia Mathematica,* dated July 1686.
5. Epicurus lived in what is now Greece from 341 B.C. to 271 B.C. In his speculations about the nature of the physical and biological world around him, he was the first to formulate a theory of matter's consisting of atoms that had substance and weight. This theory was developed in his work of 37 volumes, *On Nature.* See Epicurus, *Letters, Principal Doctrines and Vatican Sayings,* Russel M. Geer, translation and notes (Indianapolis: Bobbs-Merrill Co., Inc., 1938).
6. H. G. Wells's *War of the Worlds* first appeared as a serial in *Pearson's Magazine,* April–December 1897. It appeared as a book the following year (London: W. Heinemann, 1898).
7. H. G. Wells's *The Time Machine* was first published as a serial in *New Review* during 1894–1895. It was published as a book in 1895 (London: W. Heinemann).
8. Aldous Huxley, *Brave New World* (New York: Harper and Row, 1932).
9. Jules Verne, *From Earth to the Moon* (1865).
10. The Heisenberg uncertainty principle can be derived directly either from the Schrödinger formulation of quantum mechanics or from Heisenberg's matrix mechanics, using the Schwarz inequality that gives the mathematical relationship between the statistical uncertainties of two conjugate variables. The two forms of the mathematical expression of the uncertainty principle are:

$$(\Delta E \cdot \Delta t) \geq \frac{h}{4\pi} \quad \text{or} \quad (\Delta x \cdot \Delta p) \geq \frac{h}{4\pi}$$

where E = energy, t = time, x = position, p = momentum, and h = Planck's constant = 6.625×10^{-27} erg-seconds. The symbol Δ (the Greek letter delta) means the extent of the range of values that a variable may take, that is, $E = (E_{max} - E_{min})$.

   The interested reader with some background in physics may wish to consult Werner Heisenberg, *The Physical Principles of the Quantum Theory* (English translation) (Chicago: University of Chicago Press, 1930). Available from Dover Publications, New York, N.Y.
11. Amniocentesis is a procedure through which, by careful penetration of the abdominal wall and the uterus of a woman in the third to the fourth month of pregnancy, amniotic fluid containing loose cells with the genetic complement of the fetus is withdrawn and analyzed. Examination of the chromosomes of the cells can reveal the sex of the infant plus a number of congenital abnormalities, including Down's syndrome (mongolism). There are also some biochemical tests that can be performed on the cells so obtained to reveal the presence of inherited metabolic diseases. Specific DNA probes could, in principle, detect a multitude of genetic defects in amniotic cells.

12. Human growth hormone is now being manufactured by a process developed by Genentech, in which the hormone is synthesized by bacteria into which the gene for the human protein has been spliced. The protein hormone is currently being evaluated in clinical trials in children lacking growth hormone.
13. Raymond B. Cattell, *The Inheritance of Personality and Ability* (New York: Academic Press, 1982), 452 pp.
14. The Nobel sperm bank, the brain child of William Shockley, who received the Nobel prize for his work on the development of the transistor and achieved notoriety for his studies claiming that blacks are, on the average, less intelligent than whites, contains the semen donations of selected brilliant men, especially the mathematically gifted, for women who wish to practice eugenics to increase their chances of having a brilliant child. As of the fall of 1982, about the time when the first baby conceived with this elite DNA was born, approximately 400 women were seeking to be inseminated by sperm bank specimens.
15. One of my successes while working for Congress was the passage of legislation creating the President's Commission for the Study of Ethical Problems in Medicine and Biomedical and Behavioral Research. There were political reasons for the excessively long title, which I won't go into. In any case, the study commission so created succeeded the highly successful National Commission for the Protection of Human Subjects of Biomedical and Behavioral Research, which examined such issues as psychosurgery and research on prisoners and children. The coup represented by the new bill was a breach in the armor of the medical establishment, which had successfully resisted federal scrutiny and had just beaten down proposed legislation to contain hospital costs. Because Dr. Tim Lee Carter, who was one of the few physicians in Congress, and whose support Paul Rogers needed and sought, was the ranking minority member of the Subcommittee on Health and the Environment, a number of the studies I had written into the early drafts of the bill that would have had the commission examine certain practices of the medical profession were struck from the bill before it came to the House floor. However, the requirement that the Commission examine the equity issue in the distribution of health care as a function of income and place of residence survived intact. It turned out to be one of the commission's more challenging and interesting studies. This report is entitled *Securing Access to Health Care,* published in March 1983, by the U.S. Government Printing Office.
16. Garland E. Allen, "The Founding of the Eugenics Record Office, Cold Spring Harbor, Long Island (New York), 1910–1940: An Essay in Institutional History." (Manuscript, provided by the author in 1982.)
17. Arthur R. Jensen, "The Current Status of the IQ Controversy," *Australian Psychologist,* **13,** 7–27 (1978); Arthur R. Jensen and Arlene R. Inouye, "Level I and Level II Abilities in Asian, White, and Black Children," *Intelligence,* **4,** 41–49 (1980); H. Eysenck, *Race, Intelligence and Education* (New York: Library Press, 1971); William Shockley, "Models, Mathematics, and the Moral Obligation to Diagnose the Origin of Negro IQ Deficits," *Review of Educational Research,* **41,** 369–377 (1971).
18. Richard J. Herrnstein, "IQ Encounters the Press," *New Scientist* (April 28, 1983). This article discusses the reports of Richard Heber, director of the Milwaukee Project, which purported to be able to raise the IQs of deprived ghetto children as much as 30 points. Largely on the basis of this study, the press claimed that IQ was obviously cultural or sociological and not genetic in origin. In spite of a profusion of press releases and a continuing popularity among federal and other granting agencies, Heber never published his results in a legitimate, refereed journal. Instead, he was convicted of funneling grant funds into a variety of bank accounts and business ventures and is now serving a prison sentence, a fact that the press has failed to note.

19. Theodosius Dobzhansky, Ernest Boesiger, and Bruce Wallace, *Human Culture—A Moment in Evolution* (New York: Columbia University Press, 1983), 175 pp.

20. Dow O. Woodward and Val W. Woodward, *Concepts of Molecular Genetics: Information Flow in Genetics and Evolution* (New York: McGraw-Hill Book Company, 1977), see especially pp. 396–408.

21. Edward O. Wilson, *Sociobiology: The New Synthesis* (Cambridge,: Harvard University Press, 1975). See also Wilson's popular book *On Human Nature* (Cambridge: Harvard University Press, 1978).

22. Camilla P. Benbow and Julian C. Stanley, "Sex Differences in Mathematical Ability: Fact or Artifact?", *Science*, **210**, 1262–1264 (1980).

23. Charles J. Lumsden and Edward O. Wilson, *Genes, Mind and Culture: The Coevolutionary Process* (Cambridge: Harvard University Press, 1981), 428 pp.

24. Daniel B. Hier and William F. Crowley, Jr., "Spatial Ability in Androgen-Deficient Men," *N. Engl. J. Med.*, **306**, 1202–1225 (1982).

25. Richard Lynn, "IQ in Japan and the United States Shows a Growing Disparity," *Nature*, **297**, 222–223 (1982).

26. Jonathan Beckwith, "Present and Future Abuses," a paper presented at the National Academy of Sciences Forum, *Research with Recombinant DNA*, held in Washington, D.C., March 7–9, 1977, pp. 240–246 of published proceedings.

27. Murray Bookchin, "Sociobiology or Social Ecology," *Harbinger*, **1**, 1–10 (1983).

28. Rupert Sheldrake, from a taped interview by Joseph Meeker for the National Public Radio series, *Minding the Earth* (unedited tape made available through the courtesy of Dr. Meeker).

29. June Goodfield, *Playing God* (New York: Random House, 1977).

30. Ted Howard and Jeremy Rifkin, *Who Should Play God?* (New York: Dell Publishing Co., 1977).

31. Werner Heisenberg, *Zeitschrift für Physik*, **33**, 879 (1925); Erwin Schrödinger, *Annalen der Physik*, **79**, 489 (1926). The proof of equivalence between matrix mechanics and wave mechanics appears in E. Schrödinger, *Annalen der Physik*, **79**, 7344 (1926). The uncertainty principle is derived in W. Heisenberg, *Zeitschrift für Physik*, **43**, 172 (1927).

32. See for example "What's a Nice Kid like John Phillips Doing wth an A-Bomb?," *New York*, **10**, 66 (July 18, 1977), or "The A-Bomb Kid Comes Back," *Newsweek*, **94**, 9 (August 27, 1979).

33. The National Commission for the Protection of Human Subjects of Biomedical and Behavioral Research was enacted into law in 1975 and expired in 1979. Under the leadership of its chairman, Dr. Kenneth Ryan, the commission published some milestone reports on the ethics of research on human subjects.

34. The President's Commission for the Study of Ethical Problems in Biomedical and Behavioral Research published, in the fall of 1982, the results of its study on human genetic intervention, *Splicing Life: A Report on the Social and Ethical Issues of Genetic Engineering in Human Beings.* (Available from the U.S. Government Printing Office, Washington, D.C.) The report endorsed developing techniques in human genetic modification for purely therapeutic purposes, but not for "improving" normal individuals. Congressman Albert Gore, Chairman of the Subcommittee on Investigation and Oversight of the Committee on Science and Technology, U.S. House of Representatives, held a hearing on November 16–18, 1982, focused on the commission's report. Several witnesses, including Jonathan Beckwith, W. French Anderson, and Liebe Cavalieri stated, for different reasons, that they were opposed to human genetic intervention for other than therapeutic purposes. Most opposed such attempts without a great deal more knowledge than we now have.

35. Matthew S. Meselson, Chairman, and James M. McCullough, Rapporteur, "The Use of Recombinant DNA Research in Biological Warfare Is Ruled Out for Nations by the Biological Weapons Convention of 1972 and the Geneva Protocol of 1925: Is It Conceivable That Terrorists or Nations May Try to Use This Technology to Develop Weapons?" Report of Workshop No. 6, The National Academy of Sciences forum *Research with Recombinant DNA*, held in Washington, D.C., March 7–9, 1977, pp. 195–198 of published proceedings.
36. O. T. Zimmerman and Irvin Lavine, *DDT—Killer of Killers* (Dover, N.H.: Industrial Research Service, 1946).
37. The reader is referred to an essay by Donald Michael entitled "Who Decides Who Decides," which considers this important question in the context of the debate over recombinant DNA research at the University of Michigan in 1976. It appears in *The Recombinant DNA Debate*, David Jackson and Stephen Stich, eds. (Englewood Cliffs, N.J.: Prentice-Hall, Inc., 1979). An updated version appears in *Reflections on the Recombinant DNA Controversy*, Burke K. Zimmerman and Raymond A. Zilinskas, eds., to be published by the American Association for the Advancement of Science, Washington, D.C. and Macmillan, New York: 1984.
38. *Convention on the Prohibition of the Development, Production, and Stockpiling of Bacteriological (Biological) and Toxin Weapons and on Their Destruction* (United Nations, Treaties in International Agreement Series, TIAS 8062, 1972).
39. The distinction here is between the physical phenomenon of electromagnetic radiation between 4000 and 7000 Angstrom units wavelength, which produces the sensation of "light" when perceived by the human eye and brain. Similarly, vibrations between 20 and 15,000 cycles per second that are propagated through matter and that reach the human ear are perceived as "sound" in a conscious individual.
40. The scientific method, as it is called, is the logical procedure that, more or less, must govern scientific investigation and the construction of coherent models for understanding the elements of nature. First, on the basis of accurate observation or measurements, a hypothesis is constructed that is more general than the data that led to its formulation. From the hypothesis, predictions can be made about other aspects of nature, which then may be tested by experiment. Experiments or observations, made to test the predictions of the hypothesis, may either confirm the theory at some level of accuracy or generalization, suggest refinements of the hypothesis, or suggest its rejection altogether. For example, Newtonian mechanics is a hypothesis, or model, of how bodies move and are accelerated under the influence of forces. The model has a high degree of accuracy for large objects at relatively low velocities (compared to the speed of light). The model may then be considered valid within certain limits of accuracy of measurement and ranges of masses and velocities. However, at very high velocities, or for very small masses, Newtonian mechanics breaks down. Thus, the refinements of quantum mechanics and of the theory of relativity were needed to describe physical observations accurately. This is an illustration of the scientific method.
41. This philosophy was espoused by the rock group Devo (short for "de-evolution"). Their first and most popular hit included the phrase "Are we not men?—We are devo."

Appendix

1. David A. Jackson, Robert H. Symons, and Paul Berg, "A Biochemical Method for Inserting New Genetic Information into SV-40 DNA: Circular SV-40 DNA Molecules Containing Lambda Phage Genes and the Galactose Operon of *E. coli*," *Proc. Nat. Acad. Sci., U.S.*, **69**, 2904–2909 (1972).

2. DNA polymerase I was first isolated by Arthur Kornberg and described in 1958. This early work is discussed in Kornberg's monograph, *The Enzymatic Synthesis of DNA* (New York: John Wiley and Sons, Inc., 1961). Kornberg, awarded the Nobel Prize in 1959 for his discovery, believed for many years that DNA polymerase I was the enzyme that replicated bacterial DNA. But this enzyme possesses properties that would make it a most unlikely candidate for the "replicase." The possibility became very dim indeed when a mutant of *E. coli* was isolated that had only 1/200 of the normal level of DNA polymerase I, but that multiplied and grew happily just the same. The principal role of this enzyme now appears to be the repair of DNA, and it may also be involved in genetic recombination. It is believed to play a chain-extending role in replication, but the complete process of replication requires a relatively large number of enzymes and other proteins to unwind the DNA and to give it its correct spatial conformation. See Arthur Kornberg, "Aspects of DNA Replication", *Cold Spring Harbor Symp. Quant. Biol.*, **43**, 1–9 (1980).

3. Stuart Linn and Werner Arber, "Host Specificity of DNA Produced by *Escherichia coli*, X: *In Vitro* Restriction of Phage fd Replicative Form," *Proc. Nat. Acad. Sci.*, *U.S.*, **59**, 1300–1306 (1968); Werner Arber and Stuart Linn, "DNA Modification and Restriction," *Annual Review of Biochemistry*, 467–500 (1969); Werner Arber, "DNA Modification and Restriction," in *Progress in Nucleic Acid Research and Molecular Biology*, Waldo E. Cohn, ed., Vol. 14 (New York: Academic Press, Inc., 1974), pp. 1–37.

4. Hamilton O. Smith and Kenneth W. Wilcox, "A Restriction Enzyme from *Haemophilus Influenzae:* I. Purification and General Properties," *J. Mol. Biol.*, **51**, 379–391 (1970); Hamilton O. Smith and Thomas J. Kelly, "A Restriction Enzyme from *Haemophilus influenzae:* II. Base Sequence of the Recognition Site," *J. Mol. Biol.*, **51**, 393–409 (1970); P. H. Roy and H. O. Smith, *J. Mol. Biol.*, **80**, 427, 455 (1973).

5. Kathleen Danna and Daniel Nathans, "Specific Cleavage of Simian Virus 40 by Restriction Endonuclease from *Hemophilus influenzae*," *Proc. Nat. Acad. Sci.*, *U.S.*, **68**, 2913–2917 (1971). This article describes the mapping of the genes of SV-40 DNA by the first restriction enzyme characterized from *H. influenzae* by Hamilton Smith, designated *Hind*II, which produces 11 fragments from circular SV-40 DNA. See also K. Danna and D. Nathans, "Bi-Directional Replication of SV-40 DNA," *Proc. Nat. Acad. Sci.*, *U.S.*, **68**, 2913–2917 (1971).

6. G. Khoury, G. Fareed, K. Berry, M. A. Martin, T. N. H. Lee, and D. Nathans, "Characterization of a Rearrangement in Viral DNA Mapping of the Circular SV-40-like DNA Containing a Triplication of a Specific One-Third of the Viral Genome," *J. Mol. Biol.*, **87**, 289–301 (1974).

7. For example, see Hiroto Okayama and Paul Berg, "A cDNA Cloning Vector That Permits Expression of cDNA Inserts in Mammalian Cells," *Molecular and Cell Biology*, **3**, 280–289 (1983).

8. J. E. Mertz, J. Carbon, M. Herzberg, R. W. Davis, and P. Berg, "Isolation and Characterization of Individual Clones of SV-40 Mutants Containing Deletions, Duplications and Insertions in Their DNA," *Cold Spring Harbor Symposia on Quantitative Biology*, **39**, 69–84 (1975); T. E. Shenk and P. Berg, "Isolation and Propagation of a Segment of the SV-40 Genome Containing the Origin of Replication," *Proc. Nat. Acad. Sci.*, *U.S.*, **73**, 1513–1517 (1976).

9. Stanley N. Cohen, Annie C. Y. Chang, Herbert W. Boyer, and Robert B. Helling, "Construction of Biologically Functional Bacterial Plasmids *In Vitro*," *Proc. Nat. Acad. Sci.*, *U.S.*, **70**, 3240–3244 (1973). For a highly readable general article discussing this work, see Stanley N. Cohen, "The Manipulation of Genes," *Scientific American*, **233**(1), 24–33 (July 1975).

10. John F. Morrow, Stanley N. Cohen, Annie C. Y. Chang, Herbert W. Boyer, Howard M. Goodman, and Robert B. Helling, "Replication and Transcription of Eukaryotic DNA in *Escherichia coli*," *Proc. Nat. Acad. Sci., U.S.*, **71**, 1743–1747 (1974).

11. A. M. Maxam and Walter Gilbert, "A New Method of Sequencing DNA," *Proc. Nat. Acad. Sci., U.S.*, **74**, 560–564 (1977); Walter Gilbert and Lydia Villa-Komaroff, "Useful Proteins from Recombinant Bacteria," *Scientific American*, **242**, 74–94 (April 1980); F. Sanger, S. Nicklen, and A. R. Coulson, "DNA Sequencing with Chain-Terminating Inhibitors," *Proc. Nat. Acad. Sci., U.S.*, **74**, 5463–5467 (1977).

12. David Baltimore and D. Smoler, "Primer Requirement and Template Specificity of the DNA Polymerase of RNA Tumor Viruses," *Proc. Nat. Acad. Sci., U.S.*, **68**, 1507–1511 (1971); D. Baltimore, R. McCaffrey, and D. Smoler, "Properties of Reverse Transcriptase," in *Virus Research*, C. Fred Fox and William S. Robinson, eds., Second ICN-UCLA Symposium on Molecular Biology, Squaw Valley, Calif., March 18–23, 1973 (New York: Academic Press, Inc., 1973), pp. 51–59.

13. Pierre Chambon, "Split Genes," *Scientific American*, **244**, 60–71 (May 1981); Francis Crick, "Split Genes and RNA Splicing," *Science*, **204**, 264–271 (1979).

14. Francis Crick, "Split Genes and RNA Splicing," *Science*, **204**, 264–271 (1979); Walter Gilbert, "Introns and Exons: Playgrounds of Evolution," in *Eucaryotic Gene Regulation*, Richard Axel, Tom Maniatis, and C. Fred Fox, eds. (New York: Academic Press, Inc., 1979); see also discussions by Roger Lewin, "How Conversational Are Genes," *Science*, **212**, 313–315; "On the Origin of Introns," *Science*, **217**, (1982).

15. Nicholas J. Proudfoot, Monica H. M. Shandler, Jim L. Manley, Malcolm Gefter, and Tom Maniatis, "Structure and *In Vitro* Transcription of Human Globin Genes," *Science*, **209**, 1329–1336 (1980); R. W. Jones, J. M. Old, R. J. Trent, J. B. Clegg, and D. J. Weatherall, "Major Rearrangement in the Human Beta Globin Gene Cluster," *Nature*, **291**, 39–44 (1981); S. H. Orkin, H. H. Kazazian, Jr., S. E. Antonarakis, S. C. Goff, C. D. Boehm, J. P. Sexton, P. G. Waber, and P. J. V. Giardina, "Linkage of Beta Thalassemia Mutations and Beta Globin Gene Polymorphisms with DNA Polumorphisms in the Human Beta Globin Gene Cluster," *Nature*, **296**, 627–631 (1982).

16. See for example Y. Nishioka, A. Leder, and P. Leder, *Proc. Nat. Acad. Sci., U.S.*, **77**, 2806 (1980); C. D. Wilde, C. E. Crowther, and N. J. Cowan, Diverse Mechanisms in the Generation of Human β Tubulin Pseudogenes. *Science*, **217**, 549–552 (1982).

17. Robert Briggs and Thomas J. King, "Transplantation of Living Nuclei from Blastula Cells into Enucleated Frog's Eggs," *Proc. Nat. Acad. Sci., U.S.*, **38**, 455 (1952). See also the review by Robert Briggs, "Genetics of Cell Type Determination," in *Cell Interactions in Differentiation*, M. Kärkinen-Jääskeläinen, L. Saxen, and L. Weiss, Eds. (New York: Academic Press, 1977).

18. John B. Gurdon, "The Developmental Capacity of Nuclei Taken from Intestinal Epithelium Cells of Feeding Tadpoles," *Journal of Embryology and Experimental Morphology*, **10**, 622 (1962); John B. Gurdon and V. Uehlinger, " 'Fertile' Intestine Nuclei," *Nature*, **210**, 1240 (1966). See also the review article by John B. Gurdon, "Transplanted Nuclei and Cell Differentiation," *Scientific American*, **219**, 24–35 (1968).

19. Beatrice Mintz, *Proc. Nat. Acad. Sci., U.S.*, **58**, 344 (1968); B. Mintz, "Clonal Basis of Mammalian Differentiation," *Symp. Soc. Exp. Biol.*, **25**, 345 (1971); see also recent work on allophenic mice and rats from Markert's lab, for example, R. M. Petters and Clement Markert, "Pigmentation Pattern of a Black and Tan A-T-Black Chimera," *J. Heredity*, **70**, 65–67 (1979); K.-I. Yamamura and C. L. Markert, "Production of Chimeric Rats and Their Use in the Analysis of the Hooded Pigmentation Pattern," *Developmental Genetics*, **2**, 131–146 (1981).

20. T. A. Stewart and B. Mintz, "Successive Generations of Mice Produced from and Established Culture Line of Euploid Teratocarcinoma Cells," *Proc. Natl. Acad. Sci., U.S.,* **78,** 6314 (1981).

21. E. F. Wagner and B. Mintz, "Transfer of Nonselectable Genes into Mouse Teratocarcinoma Cells and Transcription of the Transferred Human Beta Globin Gene," *Mol. Cell Biol.,* **2,** 190–198 (1982); E. F. Wagner, T. A. Stewart, and B. Mintz, "The Human Beta Globin Gene and a Functional Viral Thymidine Kinase Gene in Developing Mice," *Proc. Nat. Acad. Sci., U.S.,* **78,** 5016–5020 (1981); B. Mintz, "Teratocarcinoma Cells as Vehicles for Transfer of Marker Genes into Mice," *J. Supramolecular Structure,* **9** (Suppl. 4), 126 (1980).

22. M. R. Capecchi, "High Efficiency Transformation by Direct Microinjection of DNA into Cultured Mammalian Cells," *Cell,* **22,** 479–488 (1980); Y. Shen, R. R. Hirschhorn, W. E. Mercer, E, Surmacz, Y. Tsutsui, K. J. Soprano, and R. Baserga, "Gene-Transfer: DNA Microinjection Compared with DNA Transfection with a Very High Efficiency," *Molecular and Cell Biology,* **2,** 1145–1154 (1982); K. R. Folger, E. A. Wong, G. Wahl, and Mario Capecchi, "Patterns of Integration of DNA Microinjected into Cultured Mammalian Cells: Evidence for Homologous Recombination between Injected Plasmid DNA Molecules," *Molecular and Cellular Biology,* **2,** 1372–1387 (1982); see also a summary by Jean L. Marx, "Gene Transfer Moves Ahead," *Science,* **210,** 1334–1336 (1980), and a more recent review by R. L. Brinster and R. D. Palmiter, "Induction of Foreign Genes in Animals," *Trends in Biochemical Sciences* (December 1982).

23. Richard C. Mulligan and Paul Berg, "Expression of a Bacterial Gene in Mammalian Cells," *Science,* **209,** 1422–1427 (1980).

24. R. D. Palmiter, R. L. Brinster, R. E. Hammer, M. E. Trumbauer, M. G. Rosenfeld, N. C. Birngerg, and R. M. Evans, "Dramatic Growth of Mice That Develop from Eggs Microinjected with Mellathionin-Grown Hormone Fusion Genes," *Nature,* **300,** 611–615 (1982).

25. G. Kohler and C. Milstein, "Derivation of Specific Antibody Producing Tissue Culture and Tumor Lines by Cell Fusion," *Eur. J. Immunology,* **6,** 511–519 (1976); C. Milstein, G. Galfre, D. S. Secher, and T. Springer, in *Ciba Foundation Symposia,* No. 66, 1979, pp. 251–276. For a readable review of Milstein's pioneering work, see Cesar Milstein, "Monoclonal Antibodies," *Scientific American,* **243,** 66–74 (October 1980). See also the popular article by Gina Maranto, "Monoclonal *What?*", *Johns Hopkins Magazine* (August 1981), pp. 26–31.

26. Dietmar Rabaussay, "Changes in *E. coli* RNA Polymerase after Bacteriophage T4 Infection," *ASM News,* **48,** 398–403 (1982). See also the review article by Michael Chamberlin, "Bacterial DNA Dependent RNA Polymerases," in *The Enzymes,* P. D. Boyer, ed., Vol. 15 (New York: Academic Press, Inc., 1982), pp. 68–86.

27. For a lucid and concise recent discussion of phage-specific RNA polymerases, see Michael Chamberlain and T. Ryan, "Bacteriophage DNA-Dependent RNA Polymerases," in *The Enzymes,* P. D. Boyer, ed., Vol. 15 (New York: Academic Press, Inc., 1982), pp. 87–108.

28. Mark Ptashne, "Specific Binding of the λ Phage Repressor to DNA," *Nature,* **214,** 232 (1967); Tom Maniatis, Mark Ptashne, K. Backman, D. Kleit, S. Flashman, A. Jeffrey, and R. Mauer, "Sequences of Repressor Binding Sites in the Operators of Bacteriophage λ," *Cell,* **5,** 109 (1975).

29. R. C. Dickson, J. Abelson, W. M. Barnes, and W. S. Reznikoff, "Genetic Regulation: The Lac Control Region," *Science,* **187,** 27, (1975).

30. For two general reviews of plant culture methods and the demonstration of totipotency, see H. E. Street, "Embryogenesis and Chemically Induced Organogenesis," in *Plant Cell and*

Tissue Culture—Princples and Applications, W. R. Sharp, P. O. Larsen, E. F. Paddock, and V. Raghavan, eds. (Columbus: Ohio State University Press, 1979), pp. 123–153; V. Raghavan, ''Totipotency of Plant Cells: Evidence for the Totipotency of Male Germ Cells from Anther and Pollen Culture Studies,'' *Plant Cell and Tissue Culture—Principles and Applications,* W. R. Sharp, P. O. Larsen, E. F. Paddock, and V. Raghaven, eds. (Columbus: Ohio State University Press, 1979), pp. 155–178.

31. M. Robertson, ''Gene Regulation: Twisting the Immortal Coil,'' *New Scientist,* 17 November 1983.

Index